Unions
and
Economic
Competitiveness

Unions
and
Economic
Competitiveness

Lawrence Mishel
Paula B. Voos
Editors

M.E. Sharpe, Inc.
Armonk, New York
London, England

Library of Congress Cataloging-in-Publication Data

Unions and economic competitiveness / edited by Lawrence R. Mishel and
Paula B. Voos.
p.   cm.
Includes bibliographical references.
ISBN 0-87332-827-2. — ISBN 0-87332-828-0 (pbk.)
1. Trade-unions—United States.
2. Competition—United States.
3. Competition, International.
I. Mishel, Lawrence R.
HD6508.U44   1991
331.88′0973—dc20
91-21335
CIP

TABLE OF CONTENTS:

Unions, Technology, and Labor-Management Cooperation 247
By Maryellen R. Kelley and Bennett Harrison

Work Organization, Unions, and Economic Performance 287
By Ray Marshall

Acknowledgments

The preparation of this publication required the assistance of many people at EPI. Amanda Barlow coordinated the paper flow among authors, editors, and publication staff and style-edited many of the papers and their bibliographies. In other words, her assistance was invaluable. Robert Blecker played a major role in the editing of the Karier chapter. Lory Camba produced several graphs. Also, several people helped by reviewing one or more papers: Steve Allen, Ron Blum, Markley Roberts, Sharon Stout, and Kirsten Wever.

Many thanks to EPI Publications Director Danielle Currier for the time she spent copy-editing and producing the final manuscript. Typesetting and design by Mid-Atlantic Photo/Type 2000.

Dedication

Lou and Paul Vogel

P.V.

Sharon Simon

L.M.

Unions
and
Economic
Competitiveness

Unions and American Economic Competitiveness

By Lawrence Mishel and Paula B. Voos

Opponents of improved social and labor legislation invariably contend that any change from the status quo will damage U.S. competitiveness. To evaluate this claim, we need to identify the symptoms of our lagging competitiveness and to examine the possible contributions of collective bargaining and other factors.

A variety of factors in the early 1980s left the impression that unions were contributing to our trade deficits. The sectors that seemed to be most affected by imports were mature, high-wage, unionized industries such as auto and steel. The frequent mass layoffs in these industries reinforced the association of unionization with job losses due to increased imports. Highly publicized Bureau of Labor Statistics (BLS) data suggested that wages in the U.S. far exceeded those of other countries. Plus, the success of nonunion, high-tech industries such as the computer industry reinforced the association of unions with decline.

Looking back, we can see how misleading these stylized facts were. Rates of unionization fell throughout the decade, with no discernable spur to competitiveness. By the end of the 1980s, our trade deficit was still substantial, but our trading position had deteriorated in unionized, mature industries (such as computers and semiconductors) *and* in high-tech, nonunion sectors. As the dollar's international value fell, U.S. wages became comparable to or even below wage levels in other advanced countries. This didn't ease our trade problems at all. Clearly, unions and union wage levels have little, if anything, to do with our lagging com-

A variety of factors in the early 1980s left the impression that unions were contributing to our trade deficits . . . Looking back, we can see how misleading these stylized facts were.

1

petitiveness. Ironically, some experts are now proposing that giving workers greater power and participation through collective bargaining might be an important avenue for increasing our competitiveness (Marshall, this volume). We find their argument convincing.

What do we mean by competitiveness? Most analysts, including the Reagan Administration's Commission on Industrial Competitiveness (1985), define competitiveness as the ability to compete in international markets while maintaining or improving living standards over time. Under this definition, both our burgeoning trade deficits and declining living standards in the past few years signalled that our competitiveness was falling relative to our competitors. This definition recognizes that improvements in trade balances achieved by the elimination of unions or by eroding wages and working conditions would impact living standards adversely. This paper employs an alternative, more narrow definition of competitiveness that is implicit in the statements of many business analysts: *the ability of domestic producers to succeed in international markets*. Even by this narrow definition—which countenances declining living standards—collective bargaining and unionization have had few, if any, adverse effects on our total competitiveness.

> **Collective bargaining and unionization have had few, if any, adverse effects on our total competitiveness.**

Cost Competitiveness versus Total Competitiveness

A rising trade deficit can be driven not only by direct firm-level cost factors such as wages and productivity, but also by "noncost" factors such as exchange rates, product design, and product quality.[1] Because unions arguably affect trade primarily through cost factors, the relative contributions of cost and "noncost" factors to our total competitiveness problem are of interest. If anything, our cost competitiveness has improved, while noncost factors have been problematic.

BLS data (Figure 1) show the trend since 1973 in U.S. unit labor costs relative to those of other industrialized countries (including Korea and Taiwan). The dotted line shows the indexed ratio of U.S. manufacturing labor costs (hourly compensation and productivity combined as unit labor costs) to the unit labor costs of other industrial countries as expressed in national currencies. This line portrays trends in our cost competitiveness: i.e., how changes in U.S.

2

and foreign manufacturing hourly compensation and productivity have differed since 1973. The solid line presents the same indexed ratio, with both terms expressed in dollars, and thus allows the rise and fall of the dollar's value to affect our relative cost competitiveness.

These data show that our underlying cost competitiveness has *improved* steadily over this time period. Unfortunately, our improved relative cost competitiveness was not due to relatively faster manufacturing productivity growth; U.S. manufacturing productivity growth has actually been below average. Rather, our cost position has improved because real hourly compensation has been rising in other countries, but falling in the U.S.

By 1989, our unit labor costs were more than 20 percent lower relative to our competitors than they were in 1973.[2] As the solid line shows, however, the sharp rise in the value of the dollar in the early 1980s meant that our competitiveness—measured in dollars—drastically eroded. Between 1980 and 1985, changes in the value of the dollar made our goods much more costly than those produced in other countries. The divergence between these trends suggests that the macroeconomic imbalances of the 1980s (slower growth abroad; tight monetary policy, high interest rates,

A rising trade deficit can be driven not only by direct firm-level cost factors but also by "noncost" factors such as exchange rates, product design, and product quality.

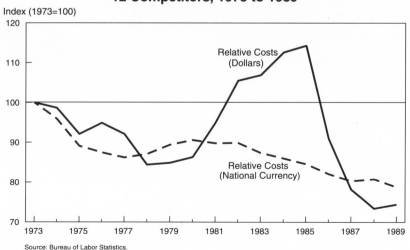

Figure 1
U.S. Manufacturing Labor Costs Relative to
12 Competitors, 1973 to 1989

Source: Bureau of Labor Statistics.

and large fiscal deficits at home) played a critical role in the rising trade deficit.

Our competitiveness problems, however, go far beyond any macroeconomic imbalance and the associated high value of the dollar. Even after the exchange rate was no longer problematic (as in 1988 and 1989), and with lower unit labor costs, the merchandise trade deficit was still a sizeable $115 billion in 1989. The intractability of the deficits suggests that noncost factors fed the burgeoning deficits of the early 1980s and persisted in driving deficits through the late 1980s.

In fact, this was the conclusion of the recent MIT Commission on Industrial Productivity (1989). They found that relative cost factors have not been the driving force behind lagging U.S. competitiveness:

> The firm's response time may be as important as the cost and quality of its products. Competitiveness may hinge on the speed at which new concepts are converted into manufacturable products and brought to market, on the flexibility with which the firm can shift from one product line to another in response to changing market conditions, or on the time it takes to deliver a product after the customer places an order. There is also the crucial question of how well the company has chosen its markets; all the efficiency, quality, and speed in the world will count for little unless the firm is producing goods that the customer wants (p. 32).

Unions, Wages, and Cost Competitiveness

Have high union wages and collective bargaining adversely affected our trade position? As we have seen, the combined effect of productivity and wage changes since 1973 have been favorable to the U.S. Moreover, current pay levels should not disadvantage U.S. producers. In 1989, the compensation of American production workers was 19 percent below the compensation of German workers, 2 percent below those of all European workers in general, and only about 10 percent above Japanese pay levels (see U.S. Department of Labor, 1990).

American workers are paid far more than those of the newly industrialized countries (NICs) such as Korea, Mexico, Brazil, or Taiwan: workers in these countries are paid

The intractability of the deficits suggests that noncost factors fed the burgeoning deficits of the early 1980s and persisted in driving deficits through the late 1980s.

4

less than 25 percent as much as average U.S. production workers. The combination of these low wages and growing productivity in the NICs is associated with a third of our total trade deficit. However, both union and nonunion domestic producers are equally vulnerable to the competitive challenge from the NICs. That is, since American workers would have to be paid less than the minimum wage to be on par with the pay levels of the NICs, the pay gap between the U.S. and the NICs has very little to do with union wage premiums in the U.S.

An examination of the geographic distribution of our 1989 trade deficits with other advanced countries offers further evidence that wages are not the problem (see Table 1). With the fall in the exchange rate since 1985, we have nearly balanced our trade with the Western European countries. The exception is the still sizeable trade deficit with Germany, a country with significantly higher wages. We also have a significant deficit with Canada, another country with higher wages.

Both union and nonunion domestic producers are equally vulnerable to the competitive challenge from the NICs.

TABLE 1
The U.S. Trade Deficit By Geographic Origin, 1989

	$Billions	Percent**
Total Merchandise Trade Deficit	$114.8	100.0%
NICs*	−37.3	32.5
Western Europe	−3.8	3.3
Germany	−8.3	7.2
Other European	4.5	(3.9)
Japan	−49.8	43.4
Canada	−9.7	8.4
OPEC	−17.6	15.3
Other Countries	3.4	(3.0)

* China, Hong Kong, Korea, Singapore, Taiwan, Mexico, Brazil.
**Parentheses indicate a trade surplus.

Source: U.S. Department of Commerce. *Survey of Current Business*, June 1990, p. 88.

Our trade deficit with Japan of roughly $50 billion represents 43 percent of our total trade deficit. Our trade problems with Japan have been widely recognized as different from our trade problems with other countries (Salvatore, 1990). No knowledgeable observer has cited U.S. wage levels as the cause of our competitive disadvantage with the Japanese.

Unionization is neither a necessary nor sufficient condition for the competitive disadvantages we observe. If unionization alone was sufficient, competitors with more heavily unionized workforces would also be suffering competitive disadvantages. However, unionization rates are far higher in other industrialized countries which are thriving in the international markets. Union representation has been stable—or even rising—in successful exporting countries such as Germany.

The declining competitive position of nonunion high-tech industries in the late 1980s makes it clear that there is no necessary connection.

If unionization were a necessary condition for our declining competitiveness, then nonunion industries should be unaffected. The declining competitive position of nonunion high-tech industries in the late 1980s makes it clear that there is no necessary connection. The sun has been setting on our so-called "sunrise" industries. According to the Office of Technology Assessment (U.S. Congress, 1988), the competitive position of 15 out of 20 high-tech industries eroded between 1972 and 1984. The computer and semiconductor industries are prime examples. Between 1983 and 1989, the U.S. market share of the computer industry fell from 81 percent to 61 percent. According to a recent commission report (National Advisory Committee on Semiconductors, 1989), Japan has taken over the lead in the semiconductor industry in the past ten years. Even the leading-edge semiconductor markets are now dominated by the Japanese. The gains made by Japanese firms in chip manufacturing have created a "serious loss of market share for U.S. semiconductors, materials, and equipment firms," with attendant losses for the suppliers of "common tools and materials used by all chip manufacturers." It is clear that our loss of competitiveness is not limited to the union sector.

Even if aggregate U.S. wage levels are not a significant disadvantage in international competition, it still may be true that union wages disadvantage firms in other ways. It is well known that union workers are paid more than equivalent nonunion workers. Common sense seems to imply that higher union wages mean higher prices and lost customers.

6

Direct econometric evidence shows that unionization is not a cause of our deteriorating trade balance. Tom Karier (1990, this volume) examined imports and exports in 360 manufacturing industries and found no statistical justification for the claim that more heavily unionized industries either attract imports or deter exports.

There are many other reasons to be skeptical of the claim that unions are associated with our competitiveness problems. Although unions *do* raise wages, they also have other effects. As Richard Freeman demonstrates in his chapter, unions affect employment relations and firm performance in ways that partially offset the effect of higher union wages on employer costs (i.e., increased productivity). Moreover, to the extent that union wage gains have come at the expense of higher profits—particularly within firms with significant market power—union wage gains do not necessarily lead to higher prices (Belman, this volume).

The impact of unions on firm costs thus depends upon the magnitude of union wage premiums and productivity improvements, and the extent to which wage gains are translated into higher prices rather than lower profits.[3] Belman (this volume) concludes his review of the existing studies on the affect of unions on firm profits and productivity:

> The negative consequences [of unions] cited by most economists—higher prices and lower employment—are largely mitigated by higher union productivity and lower rates of profit. . . This should be heartening to those who have always seen the gain from unions—greater democracy in everyday life—purchased at the expense of reduced economic efficiency. The cost of economic democracy appears smaller than previously believed.

Keefe (this volume) shows that nonunion firms are no more likely to modernize and adopt new technologies than union firms. Work rules are as evident in nonunion workplaces as in union ones. This is one reason why nonunion companies have experimented with employee participation programs and other workplace innovations in recent years. Yet, Eaton and Voos (this volume) show that unionized companies are, if anything, more likely to use workplace innovations that have proven to be the most likely to yield greater efficiency, especially team production and productivity gainsharing plans. Nonunion firms tend to focus on profit-sharing or other plans which do not have as much impact

There are many other reasons to be skeptical of the claim that unions are associated with our competitiveness problems. Although unions do raise wages, they also have other effects.

7

on productivity. Indeed, there is reason to question whether or not worker participation and other workplace innovations even have a positive effect on efficiency in the typical nonunion company. Kelley and Harrison (this volume) point out that much of the prior research indicating that these programs have a positive productivity effect typically involved studies of unionized companies. In the absence of unionization, their findings suggest that workplace committees may have negative productivity effects in nonunion companies.[4] Whether or not that rather surprising finding is substantiated by further research, it is clear that union status may be a very important determinant of the degree to which workplace innovations of various types actually result in enhanced productivity and competitiveness. Moreover, Belman (this volume) points out that even the union impact on productivity depends heavily on the labor relations climate. When management battles unionization and the two parties are locked in a pattern of adversarialism, competitiveness tends to suffer.

Empowering and Involving Workers

If unions are not the source of our competitiveness problems, what is? As Ray Marshall (this volume) explains, it is the low-wage, mass production, nonunion strategy that is still the darling of so much of American industry that is increasingly outmoded and noncompetitive. Instead, it is quality, productivity, and flexibility which are the keys to economic success in the new world marketplace. Marshall, following Piore and Sabel (1984) and other proponents of a flexible specialization strategy for America, points out that there are alternatives to mass production that provide both high wages and international competitiveness. One possibility involves producing high-quality, high value-added goods, and using cutting-edge technology which permits flexible shifts in products and production methods. The corresponding workforce must be highly skilled, involved, and motivated—willing to be deployed and redeployed flexibly to accommodate shifting markets. Unions are a positive force in that they can facilitate a key ingredient of this high-performance business system: a secure, motivated, and participative workforce. Such a secure union workforce can be more readily trained in new skills. At the same time, unions can help ensure that new technology enriches rather than impoverishes the quality of worklife. For instance, recently

Unions are a positive force in that they can facilitate a key ingredient of this high-performance business system: a secure, motivated, and participative workforce.

adopted numerical control technology tends to be skill-enhancing for blue collar workers only in the presence of unionization (Kelley and Harrison, this volume).

In the search for such a high productivity, high-skill, and high-wage solution to the American dilemma, it is important to look to Europe as well as to Japan. Turner (this volume) argues that, because of the great similarity between American and Western European work culture and institutions, European models of competitive success may well be more transplantable to the American system than Japanese ones. A close examination of West German economic success indicates that "productivity-enhancing work organization, including various forms of participation and teamwork, is not only compatible with but may even be enhanced by strong, independent unionism." Turner documents how flexibility and productivity-enhancing work reorganization in the West German auto industry have been reinforced by an interlocking system of worker representation involving both strong, independent unions, and works councils at the enterprise level. Unions are involved in management decision processes in a way that contributes to competitiveness without undermining their role as an independent representative of worker interests. The result combines national economic success, high wages, and industrial democracy.

Closer to home, there is reason to believe that the union sector is beginning to outpace the nonunion sector with regard to experimentation with the type of serious workplace innovations that have a potentially large impact on productivity (Eaton and Voos, this volume). Nonunion companies pioneered quality circles, other participation programs, and compensation-based efforts to raise worker motivation—especially profit-sharing plans. Nonetheless, by the end of the 1980s, the large union employers either equaled or surpassed the large nonunion employers with regard to virtually all flexibility and productivity-enhancing workplace innovations, with the sole exception of profit-sharing. Indeed, union companies are more heavily involved at present with extensive innovations like productivity gainsharing or team production systems which experts believe have the largest potential for increasing firm performance. Eaton and Voos (this volume) suggest that this is both a continuation of a long tradition of productivity bargaining by U.S. unions—which has permitted them to maintain employment in the face of union wages—

The union sector is beginning to outpace the nonunion sector with regard to experimentation with the type of serious workplace innovations that have a potentially large impact on productivity.

9

and a reaction to the difficult competitive environment of the early 1980s. Moreover, they explain that there are theoretical reasons to believe that worker involvement has more ultimate potential in unionized workplaces. Levine and Tyson (1990) argue that formal participation programs are more likely to result in increased productivity when:

(1) workers share the benefits in the form of higher wages, for instance through gainsharing or profit-sharing;

(2) inter-firm wage differentials are relatively narrow;

(3) long-term employment guarantees exist; and

(4) workers are protected from unjust dismissal.

As Kelley and Harrison point out, and Eaton and Voos elaborate, these conditions are far more prevalent in unionized companies. Collective bargaining agreements guarantee that workers share in the economic success of organized companies, and that individuals are protected from discipline or discharge except where there is just cause. Employment tenure is much longer in the union sector, and wage differentials are strikingly lower (Freeman, this volume). All this suggests that workplace innovations are more likely to result in increased productivity in the organized environment.

The fundamental point is that high productivity, worker rights, flexibility, unionization, and economic competitiveness are not incompatible. In actuality, they may be highly compatible components of a high performance business system. Mass production, with its top-down management of noninvolved, low-skill workers is moving to low-waged, newly industrialized countries. It is not surprising that America cannot compete with Singapore or Sri Lanka for this type of employment. And if we could compete by ever lowering wages, we wouldn't want to.

The fundamental point is that high productivity, worker rights, flexibility, unionization, and economic competitiveness are not incompatible. In actuality, they may be highly compatible components of a high performance business system.

Conclusion

We increasingly see evidence that a system based on collective bargaining and a strong independent voice for workers is not only important to our democratic institutions but also may make a positive contribution to our economic future. We have a choice. We can continue to try to compete based on mass production at ever lower wages. But that is not the industrial—or the industrial relations—system that is most appealing to us, or to most Americans. Alternatively, we can try to enhance productivity through more investment in highly skilled and motivated labor, people who are willing to be utilized flexibly by their employers because they are economically secure and have an independent voice in their future.

However, this more appealing scenario requires that American employers stop fighting collective bargaining and instead work with unions to make the production choices that will enable this country to compete in world markets without lowering living standards. Unions and other mechanisms to empower and involve workers need to be enhanced, rather than hindered (Freeman, this volume). As the MIT Commission (1989) recommended, business leaders should:

> ... support diffusion of cooperative industrial relations by accepting labor representatives as legitimate and valued partners in the innovation process. American managers must recognize that unions are a valued institution in any democratic society. Resources traditionally devoted to avoiding unionization need to be reallocated toward promoting and sustaining union-management cooperation (p.150).

The challenge is to construct an economic future that ensures both a high and rising standard of living, and a high quality of working life through workplace participation and simultaneous economic representation through collective bargaining. This is possible through an economic strategy that stresses high quality, high value-added production by a flexibly skilled workforce. The future can be high waged and it can be union. Indeed the two go together.

We increasingly see evidence that a system based on collective bargaining and a strong independent voice for workers is not only important to our democratic institutions but also may make a positive contribution to our economic future.

Endnotes

[1] Of course, these factors are also cost factors. The distinction is that they are either not controlled by the firm (i.e., exchange rates) or they are not captured in productivity statistics.

[2] The manufacturing productivity trends in this BLS series is overstated (see Mishel, 1989). However, even with a "corrected" series, our relative position has improved considerably.

[3] It should also be noted that a significant part of the payroll of unionized firms is not covered by a union contract; i.e., the white collar workforce.

[4] Ironically, the most productive companies in the Kelley and Harrison study were unionized, but without committees! Whether this is because committees were instituted by firms experiencing problems with productivity or for other reasons requires further research.

PART I

UNIONS
and the
ECONOMY

Trade Deficits and Labor Unions: Myths and Realities

Thomas Karier

During the 1980s, the rapid growth of imports sent some U.S. industries reeling, culminating in massive layoffs and plant closings. Although the surge of imports was generally blamed on misguided macroeconomic policies which created grossly distorted exchange rates, all industries were not affected equally. Imports had a particularly devastating effect on some manufacturing industries while leaving others virtually untouched. Although unions are frequently cited as one of the reasons for this failure in international competition, the evidence has usually been anecdotal and unconvincing.

The U.S. has one of the lowest unionization rates in the world today. Thus, imports are likely to originate in countries with higher unionization rates. It is especially difficult to argue that unions have impaired U.S. competitiveness when much stronger unions in Japan, Canada, and West Germany seem to have had no such effect.

The best way to ascertain the contribution of unions to import penetration is to compare the characteristics of particular industries. If industries with high import penetration were also consistently highly unionized, one could make the case that the two are related. However, the analysis in this report finds no evidence to support this hypothesis. There is no statistical justification for believing that unions either attract imports or deter exports.

The possibility remains that American unions have caused firms to relocate their production abroad. The effect on U.S. domestic industries could be just as deleterious,

There is no statistical justification for believing that unions either attract imports or deter exports.

15

causing imports to rise and/or exports to fall. However, a statistical review of industry-level data shows that unionization does not appear to be a general characteristic of the industries which rely heavily on foreign production. Other factors, in particular the degree of monopolization of an industry, seem to be more important in explaining foreign investment by U.S. firms.

This report concludes that since unions have not contributed significantly to the erosion of U.S. industrial competitiveness, it must be attributed to other causes.

> *Since unions have not contributed significantly to the erosion of U.S. industrial competitiveness, it must be attributed to other causes.*

Introduction

The deteriorating international position of many U.S. industries in the past two decades has precipitated some important controversies. Among these is whether or not U.S. manufacturers are losing their technological edge in manufacturing high quality goods at low prices. And if U.S. competitiveness really is at risk, are unionized workers partially to blame for pricing themselves out of international markets, in effect "doing themselves in"?

Some recent studies have argued that unions make U.S. firms less competitive. For example, a Federal Trade Commission (FTC) staff report, "International Competitiveness and the Trade Deficit" (Hilke and Nelson, 1987), concluded that although high union wages and union work rules did not account for the increase in the U.S. trade deficit in the 1980s, they are still significant factors in explaining import penetration rates in individual industries. Linneman and Wachter (1986, p. 104) asserted that "[L]arge and increasing union wage premiums . . . have an important impact on which firms can successfully compete in domestic and international markets." They based their claim on the assumption that higher union wages, generally placed at 20 to 30 percent above nonunion wages, are passed on in higher prices. Therefore, they reasoned that unionized firms should find it difficult to compete with nonunion domestic and foreign firms with lower labor costs.

But how much of the union wage premium actually gets passed on in higher consumer prices? Recent research has called into question the simple assumption that higher wages translate into higher prices. For instance, some of the union wage differential may be offset by higher productivity of union workers (Belman, this volume). Several studies cited by Freeman and Medoff (1984) suggest that union-

16

ized workers may be more productive than comparable nonunion workers, although most estimates for manufacturing are marred by technical problems involved in separating productivity from price effects. In any event, these studies illustrate the possibility that higher productivity among union workers could reduce or even eliminate the need for higher prices on goods produced by union firms.

There is yet another factor that could reduce the need to charge higher prices for union-made products. Numerous studies have shown that a large part of the higher wages paid to union workers are provided by reduced monopoly profits (Karier, 1985 and 1988; Voos and Mishel, 1986b). Every dollar of the union wage premium that is paid for out of monopoly profits reduces the amount passed on in higher prices. If the union wage premium was entirely covered by some combination of higher productivity and lower monopoly profits, the price differential between union and nonunion firms would vanish. Consequently, it is not certain that unions cause a disadvantage in international competition.

This chapter explores three primary ways in which unions can influence industry trade patterns. First, it is possible that aggregate trade flows between particular countries are affected by international variations in unionization rates. The evidence cited below demonstrates that, because American unionization rates are actually below those of most of our competitors, unions cannot be blamed for the overall U.S. trade deficit. Second, unions are often blamed for the poor trade performance of individual industries. The statistical analysis shows that, in fact, unionization rates are not correlated with higher imports or lower exports at the industry level. And finally, unions could indirectly affect trade flows if they increased the propensity of U.S. firms to move production abroad. While this effect cannot completely be ruled out, the last section of this report shows that factors other than unions are more important in driving American firms to invest abroad.

Higher productivity among union workers could reduce or even eliminate the need for higher prices on goods produced by union firms.

Unions and the Trade Deficit

One obvious symptom of America's problem of competitiveness is the merchandise trade deficit. While conventional thinking assumes that the trade deficit is due only to mismanaged fiscal policies (i.e., the budget deficit) and incorrectly aligned exchange rates, the evidence shows that these explain only part of the rise in the trade deficit in the 1980s (see, e.g., Helkie and Hooper, 1988).

It is frequently asserted that a sufficient depreciation of the dollar could always offset declining competitiveness, albeit at the expense of raising the domestic cost of living and thus reducing the standard of living (e.g., Dornbusch, Krugman, and Park, 1989). However, recent experience should give pause to those who attribute the trade deficit mainly to exchange rates. According to conventional wisdom, high U.S. interest rates in the 1980s attracted the attention of foreign investors, who then proceeded to buy dollars to take advantage of these high returns. Through this process, they bid up the relative value of the dollar. The strong dollar in turn raised the effective price of U.S. merchandise exports and reduced the price of imports, leading to the trade imbalance. There were few surprises until after 1985 when the falling dollar failed to reduce imports as readily as the high dollar had increased them. Although the persistence of the trade deficit can be explained partly by the lagged response of demand and limited "pass-through" of exchange rate changes into import prices, the resilience of imports in the face of a devalued dollar was greater than most analysts expected. The failure of conventional analysis to anticipate the asymmetrical effects of a rising and falling dollar serves as a reminder that exchange rates are only one of many factors influencing trade flows.

The question naturally arises whether unions could be one of the other factors affecting the trade balance. Table 1 compares the wages (hourly compensation) and unionization rates for the U.S. and thirteen of the United States' major competitors. The countries are listed in descending order of the U.S. bilateral trade deficits. With regard to wages, it is important to notice that Japan, Canada, and West Germany are high-wage developed countries which together accounted for 63 percent of the total U.S. trade deficit in 1988. The five low-wage countries (Taiwan, South Korea, Hong Kong, Mexico, and Brazil) are farther down the list and accounted for only 28 percent of the total deficit. Cheap,

Mismanaged fiscal policies and incorrectly aligned exchange rates . . . explain only part of the rise in the trade deficit in the 1980s.

TABLE 1
Characteristics of Countries
Contributing to the U.S. Trade Deficit

Country	1988 Trade Deficit with the U.S.[a]	1988 Hourly Compensation[b]	Percentage Union[c]
	($ billion)	(dollars)	
1. Japan	52.1	13.14	30 (32)
2. Taiwan	12.7	2.71	18
3. West Germany	12.2	18.07	34 (42)
4. Canada	11.7	13.58	31 (36)
5. South Korea	8.9	2.46	10
6. Brazil	5.0	1.49[d]	50
7. Italy	4.8	12.87	42 (51)
8. Hong Kong	4.6	2.43	15
9. Mexico	2.6	1.57[d]	35
10. Sweden	2.3	16.85	90 (89)
11. France	2.1	12.99	20 (28)
12. Switzerland	0.4	17.94	20 (36)
13. United Kingdom	−0.4	10.56	42 (58)
United States	120.9	13.90	18

[a]*Source:* OECD, *Monthly Statistics of Foreign Trade*, April 1989, and author's calculations. A negative deficit is a surplus. The U.S. total deficit includes all countries.
[b]Average for manufacturing production workers. *Source: Handbook of Labor Statistics*, Bureau of Labor Statistics, 1989.
[c]*Source: The World Factbook*, Central Intelligence Agency, 1987. The figures in parentheses are estimates from Freeman (1988). The U.S. figure is for 1985.
[d]Figure is for 1987 since 1988 data were not available.

unskilled labor may provide a comparative advantage for some countries in some industries. It cannot, however, explain the evolving trade relations with many developed countries, such as West Germany, Sweden, and Switzerland, that pay even higher wages than the U.S. at current exchange rates. Deficits were also run with several countries, such as Japan, Canada, Italy, and France, whose wages were within 8 percent of the U.S. average.

Even more revealing are the unionization rates listed in the final column. In comparison to its major trading partners, the U.S., with a unionization rate of 18 percent in

19

1985, is a relatively low union country. Only South Korea and Hong Kong fall below the U.S. unionization rate. If unionization is a disadvantage, then it is one that should have had a larger effect on Japan, Canada, and West Germany—the three countries which account for 63 percent of the U.S. trade deficit—than on the U.S. In reality, unionization rates in the U.S. are more comparable to the Bahamas (25 percent), Honduras (25 percent), and Tunisia (20 percent), than to other industrialized countries.

Even if some U.S. goods are more costly because of union labor, part or all of this disadvantage can be offset by higher union wages abroad. As long as the effect of foreign unions on wages and their distribution across industries are comparable to the U.S., then any union disadvantage will be largely neutralized. In fact, given the higher unionization rates in Japan, Canada, and West Germany, foreign union workers are more likely to be competing with nonunion U.S. workers than vice versa. Because the U.S. has experienced the largest decline in unionization rates among major developed countries, developments since 1980 have only served to reinforce this situation (Freeman, 1988a).

Industry Evidence

While unions do not appear to hurt American competitiveness in general, it can be argued that their effects are felt at the level of the individual industry. There exists a wide variation in the relative importance of imports and exports among U.S. manufacturing industries. Some have been very successful, expanding export production and fending off imports, while others have lost large shares of their domestic and international markets to foreign producers. By making inter-industry comparisons, we can investigate whether unions are one of the distinguishing characteristics of industries in which the U.S. has a comparative disadvantage.

Some general observations can be made from Table 2, which summarizes the import share in 1985 for twenty major U.S. manufacturing industries. The magnitude of each industry's losses to imports, measured by the ratio of imports to domestic production, varies widely from 0.91 for leather and leather products (primarily shoes, boots, and purses) to zero for tobacco products. Among the most widely publicized industries, apparel suffered the third largest losses, autos fell into the fourth category (transportation

In comparison to its major trading partners, the U.S., with a unionization rate of 18 percent in 1985, is a relatively low union country.

20

equipment), and steel placed sixth within primary metal industries.

Also included in Table 2 are unionization rates for 1968 to 1972 and four-firm concentration ratios. Union data from the early 1970s are used to determine whether or not unions affected the growth of imports and trade deficits. Since unions themselves have been affected by the trade deficits, more recent union data would raise the issue of causality.[1] It is evident from Table 2 that, with the exception of primary metals, the unionization rates of the high import industries were not much different from those in the sectors where import shares were minimal. At least for these broad categories, there is no striking evidence that imports are positively related to unions.

Table 3 gives a sample of more detailed industries with the highest and lowest net imports in 1981. Net import shares are defined as imports less exports divided by U.S. production plus imports. Once again, trade had a wide-ranging impact, with net imports as high as 76 percent for jewelers' materials and as low as −64 percent for rice milling. The unionization rates do not appear to be systematically higher in the industries with high net imports than in the industries with low net imports (high net exports).

The relationship between industry trade flows and unions cannot be measured solely by identifying simple correlations. Many other factors that can affect trade must be accounted for before the union-trade relationship can be accurately identified. The econometric method of regression analysis can be used to control for these factors in order to measure the relationship between unions and trade flows. The details of this statistical analysis are presented in the Appendix; the main results are summarized here.

The econometric analysis clearly rejects the hypothesis that unions have a positive effect on imports, either total imports or net imports (imports minus exports) expressed as a percentage of domestic supply. The econometric results also allow us to reject the hypothesis that unions have a negative effect on exports, measured as a percentage of domestic supply. Once other factors are accounted for, neither imports nor exports are significantly affected by the unionization rate.

Other implications of the econometric analysis are also of interest. The results confirm that imports are relatively higher in more concentrated industries. The reason for this is either that foreign rivals are attracted by the monopoly

Unionization rates do not appear to be systematically higher in the industries with high net imports than in the industries with low net imports.

TABLE 2
Import Penetration by Two-Digit Industry

SIC	Industry	1985 Import Share[a]	Union[b]	Concentration[c]
31	Leather and leather products	0.91	0.53	0.27
39	Misc. manufacturing industries	0.42	0.41	0.28
23	Apparel, other textile products	0.27	0.48	0.25
37	Transportation equipment	0.22	0.63	0.73
36	Electric, electronic equipment	0.20	0.41	0.47
33	Primary metal industries	0.19	0.72	0.44
35	Machinery, except electrical	0.15	0.41	0.36
38	Instruments and related products	0.14	0.33	0.49
24	Lumber and wood products	0.11	0.32	0.22
25	Furniture and fixtures	0.10	0.41	0.21
29	Petroleum, coal products	0.10	0.43	0.30
32	Stone, clay, glass products	0.08	0.62	0.36
26	Paper and allied products	0.08	0.55	0.31
22	Textile mill products	0.07	0.23	0.34
30	Rubber, misc. plastic products	0.07	0.41	0.29
28	Chemicals and allied products	0.07	0.43	0.39
34	Fabricated metal products	0.06	0.45	0.30
20	Food and kindred products	0.05	0.53	0.34
27	Printing and publishing	0.01	0.35	0.19
21	Tobacco products	0.00	0.59	0.77

[a] Imports divided by domestic production. *Source: United States Imports and Merchandise for Consumption and General Imports of Merchandise*, Census Bureau, 1965–1986.
[b] Percentage of industry workers covered by collective bargaining agreements from 1968 to 1972. *Source:* Freeman and Medoff (1979).
[c] Weighted average of 1972 four-firm concentration ratios for four-digit SIC industry categories. *Source: Annual Survey of Manufacturers*, Census Bureau.

TABLE 3
Net Imports by Four-Digit Industries

SIC	Industry	1981 Net Imports[a]	Union[b]	Concentration[c]
Highest Net Imports				
3915	Jewelers' materials, lapidary work	0.76	27	17
3263	Fine earthenware, food utensils	0.71	55	68
3021	Rubber and plastics footwear	0.69	52	58
2279	Carpets and rugs, nec.	0.57	15	69
3751	Motorcycles, bicycles, and parts	0.56	44	66
3149	Footwear, except rubber, nec.	0.55	27	24
3962	Artificial flowers	0.48	27	38
3333	Primary zinc	0.47	54	81
3873	Watches, clocks, and watchcases	0.43	35	58
2386	Leather and sheep-lined clothing	0.42	34	16
Lowest Net Imports (*Highest Net Exports*)				
2044	Rice milling	−0.64	35	51
3795	Tanks and tank companies	−0.44	44	87
3531	Construction machinery	−0.35	45	47
3721	Aircraft	−0.34	40	59
2875	Fertilizers, mixing only	−0.27	24	21
2874	Phosphatic fertilizers	−0.27	24	35
2077	Animal and marine fats and oils	−0.27	31	28
2075	Soybean oil mills	−0.25	31	54
3728	Aircraft equipment	−0.24	40	45
3511	Turbines, turbine generator sets	−0.24	60	86

[a] Equal to imports less exports divided by domestic production plus imports. FTC Report, 1987.
[b] Percentage of union production workers from 1973–75 based on the three-digit SIC industry category.
Source: Freeman and Medoff (1979).
[c] For source see Table 2.

profits or that productive efficiency has atrophied from lack of competitive pressure. There is also the possibility that firms in concentrated industries are more likely to import materials and finished products from their foreign affiliates, essentially trading with themselves. Unfortunately, the available data do not permit any deeper probing into these possibilities. It is worth noting, however, that higher imports in concentrated industries are partially offset by higher exports, but the latter fails the test for statistical significance.

The other results tend to reinforce conventional views concerning the sources of comparative advantage for the United States. Imports are significantly higher in industries which are either labor-intensive or rapidly expanding. Imports are lower for products which are protected by tariffs or produced by high-wage industries abroad. Exports are strongest in U.S. industries characterized by workers with high education levels and by high expenditures on research and development. There is also some evidence that imports are higher in energy-intensive sectors and that net imports are higher in sectors which are dependent on nonrenewable resources (excluding petroleum). These results confirm that many industry characteristics, with the notable exception of unions, are important in determining U.S. trade flows.

The data for this study were largely drawn from a similar one conducted by the U.S. Federal Trade Commission (Hilke and Nelson, 1987). The FTC study differs from the one conducted here in a number of respects which are discussed in more detail in the Appendix. One key difference is that the FTC study found unions to be positively related to imports and net imports. However, the FTC also included a variable intended to measure "human capital." The human capital variable used in the FTC study is nothing more than a modified wage rate, which is naturally correlated with unions, and which is affected by many factors other than true human capital investment. The inclusion of this human capital measure biases the results of the FTC study. When the FTC's variable is replaced by a more direct measure of human capital—median years of education—the positive effect of unions on imports disappears.

These results correspond well with the results of another study I conducted using slightly less detailed industry categories (three-digit SIC) and controlling for a similar set of industry characteristics (Karier, 1991). For a sample of 135 manufacturing industries, I found that unionized industries

> **Many industry characteristics, with the notable exception of unions, are important in determining U.S. trade flows.**

24

were generally associated with lower than average imports and higher exports, although the difference was never statistically significant. Using data for twenty-seven industries in 1966, Robert Baldwin (1979) found that the extent of unionization was largely unimportant in determining whether U.S. industries were net importers or exporters with particular countries. Japan and Libya were two exceptions who had higher net exports to those U.S. industries that were highly unionized. Australia, Greece, and Thailand, however, fared more poorly against those same highly unionized industries, importing more than they exported. For the remaining twenty-two countries in Baldwin's study, the extent of unionization did not make any significant difference in the balance of trade.

The findings of this statistical examination do not necessarily correspond with popular beliefs about particular industries, such as steel. In 1983, unionization rates and wages in this industry were among the highest in the country. Yet it also lost more than 200,000 production jobs and 20 percent of its market to imports. Are unions to blame? According to a study by Grossman (1986), rising wages in the steel industry were responsible for no more than 3 percent of the employment losses from 1976 to 1983. Structural factors independent of changes in steel prices, such as lower demand for steel products, were responsible for the majority of the jobs that were lost in the 1970s. Import competition was the major source of job losses in the early 1980s, but this could be almost entirely explained by the exchange rate changes during these years.

The long-run neglect of the capital stock which characterized this traditionally concentrated industry must be added to the short-run domestic factors emphasized by Grossman. As per the results of the empirical analysis, the particular vulnerability of concentrated industries to imports may be associated with their pattern of sacrificing long-run investments in modernization for short-run profits.[2] In sum, unions should not be blamed for the ill fortunes of the steel industry when exchange rates, falling demand, and the ravages of monopoly neglect are sufficient explanations. Moreover, any explanation of steels' ill fortunes must examine not only domestic factors but external factors such as the rise of low-wage Third World competitors, foreign subsidies, industrial policies, and the inevitable catch-up in productivity.

The extent of unionization is largely unimportant in determining whether U.S. industries are net importers or exporters with particular countries.

Unions and high
wages have not
been responsible
for the competitive
disadvantage of
the U.S. auto
industry.

The auto industry is another sector in which high union wages have been blamed for rising imports. In the early 1970s, union coverage of 70 percent in the auto industry was among the highest in manufacturing, and wages were 37 percent above the manufacturing average. In this same industry, imports captured 23.5 percent of the market by 1984, with Japanese producers firmly in control of 18.3 percent. By 1989, imports captured 29.6 percent of the market with the Japanese in control of 20.3 percent.

Unions and high wages have not been responsible for the competitive disadvantage of the U.S. auto industry. The U.S. deficit in automobiles remained large although the total hourly compensation of Japanese autoworkers rose from 44 percent of their American counterpart in 1980 to 76 percent in 1987. These wage differences are entirely in line with the average production wage differential existing between the two countries. In other words, compensation for U.S. autoworkers was consistent with the general wage differential existing between U.S. and Japanese workers, and therefore cannot account for a specific competitive disadvantage in the auto industry.

In any event, relative costs of production are not determined by wage levels alone; relative productivity levels must also be taken into account. Anderson and Kreinin (1981) showed that, from 1957 to 1977, productivity growth in the U.S. auto industry was sufficiently rapid to keep American unit labor costs (wages times hours per unit of output) from rising relative to the average for all manufacturing. Hence, they concluded that the U.S. auto industry did not suffer from a labor-cost disadvantage.

Other factors besides wages have affected our competitiveness in automobiles. The U.S. auto producers lost their absolute productivity advantage in the 1970s. This was the result not only of domestic developments but also of the rapid convergence of U.S.-Japanese productivity levels which resulted from Japanese government and private sector initiatives.

Although U.S. consumers demanded small cars, U.S. companies failed to redirect their production. Anderson and Kreinin (1981) cite this error as a primary reason for the growth of auto imports until 1980. By producing the wrong combination of large and small cars and doing it less efficiently than their rivals, the U.S. auto companies ensured themselves of declining market shares.

26

The fact that U.S. auto workers are well compensated for their labor can largely be attributed to the strength of the United Auto Workers union. If there had not been a UAW, there is little reason to expect that prices would have been significantly lower or production more efficient. The historic monopoly position of the auto industry has allowed them to maintain prices, regardless of production costs. Evidence from a number of studies shows that without unions, concentrated industries would be more likely to collect higher profits than to reduce prices for the benefit of consumers (Karier, 1988; Voos and Mishel, 1986a). Further supporting this claim is the failure of the automakers to take advantage of the falling dollar (relative to the yen) to price aggressively and build up their market share.[3]

Foreign Expansion

Direct foreign investment (DFI) by U.S. firms in production abroad is another source of the deteriorating trade position of certain industries. By replacing U.S. exports or adding to U.S. imports, thereby displacing domestic production, DFI contributes to negative trade flows. If foreign affiliates sell their products abroad, they may replace U.S. exports, but if the products are shipped to the U.S. they are counted as imports. Relative to U.S. trade, the magnitude of U.S. foreign production is hardly insignificant. In 1982, foreign affiliates of U.S.-based companies were responsible for 22 percent of all manufacturing imports and could have easily displaced an even larger share of exports by selling directly in foreign markets. The question in point is whether or not unions are an important factor in a firm's decision to transfer production from domestic to foreign operations.

While it is commonly believed that U.S. firms often go abroad in order to avoid high-wage union labor at home, the data on direct foreign investment do not generally support this belief. As of 1986, the vast majority (69 percent) of U.S. foreign investments were in other industrialized countries, rather than in the low-wage, largely nonunion developing countries. The countries on the receiving end of U.S. investment include the United Kingdom (15 percent), Canada (14 percent), and Japan (8 percent), all of which have higher unionization rates than the U.S. (see Table 1). Investments by U.S.-based companies in these par-

While it is commonly believed that U.S. firms often go abroad in order to avoid high-wage union labor at home, the data on direct foreign investment do not generally support this belief.

27

ticular countries reflect more interest in gaining shares of their large consumer markets than in avoiding the costs of union labor.

Investments in less developed countries were relatively smaller but not insignificant from the perspective of the foreign country where small investments by U.S. standards often dwarf those of foreign nationals. In these countries, U.S. firms can combine the advanced technologies of the First World with the extraordinary low labor costs of the Third World to generate unusually high profits. In these cases, a firm's interest in avoiding higher U.S. labor costs may have been at least partial motivation for foreign investments. But even here, the U.S. union wage differential, which averages 20 percent, may be largely irrelevant when compared to the overall wage differential existing between the two countries. Recall from Table 1 that the average U.S. wage ranges from six to nine times the wages in Taiwan, South Korea, Hong Kong, and Brazil—and these are not the lowest wage countries in the Third World. Consequently, unions can only marginally add to the labor-cost incentive for Third World investments.

In order to test for the effects of unions on DFI more rigorously, we need to begin by measuring the level of foreign economic activity of U.S. firms. This is complicated not only by the difficulties of translating from foreign to U.S. values, but also by intentional misreporting. For example, if a U.S. oil company extracts oil in a country with a low profit tax and ships the unrefined oil in another country with a higher tax rate, it has a clear incentive to elevate the transfer price of the crude oil to minimize its total tax burden. The firm's sales and net income will therefore be overstated in the first country and understated in the second. Similarly, foreign taxes based on assets or sales will create different incentives leading to other kinds of distortions. The fact that the value of particular capital goods abroad may differ from identical ones in the U.S. due to different purchase prices, exchange rates, or depreciation schedules further complicates matters. Price deflators are generally unavailable for data on U.S. foreign assets. Since no one measure is error-free, the best practice is to rely on a variety of different measures.

As was the case for imports, the level of foreign activity varies widely by industry. Table 4 shows U.S. foreign investments for twenty-two general manufacturing industries

> U.S. firms can combine the advanced technologies of the First World with the extraordinary low labor costs of the Third World to generate unusually high profits.

TABLE 4
Direct Foreign Investments by U.S. Firms

		U.S. Foreign Investments as measured by:				
SIC	Industry	Share of Income[a] (1981)	Employment[b] (1985)	U.S. Imports[c] (1982)	Union	Concentration
25	Furniture and fixtures	0.01	0.03	0.07	0.41	0.21
31	Leather and leather products	0.02	0.03	—	0.53	0.27
21	Tobacco products	0.06	2.05	1.00	0.66	0.79
27	Printing and publishing	0.07	0.02	0.62	0.35	0.19
22	Textile mill products	0.07	0.05	0.01	0.23	0.34
39	Misc. manufacturing industries	0.08	0.16	0.04	0.41	0.28
23	Apparel, other textile products	0.10	0.05	0.01	0.48	0.25
24	Lumber and wood products	0.14	0.03	0.07	0.32	0.22
30[e]	Rubber products	0.15	0.60	0.33	0.55	0.52
30[e]	Plastic products	0.15	0.09	0.01	0.32	0.07
34	Fabricated metal products	0.17	0.12	0.08	0.45	0.30
20	Food and kindred products	0.18	0.28	0.08	0.53	0.34
32	Stone, clay, glass products	0.21	0.22	0.10	0.62	0.36
36	Electric, electronic equipment	0.29	0.34	0.22	0.41	0.47
26	Paper and allied products	0.31	0.23	0.23	0.55	0.31
38	Instruments and related products	0.32	0.26	0.09	0.33	0.49
33	Primary metal industries	0.37	0.13	0.11	0.72	0.44
28	Chemicals and allied products	0.38	0.70	0.31	0.43	0.39
35	Machinery, except electrical	0.44	0.29	0.19	0.41	0.36
29	Petroleum, coal products	0.54	1.25	0.22[d]	0.43	0.30
37[e]	Motor vehicles and equipment	0.66	1.19	0.46	0.72	0.81
37[e]	Aircraft, ships, railroad, motorcycles, missiles	0.72	0.05	0.28	0.55	0.55
	Manufacturing Totals	—	0.25	0.22	0.47	0.39

[a]Ratio of taxable income by U.S.-based firms from foreign sources to U.S. taxable income. *Source:* FTC Staff Report, 1987.

[b]Ratio of foreign employment of U.S.-based firms to domestic employment. *Sources:* "U.S. Direct Investment: Operations of U.S. Parent Companies and Their Foreign Affiliates," U.S. Dept. of Commerce, Revised 1985, and Annual Survey of Manufacturers.

[c]Ratio of U.S. imports accounted for by U.S. foreign affiliates to total industry imports. *Sources:* Barker (1986) and "U.S. Imports of Merchandise for Consumption and General Imports of Merchandise," U.S. Bureau of the Census.

[d]This ratio and manufacturing total include oil and gas extraction (SIC 13).

[e]Includes part of this SIC category.

both by the share of taxable income generated by foreign affiliates in 1981 and the ratio of foreign to domestic employment in 1985. Although the two measures correspond well for most industries, there are three exceptions: tobacco and rubber, where the employment measure indicates substantially higher levels of foreign activity, and primary metals and transportation (other than autos), where foreign activity is higher according to the income measure. In all three cases, the employment share is the preferred measure since employment is easier to count and less susceptible to cyclical variations.

Some industries, such as furniture and fixtures, printing and publishing, textiles, apparel, lumber and wood, leather, and plastics, had relatively low foreign income and employment. In each case, foreign income was 15 percent or less of its domestic income and employment was 6 percent or less. These industries are also among the least concentrated in manufacturing and have relatively low unionization. At the other end of the spectrum are key industries with substantial foreign production. The foreign operations of U.S. automakers employed more workers than their home operations and generated two-thirds as much income. The ratio of foreign to domestic employment and income ranged roughly from a fourth to a half for many other important industries including petroleum, machinery (electrical and nonelectrical), chemicals, primary metals, instruments, and paper products.

There is also the question of whether or not the products of U.S. foreign affiliates are sold abroad or shipped back to the U.S. The third column in Table 4 reports the ratio of U.S. imports shipped by U.S. affiliates to total imports for each industry. Some caution must be used in comparing these two figures because different methods were employed to collect the two sets of data. Even allowing for a high margin of error, however, the results suggest that affiliates play a major role in U.S. imports.

For all manufacturing industries in 1982, the affiliates of U.S.-based companies accounted for more than a fifth of all U.S. imports. The shares for tobacco, printing, and publishing are high but less important because imports were so low in these cases. The same cannot be said for the automobile industry, where U.S. firms' own-imports account for nearly half (46 percent) of the value of all imports. Foreign operations of the U.S. auto companies are substantial and have been a major source of parts and semi-finished automobiles entering the country. Other industries with high shares of own-imports include rubber (33 percent), chemicals (31 percent), paper products (23 percent), electric and electronic equipment (22 percent), and petroleum (22 percent). Even in the beleaguered U.S. primary metal industry, U.S. firms accounted for 11 percent of imports. As Bulova's president, Harry B. Henshel said, "We are able to beat the foreign competition because we are the foreign competition" (Barnet and Muller, 1974, p. 305).

While U.S. own-imports are substantial, especially for certain industries, the vast majority of U.S. goods produced abroad are sold abroad. According to figures for 1984, only 7 percent of the value of U.S. manufactured goods produced abroad was shipped back into the U.S. (Brereton, 1986). The greatest potential impact of DFI on trade flows is the suppression of exports rather than the growth of imports.

The greatest potential impact of DFI on trade flows is the suppression of exports rather than the growth of imports.

Data limitations have hindered the investigation of why some industries invest in more foreign production than others, but the available results offer some interesting preliminary conclusions. According to Baldwin (1979), concentration is typically found to be a powerful determinant of foreign activity. Even for the general industries listed in Table 4, there is a strong, positive correlation between both measures of foreign activity and concentration: 0.45 for income shares and 0.76 for employment shares. Foreign activity is also positively correlated with U.S. unionization rates, but the relationship is weaker than that with concentration. While either factor alone would be a statistically significant determinant of foreign activity, only concentration remains significant when their effects are tested by multiple regression. The problem is that for such general industries, the correlation between unionization and concentration is simply too strong to tell whether firms are investing abroad because they are concentrated or because they are concentrated *and* unionized.

In a comprehensive analysis of U.S. foreign investment in 1982, I found no evidence that unions motivate U.S. firms to produce abroad (Karier, 1990b). The tendency for some industries to pursue foreign expansion could be traced to several characteristics of the domestic market, including concentration, R&D intensity, and education levels, as well as import tariffs in the host country. But unions were not a significant factor in any of the multivariate statistical tests.

The importance of concentration in determining U.S. foreign investment has been recognized by observers for some time. Due to their monopoly position at home, more highly concentrated industries generally have a larger pool of investable funds as well as more reasons to want to restrict investment in the domestic market. At least prior to the Reagan era, horizontal or vertical combinations were likely to raise serious anti-trust concerns, and too much investment in their own domestic industry could undermine monopoly profits. Any increase in output would threaten to bring down prices and profits or, even worse, lead to mutually destructive price-cutting among industry leaders. Foreign investment, on the other hand, not only provides an outlet for oligopolistic surpluses, but also increases U.S. firms' shares of world markets.

It is interesting to trace the change in U.S. DFI over time. According to Department of Commerce data, the equity value of U.S. DFI rose at an average annual rate of 8.4 percent from 1966 to 1986. This significant growth showed signs of slowing during the 1980s when the rate dropped to 3 percent, primarily because of lower inflation rates (these rates are not corrected for inflation) and the recession of 1982 which suppressed investments in general— domestic and foreign. At the very least, it is safe to assume that DFI did not accelerate during the 1980s, which itself leads to two tentative but important conclusions. First, DFI may have contributed to the declining net exports of some industries during the 1970s and 1980s, but has probably not been particularly responsible for the sharp downturn since 1983. And on a related issue, DFI may have played a role in the steady erosion of unionization rates during the past thirty years, but cannot be held responsible for the accelerating decline in the 1980s.

Summary

The purpose of this report has been to evaluate the claim that unions are responsible for some of the trade-related losses of U.S. industries. While this proposition appears reasonable on the surface, a closer examination fails to provide much support. If unionization is a disadvantage, it should be more of a concern for our major competitors, since they have equal or higher unionization rates, and some of them even have higher average wages. Even if unionization were a disadvantage for the U.S., it would be a minor one since the union percentage has now sunk to its lowest level in forty years.

If unionization is a disadvantage, it should be more of a concern for our major competitors, since they have equal or higher unionization rates.

The industry-level study conducted in this report also fails to substantiate the claims that unions impair U.S. competitiveness. Imports are not higher in heavily unionized industries nor are exports lower, making it difficult to blame unions for the trade problems of individual U.S. industries. Even in the case studies for steel and autos, the effects of unions are overwhelmed by many other factors.

There remains the possibility that unions are indirectly linked to industry trade flows because of U.S. foreign investments. If U.S. businesses are choosing to invest abroad rather than maintain or expand domestic production because of unions, then in a sense unions do have a negative effect on domestic net exports. However, the statistical evidence does not support this view. Any effect that unions may have is eclipsed by the more important effects of concentration, trade policies, and overall international wage differentials (which are much larger than domestic union wage differentials). A more important motivation for foreign expansion appears to be the effort of U.S. corporations to increase their shares of world markets while protecting oligopolistic positions at home.

To conclude from this study that unions are not responsible for the rapid increase in net imports does not in any way imply that imports are unrelated to changes in union membership. Increased imports accelerated industrial restructuring, leaving some industries with a smaller domestic workforce, heavier reliance on subcontracting, and more production facilities located in the predominantly nonunion South. This restructuring not only motivated extensive layoffs in many U.S. industries, but also provided an additional weapon for firms in reducing their exposure to unions. Under import pressure, union plants were often selected for closure because they were the oldest, most technologically backward, and in some cases, simply because they were union. Consequently, it is important to distinguish between unions as a cause of the import explosion, the theory challenged by the findings in this report, and imports as a cause of the union decline, which is less controvertible.

Endnotes

[1] It is important to note that unionization rates were falling for a long time *before* import shares rose in many U.S. industries. The union share of the private labor force peaked at 38 percent in 1954, at a time when imports were only 4 percent of GNP and the balance of trade was in surplus. The overall unionization rate had fallen to 23 percent by 1980.

[2] Commenting on the record number of steel plants closed after 1977, Walter Adams and Hans Mueller (1986) claimed that "[S]ome of the plants that were partially or completely closed were originally built in the last century. Although their technology and scale had been updated to some extent, many of their structural features—such as location and flow of materials—reflected the best-practice standards of a bygone era" (p. 83). In his study of the U.S. steel industry, Karlson (1986) found that nineteen out of forty-eight steel plants in his sample had failed to adopt either the basic oxygen or large electric furnace technology as late as 1980.

Karlson argues that steel producers were justified in waiting to invest in basic oxygen furnaces and large electric furnaces until these new technologies had reached a sufficiently large scale. But the scale was determined by their own investments in developing the new technology. Thus Karlson's justification is circular: the steel industry did not invest in the new technologies because they had not yet invested enough in them.

[3] Kwoka maintains that the automakers "deliberately kept prices high enough to permit continued imports, because by doing so they maximized their profits" (quoted in Nader and Taylor, 1986). Bussey (1988) noted that, even with the dollar falling from 240 yen in the mid-1980s to nearly 120 yen in 1988, Detroit failed to recover any lost market share. In fact, the market share of domestic producers fell to 69.9 percent as the "[B]ig three automakers aggressively raised prices right behind the Japanese in a determined—and remarkably successful—effort to increase profits."

Appendix

This appendix describes the econometric tests used to evaluate the impact of unions and concentration on U.S. imports and exports. Models for both imports and exports were specified and tested using data for 360 four-digit industries (Standard Industrial Classification) in 1981. Most of the data were obtained from a 1987 Federal Trade Commission Staff Report, "International Competitiveness and the Trade Deficit" (Hilke and Nelson, 1987). More specific descriptions of the data can be found in that report. An additional variable, the four-firm concentration ratio for 1977 from the *Annual Survey of Manufacturers,* was appended to this basic data set.

The models tested in this analysis are based on the original FTC study with several important differences. First, the FTC study included a large number of variables which were statistically insignificant. For example, variables identifying industries targeted for development by Japanese manufacturers and industries with relatively short shipping distances did not reveal any significant impact on trade. Consequently, these and other variables which were not significant were omitted from the statistical tests.

Two additional variables were also dropped because they were poor proxies for what they were intended to measure, as well as because they were highly correlated with other variables in the study. The first one, called "human capital intensity," is actually the product of labor intensity and a capitalization of the average industry wage. Although human capital does influence the industry wage, so do a number of other variables including unions, discrimination, monopoly power, and firm size. The FTC variable, derived from the industry wage, is no more representative of human capital than it is of unions or any of the other variables that influence wage levels. In particular, it is highly correlated with the union variable (correlation coefficient = 0.41) and its inclusion significantly alters the significance of the union variable. A more direct measure of human capital is the median education level which I used in place of the FTC variable.

The second questionable variable, identified as minimum efficient scale (MES), measures "the average proportion of the market served by the largest plants making up 50 percent of industry output" (Hilke and Nelson, 1987, p. 163). In reality, the optimum scale for production will vary widely by industry and should be calculated by comparing average costs for different size plants within each industry. The simple definition employed by the FTC allows for facile calculations without any clear economic meaning. Besides, if the goal is to identify entry barriers due to economies of scale, then the measure should be in absolute terms such as the expenditure required to build an efficient plant rather than a relative measure such as the market shares of large plants. Since the FTC's measure is in terms of relative size (market shares) rather than absolute size (dollar cost), it is more of a concentration measure than a measure of economies to scale. It is not surprising that industries with relatively large plants (high MES) also tend to have relatively large firms (high concentration). Consequently, there is a very high correlation coefficient between MES and the Herfindahl index of concentration (0.65) as well as between MES and the four-firm concentration ratio (0.71). For these reasons, the MES variable is not included in this analysis.

Finally, the four-firm concentration ratio was used in place of the Herfindahl index. Both are measures of the degree of competition within industries and both are commonly used in empirical analyses. The difference between the two is that the concentration ratio focuses on the market shares of the four largest firms whereas the Herfindahl index is based on squaring the market shares of all firms in the industry. The choice of the four-firm concentration ratio in this study clearly places the emphasis on the market power of the largest firms without the nonlinear effects of squaring the market shares.

Other variables included in the import model are energy intensity (the ratio of industry energy costs to value added), depleting natural resources (identified by Baldwin, 1970), labor intensity (industry labor compensation divided by value added), consumption growth (percentage change in U.S. consumption from 1972 to 1981), U.S. tariffs, and foreign pay of Japanese workers. The only additional variable introduced in the export model is research and development expenditures calculated as a percent of value added.

The results of this regression analysis are reported in Table A-1. Each of the three dependent variables (imports, exports, and net imports) is converted to a ratio by dividing by domestic supply, equal to domestic production plus imports. The coefficients presented in Table A-1 were estimated by ordinary least squares and measure the effect of each variable on imports, exports, and net imports. The t-statistics in italics indicate the statistical significance of each coefficient. The union effect is small and falls far short of statistical significance in every case, suggesting that unions are not an important factor in regulating trade flows.

Additional regressions were run to evaluate the potential effect of multicolinearity between concentration and unions on the coefficients. For each of the three trade measures, the union and concentration variables were alternately omitted to see if omitting one had any effect on the coefficient of the remaining one. All the variables from Table A-1 were included in the tests, but only the coefficients for unions and concentration are reported in Table A-2. Multicolinearity does not appear to be a problem since the estimates are hardly affected by omitting one of the variables. This is consistent with other studies which find that multicolinearity between these two variables is much less severe when four-digit industry data are used.

TABLE A-1
Regressions on 1981 Trade Measures
360 Four-Digit SIC Industries

Independent Variable	Dependent Variable		
	Imports[a]	Exports[b]	Net Imports[c]
Unions	0.05	0.02	0.04
	0.80	*0.53*	*0.53*
Concentration	0.07*	0.03	0.04
	2.13	*1.13*	*1.07*
Energy Intensity	0.001*	—	0.001
	1.89		*1.57*
Depleting Resources	0.05	−0.20	0.09**
	1.56	*−1.20*	*2.39*
Labor Intensity	0.14**	−0.05	0.18**
	2.55	*−1.27*	*2.68*
Consumption Growth (1972–1981)	0.04**	—	0.03*
	2.71		*2.05*
U.S. Tariffs[d]	−.61*	—	−.61*
	−2.01		*−1.76*
Foreign Pay	−0.02**	—	−0.02**
	−3.64		*−4.00*
Median Education	−0.002	0.015*	−0.01
	−0.23	*2.24*	*−.98*
Research & Development	—	0.004**	−0.004*
		4.11	*−2.00*
Intercept	0.11	−0.11	0.20
	0.95	*−1.27*	*1.35*
R^2	0.09	0.14	0.15

Note: *t*-statistics are in italics.

[a] Ratio of imports to domestic production plus imports.

[b] Ratio of exports to domestic production plus imports.

[c] Ratio of imports less exports to domestic production plus imports.

[d] Tariffs multiplied by one million.

* Significantly different from zero at the 0.05 level.

**Significantly different from zero at the 0.01 level.

TABLE A-2
Tests for Multicolinearity
Between Unions and Concentration

Dependent Variable	Unions	Concentration
Imports	0.07	—
	1.24	0.08
	—	*2.33*
Exports	0.03	—
	0.83	0.03
	—	*1.30*
Net Imports	0.05	—
	0.80	0.05
	—	*1.23*

Source: Author's calculations.

Note: *t*-statistics are in italics.

Unions, the Quality of Labor Relations, and Firm Performance

Dale Belman

Introduction

Who pays for the higher wages and benefits received by union members? Is it consumers, forced to shoulder a burden of higher prices and lower consumption? Is it those unable to join unions, thrust into sectors with lower wages and decreased employment security? Or is it the owners of capital, receiving reduced returns from their investments? Alternatively, could it be the union workers themselves who earn their higher wages and benefits through greater productivity? As the weak response of American firms to increased foreign competition has created economic and social problems over the past decade, the question of who pays for union gains has taken on a new urgency. For example, the *1983 Economic Report of the President* states:

> "If foreign firms can continue to produce goods at lower costs than U.S. firms, either domestic production will contract, forcing workers to leave the affected industries, or workers will have to accept constant or even declining real wages. The former option is particularly painful in industries like automobiles and steel where workers have become accustomed to high standards of living. Because wages in these industries are substantially higher than wages in other manufacturing industries, workers find it difficult to locate suitable alternative jobs" (p. 46).

The question of who pays for union gains has taken on a new urgency.

41

The steel and automobile industries are highly unionized and their unions are two of the more influential unions in the United States.

Critics of unions follow a line of logic that links higher wages and benefits to escalated costs and prices, which leads to an inability to compete in an open market. This logic proceeds as follows: higher wages are assumed to lead to increases in labor costs and consequent increases in the costs of production; firms will pass these costs on to the consumer in the form of higher prices; consumers, faced with these higher prices, will reduce their demand for the product; competitors with lower labor costs may be able to enter the market, further reducing consumer demand; eventually, burdened with wages which cannot be cut because of the union, firms will reduce output and lay off workers.

> *Unions can break the link between wages and labor costs if union employees are more productive than other workers.*

There is undisputed evidence for only the first of these three linkages: unions do raise wages and benefits. Although critics would contend that the other linkages are theoretically sound, the theory is disputed. Unions can break the link between wages and labor costs if union employees are more productive than other workers. Even if higher productivity does not completely offset higher union wages, increases in costs may not have tangible price effects if they are absorbed by reductions in profits.

Theoretic disputes over how unions affect the economic performance of firms have been in progress for at least seventy-five years. Re-examination of the issue could not provide new insights were it not for two parallel developments of the past fifteen years. First, since 1978 economists and industrial relations scholars have applied quantitative techniques to the measurement of the effect of unions on productivity, costs, and profits. There are more than fifty published articles on these topics, and they provide new and more general insights than earlier case studies. The re-emergence of programs for labor-management cooperation has also added depth to the new research by focusing interest on how the quality of labor relations affects firm performance.[1] Conceived as a response to the restiveness of labor in the late 1960s and the productivity concerns of the 1970s, experience with cooperative programs shows that there is no one union effect on firm performance. The labor relations environment (the structure of labor relations and consequent attitudes) mediates how unions influence productivity, costs, and profits.

42

This review begins with a summary of theories about unionization and firm performance; proceeds to a discussion of research on unions' influence on productivity and costs, productivity growth, and profits; and concludes with a look at the emerging quantitative literature on the labor relations climate. Although the purpose of this report is to synthesize the results from these studies into broad conclusions, some attention must be paid to methodological differences between studies. Bitter disputes over results often turn on differences in data, definitions, and techniques. As many of the technical details as possible have been placed in summary tables. Because of the difficulty involved in measuring output and costs in the public sector as well as the complexity of public sector labor relations, this review will be limited to studies of the private sector.[2]

The structure of labor relations and consequent attitudes mediates how unions influence productivity, costs, and profits.

Unions and Firm Performance: An Overview of the Theories

In the simplest neoclassical economic model, unions cannot improve firm performance. Under the assumptions of the model, the discipline of the competitive market compels firms to operate as efficiently as possible. The best intentioned union can only interfere with a firm's adaptation to the market, lowering productivity, increasing costs, and raising prices. Productivity will decline further if unions establish rules restricting managerial authority or causing managers to divert limited resources and time to labor relations functions. In the absence of barriers to competition or unionization of all competitors, organized firms will eventually be driven from the market by lower-cost nonunion companies.

These results are modified only slightly if firms adapt their production techniques to the presence of a union. Firms may respond to higher union wages and benefits by investing in additional capital and using the higher wages to attract more productive employees. Since better workers would be using more capital, organized firms would have higher productivity. But because firms would not be using the least-cost combination of capital and labor, costs would remain higher and profits lower than those of a nonunion firm.[3]

Other economists propose that the representative and protective functions of unions increase productivity, reducing the adverse impact of unions on costs and profits. Freeman and Medoff (1984) argue that workers can address on-the-job problems through two alternative social mechanisms: exit or voice. Under the first mechanism, dissatisfied employees leave their current firm for another. This creates a constant flow of employees between firms, an ongoing loss of skilled workers, and considerable costs associated with the hiring and training of replacement workers. Because the firm is continually having to attract new workers, it fashions its employment package to appeal to new workers rather than its existing workforce. This creates additional dissatisfaction among the experienced labor force.[4]

Alternatively, workers can address job issues with their employer through voice: "direct communication to bring actual and desired conditions closer together." Freeman and Medoff argue that the voice mechanism is superior to the exit one because, as firms address the concerns of their existing labor force, workers are more likely to remain with the firm. There is less turnover of skilled employees, reducing the cost of hiring and training new employees. Skills (firm-specific human capital, to put it technically) are preserved, and indeed, enhanced insofar as firms find it economically feasible to offer more training to the stable workforce. Voice is particularly important in an economy in which there are a multitude of deferred benefits such as pensions. By raising the costs of exit, such benefits reduce its effectiveness as a mechanism for addressing employee problems.

Collective voice—workers communicating with management as a group—is also superior to individual efforts to communicate with employers. The power imbalance between employers and employees, and an individuals' inability to establish readily enforceable agreements with employers restrict the effectiveness of individual voice. Provision of binding rules for promotion and due process, commonly associated with unions, can increase efficiency. Without such arrangements, workers will hoard knowledge to provide job security and increase opportunities for promotion. With enforceable arrangements for seniority and due process, workers will be more willing to share production knowledge, increasing efficiency. Collective voice is also more effective for addressing problems with common working conditions. Many conditions at a worksite cannot be changed without affecting all employees at the site. Employers are unlikely to respond to individual requests for change, but will respond to requests by the majority of workers.

Provision of binding rules for promotion and due process, commonly associated with unions, can increase efficiency.

Finally, by compelling employees to develop shared priorities, collective voice relieves the employer of making decisions which would lead to discontent were the workers themselves not involved in making the tough tradeoffs.

The exit/voice theory indicates that union labor will be more productive than nonunion labor. The effect of unions on costs and profits will be determined by the relative magnitude of the opposing productivity and wage effects.

Unions may also "shock" management into more efficient production (Slichter, 1941). Firms may not use labor efficiently when the costs of inefficiency seem small. When firms are organized, the new work environment and higher labor costs lead firms to restructure and become more businesslike. Firms may hire better managers, improve the training of supervisors, and implement production standards along with monitoring and review processes. As with voice, unionization is associated with increased productivity, but the effect on costs and profits is ambiguous.

This ambiguity is reinforced in situations in which unions lower some costs at the same time that they raise others. Employers of short term labor must constantly recruit and screen employees. There are usually no quick means for informing potential employees when work is available and no method (other than trial and error) to determine if employees have requisite skills. Unions, notably those in construction, reduce these costs through hiring halls and apprenticeship programs. Hiring halls, along with other means of disseminating information on jobs outside of local labor markets, allow contractors to assemble the crews rapidly. Ready access to skilled labor also reduces the need to carry large crews through periods of slack work. By assuring a minimum level of competence, apprenticeship programs reduce contractors' screening and training costs.

Finally, the relationship between unions and firm performance may be influenced by the industrial relations climate. The structure of bargaining, the history of labor management relations, the environment in which firms and employees operate, and the consequent attitudes of labor and management affect firm performance. In plants and firms in which there is little trust between employers and employees, in which production workers are largely excluded from decisions affecting them, and in which there is ongoing conflict over the boundary between subjects of bargaining and those under unilateral managerial control,

The relationship between unions and firm performance may be influenced by the industrial relations climate.

there will be little incentive for workers and managers to share information, workers will only produce under compulsion, and the rules of the work site—originating from conflict—will be used to assert or limit control rather than improve output. In contrast, in environments in which there is high trust, where employees and their unions are integrated into the decision process, and in which the parties accept the legitimacy of one another's goals, productivity gains and cost reduction can be realized through creative bargaining, cooperation in development of better production techniques, and a reduction in the use of restrictive work practices and monitoring. If this view is correct, there will be no simple relation between unionization and firm performance. Instead, measures of the industrial relations climate will be the critical determinants of firm performance.

The labor movement's drive for higher wages has been accompanied by demands for shared control of decisions which affect labor.

Evidence Regarding the Actual Effect of Unions on Productivity and Costs

Most fundamentally, the different views about unions' effect on productivity and costs have their genesis in the radical difference between the positions of union and nonunion employees concerning the production process. Since its founding, the labor movement's drive for higher wages has been accompanied by demands for shared control of decisions which affect labor. In the organized workplace, these demands have been translated into detailed rules regulating the labor process. While most of the rules address promotion, discipline, production standards, working rules, and contract enforcement, labor has also established the right to discuss decisions which affect employees. These rules provide substantial control over the production process and are the foundation of bilateral decisionmaking in organized worksites. In contrast, nonunion employees have limited control over production decisions. Although afforded rights by law, these are restricted in scope and enforceability. Informal shop floor organization may also provide limited control over the immediate worksite. Largely unbound by the type of rules faced by organized employers, nonunion management has greater latitude in decisionmaking.

Does bilateral decisionmaking improve or degrade firm performance? As outlined earlier, one view is that union

46

work rules, the clumsiness inherent in decentralized decisionmaking, and the reallocation of managerial resource to labor relations causes reductions in productivity. In combination with union wage gains, this raises costs and reduces profits. Others suggest that unions may, by providing employees with greater security, protecting them against arbitrary actions, improving communications between managers and workers, and compelling firms to adopt better management practices, be a source of increased productivity and have little or no influence on costs or profits. Until recently, discussion of these issues has been based on case studies and anecdotal information; neither side was convinced by the arguments and information brought forward by the other.

Does bilateral decisionmaking improve or degrade firm performance?

Recently, the debate has been widened by attempts to measure the relation between unions and productivity. These are predominantly derived from estimates of production functions. These functions specify a relationship between inputs (including labor and capital) and output. Rearrangement of the production function makes labor productivity (the ratio of output to labor input) a function of factors such as the capital to labor ratio, firm and industry structure, and union penetration. Unionization (the proportion of employees belonging to or represented by a union) is the typical measure of union bargaining power and other relevant dimensions of labor relations. Other variables, such as the capital to labor ratio, measures of firm and industry structure, and labor quality control for additional forces influencing productivity. Such controls are needed to obtain unbiased estimates of the effect of unions.

Productivity may be measured as physical output or value-added per unit of labor. Physical measures can be used only when output is homogeneous, restricting their use to studies of single industries or segments of industries. Value-added is the difference between the value of shipments and the costs of inputs exclusive of capital and labor. Appraised in dollars per unit of labor, value-added is readily comparable across industries. Unfortunately, value-added measures overstate productivity where there is monopoly power. If it is suspected that firms or industries possess power over price, measures for the monopolized markets should be deflated or the production function should incorporate controls for the competitiveness of markets.[5] Labor input has been variously measured as annual hours of production employees, annual hours of all employees, average annual production employment, and average annual total employment. Although none of these measures is inherently preferable, use of different measures can produce diverse estimates of labor productivity. Because unions regulate overtime and the use of part-time workers, different measures of labor input may produce systematic differences in the estimated effect of unions.[6]

The first quantitative study of union productivity effects was "Trade Unions in the Production Process" by Charles Brown and James Medoff (1978).

Cost functions have also figured into the debate. Cost functions measure the relationship between input prices and the cost of output. They are estimated in much the same manner as production functions except we explain cost per unit of labor input and use input prices rather than quantities. While production functions only consider the effect of unions on output per unit of labor (a measure that can be compared to a separately estimated effect of unions on wages), cost functions incorporate the effect of unions on both productivity and wages.

Production and cost functions have been estimated across industries, within industries, and within firms. Inter-industry studies are the most common, so we turn to these first. Details of these studies may be found in Appendix I.

Inter-Industry Studies

The first quantitative study of union productivity effects was "Trade Unions in the Production Process" by Charles Brown and James Medoff (1978). Productivity was measured by value-added per production employee hour for different manufacturing industries within each state (observations are industries for particular states, as defined by the Department of Commerce's two-digit SIC codes). Without controls for labor quality, organized establishments were estimated to be 24 percent more productive than equivalent nonunion establishments. With indirect controls for quality, the productivity differential fell to 22 percent.[7] One-fifth of the union effect on productivity was attributed to the lower quit rates of organized establishments. Even with controls for quit rates and labor quality, organized establishments showed a 19.5 percent productivity advantage. As the authors noted, however, a limitation of their method is that monopoly price effects may elevate value-added. And as with most productivity studies, percent organized was the sole measure of labor-management relations.

The only other inter-industry study (Clark, 1984) using value-added divided by total employment as the dependent variable found no consequential relationship between

48

unionization and productivity. The study was based on the PIMS survey of the product lines of over 250 very large firms. This measure provides superior controls for market structure and the age of capital, but uses an unrepresentative sample and somewhat mismatched data on employee quality.[8] Using several variants on a percent organized measure of unionization, Clark found a negative relationship which is too small to be of economic importance: on average, productivity was one-half of one percent lower in union than nonunion firms.

How do we reconcile the positive effect found by Brown and Medoff with Clark's finding of no effect? If we believe that union productivity gains are due to shock effects, it is possible that both studies are correct. Unions raise productivity for the average firm, but the professionalism of managers in very large firms precludes shock effects. More likely, the results were produced by differences in samples, in the level of aggregation, in the form and accuracy of the controls, and in the definitions of productivity. Whichever is more convincing, neither indicates that organized firms suffer a serious productivity disadvantage.

Even with controls for quit rates and labor quality, organized establishments showed a 19.5 percent productivity advantage.

Industry Studies

Union productivity effects have been studied in the cement, construction, hospital, banking, furniture, and coal industries. Although, unlike the inter-industry studies, these studies cannot tell us about the entire economy, they have several advantages. The use of physical measures of output or the adjustment of value-added measures for inter-regional price differences reduces the chance of confusing price and output effects. Their narrower focus also permits adapting the estimating equation to the industry under study.[9]

The cement industry, the subject of two studies by Clark (1980b, 1980a), produces a single output readily measured in physical units. In the *Quarterly Journal of Economics* study, estimates of a production function for 119 union and 9 nonunion plants for four years in the early 1970s demonstrated that union plants had a 6 to 8 percent productivity advantage. With controls for firm-specific productivity differences, such as the quality of plant management, this figure increased to 10 percent. The measure of productivity of nonunion plants may be escalated because they are newer and equipped with modern capital. After allowing for the effect of capital vintage, there is no difference in the productivity of pre-1957 union and nonunion plants, but new union plants have a 10 percent productivity advantage.[10] Capital vintage has a large impact on productivity; its effect is five times the size of the union effect. This suggests that studies lacking controls for the vintage of capital may underestimate the impact of unions on productivity.

In his 1980 publication in the *Industrial and Labor Relations Review*, Clark measured the effect of unionization on productivity in six plants organized between 1953 and 1976. Organization was followed by a 6.9 to 12.1 percent increase in productivity, the exact estimate depending on assumptions about the production process. Case studies of the plants indicated that, although organization was associated with a decrease in quits and a decline in discipline problems, the major source of productivity gain was more professional operation by management. Organization spurred replacement of upper plant management and increased training of supervisors. Internal practices were improved through the implementation of production goals and procedures for monitoring and review. Management was "shocked" into greater efficiency.

The construction industry has been the subject of a series of studies by Allen (1984, 1986a, 1986b, 1987, 1988a, 1988d). Following Brown and Medoff, the 1984 study divided construction into four-digit SIC categories across states and used the percentage organized to measure unionization. Allen used both a conventional and price-deflated measure of value-added per employee to measure productivity. The undeflated measures of productivity indicated that union workers were 44 to 52 percent more productive, the deflated effect being 17 to 22 percent.

Allen also estimated productivity and cost equations in the areas of commercial office, retail, school, and medical construction (Allen 1986a, 1986b, 1987, 1988d). Productivity is measured by value-added and square footage per employee; the cost functions used square footage per employee. In addition to the orthodox controls, the production function estimates included measures of building characteristics, the scale of the project, and labor quality. The cost functions included the prices of capital, labor, materials, and the size of the contracting firm. Union workers were shown to be between 36 percent (value-added) and 37.8 percent (square footage) more productive than nonunion workers in office construction. Despite an average union/nonunion wage differential of 54 percent, union construction costs were 20 percent lower. Cost advantage is

> **Union workers were shown to be between 36 percent (value-added) and 37.8 percent (square footage) more productive than nonunion workers in office construction.**

related to project size: union costs are lower for buildings in excess of 70,000 square feet.

Similar results were found in the study of retail construction. Union labor was between 48 percent and 51 percent more productive per hour and had lower costs in projects above 181,000 square feet. Despite higher wages in the union sector, price per square foot of retail space was equal in union and nonunion projects, as were profits. In school construction, union employees created 9.5 percent more value-added in elementary school and 41.2 percent more in secondary school construction. With square foot measures, unions were 5.6 percent less productive in elementary schools but 36.5 percent more productive in secondary schools. The cost estimates, without controls for the type of school, indicated that union labor was 16 percent more expensive in school construction.

Although the estimates are inexact because of a small sample size, union labor appears more productive and suffers no cost disadvantage in private medical construction.[11] Allen's findings indicated that unions have a productivity advantage in larger and more complex projects. Competitive conditions in the private sector projects play an important role in spurring unionized firms to greater efficiency.

In a study of surface mines in the Midwest and West, Byrnes et al. found that unionized mines had substantially higher productivity than nonunion mines.

The bituminous coal industry, one of the first non-craft industries to be organized, has been studied by Byrnes, Fare, Grosskopf, and Lovell (1987), Boal (1990), and by Connerton, Freeman, and Medoff (1983). In a study of surface mines in the Midwest and West, Byrnes et al. found that unionized mines had substantially higher productivity than nonunion mines and that mines organized by unions other than the United Mine Workers (UMW) had the highest productivity levels. The lower productivity of the nonunion mines was attributed to their smaller size and consequent problems with meeting safety and environmental requirements. Looking at 83 coal mines in West Virginia in the 1920s, Boal found that unions had no effect on productivity in large mines but a substantial negative effect in the smallest bituminous mines. Boal explains the outcome for larger mines as a result of the parties being relatively skilled in labor relations. However, this finding is also consistent with the explanations from the previous studies. Mine safety enforcement was quite weak in the 1920s, particularly in smaller mines. It is likely that the lower productivity in smaller union mines is attributable to the efforts of local unions to obtain and enforce safe conditions.

51

When it occurs, industrial conflict is more severe in coal mining than in any other industry in the United States. The severity of the conflict has notable effects on productivity. Connerton, Freeman, and Medoff (1983) found that productivity in bituminous coal mining was responsive to the state of industrial relations in the industry. While productivity in organized mines was 30 percent higher than nonunion productivity in the 1960s, it hovered around -15 percent in the 1970s. This radical change in relative productivity is explained by the shift from a climate of compromise under the leadership of John L. Lewis to one of open hostility and industrial warfare in the following decade.[12]

These results provide some additional insights to the other studies of the bituminous coal industry. The high productivity achieved in organized surface mines may be attributed to differences in conditions in surface and underground mines. Surface mines, lacking the extreme safety hazards of underground ones, may be less likely to suffer the ongoing conflict over safety which characterizes many underground mines. The lower levels of conflict allow the emergence of a positive union effect on productivity. Similarly, Boal's study looked at one of the most conflictual locales and periods in the adversarial history of coal mining. The "long strike" of the early 1920s, the Matewon Massacre, the Battle of Beal's Mountain and its consequent intervention by the U.S. military, and the Red Jacket Coal decision on yellow dog contracts all originated in West Virginia in the 1920s.

The coincidence of rapid price inflation in medicine and expanding medical unionism has generated interest in the relationship between unions and medical costs. Early research indicated that unions raise costs between 2 and 5 percent and that strikes by hospital employees increase costs by 6 to 7 percent (see Sloan and Steinwald, 1980; Miller, Becker, and Krinsky, 1977; and Salkever, 1982). Sloan and Adamache (1984) and Register (1988) provide more recent estimates which differentiate consequences for costs from those of productivity.

Both studies used multi-equation systems. Sloan and Adamache (1984) first estimated the effect of unions on wages and then used a cost equation including both an indicator of the hospital's union status and the estimated wage. The estimates were based on two alternative measures of costs: cost per patient per day and cost per admission. Register used a more elaborate approach, estimating a

> *Surface mines, lacking the extreme safety hazards of underground ones, may be less likely to suffer the ongoing conflict over safety which characterizes many underground mines.*

system of productivity, wage, and cost equations with cost measured as total expenditures per day. Both studies contained extensive controls for the mix of services and patient characteristics, hospital size, and region. Sloan and Adamache's work contained variables for previous hospital strike activity and regional labor relations conditions. The two studies used data from American Hospital Association surveys of member hospitals; Sloan and Adamache using 367 hospitals in 1974 and 1977, Register using 275 hospital's in 1984.

Sloan and Adamache found that unions raise hospital wages between 5 and 10 percent and hospital costs between 3.5 and 4.1 percent. The cost effect is due to the increase in wages caused by unionization; unions have no influence on productivity. Hospitals with recent strike activity had 9 to 10 percent higher costs. In contrast, Register found that the unions raised productivity by 16 percent and wages by 5.5 percent, but lowered costs by 9 percent.

Studies produce different results because of differences in the measures of unionization.

How could two studies produce such different results? While this difference could have been caused by the difference in the time period, it was probably due to differences in the measures of unionization. In Sloan and Adamache, a hospital was recorded as being organized if any collective bargaining agreement existed with any group of workers at the site. Lacking information on organization at the hospital level, Register counted a hospital as organized if it was located in an urban area in which more than 70 percent of hospital workers belonged to a union, and nonunion if it was in a metro area in which less than 1 percent of hospital employees were union members. Hospitals in urban areas falling between these criteria were excluded from the sample. Neither definition of unionization is satisfactory: Register's definition threw away much of the sample and confused metro area effects with the effects of unions, while Sloan and Adamache's definition aggregated different degrees of organization and radically dissimilar bargaining structures.

Subsections of both studies demonstrated that measures of unionization can influence results markedly. When Sloan and Adamache estimated their system for departments for which they had a precise measure of the collective bargaining status, they found no productivity effect and, in three out of four cases, no wage effect. In a study of Ohio hospitals with a hospital-specific measure of bargaining coverage, Register found that unions raised productivity but did not affect costs.

For these and other reasons, the estimates obtained from these studies are not entirely convincing. Nevertheless, they may be seen as favorable to unions. In contrast to manufacturing, where labor costs are only 18 percent of total costs, hospital labor costs represent at least 60 percent of total cost. Thus, if unions increase costs, it should be apparent in a hospital environment, but neither study indicates this. At worst, unions have a small positive influence and, more likely, have no effect at all. Additionally, if we take strike activity as a measure of discord between labor and management, the effect of discord on costs is at least as important as organization *per se.*

There are several additional industry studies. Graddy and Hall (1985) looked at union effects in commercial banking. Although they argue that their findings show a negative effect, the conclusions were based on weak statistical tests. Even if we accept these tests, their findings indicate that the negative effect was limited to two banks with markedly antagonistic labor relations; the other unionized banks were as productive as their nonunion counterparts. Frantz (1976) reported that unionized wooden household furniture firms have a 15 percent productivity advantage over nonunionized ones. Machin (1988a) found that, overall, unions do not influence productivity of British engineering firms, but may have negative effects in very large firms. (Given the differences in the legal structure, institutions, and values of the British and American industrial relations system, the relevance of the British experience to American conditions is uncertain.) Finally, Kelley (1990a) found that unionized plants using programmable automated systems have lower unit production time than nonunion plants, as do plants with formal seniority systems. However, the positive union productivity effect does not occur in unionized plants with formal employee participation programs. Kelley suggests that this latter puzzling negative effect may be due to a tendency to implement formal participation programs in "troubled" plants.

Firm Studies

Narrowing the focus further, Mefford (1986) found positive union productivity effects in the foreign plants of a large consumer goods manufacturer. The 126 plants in the study used similar technologies not requiring a highly

Unionized plants using programmable automated systems have lower unit production time than nonunion plants, as do plants with formal seniority systems.

skilled labor force. Productivity was measured as the ratio of actual to engineering standard labor hours per unit of product. In addition to conventional controls, the study included measures of management performance, absenteeism, and turnover as well as controls for cultural, economic, and social factors. Unionized plants were estimated to be 13 percent more productive. Their productivity was further enhanced by unions' effect on the performance of management and the capital invested in the plant.

Evidence regarding unions, productivity, and costs is incomplete. There are few general studies and a limited set of industry studies. These studies provide no evidence that unions *per se* reduce productivity: the majority of studies indicate that unions are associated with more efficient production. The limited evidence on costs is mixed. Unions are associated with lower cost production in private construction but higher costs in public construction. Evidence on hospital costs is contradictory. Research on the coal and hospital industries provides evidence that the character of the relationship between labor and management may be the critical link explaining how unions affect productivity and costs.

The majority of studies indicate that unions are associated with more efficient production.

Unionization and the Rate of Growth of Productivity

In a dynamic economy, productivity growth over time is as important as achieving high levels of productivity at a specific point in time. Industries with high rates of productivity growth will inevitably overtake those which start with high levels of productivity but experience low rates of growth. Kendrick and Grossman (1980) suggested that productivity growth is related to a range of factors including organized research and development (R&D), improvements in labor quality, changes in the inter-sectoral allocation of resources, changes in the utilization of capacity, the provision of government services to business, and the legal, institutional, and social environments.

Besides Allen (1988a), there is little theoretic work on the linkage between unions and productivity growth. Most researchers are either atheoretic or assume that the theories linking unions and productivity are also applicable to productivity growth.[13] The methodology for measuring the relation between unionization and productivity growth is also, in theory, similar to that used in productivity studies. A measure of the average annual change in productivity between two years is regressed on measures of various factors, including unionization, which are believed to influence productivity change.

In practice, techniques and measures used in the productivity growth literature are different from those used in productivity studies. Productivity studies of the type reviewed in the previous section use measures of labor productivity, adjust for capital input by including a capital/labor ratio among the explanatory variables, and often use production labor as the measure of labor input. In the growth literature, productivity is measured as total factor productivity (TFP), the ratio of value-added to an index of the amount of labor and capital used in an industry or sector.[14] Labor input is universally measured as total employment or hours. Growth studies also use a different set of explanatory variables: most include measures of R&D activities and few have the indices of labor quality common to productivity studies. The incompatibilities between the two types of literature are a source of the differences in results noted by some authors.[15]

Techniques and measures used in the productivity growth literature are different from those used in productivity studies.

Cross-Section Studies

Despite the suggestions of Kendrick and Grossman, there is little consensus on the variables that should be included in growth studies. Unionization is the only variable which appears in all of the studies in this review. Most have measures of R&D and a number have some control for the sensitivity of output to the business cycle. Studies also differ in their measures of unionization, with some using levels (typically the percent organized) and some using changes (typically the change in percent organized), over the period under examination.[16] Details of these studies may be found in Appendix II.

As part of a broad study of productivity growth in the United States from 1948 to 1976, Kendrick and Grossman (1980) estimated a series of growth equations across 19 industries. The study included several industrial relations variables; percent organized, change in percent organized, and average days lost to strikes. The effect of unions on productivity growth was sensitive to specification and time period. When the strike measure was included, percent organized did not influence growth. High levels of strike activity were associated with reduced levels of productivity growth. This reinforces evidence from productivity studies that high conflict union-management relations, rather than unions *per se*, impede productivity. In an equation which omitted the strike measure, unionization reduced productivity growth, but change in unionization had a positive effect. The results were also sensitive to the period under consideration; unions had a negative effect on growth from 1948 to 1966, but a positive effect from 1967 to 1976. The authors believe high levels of correlation among their explanatory variables make it difficult to interpret their results.

Mansfield (1980), Link (1981, 1982), Terleckyi (1980, 1984), Hirsch and Link (1984), Sveikauskus and Sveikauskus (1982), and Freeman and Medoff (1984) have produced less elaborate studies. Using Kendrick's 1948–1966 sample and measures of basic and applied R&D and percent organized as the sole explanatory variables, Mansfield found that increases in unionization decreased TFP growth. In his 1980 and 1984 studies, Terleckyi found either no relationship or a slight negative relation between unionization and growth, the exact result depending on the data set, specification, and period covered by the study. Employing a variant on Mansfield's specification with a sample of fifty-one firms in seven manufacturing industries for the years 1973–78, Link estimated that unions had a weak negative effect on TFP growth. In his 1982 study, Link found a 10.3 percent lower rate of productivity growth with a sample of ninety-seven firms from three industries in the period 1975–79. Looking at the relationship between unionization, the change in unionization, and TFP growth in the nineteen two-digit SIC manufacturing industries for the period 1957–1973, Hirsch and Link found (in contrast to Kendrick and Grossman) that both unionization and the change in unionization reduced productivity growth. In contrast, with more disaggregate data on 144 three-digit manufacturing industries for the period 1959–1969, while controlling for industry structure and R&D employment, Sveikauskus and Sveikauskus showed that unions had no effect on productivity growth. Using average annual change in labor productivity rather than TFP, Freeman and Medoff reported no relation between unions and productivity growth for three-digit, four-digit, or for two-digit industries across states.

Allen (1988a) provided contrasting results for the manufacturing and construction industries. Employing an index of growth of physical labor productivity for seventy-four manufacturing industries from 1972–1983, he found no

Unions had a negative effect on growth from 1948 to 1966, but a positive effect from 1967 to 1976.

57

relation between either unionization or changes in unionization and productivity. In contrast, with a TFP measure of output in three divisions of the construction industry in twenty-seven states for 1972 to 1982, both unionization and the change in unionization were negatively related to productivity. Allen suggested that the differences between the manufacturing and construction industries may result from difference between industrial and craft unionism. Although industrial unions are typically not resistant to innovation, craft unions can be resistant to changes in work rules or techniques for a variety of reasons. Allen also argued that the negative relation in construction has its source not in an increase in the efficiency of nonunion workers but in conditions which have forced more skilled union workers into nonunion jobs. *Situs picketing* restrictions and rulings on double breasting have made it easier for contractors to use nonunion labor. The consequent decline in the demand for union labor has forced skilled union workers into the nonunion sector. This dynamic raises measured nonunion productivity, but does not indicate that the nonunion sector is able to improve productivity on its own (Allen, 1988a, 1988d). Current research cannot support comprehensive conclusions about the effect of unions on productivity growth. The variability of findings across studies using differing definitions of variables, specifications, time periods, industries, and levels of aggregation does not allow us to conclude there is an effect, much less specify its direction and magnitude.

It may be that there is no unitary relationship between unions and productivity growth. Historically, union policies toward new technologies and job practices have ranged from strong opposition to active support. There are instances in which unions have attempted to preserve the jobs and skills of its members by obstructing new technologies. In contrast, the International Ladies Garment Workers introduced time study and other industrial engineering methods into the needle trades in the 1930s. The United Mine Workers actively supported mechanization of the coal industry in the 1940s and 1950s, despite the loss of jobs. The work of Allen (in addition to Freeman's research on coal) suggests that union productivity growth effects may well vary with union structure, industry structure, economic conditions, legal context, and the labor-management climate. Conflicting results in the productivity growth literature may be the consequence of forcing complex social relations into a simplistic framework.

Current research cannot support comprehensive conclusions about the effect of unions on productivity growth.

Time Series Studies

The effect of unions on productivity and productivity growth can also be estimated with time series data; Appendix III summarizes the most important research utilizing this approach. Time series-based studies regress productivity measures; either annual productivity or the annual change in productivity on annual measures of unionization and other variables.

The time series work of Warren (1985) and Lovell, Sickles, and Warren (1988) is sometimes seen as a counterweight to the generally positive union productivity effects found in cross-section studies.

> The suggestion of widespread beneficial union productivity effects is further undermined by Warren's (1985) findings. Warren estimates an economy-wide time-series variant on the Brown-Medoff Cobb-Douglas production function for the U.S. over the period 1948–73. He obtains a negative and statistically significant coefficient on union membership, suggesting that increases in unionization markedly decrease labor productivity. The finding that union labor is less productive than nonunion labor contradicts the results reported above obtained with cross-section manufacturing data (Hirsch and Addison, 1986, pp. 198–99).

Regressing a measure of private sector labor productivity on the private sector capital to labor ratio, capacity utilization, a time trend, and percent organized in the public and private sectors, Warren finds a union productivity effect of − 0.50 percent, which suggests that adding union workers decreases total output. Use of a more sophisticated procedure indicated that union labor is one-hundredth as productive as nonunion labor (Lovell, Sickles, and Warren, 1988). These estimates are extreme and seem "implausibly small" (Addison and Hirsch, 1989). Using the same data and model, Belman and Wilson (1989) demonstrated that estimates with this data set and method were exceptionally sensitive to the definition of unionization and the measure of cyclical movement in the economy. Depending on specification, estimates range from Warren's negative to Brown and Medoff's positive correlation. The majority of specifications show no relation between unions and productivity over time. The authors conclude that this model and data cannot produce meaningful results.

Maki (1983) looked at the relation between annual TFP

The majority of specifications show no relation between unions and productivity over time.

59

growth and unionization for Canada from 1926 to 1978. The model distinguishes shock effects, which are argued to be related to changes in unionization over time, from longer term effects related to the level of unionization. There are controls for strike activity, the business cycle, and median education. However, changes in occupational, industrial, and demographic characteristics, and the effects of World War II are ignored. The inclusion of the public sector in the TFP variable is also problematic because of the difficulty of measuring public sector output. Maki finds a positive shock effect: higher rates of unionization increase productivity growth. Although unionization and strike activity individually have a negative effect on productivity growth, their effects cannot be distinguished from one another when both are included in an equation. Again, labor-management discord rather than unions may be the source of negative growth effects. As with Warren's work, Maki's results are sensitive to specification.[17]

In sum, it would appear that the results of time series analysis are not robust enough to counter cross-section findings; that, without high industrial conflict, unionization does not reduce productivity appreciably and may even enhance it.

Labor-management discord rather than unions may be the source of negative growth effects.

Unions and Firm Profits

It would appear that union workers finance their wage increases at least in part through higher productivity. Assume that this effect does not fully compensate for the higher wages received by union workers. Who then pays the wage premia? Is it consumers and other workers, or do firms absorb part of the cost out of profits? If firms are able to pass increased wages on in higher prices, they will maintain their rate of profit. Consumer demand will fall, reducing employment. Workers who can no longer find union jobs are forced into unemployment or lower wage nonunion jobs. The union wage premia are footed by consumers and those who cannot find work in the union sector. If firms are unable to pass on the full increase in costs, their profits will be reduced and there will be smaller negative consequences for consumers and other workers. A negative relation between unionization and the rate of profit indicates that firms are absorbing part of the wage premia.[18]

A related question is whether unions reduce the profits of all firms or just firms which are earning extraordinary profits. Where firms are earning above-normal rates of return due to market power or access to particularly productive resources, unions can bargain for a part of these rents without deleterious effects on employment or prices. If wage premia are due to the sharing of these rents, we would expect the effect of unionization on profits to be larger in industries which earn substantial rents.[19]

Profit equations may be estimated with either industry or firm data. Industry data are advantageous as they cover all firms (large and small), are readily matched to worker characteristics, and minimize measurement problems associated with firm diversification. With industry data, profits are measured as a price-cost margin (PCM), where the PCM is defined as

$$\frac{\text{sales} - \text{payroll} - \text{materials costs.}}{\text{sales}}$$

PCM equations require controls for the capital to sales and advertising to sales ratio.[20]

Data are also available on large publicly traded firms. Although unrepresentative of entire industries, these surveys include firms which account for a large share of output. Firm data provide a broader set of measures of firm characteristics at the cost of mismeasuring variables, such as employee demographics, which are only available by industry.[21] Differences between firm and industry characteristics and diversification of firms across several industries can cause problems where such firm-industry matches are used to generate key variables. This poses a particularly thorny problem insofar as unionization measures are usually only available by industry.[22]

Firm rates of return may be measured as a price-cost margin or as Tobin's q, the ratio of the value of firms' equity and debt to the replacement cost of their assets. Some argue for the superiority of q as a long-run measure of profitability as it is less subject to measurement error and contains adjustments for risk (Salinger, 1984). Others are dubious because q's validity depends on the accuracy of stock market valuations and measures of replacement costs, the latter being subject to distortion during inflation or when assets change hands (Scherer, 1980).[23] As firm-level profit measures include income from foreign subsidiaries, controls for the income originating abroad or the extent of foreign operations are also required.

Where firms are earning above-normal rates of return . . . unions can bargain for a part of these rents without deleterious effects on employment or prices.

61

Industry Studies

Thomas Karier (1985, 1988) has published two industry studies on the relation between unionization and monopoly profits. (Details of the profit studies may be found in Appendix IV.) Using 1972 data on the 19 two-digit manufacturing industries, he found price-cost margins increased with market concentration, but decreased with unionization. A completely organized industry would have a 6.6 percent lower PCM than an industry with no union employment. Union effects on profit are sensitive to a firm's power over price. Industries with concentration ratios greater than 60 have 14 percent lower PCM's with complete unionization, 8.5 percent lower PCM's with moderate concentration, and PCM's indistinguishable from zero with low concentration. This pattern of effects suggest that unions share monopoly rents where they exist. The second study (Karier, 1988) uses data for 107 three-digit manufacturing industries for the period 1965–1980. Although unionization has no effect on the PCM in and of itself, it does have a negative effect if firms possess market power. Karier argues that unions only lower the profits of firms earning monopoly rents and estimates that somewhat less than 47 percent of these rents accrue to unions.

Using 1972 data on 139 three-digit SIC manufacturing industries, Voos and Mishel (1986b) found that a fully unionized industry had a 22 percent lower price-cost margin than an unorganized industry. The estimate increased to 35 percent when unionization and profits were treated as simultaneous. Freeman (1983) also found a negative relation between unionization and profitability; results are summarized in Freeman and Medoff (1984). Using several different data sets from the Annual Survey of Manufacturers and the Internal Revenue Service, price-cost margins were found to be between zero and 37 percent lower due to unions, while return on capital was reduced between 9 and 32 percent. More importantly, when estimates were made separately for industries with high and low levels of concentration, unionism was found to have "no impact on the profitability of competitive firms" (Freeman and Medoff, 1984, p. 186). In contrast, profitability is reduced 17 to 26 percent by unions in highly concentrated sectors leading the authors to conclude, "What unions do is to reduce the exceedingly high levels of profitability in highly concentrated industries toward normal competitive levels" (p. 186).

This pattern of effects suggest that unions share monopoly rents where they exist.

62

Firm Studies

Studies with firm data have produced varied results. Using a sample of 175 COMPUSTAT firms and an idiosyncratic specification, Salinger (1984) found that union workers captured 77 percent of monopoly rents. Hirsch and Connolly (1987) used a sample of 367 Fortune 500 firms with extensive controls to test whether the reduced profits of organized firms are caused by unions capturing rents from investment in intangibles such as research and development (R&D). In an initial model, higher levels of unionization are associated with a reduction in q. This disappears when a measure of R&D expenditure is included among the explanatory variables. After allowing for interactions between unionization and R&D, concentration, and market share variables, Hirsch and Connolly found that, in the presence of large investments in R&D, unions have a substantial negative effect on firm profits. There is no evidence that union effects on profits are mediated by market power.

These results are sensitive to the measure of profits, however. Surprisingly, there is no relationship between unionization and profits in equations in which price-cost margins are used in place of q. Despite the difference in findings with q and price-cost margins, the authors interpret their results as demonstrating that unions reduce the gains from intangible capital. Connolly, Hirsch, and Hirschy (1986) reached similar conclusions in a study which, using the same data set, found that excess valuation, a measure similar to q, had a strong negative relation to the interaction of R&D and unionization.[24] Using a sample of 300 manufacturing firms, measures of firm and industry unionization, and either excess valuation or price-cost margins, Becker and Olson (1990) also found a strong negative relation between firm unionization and profits which may be related to unions capturing rents on intangibles. The results of all of these firm studies are compromised by the failure to control for the effects of foreign income on rates of profit.[25]

Clark's (1984) study of productivity also considered how unions affected profitability as measured by return on investment and return on sales (an analog of the industry price-cost margin). The data set covers the product lines of 250 large firms and, as with the previous study, contains extensive controls for firm and market structure, including variables for concentration and market share but lacking R&D measures. Clark found that unions reduced return on sales by 16 percent and return on capital by 19 percent.

What unions do is to reduce the exceedingly high levels of profitability in highly concentrated industries toward normal competitive levels.

63

There are two studies of firms within specific industries. Looking at supermarket chains in urban markets, Voos and Mishel (1986b) reported that unions had a larger negative effect on profits in concentrated markets, but could not distinguish this from a general negative relationship between unionization and profits. Contrary to almost all the research in this field, Allen (1988) found that unions do not reduce profits in private construction.

Looking at
supermarket
chains in urban
markets, Voos and
Mishel reported
that unions had a
larger negative
effect on profits in
concentrated
markets.

Stock Market Studies

Another approach to measuring the effect of unions on profits is to consider how unions affect short term returns in the stock market. Assuming that the stock market processes information efficiently, these returns will reflect the true value of a firm. As new information about a firm becomes available, the price of its stock will change to reflect the new knowledge. If unions affect firm performance, then a change in the firm's relationship with unions—in bargaining status, in the terms of the labor contract, and so on—will be reflected in shifts in market valuation.

Looking at the effect of National Labor Relations Board (NLRB) election petitions and certifications on the returns to 253 member firms of the New York Stock Exchange, Ruback and Zimmerman (1984) found that election petitions had a negative and significant influence on returns. If a union wins an election and is certified, the average stock holder loses 3.8 percent of the value of the stock; if the union loses, the loss is 1.3 percent. Becker and Olson (1986) found that, on average, strikes caused a 4.1 percent decline in shareholder equity for firms listed on the New York or American exchanges. Similar results were reported by Greer, Martin, and Reusser (1980). Becker (1987) found that concessionary contracts raise the value of stock holdings by 8 to 10 percent. Abowd (1989) found a dollar-for-dollar trade-off between shareholder's wealth and unexpected changes in collectively bargained labor costs, in both a positive and a negative direction. Employing data on 1,000 firms from 1971 to 1981, Becker and Olson (1986) reported that unionized firms realized lower returns on investment.

How should we interpret these studies? Although some authors argue that reduced stock market valuation is a consequence of reduction in the total value of the firm to stockholders, employees, and bondholders (from supposed inefficiencies associated with unionism), this is only one possible explanation. Lower returns could be caused by the redistribution of income from shareholders to employees. Becker argues that the increase in valuation associated with concessions is not founded on changes in the value of the firm, but an enlargement of the shareholders' value at the expense of the workers. This is consistent with the view that union wage gains come out of profits rather than escalated prices. Becker and Olson's findings on strikes provides additional evidence that negative effects on firm performance may be due to labor-management strife rather than unions *per se*.[26] Labor problems may also be a result rather than a cause of declining firm economic performance. In Ruback and Zimmerman's study, the largest part of the decline in the value of the firms occurred considerably before the filing of the election petition. Unless the market is unusually prescient, the firms were experiencing economic problems prior to the organizing drive. Employee support for unions may be a response to efficiency and cost-cutting measures implemented by troubled companies (Becker and Olson, 1986).

The findings of the profits literature should affect our assessment of the economic consequences of unions. This will attenuate any effects of unions on prices, demand, and the employment conditions of nonmembers. If, as the productivity literature indicates, unions are also funding part of their premia through increased productivity, then the negative economic consequences of unions for consumers and workers must be quite small. A negative effect on the profits of organized firms may however have deleterious consequences for the unions themselves. If organized firms realize lower long-run returns on investment, there is an incentive for investors to shift funds to nonunion firms and for partially organized firms to shift investment into their nonunion segments. Unless unions are able to organize new nonunion plants, they will become isolated in older facilities and lose membership as these facilities are closed. Part of the decline in union membership over the past twenty years may be due to such shifts in investment.

Industry, firm, and stock market studies indicate that part of the union wage premia is being absorbed by firms.

Effects of the Industrial Relations Climate

Firm performance will be greatly influenced by the role taken by a union.

The tenor of relations between labor and management varies widely by firm and industry. It is not unprecedented to have both prolonged industrial warfare and cooperative efforts within the same industry. Multiple factors (worker and management attitudes, the structure of bargaining, the goals and strategies of the parties, the organization of work, the history of conflict resolution) mediate the relation between unions, their members, and firm performance. In their role as employee representative, unions can inform members about new programs, encourage open discussion, and obtain commitment to change. In their other role as opposition to management authority, unions can hamper implementation of management programs. Firm performance will be greatly influenced by the role taken by a union.

The importance of the labor relations climate has been reflected in studies discussed in previous sections. Recent strike activity—an indicator of industrial conflict—was shown to increase hospital costs by 7 to 9 percent. Kendrick and Grossman's research suggested that days idled during strikes had a negative relation to productivity growth. Maki's work found a negative relation between strike activity and productivity growth. Becker and Olson showed that stock market returns fell 4.1 percent as a consequence of strikes. The union productivity advantage in bituminous coal declined from + 30 percent to − 17 percent as labor relations deteriorated in the 1970s. High levels of conflict in commercial banking reduced productivity 25 percent.

Renewed interest in the climate of labor relations has been associated with the expansion of programs for labor-management cooperation such as gainsharing, quality of worklife, quality circles, and labor-management committees.[27] Initially introduced to address ongoing problems such as safety conditions and employee dissatisfaction, these programs are currently touted as a method of increasing productivity, raising quality, and lowering costs. The mechanisms through which these programs act remains a matter of discussion. These programs do not appear to resolve fundamental differences between the interests of labor and management. Rather, they provide new means to address these differences. By raising the level of trust in the workplace, they provide a foundation for a cooperative (problem solving) approach to differences and conflicts. Thus, the programs improve the effectiveness of the industrial relations system and the economic performance of the firm (Katz, Kochan, and Gobeille, 1983; Kochan, Katz, and Mower, 1985).

The United Automobile Workers and the General Motors Corporation have, under the rubric Quality of Worklife (QWL), conducted extensive experiments with cooperative programs since the early 1970s. Looking at these programs in eighteen plants in the mid-1970s, Katz, Kochan, and Gobeille (1983) tested their hypothesis that plant-level economic performance (quality of output and the ratio of actual to standard labor hours) is an outcome of the industrial relations climate (managers' views on trust and cooperation) and the performance of the industrial relations system (grievance levels, absenteeism, disciplinary actions, time spent in negotiations, and the number of contract demands at negotiations). The measures of the industrial relations climate were positively correlated with both better industrial relations outcomes and better economic performance. After allowing for the effects of the business cycle and differences among plants, quality was shown to be positively influenced by the climate and lower levels of grievance activity. There was little effect on labor efficiency.[28]

A study of twenty-five GM plants employing 50,000 workers indicated that positive attitudes (salaried worker attitudes and participation in suggestion programs), effective conflict management system (grievance rates, disciplinary actions rates, and absenteeism rates), and high levels of participation in QWL programs had beneficial effects on both productivity (direct labor efficiency) and quality (Katz, Kochan, and Weber, 1985). With controls for environmental factors (overtime and plant size) and plant effects, the researchers found that, although the effects of the attitudinal and conflictual measures are not distinct, they have a large joint effect on both economic performance variables. However, QWL did not have an effect on either dimension of performance. It may be that, as the authors argue, plants with good industrial relations performance are likely to have high QWL participation rates but that the programs have no effect in and of themselves. Alternatively, these results may indicate that attitudes, conflict management, and QWL participation are so closely linked that distinct measures for individual variables cannot be obtained.

The measures of the industrial relations climate were positively correlated with both better industrial relations outcomes and better economic performance.

67

Norsworthy and Zabala (1985) examined the relation between attitudes, behavior, and productivity in the automobile industry at a more aggregate level. Using industry data for the period 1959–1976, the authors estimated a cost function which included measures of worker attitudes toward their work and their firm: filed grievances, unresolved grievances, unauthorized strikes, and quit rates. These measures were positively associated with increased production costs. If they are combined into an index of worker attitudes, a 10 percent improvement in attitudes was estimated to reduce production costs by 4 to 5 percent.

> *There is evidence of linkages between the availability of grievance arbitration and factors known to have a beneficial effect on productivity.*

Grievance/arbitration procedures provide an orderly means of communicating and resolving industrial discord between employers and employees. Where these procedures are available, levels of conflict should be lower and the employment relationship more productive. In their absence, alternative means of resolving disputes, exit by individuals, and job actions by work groups are disruptive and costly (Ichniowski and Lewin, 1987). There is evidence of linkages between the availability of grievance arbitration and factors known to have a beneficial effect on productivity. The availability of grievance procedures reduces turnover of nurses by approximately 15 percent in both unionized and nonunionized hospitals. Arbitration procedures are associated with an additional 2 percent reduction (Ichniowski and Lewin, 1987). This is consistent with Freeman's 1976 finding that organized employees had lower turnover and longer tenure.[29]

Grievance procedures also meter the level of industrial conflict. High levels of grievance activity may evidence an inability to resolve conflict (Katz, Kochan, and Weber, 1985). Katz, Kochan, and Gobeille found escalated grievance filing associated with reduced quality; Kochan, Katz, and Mower found a strong negative correlation between grievance activity, disciplinary actions, and both productivity and quality; Norsworthy and Zabala found that productivity declined with increased numbers of filed and unresolved grievances; Spencer (1986) found higher grievance rates associated with higher turnover among registered nurses. Studying the paper industry, Ichniowski (1986) found that grievance-free paper mills were 1.3 percent more productive and 16.7 percent more profitable than mills operating with a "normal" level of grievances. Although the analysis shows that union plants never operate far below full labor productivity, a nonunion plant was estimated by

Ichniowski to be functioning 19.5 percent below full labor efficiency due to implicit grievances. The length of the collective bargaining agreement—a crude measure of labor-management distrust—also has a strong negative relation to productivity (Ichniowski, 1984b). Similar results were reported by Kelley (1990a) who found that codified work rules and procedures were associated with slower production and lower productivity in automated plants. Brett and Goldberg (1979) found that resolution of grievances in early, informal steps of the procedure reduced wildcat strike activity in bituminous coal mining. Favorable attitudes between labor and management, corporate policies which permit foremen to settle grievances, and management accessibility and willingness to discuss grievances informally also had favorable effects on wildcat strike activity.

Schuster (1983) combined quantitative and case study approaches to evaluate the productivity and employment effects of gainsharing programs in ten plants over a five-year period. The author found that productivity rose in six of the eight plants after the introduction of gainsharing. Employment did not change in the eight firms providing employment figures. The effectiveness of the programs was closely linked to the implementation process. Successful programs required sustained commitment from employees and managers. Plans cannot be imposed from above, must be supported by the full plant community, and must not be perceived as being subject to manipulation.

Negative worker attitudes, as measured by the volume of "wildcat" strikes, also affect productivity. Using quarterly data for the period 1961–1981, Flaherty (1987) found that wildcat strikes had a strong negative relation to productivity levels. A 1 percent increase in inter-contractual strikes caused a 2.9 percent decrease in productivity. However, omission of a unionization variable precludes distinguishing the effects of worker attitudes from those of changes in union strength. In a study of forty-six manufacturing plants in seven industries, Bemmel (1987) found, in keeping with other research on high conflict environments, that strike activity reduces productivity. Unions by themselves have no effect on productivity except to reduce the effectiveness of incentive pay systems.

Because they focus on organized firms and industries, studies of labor climate are narrower in scope than other productivity studies. Nevertheless, the results indicate that there is substantial variation in the effect of unions on firm

Negative worker attitudes, as measured by the volume of "wildcat" strikes, also affect productivity.

performance and this variation is caused by differences in the relationship between labor and management. Low trust/high conflict environments, rather than unions, are the source of reduced productivity. Higher levels of trust are associated with reduced strife and, consequently, with both greater productivity and higher product quality. Further, although the level of conflict is affected by the conditions and history of a plant, firm, and industry, the parties can reduce the level of conflict and share the gains from improved efficiency and quality.

Summary and Conclusion

What have we learned from a decade of quantitative research? *First*, contrary to the fears of neoclassical economists, unions do not of themselves lower productivity. The majority of studies find that unions are associated with higher productivity. Of those which have not found positive effects, there is typically either no effect or a negative effect associated with a poor labor relations climate. *Second*, organized firms have lower rates of profit than nonunion firms. This negative relation is found in virtually all data sets and specifications. *Finally*, although the findings are tentative, the labor relations climate appears to determine the effect of unions on firm performance. Unions can improve or degrade firm performance, depending on the relationship between workers and managers. These topics aside, there are either too few studies or too little agreement among the varied studies to reach conclusions on other matters.

These results should alter our views on the economic consequences of unions. The negative consequences cited by most economists—higher prices and lower employment—are largely mitigated by higher union productivity and lower rates of profit. It would be useful to establish employment and price effects directly, but the evidence indicates that they will be small. This should be heartening to those who have always seen the gain from unions—greater democracy in everyday life—purchased at the expense of reduced economic efficiency. The cost of economic democracy appears smaller than previously believed.

Another finding is that it is the handling of conflict, not unions, which affects productivity. Managers and employ-

Low trust/high conflict environments, rather than unions, are the source of reduced productivity.

ees have shared interests, but also legitimate differences in interests. It is these differences which underlie conflict in the workplace. The institutions and procedures for managing conflict that govern employee and managerial behavior thereby regulate firm performance. Low trust/high conflict environments, environments with elevated levels of grievance activity, work stoppages, and dissatisfaction are not conducive to employees doing more than is required to earn a paycheck and avoid dismissal. Employers, lacking the support of their labor force, cannot avail themselves of employee loyalty and intelligence to improve the product or production methods. Conversely, high trust/low strife environments provide a foundation for improving efficiency. By developing trust, emphasizing problem-solving, and respecting the divergent and conflicting interests of the parties, these joint programs make it possible to implement new technologies, job practices, employment relations, and management structures in a manner consistent with the concerns of both labor and management.

High levels of conflict are not inherent in employment relations. Although discord is often deeply rooted in the history of the parties, less conflictual and more productive relationships can be achieved by deliberate efforts to promote problem solving. More companies and unions, convinced that there are better ways to work with one another, are trying cooperative programs. At the national level, the most extensive cooperative program is the set of initiatives developed between the UAW and two auto companies, Ford and GM. This effort includes restructuring work, improving workers' knowledge of the industry, and protecting the jobs of employees. The Amalgamated Clothing and Textile Workers and the Xerox Corporation have a successful program which, through a mixture of hard bargaining and problem solving, has been able to reduce costs and increase job security. The United Steelworkers and the major steel companies have been engaged in joint training to ease the shift to team work structures. The A&P corporation and the United Food and Commercial Workers are also trying QWL programs as a means of addressing nonunion competition in several locations.

These programs do not mean that all differences between labor and management have been resolved. The parties remain in contention over issues such as wages, benefits, profits, and job security. The programs involve both sides in an ongoing process of balancing effective rep-

More companies and unions, convinced that there are better ways to work with one another, are trying cooperative programs.

71

resentation of their interests with a need to work together. What the cooperative programs provide are new tools for managing conflict, maintaining a productive relationship, and differentiating between joint issues and those which are contentious. They provide an additional means of addressing many of the current problems faced by firms and labor.

Historically, labor-management cooperation has received more praise than support. Cooperative programs are difficult to start, place great strains on those leading the programs, and when they succeed, are hard to institutionalize. The industrial relations traditions and legal structure of the United States emphasize limiting conflict over developing cooperation. The U.S. Department of Labor and federal Mediation and Conciliation Service support cooperative efforts through state conferences, guidance in establishing programs, training for participants, and advice in solving ongoing problems. These programs, the only resource available to many unions and firms, are small and do not have resources adequate to meet the ongoing needs of the existing cooperative ventures. More active federal support for cooperation, both in increased availability of training and promotion of the advantages of cooperation, would encourage those who are unaware of these gains or are reluctant to begin without the availability of expertise.

It is typical to end with the suggestion that more research, preferably supported by substantial grants, would greatly add to our knowledge and provide a sounder base for policy. The need for more considered research has been adequately documented in the body of this paper and does not bear repeating. Rather, there is a need to be clearer about what we are measuring. By focusing on productivity, costs, prices, and profits, we have neglected the fundamental reasons for the existence of unions: protection of the economic interests of employees, provision of due process, and the betterment of the physical and moral work environment. Better firm performance can be the outcome of skilled workers operating with superior capital in a wholesome environment. Better performance can also be founded on sweated labor driven to higher output by necessity and insecurity. It is to be hoped that we do not believe these two examples to be equally acceptable so long as they are equal in productivity, cost, and profit. Yet, based on disembodied numbers which veil labor conditions, such a conclusion would be possible.

> **By focusing on productivity . . . we have neglected the fundamental reasons for the existence of unions: protection of the economic interests of employees, provision of due process, and the betterment of the physical and moral work environment.**

Endnotes

1   Programs for labor-management cooperation and research on the labor relations climate previously received particular attention in the 1920s, 1940s, and 1950s.

2   Other recent reviews of this literature are provided by Addison and Hirsch (1989) and Allen (1988a).

3   There are theoretical and empirical reasons to question the importance of these adjustments. In models predicting that firms alter worker quality, capital/labor ratios assume that unions bargain wages and then naively allow the firm to adjust employment. Other models indicate that unions, in an effort to preserve employment, allow firms to pay competitive wages and then bargain for a share of firm profits. The firm has no incentive to alter employment or capital stock. Of equal importance in the real world, Scherer (1980) reports that capital to labor ratios are invariant to the relative costs of capital and labor.

4   The effectiveness of the exit mechanism also depends on the efficiency of labor markets and the ease with which workers can find alternative employment.

5   Value-added is not an accurate measure of labor productivity if differences in value-added are associated with the ability of firms to charge higher prices for identical products. Firms with power over price, located in markets with weak competitive conditions, will have an escalated value of shipments and appear to have higher value-added per unit of labor. This measurement problem is particularly serious if we believe that organized firms—firms which generally have higher labor costs—have the ability to pass escalated costs into their prices. Price effects are not a problem in competitive markets because firms are unable to pass on increased costs. Controls for the degree of competitiveness, such as four-firm concentration ratios, will reduce price effect bias in the measure of union effects on productivity.

6   Consider the case of an organized and unorganized firm with equal labor productivity. If the unionized firm has fewer part-time workers than the nonunion firm, the union firm will appear to have higher productivity when it is measured per worker. If union workers work less overtime than their nonunion counterparts, union productivity will be lower when measured per worker. Measures of output per employee hour will not be subject to these biases.

7   These are the coefficients on the fraction unionized in the Brown-Medoff study. These results were not changed when controls for material inputs and different types of labor were added. If these gains are attributed exclusively to the labor input, then the union effect on productivity equals the coefficient on unionism divided by 1 minus the coefficient on the capital-labor ratio, and there is a union labor productivity effect of about 30 percent.

8   The PIMS sample differs from the industry sample in that it does not represent all firms or even all large firms. Because there may be multiple observations on some product lines (GM, Ford, and Chrysler all produce cars) and none in others

(no large firms produce carbon blacking), the weighing of observations is very different from industry data sets.

9   The Kaufman and Kaufman (1987) study of the auto-parts industry is omitted because response rate for their survey, less than 10 percent, is well below the 50 percent rate required to avoid response bias (Babbie, 1973).

10 Clark is skeptical about the results for the older plant equation because the non-union sample is very small and the organized plants in the sample have substantially older capital stocks than the nonunion plants.

11 Allen suggests that the competitive market in private construction serves to hold down the costs of union labor. In the public sector, restriction on materials and area wage standards legislation serves to increase the cost of union labor.

12 The deterioration of the industrial relations climate was due to the flow of younger workers into the industry, problems within the United Mine Workers leadership, and an effort by the industry to reduce the power of the union. During 1977, mining, which accounted for 1 percent of total employment, accounted for 20 percent of all strikes and 25 percent of all participants in strikes. This was also the year when coal miners defied their leadership and a Taft-Hartley injunction by remaining on strike against the Bituminous Coal Operators Association for 120 days.

13 If firms respond to union wages by adjusting capital and labor quality, growth rates of organized firms will be higher during the period of adjustment. After the adjustment, growth rates will be unchanged so long as the relative union wage advantage is stable.

14 The index is constructed by converting the measures of capital and labor into indices. The final index number for each year is computed by weighing the capital and labor indices by their factor shares, the proportion of income going to capital and labor, and summing the result.

15 While results with TFP indices and labor productivity indices should be similar, the TFP imposes the annual factor share parameters which are estimated in the labor productivity studies. The difference in the share parameters used in TFP studies and those found in the labor studies are large, suggesting that the studies will produce different results.

16 If we consider the growth equations as extensions of the productivity level equations across time, then changes rather than levels in the explanatory variables provide the appropriate formulation. The use of level measures is, however, common.

17 Maki reported problems with the study when he used a measure of unemployment to control for business cycle movement.

18 In the short run, rates of profit will fall no matter who pays for the wage premium. Only when firms have had the opportunity to adjust their capital stock does the rate of profit provide information on the impact of higher union costs. As the patterns of private sector unionization have been stable for thirty years, it

is reasonable to presume that the studies are estimating long-run relationships.

[19] Increased market power is associated with both higher wages and an increase in the differential between union and nonunion wages (Belman, 1988).

[20] In some of the literature, the technical term—the value of shipments—is employed in place of sales.

[21] Typically, where data is not available by firm, data on the firm's primary industry is substituted.

[22] Unless there are other mismatched industry variables in the equation, the measure of organization will pick up all of the "effects" associated with the firm's primary industry rather then union effects. It will misrepresent the effects of unions.

[23] Becker and Olson (1986) provided an extensive review of the research on profitability effects using stock market measures. Their explanation of event history studies is particularly accessible.

[24] Contrary to the authors' thesis, the interaction between advertising expenditures—another form of intangible capital—and penetration had a positive relation to profits. The authors claim that, because advertising is a short term investment, unions cannot lay effective claim to the increased revenues.

[25] These firm studies are compromised by the failure to control for income originating from foreign subsidiaries. This income is included in the profit measure of the firms, many of which are multinationals receiving substantial portions of their income from abroad. If there is any correlation between foreign profit levels, the extent of foreign operations, and unionization, the measured relation between unions and profits will be biased.

[26] If strikes are a means through which workers and managers determine the allocation of profits, then the lower returns during strikes could reflect concerns about future redistributions.

[27] Gainsharing plans—Scanlon and Rucker plans and their variants—provide a formula for sharing increased productivity (or cost reductions) resulting from employee efforts to improve efficiency. Quality of worklife programs are intended to establish direct channels of communication between workers and their supervisors and involve workers in shopfloor decisionmaking. Quality circle programs establish voluntary teams of managers and employees which discuss production problems and develop improvements. Labor-management committees address issues such as safety which are of mutual concern to labor and management and are more amenable to problem solving than negotiation.

[28] The authors suggest this latter result may be due to the sample of plants included in the survey.

[29] Although the availability of grievance procedures reduces turnover, use of those procedures is associated with escalated turnover. This is not surprising as a large proportion of grievances are filed over issues of discipline and dismissal (see Lewin, 1987; Lewin and Peterson, 1987).

APPENDIX I
Studies of Union Productivity Effects

Reference	Key Finding	Type of Study
	INTER-INDUSTRY STUDIES	
Brown & Medoff (1978)	Unions increase productivity 19–24 percent.	Inter-industry production function; 20 manufacturing industries in various states.
Clark (1984)	Unions have a small negative effect on productivity in the −2 to −3 percent range. Clark doubts unions have any effect on productivity.	Inter-industry production function; 250 very large firms from the PIMS data set. Data is organized by product line within firm.
	INDUSTRY STUDIES	
Clark (1980a)	Organized cement plants have 6 to 8 percent higher productivity. Newer union plants have 10 percent higher productivity.	Industry production function: estimated with data on 119 union and 9 nonunion plants for four years in the early 1970s.
Clark (1980b)	Cement plants experience a 6.9 to 12.1 percent improvement productivity when they are organized. This is due, in large part, to shock effects.	Industry production function for six cement plants from in 1953 to 1976.

Variables	Comments

INTER-INDUSTRY STUDIES

PRODUCTIVITY: Value-added per production employee hour.
UNIONIZATION: Percent organized by industry and state.
CONTROLS: Capital per employee, an index of labor quality, establishment size, investment flow, industry and region dummies.

Value-added may not be an accurate measure of productivity if firms have power over price.

PRODUCTIVITY: Ratio of value-added or sales to total firm employment.
UNIONIZATION: Percent organized by firm product line or dummy variables derived from percent organized.
CONTROLS: Market structure and the age of capital. Demographic controls based on three-digit industry averages.

Sample is not representative of all firms in industry and may not be representative of large firms. The demographic variables, three-digit industry averages, may not be closely to the characteristics of the firm's workforce. Differences in the measures of productivity and universe of firms makes comparisons with Brown & Medoff tenuous.

INDUSTRY STUDIES

PRODUCTIVITY: Tons of cement per production worker.
UNIONIZATION: Dummy variable to indicate whether the plant was organized.
CONTROLS: Ratios of capital to labor and supervisors to labor, size of the facility, average utilization, vintage, and plant-specific effects.

The study lacks controls for labor quality. As cement plant labor is relatively homogeneous across plants, omission may not affect the results.

PRODUCTIVITY: Tons of cement per employee.
UNIONIZATION: Dummy variable indicating when the plant was under contract.
CONTROLS: Capital to labor, supervisors to labor, capacity utilization, total production manhours, vintage, regional, time, and firm effects. Production functions were estimated under various assumptions.

The study was based on a very small group of plants. The results may be specific to these plants or to the cement industry.

Reference	Key Finding	Type of Study
Allen (1984)	Union construction workers have between 17 to 22 percent higher productivity.	Industry production function for the construction industry. Data are divided into state by four-digit industry cells.
Allen (1986a, 1986b, 1987)	Union construction workers are from 36 to 38 percent more productive and 20 percent less expensive for office construction. The union productivity advantage in school construction varies with the measure of productivity and type of school. Union-built schools are 16 percent more expensive.	Industry production and cost functions for the office, school, and medical construction industry. Data are on individual projects.
Allen (1988b)	Union workers are 51 percent more efficient in retail construction. Costs, prices, and profits are equal across the two sectors.	Productivity, cost, and profit study covering 42 retail stores and shopping centers. The productivity and price study uses a Cobb-Douglas function. The cost and profit comparisons are obtained from a translog cost function.

Variables	Comments
PRODUCTIVITY: Value-added and deflated value-added. UNIONIZATION: Percent of employees organized in state by four-digit industry cell. CONTROLS: Capital to labor ratio, firm size, labor quality, regional and industry effects.	Productivity studies are often criticized because they fail to distinguish the productivity effect of unions from their effect on price. This study removes price effects by using deflated value-added. Although the union productivity advantage declines, it remains substantial.
PRODUCTIVITY: Productivity is measured as value added per employee and square feet of construction per employee. In the cost function, the dependent variable was square footage per employee. ORGANIZATION: Productivity estimates used dummy variables to indicate union projects. Separate cost functions were estimated for union and nonunion projects. CONTROLS: For the productivity studies, controls included a capital to labor ratio, the size of the project, an index of labor quality, and building characteristics. The study of schools included a dummy for secondary schools. In the medical study, controls for public construction and nursing homes are included. The cost estimates were derived from a translog function various restrictions.	Unions are shown to have higher productivity and lower costs on larger and more complex projects. Allen believes that the union cost advantage in private sector construction is related to greater competition and fewer restrictions on materials and construction techniques.
DEPENDENT VARIABLE: In the productivity study, value added per hour or square feet per hour. In the cost estimates, the dependent variable was cost per hour. UNIONIZATION: In the productivity and price studies, a dummy variable indicated whether the project used union labor. The translog was estimated separately for union and nonunion projects. CONTROLS: In the productivity equation, the capital to labor ratio and project size. In the translog, labor and input prices and project size.	As with Allen's other studies of unionized construction in the private sector, it appears that union workers pay for their higher wages with substantially higher levels of productivity. The large productivity differential is somewhat surprising as retail construction requires fewer skills than office construction.

Reference	Key Finding	Type of Study
Sloan & Adamache (1984)	Unions have no effect on productivity and raise hospital costs by 3.5 to 4.1 percent. Measured at the departmental level, unions do not affect productivity or costs.	Provides estimates of the effect of union wages and productivity practices on hospital costs. Sample of 367 hospitals from the 1974 and 1977 American Hospital Association Survey.
Register (1988)	In a national sample, unions raised hospital productivity 16.1 percent and lowered costs by 9.5 percent. In a sample of Ohio hospitals, unions had a positive effect on productivity and no effect on cost.	Provides estimates of the effect of unions on hospital productivity, wages, and costs. Sample of 250 hospitals from the 1984 American Hospital Association Survey
Machin (1988)	Results vary with specification. Overall, unions have no effect on productivity. With controls for firm size, unions have no effect on small firm productivity, but reduce productivity in firms of more than 1000 employees.	A production function study of the British engineering industry. The sample covered 52 firms for the period 1978–1982.

Variables	Comments
COST: Cost per patient day or cost per admission. UNIONIZATION: The union status of the hospital. Hospitals considered organized if any employees have bargaining rights. CONTROLS: Hospital size, the mixture of services and sources of payments, region, public/private status. OTHER: Estimated as a two stage system. Estimated wages were included in the cost equation to measure the effect of union wages on costs.	There are several problems. The measure of union status does not adjust for partial organization of a facility or differences in bargaining structure. The wage equation uses a measure of average employee benefits but fails to adjust for the skill composition of the staff. This may bias estimates of union wage effects. The study does not use conventional cost equations, raising some concern about the meaning of their measures.
PRODUCTIVITY: Productivity is inpatient days per employee while cost is measured as average costs per patient day. UNIONIZATION: Hospital considered organized if located in a city with more than 70 percent of health care workers organized. Considered unorganized if in a city with less than 1 percent organized. CONTROLS: In the productivity equation, conventional controls plus measures of the mixture of services and regional dummies. In the cost equation, measures of the mixture of services, regional dummies, and patient care characteristics.	As in the Sloan and Adamache study, the measure of organization is only weakly associated with union presence or bargaining power. The definition of unionization removes some hospitals from the study. While inclusion of controls for the skill level of the staff provides better wage estimates, Register uses a less extensive and sophisticated set of controls in the cost equation. The cost equation is not estimated in a conventional form.
PRODUCTIVITY: Value-added per employee deflated for by an industry price level index. UNIONIZATION: Either an index of unionization constructed from measures of union security arrangements, percent of employees unionized, and the number of production and white collar unions in a firm or a dummy variable indicating whether there was a closed shop. CONTROLS: Capital to labor ratio, pay incentive schemes, technology, plant size, and proportion of employees in skilled trades.	The use of an unusual index of unionization and interactions between this index and firm characteristics makes interpretation of results difficult. When an indicator of the union security arrangement is used there is no evidence of a union productivity effect. The results are also problematic because the study includes a single nonunion firm and fails to control for plant or industry effects.

Reference	Key Finding	Type of Study
Graddy & Hall (1985)	Bank productivity is not influenced by unionization. There is weak evidence that conflictual labor relations reduce productivity by up to 25 percent.	A firm level labor productivity study using 60 banks: 30 union banks matched to 30 nonunion banks. The authors are interested in determining whether different unions have differential effects on productivity and whether the union sector had the same production function as the nonunion sector.
Connerton, Freeman, & Medoff (1983)	Union productivity effects in bituminous coal change from a positive 25 percent in the 1960s to a negative 25 percent in the mid 1970s. The shift is due to changes in the industrial relations climate in bituminous coal	
Boal (1990)	Unions had no influence on productivity in large underground mines, but decreased productivity in smaller mines.	Production function study of output on 83 mines in West Virginia over four years in the 1920s. The study used both Cobb-Douglas and translog functions.

Variables	Comments
PRODUCTIVITY: The ratio of interest and fees on lending output divided by the total non-supervisory labor force. UNIONIZATION: Depending on the equation, a dummy variable indicating whether bank employees have union representation or union specific dummy variables for organization by OPEIU, UFCW, Teamsters, ACTWU, other international unions, or independent unions. CONTROLS: Capital to labor and supervisory to non-superivsory labor ratios. Equations for the union sector include number of years since organization and percent of employees belonging to the union.	Although the authors believe their study indicates a negative relation between unionization and productivity, the hypothesis of a non-negative effect can never be rejected in any conventional test of significance. Further, even accepting the authors' weak tests, negative effects are isolated in two banks with notably conflictual labor relations.
PRODUCTIVITY: Apparently tons of coal produced by a mine on an annual basis. UNIONIZATION: Whether the mine was under contract in the year in question. CONTROLS: Number of miners, number of other workers, number of maintenance workers, number of mining machines, mine locomotives, and mules. In addition, the models controlled for geological conditions, mine age, and structure. The model was estimated in a panel data framework.	The authors' data covers a particularly conflictual period in labor history in West Virginia. All of the mines in the sample were nonunion by the end of the period under study. This suggests that the result may be due to high levels of conflict rather than unionism per se.
PRODUCTIVITY: Output of coal per unit of input. UNIONIZATION: Whether a mine was covered by a collective bargaining agreement. CONTROLS: Labor input, earth-moving capacity, number of drills and related equipment, the number of bulldozers and related equipment, the thickness of the seam, and amount of overburden.	

Reference	Key Finding	Type of Study
Byrnes, Fare, Grosskopf, and Lovell (1987)	Unionized surface coal mines have higher productivity than nonunion mines. The inefficiency of nonunion mines is due the small size of the mines increasing the costs of meeting safety envi-ronmental regulations.	The study looked at 84 midwest-ern surface mines in 1978 and 64 Western surface mines for the period 1975–1978. Actual levels of output were compared with optimal levels based on non-parametric production function analysis.
Kelley (1990)	Unionization and seniority procedures reduced the time required for a production run in automated machine shops. Extensive rules for operations had the reverse effect.	The data set included 2,044 dis-tinct jobs in 1,015 plants of which 817 were crafted solely with programmable technology. Results are obtained from an OLS regression using 605 observations.
Frantz (1976)	Unions raised productivity by 15 percent in the wooden household furniture industry.	

FIRM STUDIES

Mefford (1986)	Unions increase productivity by 13 percent. This increase is associated with improved management performance and increased capital investment.	A production function study of 126 plants in an international consumer products firm. All plants use similar technologies and have similar workforces.

Variables	Comments

PRODUCTIVITY: Time taken for a production run.
UNIONIZATION: Whether a plant was organized.
CONTROLS: Product specific attributes, plant specific technology, technology expertise, management practices, and labor characteristics.

FIRM STUDIES

PRODUCTIVITY: Actual output to standard output as determined by engineering studies.
UNIONIZATION: Union status of the plant.
CONTROLS: Capital to labor ratio, total employment, absences, turnover, management performance rating, and controls for cultural, economic and social differences between countries.

Findings may be firm-specific. Omission of labor quality variables may cause the union variable to pick up some of the effects of labor quality. The author contends that labor is homogeneous across plants, alleviating this problem.

APPENDIX II
Studies of Union Effects on Productivity Growth

Reference	Key Finding	Type of Study
	CROSS-SECTION STUDIES	
Kendrick & Grossman (1980)	Findings vary with specification and time period. Unions had a negative relation to productivity growth for the period 1948 to 1966, but a positive relation for the period from 1967 to 1976. Inclusion of strike measures eliminate the effect of unions on productivity growth.	Productivity growth in 22 two-digit industries from 1948 to 1976.
Mansfield (1980)	A completely organized industry will have a 5 to 6 percent lower rate of productivity growth.	Similar to Kendrick & Grossman. Data for 22 manufacturing industries for the period 1948–1966.
Link (1981)	Unions reduce productivity growth by 2.5 percent.	Applies Mansfield's specification to 51 major manufacturing firms.

Variables	Comments

CROSS-SECTION STUDIES

GROWTH: Change in total factor productivity from 1948 to 1976 and various intermediate years.

UNIONIZATION: Percent of two digit industry organized in 1958, 1968, or 1972. The annual rate of change of the percent organized and average annual man days lost in strikes.

CONTROLS: Varies between equations. May include capacity utilization, variance of utilization, median education, private R&D, market concentration, pollution abatement expenditures, labor force composition by gender, age and skill, layoff rate, quit rate, and change in sectoral employment.

Estimates of statistical significance are not valid, as specifications have been determined by t-statistics. The authors also note substantial problems with multi-collinearity make casual interpretation of coefficients suspect.

GROWTH: Same as K&G.

UNIONIZATION: Percent of two-digit industry organized in 1958.

CONTROLS: Ratio of basic R&D research to value added, applied R&D to value added, additional R&D measures.

As it is unlikely that only R&D and organization affect productivity, there is potential for substantial omitted variable bias. Estimated coefficients are unlikely to be accurate.

GROWTH: Change in average annual total factor productivity from 1973 and 1978.

UNIONIZATION: Percent organized in the firms major three-digit industry.

CONTROLS: Four measures of expenditures on R&D.

As with Mansfield, the specification is too parsimonious to provide unbiased measures estimates. In addition, the measure of unionization is mismatched since firm organization may be quite different than industry average organization. Omission of controls for industry effects may also bias estimates of the effects of unions on productivity growth.

Reference	Key Finding	Type of Study
Link (1982)	TFP would fall by 10 percent if an unorganized firm became fully organized.	Change in TFP between 1975 and 197 for 32 chemical, 51 machinery, and 14 petroleum firms in the COMPUSTAT data base.
Hirsch & Link (1984)	Both percent organized and change in percent organized have a negative effect on productivity growth.	Total factor productivity growth in 19 two-digit manufacturing industries from 1957 to 1973.
Terleckyi (1980, 1984)	In four equations, the level of unionization has no effect on productivity growth. In three specifications, it reduces growth between 1 percent and 4 percent.	TFP growth from 1948–1966 in 20 two-digit industries (1980). TFP growth in 27 two- and three-digit industries from 1969–1976.

Variables	Comments
GROWTH: The ratio of change in net sales from 1975 to 1979 to an index of the change in total employment and deflated tangible fixed property. UNIONIZATION: The percent of employees belonging to a union in the firm's major industry. OTHER VARIABLES: The ratios of environmental and non-environmental R&D to sales.	The use of industry unionization measures for firm data sets is problematic both because it may be unrepresentative of firm characteristics and because, in the absence of controls for other industry conditions, may may be biased by the effects of demand shifts and other industry-specific effects.
GROWTH: annual total factor productivity growth from 1957 to 1973 from Kendrick & Grossman and from Gollop & Jorgensen. UNIONIZATION: Percent of industry organized in 1958. CONTROLS: Ratio of R&D to sales, market concentration, proportion of sales going to the private sector, cyclic instability of sales.	The results are only obtained from a specification with both unionization and change in unionization. When the unionization variable is dropped, the change variable has no effect on productivity growth.
GROWTH: The 1980 study uses various TFP measures developed by Kendrick, Gollop & Jorgensen, and Kendrick & Grossman. The 1984 study uses the TFP measures of Grillches & Lichtenberg. UNIONIZATION: The 1980 study uses Terleckyi's own data on levels of unionization; the 1984 study uses Freeman and Medoff's data. CONTROLS: The 1980 study uses measures of various levels of R&D intensity, a measure of cyclic variation in output, and government sales. The 1984 study uses several measures of R&D.	The 1980 results are notably sensitive to the data set and construction of the variables. The 1984 results generally are non-significant or indicate a very small negative effect.

Reference	Key Finding	Type of Study
Sveikauskus & Sveikauskus (1982)	Percent organized has no effect on productivity growth.	Total factor productivity growth in 144 three-digit manufacturing industries from 1959 to 1969.
Freeman & Medoff (1984)	Percent organized has no effect on productivity growth.	Average annual growth in labor productivity for various periods and levels of aggregation of the data.
Allen (1988c)	In manufacturing, there is no evidence that percent organized affects the growth of labor productivity. In construction, high initial levels of organization or growth of organization are associated with lower rates of productivity growth.	In manufacturing, the annual change in physical labor in 74 three- and four-digit industries from 1972 to 1983. In construction, the change in TFP in 3 two-digit industries across 27 states between 1972, 1977, and 1982.

Variables	Comments
GROWTH: Average annual total factor productivity.	This study uses a comprehensive set of controls. Use of less aggregate industry data than other studies also provides a better match between the growth variable the explanatory variables.
UNIONIZATION: Either the percent of workers or the percent of production workers belonging to a union.	
CONTROLS: Percent of employees in large firms, percent of employees in small firms, market concentration, percent of employees in R&D, and a durable goods dummy.	
GROWTH: Average annual value-added per worker for three-digit industries for 1958–1976, for four-digit industries for 1958–1978, or for two-digit industries by state cells for 1972–1977.	
UNIONIZATION: Percent organized.	
GROWTH: In manufacturing, the average annual change in an index of physical output per employee for 1972 to 1983. In construction, it is the change in the ratio of real value added to an index of real labor and capital input for the periods 1972–1982, 1972–1977, and 1977–1982.	The manufacturing study provides additional evidence that productivity growth results are sensitive to the measure of output and to the level of aggregation of the data. Allen believes the negative productivity growth relation found in construction is due to migration of skilled union workers to nonunion jobs.
UNIONIZATION: Both studies include a measure of the initial level of unionization as well as a measure of change in the level of unionization for the period under consideration.	
CONTROLS: In manufacturing, concentration and R&D. In construction, the level and change in labor quality establishment size.	

APPENDIX III
Time Series Studies of Union Effects on Productivity and Growth

Reference	Key Finding	Type of Study
Maki (1983)	On average, growth of the Canadian economy is 40 percent lower because of unions. It is reduced a further 15 percent because of strike activity.	Time series regression of change in total factor productivity for Canada from 1926 to 1978.
Warren (1985), Sickles, Sykes & Warren (1988)	Unions not only slow national productivity growth, they reduce total output. The 1988 estimates indicate that union workers are one-tenth as productive as nonunion workers.	Time series regression of labor productivity of the United States for the period 1947 to 1973.
Belman & Wilson (1989)	Warren specification is excessively sensitive to changes in the measurement of unionization and the business cycles.	Identical to Warren.

Variables	Comments
GROWTH: Change in total factor productivity. UNIONIZATION: Percent organized, change in percent organized, average annual man-days lost in strikes. CONTROLS: Percent change in output, median education.	The specification leaves out demographic, economic, legal and historic factors, such as World War II, which likely affected productivity growth. There is evidence that alternative measures of the business cycle produce different results. Estimates of productivity and union membership include the public sector, potentially biasing results.
GROWTH: Ratio of total private domestic product to quality adjusted labor input. UNIONIZATION: Percent of the non-institutional labor force belonging to unions. CONTROLS: Capital to labor ratio, time trend, deviation of actual output from potential output. COMMENT: In the 1988 article, the authors used non-linear least squares to obtain more accurate estimates of the union effect.	See the conclusions of Belman & Wilson for details.
GROWTH: Same as Warren. UNIONIZATION: Warren's definition, percent of non-agricultural labor force organized, percent of the private non-agricultural labor force organized. CONTROLS: Warren's business cycle variable, unemployment, capacity utilization, average hours of production workers, percent of women in the labor force, percent employment in manufacturing.	Effect of unionization on national labor productivity varies from negative to positive depending the specification. Results from the system are not sufficiently stable to be reliable.

APPENDIX IV
Studies of Union Effects on Profits

Reference	Key Finding	Type of Study
	INDUSTRY STUDIES	
Karier (1985)	Total organization of an industry decreases price-cost margins (PCM's) by 6.6 percent. Unions decrease PCM's by 14 percent in high concentration industries, but have no effect in low concentration industries.	Profit study using price costs margins for 119 two-digit manufacturing industries for 1972.
Karier (1988)	Unions only reduce the PCM of firms with high market concentration. Approximately 47 percent of monopoly profits accrue to organized workers.	Price-cost margin study for 107 three-digit industries for the period from 1965 to 1980.
Voos & Mishel (1986)	Fully organized industries have a 22 to 35 percent lower PCM than industries with no union members.	Price-cost margin for 139 three-digit industries in 1972.
Freeman (1983)	Unions lower PCM by 0 to 14 percent. Return on capital is reduced by 9 to 27 percent.	Price-cost margin and return on capital regressions from (1) inter-industry data, and (2) state by two-digit industry data.

Variables	Comments

PROFIT: Price-cost margin. UNIONIZATION: Percent organized by industry. CONTROLS: Capital stock, advertising, sales growth, regional dummies, and dummy variables indicating whether market concentration was greater than 60 percent, or between 45 to 60 percent.	The high level of aggregation of the data may obscure relations among the variables. Use of discrete rather than continuous measures of market concentration may also influence the results.
PROFIT: Price-cost margin derived from Census of Manufactures data. UNIONIZATION: Percent organized by industry. CONTROLS: Capital to sales ratio, demand growth, advertising expenditures, average firm size, import to sales ratio.	Use of a continuous measure of concentration, a larger set of controls, and less aggregate data is an improvement over the 1985 study.
PROFITS: Price-cost margin constructed from Census of Manufactures. UNIONIZATION: Percent of industry labor force covered by collective bargaining. CONTROLS: Market concentration, capital to sales ratio, advertising to sales, import penetration, proportion of employees in medium, large, and very large establishments, dummies for barriers to entry, sales growth.	Use of a collective bargaining coverage rather than membership to measure unionization provides a superior indication of the extent of union effects. The range of estimates depends on whether the PCM equation is estimated by itself or treated as simultaneous with coverage. Inclusion of adjusted concentration and barriers to entry variables is controversial and may make the results less credible to some.
PROFITS: Price-cost margin & returns on capital from the Survey of Manufactures & IRS data.	At variance with prior studies, concentration reduces profitability in some equations without the unionism-concentration interaction in SofM but not IRS data.

Reference	Key Finding	Type of Study
	FIRM STUDIES	
Salinger (1984)	Unions capture 77 percent of the monopoly profits.	Regression of q, the ratio of firm's market value to replacement value, for 175 COMPUSTAT firms in 1979.
Hirsch & Connolly (1987)	Unions reduce profits from R&D activities when profits are measured by q. Unions have no effect on profits when profits are measured with a price-cost margin.	Study of the profits of 367 Fortune 500 firms.
Connolly, Hirsch, & Hirschy (1986)	Excess valuation is decreased in organized firms with high R&D expenditures.	Same as H&C (1987).
Becker & Olson (1990)	Completely organized firms have 30 percent lower price-cost margins and 18 percent lower stock market returns than unorganized firms.	Regression of price-cost margins or a measure of excess valuation on firm and industry variables for a sample of almost 300 firms.

Variables	Comments

PROFITS: q as constructed by Salinger and Summers (1983).
UNIONIZATION: Percent of production covered by collective bargaining in 1974.
CONTROLS: Several concentration measures, minimum efficient scale, advertising to capital, R&D to capital, sales growth.

The specification chosen by Salinger is idiosyncratic and highly constrained. As with all workers firm studies there is a mismatch between firm organization and the industry unionization measures used to proxy organization. Studies using q also assume that stock market valuations accurately reflect the true value of the firm.

PROFITS: q and return on sales.
UNIONIZATION: Percent organized in the firms major three-digit industry.
CONTROLS: Market share, market concentration, R&D, import penetration, advertising, firm growth, capital stock.

Authors emphasize results with q support their belief that unions capture intangible rents. These results are not obtained when a return on sales ratio is used. As in the Salinger study, the unionization measure and q may be problematic.

PROFITS: Excess valuation, the ratio of firm's book value to sales. It is closely related to q.
UNIONIZATION: Same as 1987 study.
CONTROLS: Same as 1987 study.

Union organization has a negative effect on profits until it is interacted with the R&D to sales, advertising to sales, and patent intensity to sales ratios. With these variables, organization no longer affects excess valuation. Organization interacts negatively with R&D, but, unexpectedly, has a positive interaction with advertising. The latter result is inconsistent with the view that unions capture intangible rents.

PROFITS: Price cost margins or excess valuation.
UNIONIZATION: Percent of employees belonging to a union as well as the percent of the firms' major three-digit industry which is organized.
CONTROLS: Four-digit market concentration, the R&D to sales ratio, the advertising to sales ratio, sales growth over five years, systematic risk, imports to sales, and two-digit industry dummies. The price-cost equations included a capital-to-sales ratio firm and omitted the systematic risk variable.

The limitations of this study are similar to those cited in Hirsch, Hirschy, and Connelly. The mismatch of industry data and omission of controls for foreign income are particularly serious. The major advantage of this study is that it uses an accurate measure of firm-level organization.
Although the results indicate a strong negative relation between firm unionization and profits, there is generally no relation between industry unionization and profits, a finding which is inconsistent with Marshallian theory.

97

Reference	Key Finding	Type of Study
Clark (1984)	Unions reduce price to sales ratios by 16 percent and return on capital by 19 percent.	Regression of return on investment and sales for the PIMS data set discussed in the productivity section.
Voos & Mishel (1986)	Unions have a negative effect on supermarket profit margins, possibly having a larger effect in concentrated markets.	Profit equation for six supermarket chains for several urban areas for 1970–1974.

STOCK MARKET STUDIES

Reference	Key Finding	Type of Study
Ruback & Zimmerman (1984)	Certification of a union by the NLRB causes a 3.8 percent decline in the value of the to stock holders. Even if the union is not certified the value of the firm declines by 1.3 percent.	Estimates the relation of election petitions and NLRB certification to cumulative abnormal stock market returns. Sample of 253 NYSE firms involved in certification elections from 1962 to 1980.
Becker & Olson (1986)	Strikes reduce shareholder equity by 4.1 percent, of which 2.8 percent occurs after the announcement of the strike.	Same methodology as Ruback and Zimmerman. Sample of 699 strikes at firms listed on the New York or American Stock Exchanges from 1962 to 1982.

Variables	Comments
PROFITS: Return on investment by firm product line. Also, return on sales, an analog of the price-cost margin. UNIONIZATION: Same as discussed in productivity section. CONTROLS: Similar to earlier discussion.	Results are similar to those obtained in industry studies despite dissimilarities in data sets. There is little difference between ROI and ROS results.
PROFITS: The ratio of profits to sales. UNIONIZATION: The union status of a chain in a city. CONTROLS: Market concentration, market growth, market size, average store size, firm growth, expenditures on entry, relative firm market share.	This study falls between those studies which indicate that unions lower all firms profits and those which indicate that unions only lower the profits of firms with market power. The similarity of the results of this industry-specific study to the inter-industry studies provides further evidence that unions reduce profits.

STOCK MARKET STUDIES

PROFITS: Cumulative abnormal stock market returns as measured by the difference between firms' actual returns and market returns. UNIONIZATION: Dummy variables indicating when an election petition was filed and when a certification order was issued. CONTROLS: Average stock market returns and industry-specific effects.	As with all stock market studies, it is assumed that stock market returns reflect the true value of the firm. The lack of controls for events other than union election activity may produce biased estimates. The sample of firms, those involved NLRB proceedings, excludes firms involved in organizing campaigns which either agreed to voluntary recognition or prevented unions from getting 30 percent of workers to sign an election petition.
PROFITS: Similar to Ruback and Zimmerman. UNIONIZATION: Dummy variables indicating the occurrence of a strike. CONTROLS: Average market returns.	As with R&Z, the omission of controls for events other than strikes may cause inaccuracy in the estimates of strike effects. For example, the portion of the firms' business which was struck might have some influence on stock market returns, but is not included in the model.

Reference	Key Finding	Type of Study
Becker (1987)	Concessionary settlements are associated with an 8 to 10 percent increase in the value of the firm for stockholders. This is due to a redistribution of existing value from workers to stockholders rather than an increase in the firm's value.	Methodology is the same as R&Z. Sample of 70 firms listed on the NYSE or ASE for which the Bureau of National Affairs collected summary information on concessionary bargaining.
Abowd (1989)	There is a dollar-for-dollar trade-off between shareholder's wealth and union member's wealth.	Similar methodology to other stock market studies. Sample of 7683 between 1976–1982. A forecasting model is used to decompose the present value of total labor costs into expected and unexpected components. The latter is related to an estimate of unexpected changes in shareholder's wealth around the date of the contract settlement.

Variables	Comments
PROFITS: Excess returns. UNIONIZATION: Dummy variable indicating. CONTROLS: Average market returns.	The sample may be unrepresentative because of data sources, concession bargaining and difficulty classifying bargaining outcomes.

APPENDIX V
Studies of the Effects of Labor Climate

Reference	Key Finding	Type of Study
Katz, Kochan, & Gobeille (1983)	Better industrial relations climates improve the quality but do not increase the quantity output.	Quality of worklife programs at 18 GM plants in the mid-1970s. Authors argue QWL will alter the labor relations climate and the results from the IR system, improving plant economic performance.
Kochan, Katz, & Mower (1985)	Better functioning conflict management systems and worker attitudes have a beneficial influence on both productivity and quality. QWL programs do not have an independent effect.	This study examines the relation between worker attitudes, conflict management, QWL involvement, and economic performance in 25 durable goods plants.
Norsworthy & Zabala (1985)	Improvements in worker attitudes are associated with decreased costs of production.	Cost function for the automobile industry for 1959 to 1976.

Variables	Comments
PRODUCTIVITY: Quality and the ratio of actual to standard labor hours. LABOR CLIMATE: Attitudes are measured by managers' and supervisors' views on trust and cooperation. Industrial relations performance is measured by grievance levels, absenteeism, disciplinary actions, time spent in negotiations, and number of demands made in negotiations. CONTROLS: Business cycle movement and plant-specific effects.	Most sophisticated study to date of of the relation of the industrial relations system to firm performance. Limitation of the study to organized plants limits its application to nonunion settings.
PRODUCTIVITY: Quality and the ratio of actual to standard labor hours. LABOR RELATIONS: Attitudes are measured by salaried worker attitudes on compensation, working, environment, relations with supervisors and subordinates, and career progress and by the proportion of employees submitting suggestions. The effectiveness of conflict management is measured by grievance rates, absenteeism, and disciplinary action rates. QWL intensity is the percent of hourly employees involved in programs. CONTROLS: Overtime hours, size of the workforce, and plant-specific effects.	Similar to Katz, Kochan, and Gobeille in its approach to analyzing the effect of industrial relations systems of economic performance. The attitude, conflict, and QWL variables exhibit common signs of multicollinearity; individual insignificance but high levels of joint significance. It may be that these factors are sufficiently closely linked to preclude distinguishing individual effects.
COST: Total unit cost of automobile industry. ATTITUDES: Measures of grievance filed, unresolved grievances, unauthorized strikes, and quits. These variables are also used, *ex post*, to form an index of worker attitudes. CONTROLS: Labor force characteristics, production technology, and trend effects.	

Reference	Key Finding	Type of Study
Shuster (1983)	Gainsharing plans increase productivity but do not affect employment.	Within-site comparisons of output and employment conducted from production records from nine plants in the fabricated steel industry. Sample covers plants with Scanlon and Rucker plans which agreed to the survey.
Brett & Goldberg (1979)	Wildcat strike activity is diminished when grievances are settled informally. Positive attitudes between labor and management, management's willingness to settle disputes informally, and the ability of foremen to resolve grievances also have positive effects.	The study covered one high and one low conflict mine in each of two coal companies. Interviews of 124 miners were conducted in addition to local committee members, foremen, and managers. Interview data was supplemented with objective information on mines and local communities.
Ichniowski & Lewin (1987)	Turnover among nurses is 14 percent and 15 percent lower for union and nonunion providing grievance procedures. Arbitration procedures reduce turnover an additional 2 percent.	Extensions of work done by Spencer (1986). Survey covered 111 hospitals. Original work by Spencer looked at the effect of voice mechanisms on turnover.
Flaherty (1987)	Shop floor confrontation as measured by wildcat strikes played a significant role in the productivity slowdown of the mid-1960s.	Time series study of productivity in the auto industry from 1961 to 1981 using quarterly data.

Variables	Comments
PRODUCTIVITY: Employee output per hour (productivity) and average number of workers employed in a month. PLAN: Fitting separate regression before and after institution of the gainsharing plan. CONTROLS: Plants are similar in size and technology.	As noted by the author, the research design may not eliminate the effect of unmeasured variables and there may be self-selection bias in the sample. The small number of sites and short period of examination may also limit the generality of results.
The study provides comparisons of the mean characteristics of high and low strike mines as reflected in interviews and other data sources.	It appears that the authors have not controlled for systematic differences between the companies. Some discussion of these differences is incorporated into discussion of the results.
TURNOVER: Voluntary turnover among registered nurses for the previous 12 months. UNIONIZATION: Dummy variable indicating whether the nurses at the hospital were unionized. CONTROLS: Not clear from the article.	The use of a linear probability model is technically inappropriate but may not affect the estimates. Some discussion of controls would also be useful as these can have large effects on estimates.
PRODUCTIVITY: Labor productivity as published by the American Productivity Center. STRIKES; BLS series on the number work stoppages during the term of the contract. CONTROLS: Change in capacity utilization, capital to labor ratio, energy to labor ratio, ratio of fuel to finished goods, and a dummy for the oil embargo of 1973–1974. COMMENTS: The productivity equation is estimated simultaneously with strikes.	Lack of a percent organized variable, usually present in studies of productivity, precludes separating the effects of worker militancy from those of union strength. As with other time series studies, the specification is very lean, raising questions about the accuracy of estimates.

Reference	Key Finding	Type of Study
Bemmel (1987)	Unions do not reduce productivity except by reducing the success of incentive pay plans. Strikes have large negative effects on productivity.	Translog production function estimated with survey data on 46 plants in 7 industries.
Ichniowski (1984a, 1986)	Increasing levels of grievance activity reduce productivity. Longer collective bargaining agreements, a measure of labor-management distrust, having similar effects.	Production function for ten paper plants with monthly data for the period 1976 to 1982.

Variables	Comments
PRODUCTIVITY: Value-added. UNIONIZATION: Percent of production workers covered by a union contract. Strikes measures included whether a strike occurred in the previous 3 to 5, or in the previous 6 to 10 years. The unionization variable was interacted with several other variables to capture their joint effect. CONTROLS: Expenditures on capital, production, and non-production labor, whether there was participative management, performance appraisals, or incentive pay.	The study may suffer from self-selection bias. Use of factor analysis to create some variables and the omission of controls for industry and firm effects may also bias estimates.
PRODUCTIVITY: Monthly output in tons. LABOR CLIMATE: Total pages in the collective bargaining agreement or number of step two grievances per 1000 production hours. CONTROLS: Major product dummies, nine categories of capital assets, number of paper machines, labor and energy input.	As noted by the author, it is necessary to assume that contract pages are associated with the number and complexity of work to interpret contract pages as a measure of labor-management conflict.

Do Unions Hinder Technological Change?

Jeffrey H. Keefe

Introduction

Unions are often portrayed as obstacles to technological change in the workplace. Many Americans have lingering negative images of the railroad firemen and the featherbedding controversy, the reluctance of plumbers to adopt plastic pipe, or the resistance of typographers to computerized typesetting in the newspaper industry. Are these images illustrative of the typical union reaction to technological change or are they the exceptions?

One school of thought claims that these examples are indeed typical. Concerned with the job and income security of their members, unions negotiate a complex web of rules that restrict the ability of management to manage. This creates inflexibility and impedes technological change. In this view, the efforts of unions to vest workers with job rights ultimately prove counterproductive. The web of work rules eventually strangles productivity, renders the unionized employer uncompetitive, and results in job loss.

In contrast to this portrait of job control unionism, many experts and several government panels have concluded that American unions have participated constructively in the introduction of new technology. True, they have been concerned with the job security of their members, but this has not impeded efficiency. Recently, some unions (the Steelworkers and the Clothing and Textile Workers for example) have actively encouraged technological modern-

Experts and several government panels have concluded that American unions have participated constructively in the introduction of new technology.

izatization as a way of retaining employment *and* maintaining competitiveness. This perspective acknowledges that American unions have generally accepted the doctrine of "high wages, high productivity, and low labor costs," as the best approach to securing income growth and employment stability for their members (Taylor, 1962).[1]

These contrasting depictions of unions and collective bargaining raise several questions which are the subject of this study:

(1) Does collective bargaining balance the concerns of the employee with the increasing need for efficiency, or does it inevitably lead to workplace sclerosis?

(2) In order to promote employment security, do unions promote or hinder productivity-enhancing change?

(3) Do unions impede or encourage the introduction of new labor-saving technology?

(4) When compared with nonunion establishments, are unionized workplaces moribund and obsolete?

To answer these questions, this study reviews the academic theories and research evidence concerned with the relationship between unions and technological change. Because they are conflicting and inconclusive, theories are surveyed only briefly. Fortunately, a growing body of empirical research has been directed toward gaining a greater understanding of the influence of unions on technological progress. A review of this research is followed by a discussion of the legal framework regulating union activities with regard to technology. The paper concludes by providing concrete examples of contemporary union responses to technological change.

This paper reviews the research about the influence of unions on technological change. Based on the evidence presented, I reach the following conclusions:

* Unions have no effect on a firm's use of advanced manufacturing and microelectronic technology.

* Unionized establishments are more likely than nonunion ones to be using advanced technology, primarily because they are larger, more likely to be part of multiplant enterprises, and operate on shift work.

Unionized establishments are more likely than nonunion ones to be using advanced technology.

110

* In most cases, unions welcome technological modernization; sometimes encouraging it, most often accepting it, infrequently opposing it, but usually seeking to protect their members.

* Both labor law and arbitration allow American businesses broad discretion over the introduction of new technology in unionized settings.

* The current legal and managerial frameworks confine unions to a reactive role in technological and organizational changes. This may impede employee participation and prevent the full utilization of new manufacturing technologies.

Theories Regarding Unions and Technology

The current legal and managerial frameworks confine unions to a reactive role in technological and organizational changes.

Not surprisingly, the academic literature offers competing models of the influence of unions on technological change. On the one hand, higher union labor costs may deprive management of capital needed for modernization, or unions may be able to capture the returns to sunk capital investment. As a result, a union firm is likely to maintain old and inefficient capital to moderate wage demands (Baldwin, 1983; Lawrence and Lawrence, 1985; Addison and Hirsch, 1989). Moreover, the union capture of quasi-rents will affect the long-term performance of a firm by deterring new investment (Addison and Hirsch, 1989).[2] Unions may also make prohibitive the adjustment costs to technological change, or they may negotiate work rules that prevent the substitution of new capital for labor.

However, other theories conclude that there are a number of reasons why unionization might actually increase the pace of modernization. First, unions clearly raise wages and benefits, which provides management with an incentive to substitute labor-saving technology for more expensive union labor. Unions may also "shock" a slack and inefficient management into tightening up and modernizing operations (Slichter, 1941). In addition, a union "voice" may provide mechanisms to protect worker interests in income and employment security, thereby reducing the resistance to change (Freeman and Medoff, 1984).

Since each of these theoretical perspectives is plausible, only empirical evidence can answer the questions previously set forth. The following review focuses on recent econometric or statistical studies of modernization in union versus nonunion facilities, and then surveys studies of union policy with regard to technological change.

Do Unions Hinder Technological Change? The Evidence

In this section, I will present summaries of five studies that investigate the impact of unions on the introduction of new technology. In order to determine whether or not unions impede technological change, each of these studies compares the prevalence of new technology at union and nonunion facilities. In addition, four studies on current union policies and responses to technological change are reviewed.

Before proceeding with the survey of the statistical research, it is important to note that the current industrial relations environment presents some difficulties in interpreting the evidence. On average, unionized facilities are older than nonunion ones. This is partly a function of management opposition to the unionization of new facilities. Verma (1985) found evidence that in multiplant companies, unionized facilities may be used as "cash cows" to finance new nonunion operations. Bluestone and Harrison (1982) argued that firms are systematically disinvesting from the union sector. New technology allows corporations to operate hundreds of smaller, geographically dispersed, nonunion plants in place of a few large unionized complexes. Only where management is faced with a large union capable of securing neutrality pledges or voluntary recognition have attempts at organizing labor been relatively successful (Kochan, McKersie, and Chalykoff, 1986). Using data collected for his American Enterprise Institute study of small metalworking plants, Hicks (1986) showed that union status is a function of plant age. A plant built fifty years ago has a better than 50 percent chance of being unionized, whereas a plant built since 1974 has a very low probability of being unionized (see Table 1). This evidence suggests that management's antipathy toward unionization may cause the unionized sector to be saddled with obsolete plants and equipment. Unfortunately, no study to date controls for plant vintage and its potential impact on modernization.[3]

TABLE 1
The Aging of Unionized Plants:
Summary of Hicks' Survey Data
on Small Metalworking Plants Using NC

Plants Built	Union	Nonunion	Percent Union
Prior to 1940	78	66	54%
1940–49	35	79	31
1950–59	52	156	25
1960–69	58	267	18
1970–79	23	264	8
1980–82	0	19	0
Totals	**246**	**851**	**22**

Note: Small is defined as less then 250 employees.

Source: Hicks, 1986, p. 77.

Statistical Studies of Technological Innovation

Benvignati on Innovation in the
U.S. Textile Industry

Using data collected from 241 textile mills, Benvignati (1982) found that unionized firms (firms with at least 10 percent of production workers represented by a textile union) were more likely than nonunion firms to pioneer the adoption of important textile machinery innovations (see Table 2).[4] Unionized firms were also more likely to adopt new textile process innovations. However, this result was not statistically significant. Her research supports the view that unionization may actually accelerate technological diffusion.

Kelley and Brooks on Programmable Automation
in U.S. Metalworking Industries

After controlling for wages, type of ownership, and firm size, Kelley and Brooks (1988, p. I-30) found that "unionization was not found to affect the adoption of computerized

Research supports the view that unionization may actually accelerate technological diffusion.

113

TABLE 2
Adoption of Capital Goods Innovations in
241 Textile Mills

Equations Probit (t-statistics)	Adopters		Pioneers	
	(1)	(2)	(3)	(4)
Union	0.437 (1.73)	0.376 (1.46)	0.576 (2.03)	0.580 (2.04)
Size	0.034 (2.57)		0.010 (0.82)	
Size^2	-0.0005 (-1.60)		0.0001 (0.13)	
Size*ConRatio		0.0015 (2.83)		0.004 (2.02)
(Size*ConRatio)^2		-0.00003 (-2.20)		-0.000007 (-1.14)
Spinning	0.971 (4.03)	1.004 (4.15)	0.388 (1.66)	0.401 (1.73)
Constant	-0.075 (-0.63)	-0.116 (-0.95)	0.107 (0.69)	0.082 (0.54)

Source: Benvignati, 1982, pp. 330-35.

Variable Definitions:
Adoption—a binary variable which takes the value 1 if the firm adopted any of the thirty-three textile capital innovations, and takes the value 0 otherwise. 66 percent were adopters.
Pioneer—a binary variable which takes the value 1 if the firm has adopted at least one innovation of the thirty-three with a speed equal to, or better than, the average speed of adoption of that innovation by all who have installed it, and takes the value 0 otherwise.
Union—a binary variable which takes the value 1 if at least 10 percent of the firm's textile workers are unionized, and takes the value 0 otherwise.
Size—firm employment divided by 10,000.
Size^2—size squared.
*Size*ConRatio*—Size interacted (multiplied) by the four-firm four-digit SIC concentration ratio.
*(Size*ConRatio)^2*—Size*ConRatio squared.
Spinning—binary variable controlling for the four-digit SIC spinning industry.

automation" (see Table 3). However, they also found that higher wages significantly increased the likelihood that a machine shop would use programmable automation. Since unions raise wages, it seems likely from this study that labor organizations have a positive indirect influence on this form of technological diffusion.

Further confounding the union effect in the study was the high correlation between union status and multiplant ownership. Although 82 percent of the surveyed establishments were single plant firms, half of all unionized establishments were part of multiplant enterprises. For their regression analysis, Kelley and Brooks used factor analysis to construct a variable—organizational complexity—indicating that large firm size, large plant size, and multiplant ownership are highly correlated in the metalworking industries. Higher levels of organizational complexity significantly increased the probability that a machine shop was using programmable automation. They concluded that given "the strong association of unionization with the multiplant enterprise, it is not surprising that we find no independent union effect on the likelihood of PA adoption" (Kelley and Brooks, 1988, p. I-14).

Unionization was not found to affect the adoption of computerized automation.

Betcherman on Use of Computerized Technology in Canada

Similarly, Betcherman (1988) found no meaningful union effect on the adoption of computerized technologies in Canadian firms between 1980 and 1985 (see Table 4). In his study, three measures were used to capture the extent of computer utilization in each establishment: expenditures on computer technology as a percent of sales; the percentage of employees working directly with these technologies in 1985; and expenditures on computerized process technologies as a percent of sales. The union coefficient in each regression was typically small, negative, and insignificant, leading Betcherman to conclude that unions do not "appear to have a significant effect on the extent to which firms introduce computer-based technologies."

Daniel on Microelectronic Applications in British Manufacturing

In contrast, Daniel's (1987) report on the British Policy Studies Institute survey of 1,853 British workplaces found that unionized manufacturing establishments were more likely to use advanced technology than nonunion ones. This

TABLE 3
Adoption of Programmable Automation
Technology in 1987

Dependent Variable: Does Establishment Use PA?
(1 = yes, 0 = no)

	All Firms	Firms with External Customers	Firms with Internal Customers
Union	−0.231 (0.311)	−0.202 (0.419)	0.210 (0.506)
Hourly Wage	0.097*** (0.030)	0.113*** (0.037)	0.023 (0.091)
Organizational Complexity	1.426*** (0.205)	1.655*** (0.288)	1.169*** (0.308)
Machining Employment Share	2.853*** (0.397)	3.098*** (0.554)	2.739*** (0.688)
Small Batch Output	−0.398 (0.250)	−0.131 (0.314)	−2.298*** (0.546)
Product Variety	0.603*** (0.213)	0.561** (0.266)	1.250*** (0.455)
Other Computer Use	0.756*** (0.201)	0.985*** (0.249)	−0.212 (0.308)
Written Work Orders	0.064 (0.205)	0.123 (0.252)	1.067** (0.502)
Customer Technical Assistance	−0.472* (0.262)		
−2 Log Likelihood	801.74	537.12	183.04
X^2	241.39	153.75	164.15
Sample size	757	500	257

Source: Kelley and Brooks, 1988.

Other variables controlled for: written media, demos/exhibits, other users experience, and vendor contact. An intercept was included in each regression.

* Significant at 0.10.
** Significant at 0.05.
*** Significant at 0.01.

TABLE 4
Adopting Innovations: Do Unions Make a Difference in Canada?

Dependent Variable	EXPTECH	WORKTECH	PROEXP
(t-statistics)			
UNION	−0.07	−1.47	
	(−0.49)	(−0.77)	
Blue Collar UNION			−0.28
			(−1.55)
Observations	337	536	329

Source: Betcherman, 1988.

Control Variables: industry, size of full-time employment, region, and type of ownership.

Data: Economic Council of Canada, Working With Technology Survey.

Variable Definitions:
EXPTECH—Expenditures on computer-based technologies as a percentage of sales during the period 1980–85.
WORKTECH—The percentage of the establishment's employees working directly with these technologies in 1985.
PROTECH—Expenditures on computer-based process technologies as a percentage of sales during the period 1980–85.

TABLE 5
Unions and Advanced Manufacturing in Great Britain
Microelectronic Applications in Manufacturing Industry

Percentages using given technology

	Union	Nonunion
All Establishments		
Any Application	52%	38%
Process Application	49	33
Small Establishments (25–99)		
Any Application	40%	35%
Process Application	38	30
Medium Size Establishments (100–499)		
Any Application	61%	54%
Process Application	58	51

Source: Daniel, 1987.

was true for both process and product applications. Unfortunately, Daniel only provided aggregate statistics which did not control for other potential determinants of modernization potentially correlated with unionization (see Table 5).

Keefe on Advanced Manufacturing Technology in U.S. Machine Shops

The general conclusion from the above-mentioned studies is that unions have a generally positive effect on the adoption of technology, but that the effect is negated once one controls for other factors, including the fact that unions raise wages. This interpretation is substantiated in earlier research done by myself (Keefe, 1991). I found that for seven major advanced manufacturing technologies in U.S. machine shops, a unionized plant is more likely than a nonunion one to have introduced each technology (see Table 6). From a statistical standpoint, the difference between union and nonunion plants is significant for five technologies: numerically controlled machine tools; machining centers; direct numerical control; computer aided design and manufacture; and robots.[5]

Unions in machine shops were found to raise wages by 16 to 21 percent and to increase the likelihood that a plant had a formal training program by 15 to 22 percent.[6] Higher wages and formal training are both positively related to the adoption of advanced manufacturing technology. However, once one controls for these factors, the union effect is generally insignificant. Table 7 reports coefficient estimates from probit models for each of the seven technologies (see Appendix for detail on variable definitions for Tables 7 and 8). The specifications include a direct measure of union status, plus measures of indirect union effects, operating through wages and training. These probit results indicate a positive effect through wages in four cases and through training in three cases. Controlling for wages and training, the union coefficient is negative and significant in two out of seven cases. When training and wages are omitted from the specification and the equations are re-estimated, the overall union effect (including that operating through wages and training) becomes more apparent (Table 8). In one case, the total union effect remains negative and significant. However, the union effect becomes positive and significant in the robotics equation. In the five other equations, the union effect is not significantly different from zero.

For seven major advanced manufacturing technologies in U.S. machine shops, a unionized plant is more likely than a nonunion one to have introduced each technology.

TABLE 6
Unions and Computerized Manufacturing
New Technology Survey of the American Machinery Industry, 1983

*Percentages based on union and nonunion subsamples**

New Technology	Percent of Establishments With New Technology By Union Status		Significant at 0.05**
	Union	Nonunion	
Numerically Controlled Machine Tools (NC)	59%	34%	YES
Machining Center [Multifunction NC] (MC)	31	19	YES
Computerized Numerical Control (CNC)	41	36	NO
Direct Numerical Control (DNC)	13	7	YES
Computer Aided Design & Manufacture (CADCAM)	21	13	YES
Industrial Robot	9	3	YES
Flexible Manufacturing System (FMS)	4	2	NO
Observations	332	498	

Numerically Controlled Machine Tools—Machine tools controlled by instructions on tape, punch cards, plugs, etc. Allows rapid parts changes by changing the control tape.
Machining Center (Multifunction Numerically Controlled Machines)—A numerically controlled machine tool with automatic tool changer. May select from 20–100 tools.
Computer Numerically Controlled—A NC machine with an onboard microcomputer that stores information and directs the machine tools.
Direct Numerical Control—A central computer that may control 100 or more NC machine tools.
Robots—A programmable multifunctional device that manipulates and transports tools, parts, or implements through variable programmed paths to perform specific manufacturing tasks or assembly.
Computer Aided Design and Manufacture—A system that uses computers to design (CAD) and manufacture (CAM). Used by large manufacturers only.
Flexible Manufacturing System—Programmable manufacturing process consisting of a series of automated machines and transfer devices. Used for mass production. Very expensive.

Source: Keefe, 1991.

* U.S. Department of Labor Bureau of Labor Statistics, 1985, Industry Wage Survey: Machinery Manufacturing, November 1983. Bulletin 2229 Source: Microdata tape, SIC industry 35. Manufacturers included are Farm Machinery, Construction Equipment (including oil field and mining equipment), Metalworking Machinery, General and Special Industry Machinery, Office Equipment (including computers), Turbines and Engines, and Refrigeration and Service Equipment.

** Chi-square test rejects, where significant, the hypothesis of similar means.

TABLE 7
Unions & the Diffusion of Advanced Manufacturing Technology: Direct & Indirect Effects

Probit Estimates (*Standard Errors*)

	NC	MC	CNC	DNC	ROBOT	CADCAM	FMS
Union	−0.113	−0.158	−0.303**	0.036	0.315	−0.278*	−0.230
	(0.11)	(0.12)	(0.11)	(0.14)	(0.19)	(0.13)	(0.22)
Training	−0.027	0.118	0.147	0.049	0.580**	0.567**	0.625**
	(0.11)	(0.12)	(0.10)	(0.14)	(0.18)	(0.13)	(0.22)
Wage	0.773**	0.858**	0.438*	0.313	−0.214	0.764**	0.615
	(0.23)	(0.28)	(0.22)	(0.33)	(0.40)	(0.30)	(0.52)
Size 11–50[a]	1.039**	0.989**	0.783**	0.623**			
	(0.11)	(0.14)	(0.11)	(0.18)			
Size 51–200[a]	1.735**	1.524**	1.137**	0.817*	0.026	0.680**	0.145
	(0.20)	(0.19)	(0.17)	(0.23)	(0.32)	(0.21)	(0.41)
Size 201[a]	1.995**	2.161**	1.126**	1.027**	0.273	1.251**	0.492
	(0.52)	(0.41)	(0.37)	(0.40)	(0.36)	(0.25)	(0.44)
Size 401[a]					0.858*	1.916**	0.809
					(0.35)	(0.25)	(0.44)
Shift 2nd	0.303**	0.349**	0.314**	0.200	0.270	0.099	0.626*
	(0.11)	(0.13)	(0.11)	(0.16)	(0.23)	(0.15)	(0.31)
Constant	−0.685**	−1.802**	−0.869**	−2.179**	−2.851**	−2.270**	−3.027*
	(0.11)	(0.14	(0.11)	(0.18)	(0.28)	(0.18)	(0.34)
# of Users	415	202	315	75	44	137	24
# of Obs.	817	816	815	815	812	813	812
−2 Log Likelihood	260	218	144	54	75	184	41

Source: Keefe, 1991.

* Significant at the 0.05 level.
** Significant at the 0.01 level.

[a] For NC, MC, CNC, and DNC Size increments are based on machine shop employment and for Robot, CADCAM, and FMS Size is based on establishment employment. Size specifications were selected using likelihood ratios, adjusted R^2, and condition numbers as criteria. These specifications scored highest on explanatory power and the lowest for multicollinearity.

TABLE 8
Union Effect on the Diffusion
of Advanced Manufacturing Technology

Probit Estimates *(Standard Errors)*

	NC	MC	CNC	DNC	ROBOT	CADCAM	FMS
Union	−0.017	−0.048	−0.237*	0.073	0.380*	−0.079	−0.044
	(0.10)	(0.12)	(0.10)	(0.14)	(0.17)	(0.12)	(0.20)
Size 11–50[a]	1.111**	1.070**	0.852**	0.671**			
	(0.11)	(0.14)	(0.11)	(0.18)			
Size 51–200[a]	1.954**	1.673**	1.249**	0.893*	−0.020	0.513**	0.013
	(0.20)	(0.19)	(0.17)	(0.23)	(0.31)	(0.20)	(0.38)
Size 201[a]	2.203**	2.428**	1.335**	1.152**	0.167	1.079**	0.342
	(0.51)	(0.41)	(0.36)	(0.38)	(0.35)	(0.23)	(0.41)
Size 401[a]					0.757*	1.736**	0.676
					(0.34)	(0.24)	(0.42)
Shift 2nd	0.290**	0.323**	0.313**	0.199	0.333	0.220	0.659*
	(0.11)	(0.13)	(0.11)	(0.16)	(0.22)	(0.14)	(0.29)
Constant	−0.694**	−1.738**	−0.826**	−2.180**	−2.612**	−1.910**	−2.588*
	(0.10)	(0.14)	(0.10)	(0.18)	(0.26)	(0.16)	(0.28)
#of Users	415	202	315	75	44	137	24
#of Obs.	831	830	829	829	826	827	826
(−2) Log Likelihood	260	212	144	55	66	162	29

Source: Keefe, 1991.

* Significant at the 0.05 level.
** Significant at the 0.01 level.

[a] For NC, MC, CNC, and DNC Size increments are based on machine shop employment and for Robot, CADCAM, and FMS Size is based on establishment employment. Size specifications were selected using likelihood ratios, adjusted R^2, and condition numbers as criteria. These specifications scored highest on explanatory power and the lowest for multicollinearity.

The main conclusion that can be drawn from econometric research to date is that union status probably has no
effect on the use of advanced manufacturing and microelectronic technology. Unionization, however, may be associated with their early adoption. In general, unionized establishments are more likely than nonunion ones to be using
advanced technology; not because they are unionized, but
because they are larger, more likely to be part of multiplant
enterprises, and operate on shift work.

Union Policies toward Technological Change

An alternative stream of research examines U.S. union
policies toward technological change historically or con-
temporaneously. Throughout the 19th and early 20th cen-
turies, one can find examples of American craftsmen resist-
ing the onslaught of new machinery and factory organization, eventually destroying themselves and their organizations. In a recent review of the literature, Cornfield (1987)
concluded that nothing could be more atypical of the contemporary American labor movement's response to technological change.

Studies beginning in 1926 consistently find that willing
acceptance is the most common American union response
to technological change (Barnett, 1926; Slichter, 1941;
Slichter, Healy, and Livernash, 1960; McLaughlin, 1979). In
recent years, three studies (McLaughlin, 1979; Weikle,
1985; Helfgott, 1988) have sought to assess the impact of
American union policies on technological change. Using
survey data from participants in collective bargaining and a
comprehensive literature review, McLaughlin concluded
that unions do not impede the rate and direction of technological change, and that "labor unions are not the major
stumbling block inhibiting increased productivity—the
ultimate objective in introducing more efficient production
methods." Her survey data revealed that "willing acceptance" was the single most common response of unions to
the introduction of new technology (49 percent of
responses). The next most common response, at least initially, was opposition (24 percent),[7] which usually gave
way to bargaining over adjustments (17 percent of those
cases which began in opposition changed to other
responses, most commonly adjustment), and 24 percent of
the initial responses sought adjustment for workers who
were adversely affected by the new technology. In the long
run, willing acceptance and adjustment constituted the

> *Studies beginning
> in 1926
> consistently find
> that willing
> acceptance is the
> most common
> American union
> response to
> technological
> change.*

most common union responses. Opposition to technical change arose only when a large segment of the membership would be adversely affected. Furthermore, unions were rarely successful in preventing technological change.

Helfgott (1988) conducted a study sponsored by the Industrial Relations Counselors, which relied upon a survey of business and labor leaders and experts in the field of automation. This was supplemented with sixteen case studies of companies planning for and implementing new computer-based technology. Helfgott concludes that "the most important finding in the labor management area is an almost total absence of union resistance to technological change" (1988, p. 102). In the vast majority of cases, effective communications programs, including long advance notice of impending innovation, combined with no layoffs lessened union fears of and built support for new technology. The study team discovered no difference between union and nonunion establishments in the ability of management to introduce new technology.

In a survey of 610 United Steelworkers of America officials, Weikle (1985, p. 224) found that their attitude toward technological change was essentially positive. More than 76 percent indicated that technological change was to be encouraged, but almost half of that number said it should be encouraged only if the union had the right to participate in the initial decision to adopt new methods *and* the work adjustment process. A positive attitude toward new technology was associated with anticipated improvements in working conditions, job security, and the competitive position of the plant or company. Experienced leaders were more likely to encourage new technology than junior ones.

A Canadian survey (Petchinnis, 1983) found that Canadian unions also recognize the desirability of technological change, and accept the inevitability of its implementation, but make their consent conditional upon negotiation of satisfactory adjustments for workers who are adversely affected.

Opposition to technical change arose only when a large segment of the membership would be adversely affected.

Research Summary

The statistical literature strongly suggests that unionized facilities are *more* technologically modern than nonunion ones. However, once differences in size and other characteristics thought to influence technological diffusion are taken into consideration, there is probably no union effect on technological progressiveness. The studies of union poli-

123

cies indicate that, in most cases, unions welcome technological modernization; sometimes encouraging it, most often accepting it, infrequently opposing it, but usually seeking to protect their members. The next two sections address why these findings are plausible, given the legal and institutional framework of collective bargaining.

The Legal Framework: Collective Bargaining & Technological Change

NLRA and the Courts

Contrary to many popular portrayals, American business has been granted broad discretion over the introduction of new technology in unionized settings. The National Labor Relations Act states that "wages, hours, and other terms and conditions of employment" are mandatory subjects of collective bargaining. In its 1958 *Borg-Warner* decision, the Supreme Court distinguished between mandatory and permissive subjects of bargaining. Insistence on bargaining over a permissive subject is considered an unfair labor practice.[8] Parties are only required to bargain over the mandatory subjects. Through their rulings since *Borg-Warner,* the courts and the National Labor Relations Board (NLRB) have placed particular issues into the mandatory or permissive categories.

The courts and the NLRB have consistently held that the effect of technological change is a mandatory subject of bargaining. If a union introduces provisions that address the impact of technological change into contract negotiations, an employer has the duty to bargain over this issue but has no obligation to accept any contractual provision. If a contract does not specifically include the issue of technology, an employer introducing new technology that will have a demonstrable, substantial, and detrimental effect on bargaining unit employees is obligated to bargain with its union about the impact of the changes.[9] Although an employer has a duty to bargain over the adverse effects of new technology, whether or not the decision to automate is a mandatory subject of bargaining has been a matter of dispute. If the proposed automation would have an adverse impact on bargaining unit employees, bargaining over the decision to automate requires an employer to notify the union in advance of the plan to automate, to confer in good faith, and to discuss any alternative plans the union may

> *The courts and the NLRB have consistently held that the effect of technological change is a mandatory subject of bargaining.*

124

propose. As with all collective bargaining, decision bargaining imposes no obligation on the employer to accept the union's proposals, but solely to engage in a full and frank discussion.[10]

In recent years, the courts and the Board have narrowed the scope of mandatory bargaining over managerial decisions affecting plant operations. In 1981, the Supreme Court's decision in *First National Maintenance* held that an employer's decision to close a portion of its operations is not a mandatory subject of bargaining. In the 1984 *Otis Elevator II* decision, the NLRB held that an employer transferring work from one plant to another has no statutory duty to bargain with the union about the decision itself, unless that decision rests solely on an attempt to reduce labor costs or a specific contract clause requires bargaining. In *Otis Elevator II*, the Board did not address the issue of new technology, and in its *First National Maintenance* decision, the Supreme Court explicitly sidestepped the issue of automation (Miscimarra, 1983).

If a collective bargaining agreement is silent on an employer's right to make a technological change, an employer's change in technology is a mandatory subject of bargaining, but *only* if that change has a significant and detrimental impact on the bargaining unit. The technological change must have a demonstrably adverse effect on the employees in the unit to trigger a bargaining requirement, and the union must request bargaining.[11] Ironically, facing a substantial and detrimental effect on its members, a union's bargaining power will probably be at a diminished state exactly at the moment when a bargaining requirement is engendered by the introduction of a new technology.

Arbitration

Most disputes over technological change arise during the life of a collective bargaining contract and during a period of business expansion. Therefore, they may not have a sufficiently adverse impact on bargaining unit employees to trigger an employer's duty to bargain. These disputes are usually settled within the contractually provided grievance-arbitration system. In general, arbitrators have recognized broad authority in management to determine methods of operation. Unless restricted by a contract, an employer has the right to determine *what* is to be produced, *when* it is to be produced, and *how* it is to be produced. An employer has the right to determine the tech-

> *The technological change must have a demonstrably adverse effect on the employees in the unit to trigger a bargaining requirement, and the union must request bargaining.*

niques, tools, and equipment by which work shall be performed in its behalf (Elkouri and Elkouri, 1985, pp. 481–82). Arbitrators have held that a union cannot block technological improvement unless there are specific contractual restrictions on the matter (Bureau of National Affairs, *Grievance Guide,* 6th ed., pp. 280–81).

Not only can employers automate during the life of a contract, but they may also introduce new methods and reorganize work in order to utilize new technology. Arbitrators are in general agreement that where substantial changes in technology have been made unless restricted by a contract, management has the right, for example, to make changes in the size of the crew, (Elkouri and Elkouri, 1985). Also, with few exceptions, arbitrators have recognized management's right to establish new jobs, eliminate obsolete jobs, or combine jobs and job classifications (Hill and Sinicropi, 1986). The mere listing of job classifications and their corresponding wage rates in the parties' contract does not preclude management from changing or eliminating the classifications, unless specifically provided by the agreement (Hill and Sinicropi, 1986).

A survey of sixty-seven arbitration cases by McLaughlin (1979, pp. 89–90) revealed that when unions won disputes concerning automation, it was due to specific contract language. Unions lost most of the cases surveyed because their contracts lacked relevant or specific language. In the absence of specific contract language, arbitrators relied on management rights clauses, permitting employers to automate, combine or eliminate jobs, assign work, set pay rates on new jobs, and determine crew sizes. Unions *have* had arbitration success in the reassignment of work outside the bargaining unit. Arbitrators reason that the transfer of work customarily performed by unit employees to others outside the unit in effect attacks one of the basic purposes of a labor agreement: to maintain employee job security (Hill and Sinicropi, 1986, p. 406). Usually, if a union can show that workers in the unit are capable of continuing the work after new machines are installed, then its grievance against transferring the work is likely to be upheld. On the other hand, if a company can show that the nature of work has changed so that workers who were previously assigned to it can no longer handle it efficiently, an arbitrator will uphold a decision to transfer work (Bureau of National Affairs, *Grievance Guide*, 6th ed., pp. 280–81).[12]

Where substantial changes in technology have been made unless restricted by a contract, management has the right, for example, to make changes in the size of the crew . . . establish new jobs, eliminate obsolete jobs, or combine jobs and job classifications.

Collective Bargaining Contract Provisions

In most situations, if a union is to directly influence the introduction of new technology, it needs to have already negotiated specific contract language addressing technological change. The available evidence indicates that only a small percentage of union contracts contain such specific language. According to a BNA survey (1986a, pp. 82–83), management rights to make technological changes are restricted in only 25 percent of the sampled contracts. The most common provision (contained in 15 percent of the contracts) requires advance notice and discussion with the union. A 1978 BLS survey found that only 11 percent of all contracts examined contained a provision requiring employers to notify the union about a technological change in advance. According to BNA, retraining is required in only 8 percent of the surveyed contracts. Technological displacement provisions, which require a company to retain displaced employees, are found in only 2 percent of the BNA surveyed contracts. The distribution of all of these provisions varies by industry, with high concentrations being found in apparel (89 percent), printing (75 percent), maritime (63 percent), textile (50 percent), and communications (60 percent) industries. Other industries with over 30 percent of the BNA-surveyed contracts containing technology provisions include rubber, chemicals, food, mining, retail, insurance, and finance contracts.

According to a BNA survey, management rights to make technological changes are restricted in only 25 percent of the sampled contracts.

In his study for the AFL-CIO, Murphy (1981) found that "the single most prevalent provision is advance notice of technological change, usually accompanied by provision for consultation or negotiation." He did not find any provisions that limited the ultimate right of management to introduce technological change, or that explicitly gave unions the right to influence the nature of the innovation itself. In general, the study found that "contract provisions centered on smoothing worker adjustment to management-initiated and management-controlled change."

It may be unfortunate in some respects that so few contracts provide for union influence over the introduction of new technology. In a recent study of a large unionized automobile company, Katz, Kochan, and Keefe (1987c) showed that greater worker and union participation in the process of introducing technology was associated with increased productivity and improved product quality (see Table 9). Their findings are consistent with an increasing amount of literature on the importance of worker participation in

TABLE 9
The Impact of Worker and Union Participation
in Technological Change on Quality and Productivity
in a Large North American Automobile Company

Standard errors are in parentheses

	Adjusted Labor Hours	Quality
Participation in Technology	−0.0536* (0.0217)	1.1066* (0.6278)
Work Group Participation	−0.0327 (0.0218)	0.7040 (0.5686)
Start-up	0.2696** (0.0606)	−5.0719** (2.0312)
Assembly	−9.4156** (1.5466)	
Body	−3.7294** (1.9745)	
Constant	1.1350** (0.0229)	137.7389** (1.3790)
R	0.36	0.40
Observations	33	79

Source: Katz, Kochan, and Keefe, 1987.

* Statistically significant at the 0.10 level, 2-tailed t test.
** Statistically significant at the 0.05 level, 2-tailed t test.

management decisionmaking as an essential ingredient for full utilization of new computerized technology (Zuboff, 1988; also see Kelley and Harrison in this volume). Excluding workers and their representatives from decisionmaking about new technology may result in under-utilization, or less productive utilization, of new technology.

The Implications for Unions and Technological Change

The contemporary collective bargaining framework usually relegates unions to a reactive role in the process of modernization, shaping both the collective bargaining relationship and the balance of power between labor and management. Union concerns about the consequences of new technology have focused on the threats to employment. In general, although there is no evidence that unions are using contract language to impede technological change, unions have been rarely able to secure contract language that specifically protects their members from the adverse consequences arising from technological change.

Contemporary Union Policies and Responses to Technological Change

After a systematic review of the literature and arbitration cases on industrial unions and technological change, this study concludes that during the 1980s, unions have either encouraged or accepted technological change and have focused on helping workers adjust to ongoing modernization. Alternative options for competition with and opposition to new technology have fallen into disuse. Concern for employment security has caused some unions to encourage plant modernization and to find ways to soften the potentially devastating effects of worker displacements.

Contemporary Union Encouragement of Technological Change

Contemporary examples of union encouragement of technological change abound. Their common objective is to re-energize the competitiveness of their plant or industry. For example, the American steel industry has been on the decline since the early 1970s. When foreign imports began to gain market share, steel production began to shift away from integrated mills to mini-mills, and the demand for steel declined as plastics and other materials were increasingly utilized. Steelworkers believe that another reason for the industry's decline has been the failure of the steel companies to modernize facilities: the companies were instead taking profits earned in steel production and using them to diversify. One example would be U.S. Steel's 1982 decision to purchase Marathon Oil rather than build a new integrated steel mill. The 1987 United Steelworkers of America-USX (U.S. Steel) agreement addressed this concern. It includes Appendix Q, which details U.S. Steel's commitment to modernize specific facilities during the life of the contract. In return for this commitment, the Steelworkers

Contemporary examples of union encouragement of technological change abound. Their common objective is to re-energize the competitiveness of their plant or industry.

129

were willing to make wage and benefit concessions. The objective of the union's technology bargaining policy for steel and other distressed industries was to "stem the tide of unemployment and make jobs more secure."[13]

Declining U.S. automobile sales and the surge of imports has stimulated a policy of technological encouragement in the auto industry. In 1985, General Motors (GM) and the United Automobile Workers (UAW) entered into the "Saturn Agreement." Under this agreement, Saturn (a new GM subsidiary) will produce small cars, using the most modern auto technology and a team system of work organization. The union will participate in all levels of management decisionmaking. The Saturn Agreement was reached prior to plant construction, reflecting the desire of GM and the UAW to build a small American car competitive with Japanese and Korean imports.

In their study of a large auto company, Keefe and Katz (1990) found that the company's modernization of particular facilities was associated with concessions made by the local union. Apparently, some UAW locals have been making work rule changes to encourage the company to select their facility for modernization. GM, for example, has effectively used facility modernization to whipsaw UAW locals into making concessions in order to remain open.

In the textile and apparel industries, employment declined by 500,000 jobs between 1973 and 1983. In 1979, the Amalgamated Clothing and Textile Workers Unions (ACTWU) joined with employers from the Clothing Manufacturers Association to launch the Tailored Clothing Technology Corporation (TC), a nonprofit research and development corporation proposed by the union.[14] Funded by the federal government, the companies, and the union, the purpose of TC has been to develop new technologies that allow the U.S. men's and boy's tailored clothing industry to compete with foreign imports. One new development is a technology that can perform 25 percent of the handling and sewing done on a suit coat, which would displace 20 percent of the workers now required to produce a coat. The union hopes that this new technology will sufficiently reduce costs and processing time, cut final prices, and cause the domestic market to expand sufficiently to offset the resulting employment.

Another example of the policy of encouragement involved the Singer Company and the International Union of Electrical Workers (IUE). In an effort to keep a New Jer-

> *The purpose of TC has been to develop new technologies that allow the U.S. men's and boy's tailored clothing industry to compete with foreign imports.*

sey Singer sewing machine plant open, IUE Local 461 made concessions to Singer. The contract specified that these labor-cost savings were to be used to modernize equipment and to keep the plant open. However, Singer chose to close the plant during the life of the agreement. In 1982 a federal court awarded Local 461 a $2 million damage settlement for the contract violation. In this case, the policy of encouragement had given way to the policy of adjustment.

The policy of encouragement is usually triggered by a declining competitive position of an industry, plant, or craft. When modernization can stem an employment decline, union encouragement is likely. However, adjustment is an even more common union policy toward worker-displacing technological change.

Contemporary Adjustment Policies and Programs

In many instances, unions do not actively encourage modernization, but instead focus on protecting the income and skills of their members. Where technological progress involves reduced employment, the emphasis is on mitigating adverse effects. Four approaches are identified and discussed: 1) contractual provisions and adjustments; 2) work preservation (featherbedding); 3) employment security through attrition and human resource planning; and 4) comprehensive adjustment programs which rely on a variety of mechanisms from early retirement to outplacement services. Basically, any successful adjustment program requires advance notification of potential displacement problems.

Contractual Provisions and Adjustment

Most unions anticipate future operating changes by negotiating labor-management agreements that include rules, procedures, and programs governing workforce adjustments. However, management usually opposes efforts to contractually specify worker adjustment procedures. Instead, employers negotiate management rights clauses in an effort to maintain broad discretion in the implementation and adjustment of changes. These clauses appear in over 99 percent of U.S. labor agreements. However, they vary considerably in both scope and specificity.[15]

Some unions provide their negotiators with "model" contract language on regulating adjustments to technological change. A good example of this approach is provided by the International Association of Machinists (IAM). The IAM has

Employers negotiate management rights clauses in an effort to maintain broad discretion in the implementation and adjustment of changes.

131

developed model contract language to govern the introduction of new programmable manufacturing technologies such as numerically controlled machine tools, robots, integrated computer-aided manufacturing, CADCAM, flexible manufacturing systems (FMS), and any other innovation which would affect employment or job content. The stated purpose of the model agreement is to encourage the use of the most efficient processes, methods, machines, and materials so that the company can effectively compete. At the same time, this protects employment, prevents the erosion of skills and working conditions, and secures the collective bargaining relationship. The model agreement defines that which constitutes new technology, requires advance notice and joint consultation, provides for the creation of new job classifications, ensures that incumbent employees will be given the opportunity to train for new jobs, restricts electronic monitoring of job performance, maintains the integrity of the bargaining unit, and provides a procedure for dispute resolution. This model contract language is introduced by IAM representatives in negotiations with management to address problems that may arise from anticipated technological changes.

Adjusting to technological change through negotiated contractual provisions is the most common union approach to worker displacement issues.

For example, a 1985 dispute between the IAM and Pratt & Whitney centered on access to retraining for incumbent employees who were being displaced by new technology. After a two-week strike, an agreement was reached that prevented Pratt & Whitney from hiring new employees while veteran employees were being laid off. Workers also won the right to bid for jobs across occupational groups. In addition, workers could receive up to $1,500 toward education tuition, and laid-off workers were given first preference to be rehired for new positions created by the introduction of new technology. The agreement called for continued labor-management consultation and discussion about the impact of new technology.

Adjusting to technological change through negotiated contractual provisions is the most common union approach to worker displacement issues. In contrast, the least prevalent adjustment approach is work preservation (or "featherbedding").

Work Preservation

One commonly held view about union objectives is dominated by the imagery of "featherbedding" or make-work practices. According to this view, unions seek to maintain traditional work methods by preventing the introduction of new technology or more efficient work practices in order to preserve the employment of their members and secure a steady stream of dues income.[16] This has been an uncommon union approach in recent years.

More commonly, we have witnessed union-management conflict over whether particular tasks will be done by bargaining unit members or by nonunion employees. For instance, Shaiken (1984) reported that when the job of parts programmer had been created by the introduction of numerical control (NC), management often tried to fill the position with a nonbargaining unit employee. Shaiken reviewed a UAW arbitration case concerning NC introduction in which the union was successful in having the work returned to an employee in the bargaining unit. However, even when a company is contractually obligated to hold advance discussions with the union, the introduction of NC may occur without the union's knowledge.

Similarly, Kelley (1989) provided evidence that management in nonunion settings is more likely to permit workers operating programmable machines to do their own programming. Management in unionized settings is more likely to create a position for a professional programmer and place programming responsibilities outside the bargaining unit. Unions naturally resist such efforts.

Employment Security Through Attrition and Human Resource Planning

Until the 1980s, agreements and polices of adjustment through attrition were common in both regulated and government-operated industries and in a few large union and nonunion manufacturing firms. But then deregulation, budgetary pressures, and foreign competition forced many union and nonunion employers to abandon guaranteed employment security policies.

Offering employment security and making adjustments to technological change through human resource planning is good for labor *and* management. However, several conditions must be met for the planning process to operate. First, there must be coordination between those planning the new technology and the labor relations and human resource staffs. Without advance knowledge of the introduction of new technology and its projected staffing levels, human resource planning is impossible. Second, if transfer opportunities are to be offered to all displaced employees,

Offering employment security and making adjustments to technological change through human resource planning is good for labor and management.

133

there must be an adequate balance between turnover and new positions. Where there is a history of stable employment, this condition usually requires that other business operations have growing employment needs *or* that workforce demographics permit an adequate number of induced early retirements. In the last decade, many firms that, historically, had been able to offer employment security through human resource planning were faced with substantial employment contractions throughout their operations. No longer able to generate sufficient openings to offer transfers to all surplus employees, a number of labor-management agreements moved toward comprehensive adjustment programs. These programs combine human resource planning with outplacement assistance for those workers who are displaced.

Between 1979 and 1984 . . . Of those who lost their jobs, 5.1 million had been employed in their jobs for at least three years, and therefore were considered officially displaced.

Comprehensive Adjustment Programs and Outplacement Initiatives

Beginning in 1979, major structural changes in the U.S. economy combined with a deep recession to cause dramatic and permanent employment declines in many basic U.S. industries. Between 1979 and 1984, 11.5 million workers lost their jobs due to plant closings, abolition of a position or shift, or lack of work. Of those who lost their jobs, 5.1 million had been employed in their jobs for at least three years, and therefore were considered officially displaced (U.S. Office of Technology Assessment, 1986).

In response to these massive displacements, a number of collective bargaining agreements adopted worker adjustment programs modeled after the Armour Automation Fund. This fund was established in 1959 through an agreement between Armour and its two unions. It underwrote various efforts to solve the employment problems created for workers when the company closed obsolete plants. Financed by a $500,000 company contribution, a joint union-management committee oversaw the effort. The committee relied on a variety of techniques, including job counseling, individual skill assessments, retraining programs, promotional campaigns to generate job offers, severance payments, interplant transfers, relocation allowances, advance notice, and planning which involved coordination with external government agencies, primarily the state employment services. Senior employees were offered several early retirement options.[17]

In 1982, for example, the UAW-Ford and the UAW-GM contracts contained pilot adjustment programs to aid workers displaced by a shutdown or the retrofitting of a plant. These programs, funded by company contributions, were later given permanent status. A number of comprehensive adjustment programs have been negotiated in the last decade. These include: joint efforts by the United Steelworkers (USWA) and the major steel producers; the International Electrical Workers (IUE) and GE; the Alliance, which is a joint program sponsored by the Communications Workers (CWA), the International Brotherhood of Electrical Workers (IBEW), and AT&T; the CWA and several regional telephone operating companies; the International Brotherhood of Electrical Workers (IBEW) and GTE; the Amalgamated Clothing Workers (ACTWU) and Levi Strauss; and ACTWU and Johnson & Johnson.[18]

Critical to the operation of many of these programs has been the availability of federal Job Training Partnership Act (JTPA) Title III funds to aid displaced workers. JTPA was passed in 1982, and in October 1983 Title III displaced worker programs were initiated. Title III was the first comprehensive government program in over 20 years that was designed specifically to offer assistance and retraining to displaced workers.[19] Although organized labor has been critical of the inadequate funding levels and program administration, unions have actively participated in the displaced worker programs. A study by Fedrau and Balfe (1989) found that the process of obtaining Title III funding often served as the catalyst in establishing plant level labor-management programs to provide displaced worker assistance. At the present time, no systematic studies have been done to evaluate the effectiveness of these JTPA-supported programs.

Although organized labor has been critical of the inadequate funding levels and program administration, unions have actively participated in the displaced worker programs.

Conclusion: Unions Do Not Hinder Technological Change

The research presented in this study indicates that unionized facilities are older but technologically more modern than nonunion facilities. However, when differences in size and other characteristics thought to influence technological diffusion are taken into consideration, there is no union effect—positive or negative—on technological modernization. The evidence strongly indicates that union-

135

ization does not hinder technological change. Union policies toward technological change encompass a wide spectrum, from opposition to encouragement. Opposition is triggered when a large proportion of members' jobs are threatened by new technology. However, the most common union responses have been acceptance and adjustment to change, and in recent years unions have been encouraging modernization to improve competitiveness and preserve jobs. Most union contracts do not contain language specifically covering the introduction of new technology.

If collective bargaining does not specifically address the introduction of new technology, the law requires unionized employers to negotiate over its introduction only when the change will have an adverse effect on the bargaining unit. Beyond the bargaining requirement, employers, unions, workers, and the public could benefit from a more active union and employee involvement in technological change.

The most common union responses have been acceptance and adjustment to change, and encouraging modernization to improve competitiveness and preserve jobs.

Endnotes

[1]   He writes, "almost without exception, union leaders recognize that increased productivity per man hour, arising from mechanization, is the key to easier jobs and improved standard of living" (pp. 88–89).

[2]   Early studies by proponents of the union-rent-seeking model found that unions adversely affect investment in new capital and R&D (Connolly, Hirsch, and Hirschey 1986; Bronars and Deere, 1988). To operationalize unionism, however, both of these rent-seeking studies used constructed measures of the extent of unionism based on three-digit SIC aggregations of the May Current Population Survey (CPS), which serve as a proxy for the firm's extent of unionism, a proxy subject to considerable measurement error.

To remedy this problem, Hirsch (1988, p. 3–3) constructed a measure of the 1977 level of unionization for 632 COMPUSTAT companies. He merged his union-ization cross-section with a 12-year COMPUSTAT panel and estimated pooled regressions to determine the union effect on capital investment and R&D. The pooled results indicate a strong negative union effect. However, once the model is purged of autocorrelation, the results become statistically not different from zero (1988, pp. 5–7, 5–12, and 5–13). The 1977 cross-section results show that union effects on capital investment, while negative, are also insignificant (1988, Table 5.2); however, union effects on R&D investment are negative and highly significant (1988, Table 5.5).

In the best designed study on the subject, Clark (1984), using a five-period panel of 902 firms, found that unionization (measured at the firm level) has little effect on growth or capital-labor substitution. Clark interprets his results as "consistent with a bargaining model of the union, in which the union affects the distribution of profits, but has little effect on output, or factors of production" (1984, p. 918).

On the whole, once problems of measurement error are addressed, these studies suggest that unionization does not exert a significant influence on capital investment.

[3]   However, based on survey data, Rees, Briggs, and Oakey (1984) surprisingly found that older plants are more innovative users of new process technologies than the newer ones. Plants built prior to 1939 show higher adoption rates than do plants built after 1940. This finding suggests that there may be differential survival rates for modernizers versus nonmodernizers, which could be another potential source of bias. For example, we may observe only modern old plants (others having shut down), whereas we observe all newer plants. Since older plants are more likely to be union plants, this may overstate a positive union effect. Or, higher union labor costs may cause unionized plants to become obsolete sooner, causing them to shut down earlier (and disappear from the sample) than comparable nonunion plants. Accordingly, a finding that union plants are more modern could mean that nonmodernizing unionized plants are more

likely to close down, and not that unionized establishments have a greater propensity to modernize.

4   Pioneer is a binary variable which takes the value 1 if the firm has adopted at least one of the thirty-three major textile machinery innovations with a speed equal to, or better than, the average speed of adoption for that innovation, and takes the value 0 otherwise.

5   The chi-square probabilities were 0.000 for NC, 0.000 for MC, 0.189 for CNC, 0.003 for DNC, 0.003 for CADCAM, 0.000 for ROBOT, and 0.290 for FMS; see Table 6 for variable definitions. In the case of flexible manufacturing systems (FMS), there are simply too few user observations to detect a significant difference, and for computerized numerical control (CNC) there is no measurable difference in utilization between unionized and nonunion facilities.

6   These estimates are from multiple regression analysis. See Keefe (1991).

7   The sources often cited only the union's initial response rather than its ultimate response. Also, this survey is not random; it deliberately oversampled the number of unions that opposed the introduction of new technology. In order to investigate the consequences of pursuing such a policy, McLaughlin actively sought out unions that had opposed the introduction of new technology.

8   That is, bargaining to impasse or using economic weapons to extract concessions on these items is an unfair labor practice.

9   Employees must be laid off, transferred to lower paying jobs, lose overtime, lose work by removal from the bargaining unit, or be faced with the permanent elimination of jobs classifications.

10 Most of the litigation about the decision to automate involves changes in typesetting technology in the printing industry, when cold type replaced hot type. Initially, the NLRB reasoned that the decision to automate was mandatory subject of bargaining in *Renton News Record* (*Renton News Record*, 136 NLRB 1294, 1962; cited in Morris, 1982). Here the employer was found to have failed to bargain in good faith when the employer refused to bargain with the union "over the intended change of operations and its effects on the composing room employees" (*Renton News Record* at 1296, 1973). Although Renton News was found guilty of refusing to bargain over the decision to automate and the effects of this refusal, the NLRB remedy ordered bargaining only over the effects of the change. Renton News was "not direct[ed] ... to reinstate the composing room employees or to bargain with the union about any proposed termination of their composing room operations ..." (*Renton News Record* at 1298).

The Board apparently retreated from its *Renton News* position, requiring decision bargaining over automation after the Supreme Court's *Fibreboard* decision in 1964 (McLaughlin, 1979, pp. 67–68). *Fibreboard* requires management to bargain over an economically-motivated decision to subcontract bargaining unit work. However, of special importance in shaping judicial thinking about

138

the issue of automation is the frequently cited concurring opinion of Justice Stewart in *Fibreboard*:

> Yet there are ... areas where decisions by management may quite clearly imperil job security, or indeed terminate employment entirely. An enterprise may decide to invest in labor-saving machinery. Another may resolve to liquidate its assets and go out of business. Nothing the Court holds today should be understood as imposing a duty to bargain collectively regarding such managerial decisions, which lie at the core of entrepreneurial control. Decisions concerning the commitment of investment capital and the basic scope of the enterprise are not in themselves primarily about conditions of employment, though the effect of the decision may be necessarily to terminate employment (*Fibreboard Paper Products Corp. v. NLRB*, 379 U.S. 203 1964).

Justice Stewart's opinion clearly places the decision to invest in labor-saving technology outside the scope of mandatory bargaining. However, some scholars reviewing NLRB and Court decisions—including the majority opinion in *Fibreboard*—called upon the NLRB to make explicit "what is already implicit in *Fibreboard* and its progeny: that where a managerial decision to automate will directly and forseeably affect union interests adversely, an employer is under a mandatory duty to bargain collectively" (Note, *Harvard Law Review*, 1971, p. 1855). In *Columbia Tribune* (*NLRB v. Columbia Tribune Publishing Co.*, 495 F.2d 1384, 8th Cir., 1974; *enforcing* 201 NLRB 538, 1973), the Eighth Circuit Court upheld the Board's ruling that the employer failed to bargain in good faith regarding the change in the type of machinery used, which resulted in the layoff of half the bargaining unit. This decision "may be read as extending the mandatory bargaining requirements of the Supreme Court's *Fibreboard* case to encompass both automation and technological change" (Morris, 1982, p. 818, fn. 257).

[11] The union request could occur after the employer introduces the new technology.

[12] However, the NLRB in *BASF Wyandotte Corp* (1985), "held that an employer did not refuse to bargain when, because of automation, employees were removed from the bargaining unit when they were made salaried technicians" (Linnick et al., 1988).

[13] Quoted from Dennis Ahlburg (1987).

[14] This brief account is based on Jocelyn F. Gutchess (1985, pp. 130–33).

[15] Partly underlying these management rights clauses is a deeply embedded belief that as a function of human nature, workers are resistant to change. Therefore, management must maintain unrestricted control to implement operational changes, otherwise technical improvements would not be possible. However, it is these same workers, in their role as consumers, who buy new cars and new consumer products (such as microwaves and VCR's) from these employers, and whom advertisers believe must be convinced that a product is "new and

improved" in order to make a sale. Can both images be right? Are worker/consumers the modern-day equivalent to Dr. Jeckel and Mr. Hyde? Do they undergo a fundamental metamorphosis between work and home? The answer is no. Workers do not inherently resist change; they resist change that they believe may worsen their circumstances; they resist change when their interests are either not adequately considered or ignored; and they are most likely to resist change that threatens their employment security. As discussed above, workers and their unions are most often willing to accept technological change.

[16] Featherbedding is a violation of the National Labor Relations Act, 8(b)(6), which is defined as causing or attempting "to cause an employer to pay or deliver or agree to pay or deliver money or any other thing of value, in the nature of an extraction, for services which are not performed or are not to be performed." What is commonly and incorrectly referred to as featherbedding is an effort by a union to preserve the employment of its members by relying on work rules rendered obsolete by change, while at the same time permitting the introduction of new technology.

[17] The Armour program was the subject of a number of evaluations, getting only mixed reviews. See especially Schultz and Weber (1966).

[18] This is not an exhaustive list.

[19] Federal and state government programs, such as unemployment insurance, the employment service, trade adjustment assistance, and retraining programs provide the principal vehicle to aid displaced workers. Employment Service (ES) administers unemployment insurance payments and provides free services such as job placement. Although the ES can offer services such as skills assessment, job counseling, job development, and referrals to suitable training programs, it is often inadequately funded and unable to make these services available. A recent study indicates that only 5 percent of people looking for work found jobs through the ES system. The AFL-CIO is a strong advocate of modernizing the U.S. Employment Service (ES) system, and for improving the levels of unemployment insurance payments. There have been several government programs aimed at aiding displaced workers. In 1962, the Manpower Development and Training Act (MDTA) was passed with active labor support; it was initially designed to assist workers who were displaced by automation. After only two years of operation, however, as unemployment rates fell and the fear of technological unemployment subsided, the program shifted its mission to aiding disadvantaged workers. During the Nixon Administration, the MDTA was replaced by the Comprehensive Employment and Training Act (CETA), which was also aimed at aiding the disadvantaged. In 1982, CETA was superseded by the Job Training Partnership Act (JTPA).

Appendix: Independent Variable Definitions for Tables 7 and 8

Union—If the majority of workers in the establishment are covered by a collective bargaining agreement, the Union is coded 1. Otherwise it is coded 0.

Training—Coded 1 if there is a formal training program or apprenticeship program in operation at the plant. Otherwise it is coded 0.

Wage—The natural log of the average hourly wage for production workers in the establishment.

Shift 2nd—Coded 1 if establishment operates a 2nd shift. Otherwise it is coded 0.

Size Control Variables for NC, MC, CNC, and DNC

Size11—If a machine shop employs between 11 and 50 machine operators, the variable Size11 is coded 1. Otherwise it is coded 0.

Size51—If a machine shop employs between 51 and 200 machine operators, the variable Size51 is coded 1. Otherwise it is coded 0.

Size201—If a machine shop employs more than 200 machine operators, the variable Size201 is coded 1. Otherwise it is coded 0.

Size Control Variables for Robots, CADCAM, and FMS

Size51—If a plant employs between 51 and 200 production workers, the variable Size51 is coded 1. Otherwise it is coded 0.

Size201—If a plant employs between 201 and 400 production workers, the variable Size201 is coded 1. Otherwise it is coded 0.

Size401—If a plant employs more then 400 production workers, the variable Size 401 is coded 1. Otherwise it is coded 0.

Is Declining Unionization of the U.S. Good, Bad, or Irrelevant?

Richard Freeman

Introduction

It is indisputable that the unionized share of the private sector workforce in the United States declined rapidly in the 1970s and 1980s. In 1970, 31 percent of all private sector workers and over half of those engaged in blue collar jobs were unionized. In 1989, only 12 percent of private sector workers and less than a quarter of those engaged in blue collar jobs were unionized.[1] An observer from the 1920s would recognize the "ghetto unionism"—pockets of organized workers and companies, often in declining industries, in a sea of nonunion labor—that characterized the private sector of the American labor market at the outset of the 1990s. An observer from the 1950s would be shocked. Where was Big Labor? What happened to collective bargaining as the nation's way of dealing with labor-management relations?

The precipitous drop in union density is arguably the most important change in the institutional structure of the U.S. labor market since the New Deal. In most member countries of the Organization for Economical Cooperation and Development (OECD), union densities tended to increase in the 1970s and stabilize in the 1980s at levels far above those in the United States (Freeman, 1990a). The United States now is much closer to the union-free nirvana of the National Association of Manufacturers (NAM) than even the most rabid union opponent would have hoped when the NAM set up its Council for a Union-Free Environ-

The precipitous drop in union density is arguably the most important change in the institutional structure of the U.S. labor market since the New Deal.

143

ment. If current patterns persist, union density will fall to single digits in the private sector in the mid- to late 1990s (Freeman, 1989). The determination of wages and working conditions will be more dependent on market forces and managerial discretion. Labor will be represented less in workplaces and on the political scene than in any other major industrial country.

How should the nation view the declining unionization of the labor market? Is a less unionized workforce good, bad, or irrelevant to our economic well-being? Will it raise or lower the efficiency of the economy? Will it alter modes of compensation and if so, how? Will it improve or worsen personnel and labor relations practices? How will it change the distribution of earnings and the profitability of firms?

How should the nation view the declining unionization of the labor market?

The answer to these questions requires reasonably accurate knowledge of the effects of unions on our economy and society. The 1984 book, *What Do Unions Do?* (written with J. Medoff), was based on research from the mid-1970s to the early 1980s. The book summarized the empirical evidence on these issues, and concluded that unions were complex social institutions. Their effects on the economy were not adequately captured by the simple monopoly model that dominated empirical labor economics in the post–World War II period (see G. Johnson, 1975, and H.G. Lewis, 1986, for summaries of this research). *What Do Unions Do?* argued that while unions raise wages in ways that misallocate labor and reduce social output—as stressed by the monopoly model—they also have a collective voice "face" that changes work relations in socially beneficial ways.[2] Unions and collective bargaining change work relations by lowering turnover and establishing stable workforces; eliciting preferences of workers for different fringe benefits and workplace conditions, producing a more efficient compensation package; providing management with information about plant level operations, increasing productivity; and reducing wage inequality among similar workers through "equal pay for equal work" policies that bring the actual distribution of wages closer to the free market ideal.

The idea that unions do more than raise wages is not new. Analysts as diverse as Sumner Slichter, Milton Friedman, Alfred Marshall, Derek Bok, John Dunlop, and H. Gregg Lewis have made similar points. The idea that collective bargaining can actually improve the operation of the labor market, with all of its imperfections, is also an old

144

theme in industrial relations (Reynolds, 1982). *What Do Unions Do?* was novel because it tried to quantify the non-wage effects of unions with as much or more rigor as commonly used by analysts to quantify the monopoly wage effects. Vague assertions about the virtues of collective bargaining and industrial jurisprudence were transformed into testable propositions about turnover, productivity, fringe benefits, wage inequality, and so on.

What Do Unions Do? concluded that the empirical evidence showed the positive effects of the collective voice face outweighed any negative effects of the monopoly wage face on the social balance sheet. The policy implication was that the nation should consider new initiatives in labor relations to arrest and reverse the decline in union representation in the private sector.

The nation should consider new initiatives in labor relations to arrest and reverse the decline in union representation in the private sector.

Have the results of *What Do Unions Do?* stood up to ensuing empirical analysis, and are they still relevant to the economic environment of the 1980s? Is the portrayal of unionism in *What Do Unions Do?* relevant to union movements in other countries, or does it apply solely to U.S. unionism?

Assessing one's own past research findings is difficult. There is the risk of being embarrassed at past blunders—was I the bozo or naif who wrote that? Even worse is the risk of finding oneself in total agreement with one's published writing—a sure sign that one hasn't learned a thing thereafter. The pieces by Belman, Karier, Keefe, Voos and Eaton, and Kelley and Harrison presented in this volume, as well as other recent assessments in the literature (Allen, 1988a; Addison and Hirsch, 1986), offer such useful grist that it seems worth the effort to undertake the task of reassessing *What Do Unions Do?* at the onset of a new decade.

This reevaluation of the effects of unions on working life and the economy confirms the following conclusions from *What Do Unions Do?*:[3]

1) *Unionism reduces the probability that workers will quit their jobs and increases the tenure of workers with firms*, producing the long-term attachment of workers to firms that many regard as one of the key features of Japanese economic success. At the same time, unionism creates a temporary layoff response pattern of adjustment to the business cycle.

145

2) *Unions alter the composition of the compensation package toward "fringe benefits,"* particularly deferred benefits such as pensions, and life, accident, and health insurance, which are favored by senior workers. As a consequence of union-created pension plans, the vast majority of unionized blue collar workers are covered by pensions, whereas most nonunion blue collar workers are not.

3) *Unions reduce the inequality of wages among workers with measurably similar skills.* Unions encourage payment through wage scales for specified jobs. They discourage individual determination of pay, and limit managerial discretion in compensation. As unions also raise the wages of blue collar workers relative to those of higher paid white collar workers, the overall inequality of wages is lower.

4) *Union workplaces operate under more explicit rules than nonunion workplaces.* Personnel decisions in union settings depend on seniority rules and grievance-arbitration procedures rather than on managerial discretion or whim.

5) *Most unions are highly democratic, especially at the local level.* They are far from being the corrupt institutions that union-baiters often allege. Because most union policies reflect the desires of the median union member, union contracts respond more to the preferences of average workers than to those of marginal workers. This means that unionized firms pay relatively more attention to the desires and needs of senior or older workers, and others who are less mobile than to the desires and needs of those who threaten to leave. Crime and corruption are less common among union officials than among business officials.

6) *The view that unions harm productivity is erroneous.* In many sectors, unionism is associated with higher productivity. In only a few sectors is unionism associated with lower productivity. Good industrial relations climates and competitive economic pressures contribute to higher productivity under unionism. However, productivity growth

rates are possibly slightly lower in union than in nonunion settings.

7) *It is erroneous to blame unionism for national macroeconomic problems*, such as wage inflation or aggregate unemployment. Union wage gains are sizeable, but the social cost of those gains is modest. Union wages tend to respond markedly to changes in economic conditions that threaten the jobs of existing members, reducing potential social losses.

8) *Union wage gains reduce the rate of profit of unionized firms, motivating considerable anti-union activity by employers.* The reduction in profitability occurs largely in concentrated or otherwise highly profitable sectors of the economy.

9) *The decline in union density is due in large part to employer opposition to union organizing in National Labor Relations Board (NLRB) representation election campaigns.* The effectiveness of this opposition (motivated by the loss of profits from unionism) gives employers a great deal of influence over the decision of workers to join unions.

In addition, recent research has established that:

1) *Unionized firms introduce modern technological innovations at least as rapidly as nonunion firms and are in the forefront of personnel and labor relations innovations.* There is no truth to the claim that unions reduce the rate of introduction of new machines or work practices.

2) *Research and Development (R&D) is less in unionized settings*, in part because unionism is concentrated in older, mature industries, but also in part because the reduction in profits due to unionism discourages firms from investing in R&D.

The decline in union density is due in large part to employer opposition to union organizing.

3) *The wages of unionized workers respond more to adverse economic conditions due to trade and other factors than the wages of nonunion workers*, as was made clear in the union concessions of the 1980s. Union wages respond more because they are higher than nonunion wages, providing workers and firms with a margin of adjustment.

4) *Union pension plans are a major form of savings among blue collar workers and a substantial contributor to the overall national savings rate*, and potentially to the rate of investment as well.

Unions as Collective Voice

The findings reported in *What Do Unions Do?* on the collective voice face of unionism—those relating to the impact of unionism on quit rates, workforce stability, the composition of compensation, wage inequality, and the democratic operation of unions—are not revisited in the other chapters of this book. They have been accepted, and have become part of the conventional wisdom about the effects of unionism on the labor market. While some analysts may disagree with the policy conclusions drawn in *What Do Unions Do?* from these findings, no one denies their factual validity for the United States. Studies of unionism in other countries suggest that these findings describe other industrial relations systems as well (Blanchflower and Freeman, 1990).

The implication of these findings is far-reaching, for the existence of the collective voice face of unionism implies that unionism can be a unique positive force in modern economies—a force for which there is no apparent substitute.

Virtually all modern studies of *turnover and mobility*— including those concerned with nonunion issues—contain union variables as controls, and invariably find that unionism significantly reduces quit rates or raises job tenure. For example, a 1990 analysis of the effects of "overeducation" on worker mobility using the Michigan Panel Survey of Income Dynamics found union status (a control variable of little relevance to overeducation) to be the single most important factor in the decision of workers to remain with a firm (Sicherman, 1989). Research on turnover in Japan (Muramatsu, 1984; Osawa, 1989), Canada (Kupferschmidt

> **Union pension plans are a major form of savings among blue collar workers and a substantial contributor to the overall national savings rate.**

and Swidensky, 1989), the United Kingdom (Elias and Blanchflower, 1989), and Australia (Kornfeld, 1990) also shows lower quit rates and greater job tenure among union than among nonunion workers. The exit-voice trade-off at the heart of *What Do Unions Do?* applies universally to unionism in industrialized countries.

The finding that unionism increases the *fringe benefit share of compensation* has been confirmed in ensuing U.S. research (Freeman, 1985b; Allen and Clark, 1988). It also has been found to hold in other developed countries. Nakamura reported that the bonus share of compensation is higher in unionized settings in Japan. Kupferschmidt and Swidensky found that unions raise the probability of having pensions in Canada. Millward and Stevens (1986) and Green, Hadjimatheou, and Small (1985) showed that unionism increases the likelihood that firms have health and safety committees and raises the probability that establishments have various fringes in the United Kingdom. Looking across countries, Green and Potepan (1987) found that the differences in vacation time received by workers in OECD countries are strongly associated with differences in union density. Sweeney pointed out that U.S. unions have taken a lead role in seeking ways to contain the skyrocketing costs of medical insurance.

That *unions reduce wage inequality* seems to be well established. Union wage policies increase the equality of wages within establishments and encourage equal pay for equal work across establishments. As unions also raise the wages of lower paid blue collar workers relative to those of higher paid white collar workers, the overall inequality of wages is lower under unionism. Recent findings, based on usual hourly earnings in 1988–89, confirm that unions reduce inequality among male workers by 15 to 20 percent (Freeman, 1990b). Although the difference in wage inequality between union and nonunion women is smaller, unions still noticeably reduce inequality (Macpherson and Stewart, 1987). Wage inequality in the public sector is also lower among union workers than among nonunion workers (Freeman, 1986b, p. 60). For both men and women, the effects of personal characteristics such as schooling and age that determine wages tend to be smaller among union workers (Macpherson and Stewart, 1987).

Studies of the relation of unionism to wage inequality in other developed countries yield similar results. In the United Kingdom, researchers have found that union work-

The existence of the collective voice face of unionism implies that unionism can be a unique positive force in modern economies—a force for which there is no apparent substitute.

ers have less wage inequality (Metcalf, 1982). In Canada, inequality of wages is lower among union workers in both cross-section and longitudinal analyses (Kupferschmidt and Swidensky, 1989). Comparisons of industrial wage inequality and union density across countries show that countries with high union density have lower wage inequality (Blanchflower and Freeman, 1990).

Unionized establishments pay workers differently. Brown (1990) has confirmed that union firms are more likely to use single wage rates or scales that reduce inequality. Freeman and Kleiner (1990a) found that plants that unionize are less likely to use merit pay (which allows firms to differentiate greatly among workers). Blanchflower and Oswald (1988b) found that union workers in the United Kingdom are less likely to be paid by merit pay systems. Eaton and Voos' summary of studies in this volume showed that union firms are less likely to have profit-sharing than nonunion workers.

That unions influence *personnel and labor relations practices* in ways likely to affect both worker well-being and firm productivity has been found in diverse studies since the publication of *What Do Unions Do?* Studying establishments that became unionized in the 1980s, Freeman and Kleiner (1990a) reported that unions obtaining only modest compensation gains for members in first contracts substantially altered the rules of the workplace, introducing stronger seniority practices, additional fringe benefits, and grievance and arbitration procedures. They concluded that these "voice" effects are more fundamental to unions than the monopoly wage effects of unions. Eaton and Voos (this volume) cite studies reporting that nonunion grievance machinery is used so little compared to union grievance machinery as to suggest "a significant difference in the protections offered in the [union and nonunion] sectors." Their review of research and their own new evidence decisively rejects the myth that unions limit experimentation in new and improved methods of work organization. Some innovations in labor relations—quality circles, for instance—are more likely to occur in union settings. Others—such as the availability to employees of an employee stock ownership plan (ESOP)—appear unaffected by unionism, while, as noted above, union firms are less likely to have profit-sharing plans. These results come as no surprise to observers of the automobile and steel industries. Unions have been in the forefront of innovations

> Unions influence personnel and labor relations practices in ways likely to affect both worker well-being and firm productivity.

in work relations ranging from joint committees (United Automobile Workers in Ford and General Motors), to Japanese-style shopfloor relations (NUMMI), to workers' ownership of companies (United Steelworkers). Whether or not one agrees with Eaton and Voos' assessment that truly productivity-enhancing innovations are used as or more often in the union sector as in the nonunion sector, union workplaces have developed new modes of work organization, compensation, and employee participation.

Knowledgeable economists have always viewed unions as democratic institutions responsive to their members. Since Dunlop (1944) first developed maximizing models of union behavior, researchers (Farber, 1986; Kuhn, 1983) have asked what is the appropriate maximand (or set of goals) for union members, and whether a median voter model or some more complicated function of preferences better describes union behavior. No one believes union leaders extract rents from members or otherwise use dues for their personal aggrandizement. While academicians with little first-hand knowledge of unions may harbor images of union leaders as Mafiosi capos or bunglers in the *I'm All Right, Jack* mode,[4] the 1980s scandals in the business community—insider trading and junk bonds on Wall Street and bankruptcies of savings and loan institutions—make it clear that there are more real crooks and incompetents in the business community than in unions.

All told, the evidence of the 1980s has supported the "collective voice" view that unions alter labor outcomes in ways that go beyond raising wages. They affect turnover, components of compensation, work rules, and the inequality of wages in ways that are generally beneficial to the economy.

Unions affect turnover, components of compensation, work rules, and the inequality of wages in ways that are generally beneficial to the economy.

Union Wage Gains and Economic Welfare

What Do Unions Do? made three points about union wage gains. First, during the 1970s, union wage gains exceeded those in earlier postwar decades, setting in place pressures that led to concessions and "givebacks" in the 1980s. Second, union-nonunion wage differentials varied among sectors depending on the elasticity of demand for labor. Unions won greater wage gains in sectors where they had organized a higher percentage of the workforce, and

151

thus faced (all else the same) lower elasticities of demand for labor. Third, the social losses associated with union monopoly wages were small. How have these results fared in the 1980s?

Union wage studies have documented that the union-nonunion wage differential was larger in the 1970s than in earlier years (Lewis, 1986). However, studies have failed to pin down the magnitude and importance of the highly-publicized concessions of the 1980s. The two primary data sources on the earnings of union and nonunion workers tell contradictory stories. The Current Population Survey (CPS) data, based on reports from individuals, do not show the union differential decreased in the 1980s; some tabulations show that the union pay advantage actually increased (Blackburn, Bloom, and Freeman, 1990). On the other hand, the Employment Cost Index survey data, based on reports from establishments, show smaller gains among union workers than among nonunion workers in the 1980s (Freeman, 1986a). These conflicting results may stem from discrepancies in accounting for hours and overtime, by the greater prevalence of self-employment in the CPS data, or by differences in the treatment of moonlighting workers. Errors in identifying industries may contribute. Until the discrepancies between the data sets are resolved, whether *What Do Unions Do?* overstated or understated the importance of wage concessions in the 1980s will remain uncertain.

> **No analyst has argued, much less demonstrated empirically, that there is a large welfare loss induced by union wages.**

The result that union wages respond to market conditions when jobs are threatened has been confirmed in ensuing work. Freeman and Katz (1991) reported that union wages are more responsive to imports—and to changes in industry sales generally—than are nonunion wages. Macpherson and Stewart (1987) estimated that increases in the import share in a sector lower the union wage differential; this import effect is smaller in sectors where unions organized a higher percentage of workers. These analyses suggest that unionized workers have the flexibility to give wage reductions in hard times because they earn economic rents. Workers in other markets cannot reduce wages, as they receive the competitive wage. Blanchflower and Oswald (1988b) take this claim to its logical conclusion, arguing that British unions smooth the distribution of economic rents to workers over time—increasing the workers' share during prosperous times, and returning rents to firms during recession. Ordinarily, unions seek to preserve the jobs of existing members.

152

Unions very rarely raise wages to extract the maximum rent when a firm begins to fail.[5]

In *What Do Unions Do?* the estimates of the welfare loss due to the union wage premium were based on partial equilibrium rather than general equilibrium analysis. As such, they were subject to possible error for failing to account for the reverberations of union-induced misallocations of labor from one sector to another. Ensuing work using a full general equilibrium model has found only small welfare loss due to union monopoly wage gains. This loss is of the same magnitude as that reported in *What Do Unions Do?* and in earlier work by Rees (1963) as well (see DeFina, 1983). Indeed, there is good reason to believe that the estimates presented in *What Do Unions Do?* of the cost of the monopoly face of unionism are upwardly biased (Ashenfelter, 1985). This is because the book ignored the possibility that unions negotiate "efficient" collective contracts by bargaining over employment as well as over wages. Under such agreements, unions shift profits to labor while maintaining competitive levels of employment: no monopoly welfare loss is created. Finally, no analyst has argued, much less demonstrated empirically, that there is a large welfare loss induced by monopoly wages.

The evidence decisively rejects the notion that unions contributed to the massive trade deficit of the 1980s.

Do Unions Cause Macroeconomic Problems?

Unions have been blamed for a wide variety of macroeconomic problems, including the trade deficit, wage inflation, unemployment, and slow productivity growth. *What Do Unions Do?* rejected all of these charges. The economic developments of the 1980s and more recent studies have, for the most part, supported this assessment.

As Karier shows in this volume, the evidence decisively rejects the notion that unions contributed to the massive trade deficit of the 1980s. The trade deficit developed while union density was plummeting. The largest U.S. deficits were incurred with countries that had unionization rates equal to or greater than the U.S. rate. Trade deficits were no more severe in industries with high unionization rates than in those with low unionization rates. Union densities by industry are independent of trade deficits. The correlation coefficient between rates of unionization and net exports across the 450 three-digit Standard Industrial Classification (SIC) code manufacturing industries is effectively zero (Abowd and Freeman, 1991). Even in the auto and steel industries—where unions have been blamed for the rising tide of imports—research shows that unions have had only slight adverse effects on the trade balance (Karier, 1990a, this volume).

Do unions cause inflation? Since aggregate wage inflation decelerated in the 1980s as union density was falling, it is plausible to argue that falling density reduced wage pressures and inflation in the 1984–1990 recovery. According to Neumark's (1989) econometric study of unionism and wage deflation in the 1980s, the argument is plausible but not true. Analyzing the linkage between density and wage changes over time, Neumark found that while declining density held down union wages—as one would expect, given that greater union density produces greater wage settlements—"the spillovers from union to nonunion wages [were] apparently too small for the decline in union strength to explain aggregate wage movements" (Neumark, 1989, p. 14).

Do union wage increases cause unemployment? On this issue, neither theory nor evidence tell a decisive story. While competitive economic analysis predicts that union wage increases will reduce employment in unionized sectors, the reduction in unionized employment may not add to aggregate unemployment: workers who might have gotten union jobs may, after all, find jobs elsewhere.[6] National unemployment rates increased from the 1950s to the 1980s as union density fell, and reached their peak in the 1980s as union density reached new lows.[7] These conflicting trends suggest that unions do not cause unemployment. The only direct empirical evidence that suggests that unions raise unemployment comes from comparisons of unemployment across states, which invariably find higher unemployment in more unionized areas (Olson, 1982; Summers, 1986; Freeman, 1988b). Gruben and Phillips (1990) found that higher unemployment in these areas did not result from greater union concentration in older industrial sectors. Moreover, CPS data show that a lower share of the population in more highly unionized states is employed, as one would expect if union wage gains reduce employment (Freeman, 1988b).

Correlation does not, however, imply causation. Additional evidence on the relation between unionism and

Conflicting trends suggest that unions do not cause unemployment.

154

unemployment across areas casts doubt on any causal interpretation of these area correlations. Changes over time in
union density are not related to changes over time in
unemployment rates across states, suggesting that the
cross-section correlations are due primarily to omitted area
characteristics. Moreover, union density by state is positively related to establishment-based employment (per per-
son of working age) by state. This conflicting evidence
makes it difficult to reach any solid conclusion about the
effects of unions (Freeman, 1988b). Perhaps most telling is
that as private sector density plummeted in the 1980s, attri-
buting the correlation across states to unions (particularly
to union wage policies) became increasingly implausible.
No one has observed spillovers of union wages to nonunion
workers of the magnitude that would be required to be
responsible for the observed unemployment rates.

In sum, recent research has not found evidence for
any of the claimed adverse impacts of unionism on
macroeconomic outcomes—the trade deficit, wage inflation, or unemployment.

*Recent research
has not found
evidence for any of
the claimed
adverse impacts of
unionism on the
trade deficit, wage
inflation, or
unemployment.*

Productivity

Slow productivity growth is yet another macroeconomic
problem that has been attributed to the effects of unionism.
Perhaps the most controversial conclusion of *What Do
Unions Do?* was that unionism did not deter firms from
reaching high productivity. This assertion was based on
econometric estimates of production functions. Production
functions have been widely used to assess the productive
input of human capital and research and development
(R&D), as well as of capital and labor. In principle, they are
as likely to yield negative as positive coefficients on union
variables. *What Do Unions Do?* reported diverse estimates
of the effects of unionism on productivity. While most analyses showed that unions raise productivity, the negative or
negligible effects obtained in some studies suggested that
"Unionism per se is neither a plus nor a minus to productivity. What matters is how unions and management interact
at the workplace."[8] For example, the markedly lower union
productivity in underground coal mining during the 1970s
period of chaotic industrial relations in coal supports this
inference (Freeman and Medoff, 1984). Whether productivity in union firms was higher or lower appeared to

155

depend on management responses to unionism, the industrial relations climate at the workplace, and the degree of competition in the product market.

Recent published studies of the union effects on productivity, reviewed by Belman in this volume (Appendix I), tend to confirm the evidence in *What Do Unions Do?* The majority of studies find that union firms have higher productivity, but there are well-documented exceptions.[9] Allen (1984) found that unionism and high productivity ran hand in hand in the construction industry. Recent studies of productivity in other sectors also found that union firms were more productive. Kruse's (1988a) analysis of a sample of COMPUSTAT companies; Ichniowski's (1990) analysis of firms in the Columbia University industrial relations data set; Byrnes, Fare, Grosskopf, and Lovell's (1987) analysis of surface coal mining; and Kelley's (1990a) study of unit production time in machine tool technology in over 600 manufacturing workplaces all showed greater productivity in unionized settings. In contrast, Clark (1984) found a slight negative union effect in his analysis of business lines, and Hirsch (1988) reported a statistically significant (though modest) negative union effect on productivity among COMPUSTAT firms. Even in this case, there were noticeable exceptions. Union firms were more productive than nonunion firms in the textile and apparel, fabricated metal products, engines, and farm and construction equipment industries. Study results varied considerably, depending on the econometric specification of the models estimated. Both Clark (1984) and Hirsch (1988) concluded that their evidence suggested that unionism has a negligible effect on productivity. No knowledgeable analyst currently endorses the pre–*What Do Unions Do?* view that union firms are substantially less productive.

An implicit premise in *What Do Unions Do?* was the theme that labor relations practices matter critically in productivity. Research on productivity has shown that union-management interaction at the workplace determines whether productivity is higher or lower under unionism. Studies that categorize workplaces by the labor relations climate invariably find that workplaces with better climates have higher productivity (see Belman's Appendix V). Studies examining related aspects of workplace labor relations—worker participation in enterprise decisionmaking (Levine and Tyson, 1990) or profit sharing (Weitzman and Kruse, 1990)—find that these practices profoundly influence productivity. At the very least, new productivity research has shown that technical production functions relating output to capital and labor—including labor skills, but excluding labor relations climate—miss the major determinant of economic efficiency. Productivity studies with omitted variables lead to erroneous analyses of the causes of poor productivity performance.

Research has not yet adequately addressed or answered the $64,000 question: how can firms and unions develop the good employer-worker relations that maximize productivity and thus benefit workers, employers, and the public? Even partial answers to this question would have a tremendous practical payoff.

There are only a limited number of studies on the effect of union productivity outside the United States, so it is difficult to determine whether unionism increases or decreases productivity in other industrial relations systems. Muramatsu (1984) found that in Japan, the value-added per worker is positively correlated with union density across industries and firms of different sizes. However, the concentration of unionism among full-time workers in large Japanese companies suggests that his estimates may not properly distinguish between the effects of unionism and the effects of large firms on productivity. Studies linking productivity to unionism in the United Kingdom are very controversial.[10] No British study has found clear convincing evidence that union firms are more productive than nonunion firms in any major sector. Metcalf (1990) concludes that at the outset of the 1980s, highly unionized enterprises had lower productivity than less unionized enterprises. However, he notes that unionized firms had greater growth of productivity through the 1980s, suggesting that any adverse effect of unions on productivity did not persist over time. Other analysts do not concede that there was a modest negative productivity effect in the first instance (Callaghan, 1990; Nolan and Marginson, 1990). While the tone of the debate differs from that in the United States, the lack of compelling evidence that union firms are less productive—even in a country whose unions have long been lambasted as inefficient—suggests, as claimed in *What Do Unions Do?*, that unionism is not inherently hostile to productivity growth.

Unionism is not inherently hostile to productivity growth.

157

Productivity Growth and Technological Change

What Do Unions Do? found a slight negative (but statistically insignificant) relation between union density in an industry and productivity growth, but did not examine the relation in any depth. Succeeding analysts (notably Hirsch and his co-authors) have examined carefully the link between unionism and productivity growth, and fruitfully delineated the three ways in which unions can affect productivity growth and technological change:

> **Most of the slower productivity growth associated with union coverage can be accounted for by the disproportionate presence of unionization in industries with slower growth.**

(1) *By raising wages*, unions can induce management to introduce new technologies more quickly than they otherwise might do. The substitution of technology (possibly embodied in capital) for labor can be socially beneficially or costly, depending on whether the introduction of that technology would have been optimal in any case—an issue of some debate in the literature on innovation.

(2) *By capturing the quasi-rents from productivity-increasing investments*, unions reduce the incentive of firms to invest in R&D and other long-lived forms of capital (Hirsch and Connolly, 1987). Because investments in R&D are critical to economic progress, this potential impact is important.

(3) *By negotiating work rules or related labor relations policies*, unions can encourage or discourage the introduction of new technologies. The belief that union work rules limit technological change underlies much traditional criticism of unionism on the productivity front.

Depending on the net result of these offsetting forces, unionism may be positively or negatively associated with productivity growth. The issue—like other economic issues relating to unionism—is an empirical question.

Belman (this volume), Keefe (this volume), Allen (1988a), and Addison and Hirsch (1986) reviewed studies of the reduced form relation between unionism and productivity growth over time, across industries, and across firms. In addition, Keefe summarized the findings of studies on the actual rate of introduction of new technologies.

158

Time-series studies relating trends in aggregate productivity growth to trends in union density are not scientifically reliable. At a crude level, the fact that productivity growth slackened in the 1970s and 1980s as union density fell might suggest that unionism is an important spur to productivity. Whether estimates produce positive or negative effects of unions on productivity appears to depend on the econometric specification of the models used in producing the estimates (Belman and Wilson, 1989).

Comparisons of productivity growth across industries provide a better assessment of possible union effects on growth because both union density and productivity growth vary widely across industries. Analyses of the relationship between industry density and productivity growth generally confirm the *What Do Unions Do?* finding that growth is lower (although statistically insignificantly lower) in unionized sectors (see Belman, 1990, this volume, Appendix IV; Allen, 1988a, Table 1). Construction is a noticeable exception: nonunion contractors have raised their productivity toward union levels, often with union workers "working with their card in their shoe." Comparisons of productivity growth between union and nonunion companies also yield generally weak negative union effects. Clark and Griliches (1984) report statistically insignificant negative coefficients on unionism in their analysis of productivity growth in business lines. Hirsch (1988) obtained significant negative effects on unionism in an analysis of COMPUSTAT firms, but found that the result depends on the specification of the model estimated. Results were not statistically significant when a two-stage regression model designed to control for a specific firm effect was used or in analyses of changes in productivity growth and changes in union density.[11] He concludes that "Most of the slower productivity growth associated with union coverage can be accounted for by the disproportionate presence of unionization in industries with slower growth." This reading of the evidence strikes me as correct.

The most likely explanation for the presence of unions in sectors with low productivity growth was their inability to organize new plants and industries in the 1970s and 1980s. The American Enterprise Institute study data (Keefe, this volume, Table 1) dramatically illustrate the concentration of unionism in older worksites. Of the plants built before 1970 included in the survey, 39 percent were union plants,

The most likely explanation for the presence of unions in sectors with low productivity growth was their inability to organize new plants and industries in the 1970s and 1980s.

but only 8 percent of the plants built in the 1970s were union plants. None of the plants built in the 1980s were unionized. If slowing productivity growth in union firms is an artifact created by marooning of aging, unionized firms in a sea of newer, nonunion firms, then other countries lacking our peculiar distribution of unionism should experience productivity growth in union firms that keeps up with or outpaces that of nonunion firms. In the United Kingdom, union density rose in the 1970s, so unions are in new plants and industries as well as in older ones. Nickell, Wadhwani, and Wall (1989) did find higher productivity growth in British union plants than in nonunion plants during 1980–84, and productivity growth was comparable in other years.

The strongest body of evidence that unionism may harm economic growth lies in analyses of the relation between unionism and spending on R&D. In the United States, spending on R&D is lower in more highly unionized industries or firms (Hirsch and Link, 1987; Connolly, Hirsch, and Hirschy, 1986; Allen, 1988a; Hirsch, 1988). In the United Kingdom, a similar pattern of lower R&D in unionized industries has been found (Ulph and Ulph, 1989). Two likely reasons for these correlations are the reduced incentives of firms to invest in R&D when unions capture quasi-rents from such investments and the concentration of unions in older plants and "mature" industries. Without good measures of the age of plants and of the maturity of industry technology, it is difficult to differentiate between these two factors. One possible way to assess their importance would be to correlate U.S. union density by industry with R&D investment by industry in a country whose firms could not possibly be influenced by U.S. unionism (say, Germany or Sweden). If higher *U.S.* unionism correlates with low R&D investment in *German* industry, this would support a mature industry interpretation of the U.S. results, whereas a negligible correlation would support the hypothesis that unionism reduces R&D by organized firms.

The evidence showing that investment in physical capital is lower in union settings than in nonunion ones is more limited. Hirsch (1988) found some evidence that U.S. firms with more unionized workforces invest less. By contrast, British data indicate that corporate investment is unrelated to unionism (Wadhwani, 1989). These conflicting results may reflect the differences between the U.S. and Britain in the ease with which unions organize newer firms, and the

> **Studies of the effects of unionism on the introduction of specific new technologies in given sectors decisively reject the claim that unions reduce investment in advanced technology.**

160

resulting distribution of unions across firms. Studies of the effects of unionism on the introduction of specific new technologies in given sectors decisively reject the claim that unions reduce investment in advanced technology (see Keefe, this volume). In this case, there is an impressive uniformity of findings for other countries as well. In Canada (Betcherman, 1988) and the U.K. (Daniel, 1987; Machin and Wadhwani, 1989), analysts found that the rate of adaptation of new technology is not measurably affected by union status.

While the evidence casually relating unionism to investment in productivity-advancing activities is thus ambiguous, the likelihood that in some situations union-induced reductions in profits will deter firms from investing cannot be dismissed, with concomitant deleterious effects on output and jobs in the long run. The argument conveys a clear message to farsighted union leaders: to be effective, a trade union cannot leave key decisions regarding investment—including long-run investment in R&D—to management.

To be effective, a trade union cannot leave key decisions regarding investment—including long-run investment in R&D—to management.

Profits

Surprisingly, in view of the obsession of economists with the monopoly face of trade unionism, the first econometric estimates of the effect of unionism on profitability appear to have been given in *What Do Unions Do?* and in Freeman (1983). Analysts examining profits from an industrial organization perspective focused on how product market factors—notably concentration ratios, regulation, and related indicators of monopoly power—affected profitability; they excluded labor market variables. Business economists studied the strategic decisions made by firms to raise profits. Experts in industrial relations considered how unionism affected working rules, not return on capital. Labor economists focused almost exclusively on estimating the "union wage effect."

As Belman's review of literature in this volume indicates, unionism substantially reduces profits. Study after study finds that the presence of a union lowers measures of firm profitability, such as price-cost margins, net revenues per unit of capital, Tobin's q, and the stock market value of firms. Activities associated with unionism—strikes and the magnitude of wage settlements—also affect stock market valuation of firms. This conclusion is consistent with estimates of the magnitude of union wage effects and of the effect of unionism on productivity. Estimated wage effects invariably exceed estimated productivity effects. Studies also indicate that unions reduce firm profits in the United Kingdom (Machin, 1988b; Blanchflower and Oswald, 1988b; Machin and Stewart, 1988).

Whether unions reduce profitability largely in sectors or firms with excess returns—redistributing monopoly rents—or whether they reduce profitability regardless of the market conditions in which the firm finds itself, is uncertain. If unions give workers a share of the firm's monopoly returns, and flexibly adjust settlements when the firm is in economic trouble, unions potentially efficiently redistribute economic rents. Few, if any, losses of economic efficiency result. If, on the contrary, unions cut into normal profitability, they can force firms out of business, thus reducing production and employment. *What Do Unions Do?* argued that unions would rarely raise wages to the point that profits were so low that the firm would close down, and presented evidence that the union-induced decline in profits occurred largely in concentrated sectors. A substantial number of ensuing studies have confirmed this claim (Voos and Mishel, 1986a; Karier, 1985, 1988; Salinger, 1984), but other studies have produced conflicting results (Clark, 1984; Hirsch and Connolly, 1987). Abowd's study showing evidence of a dollar-for-dollar trade-off between payments to workers in collective bargaining agreements and shareholder's wealth would seem to favor the efficient rent extraction model, but his study is limited to surviving firms. If union-induced reductions in profits are more likely to force the closure of firms lacking market power, studies of the profitability of existing firms may give a misleading picture of unions' effects on profitability in competitive sectors. Without definitive evidence concerning the effects of unions on the solvency of firms or establishments, the issue cannot be resolved.

> **If unions give workers a share of the firm's monopoly returns, and flexibly adjust settlements when the firm is in economic trouble . . . Few, if any, losses of economic efficiency result.**

Union Effects on Aggregate Savings and Investment

If unionism does in fact lower investment or spending on R&D in organized sectors, then do unions reduce national R&D activity or investment and long-term economic growth? Not necessarily.

Even if the microeconomic evidence were unambiguous, there are two difficulties in generalizing from the claim that unionism reduces investment by organized firms to the effects of unionism on aggregate R&D or investment. First, any such reductions in organized sectors may be largely or entirely offset by increases in R&D or investment in non-union sectors.[12] If so, the observed patterns among firms will largely reflect shifts in the locus of investments, producing at most small economic inefficiencies. Such shifts in activity may help explain the decline of union density in the United States, but would not help explain national output. Second, national investment at the macroeconomic level depends critically on national savings. Arguably, unions increase savings through the creation of pension funds (Freeman, 1985b)—a union impact that is largely ignored. Labor economists have deep suspicions about macroeconomics, and macroeconomists generally know little about unions.

Arguably, unions increase savings through the creation of pension funds.

The argument that unions raise national savings hinges on three propositions: One, unions increase the pension contributions of organized workers compared to otherwise similar nonunion workers; two, relatively few blue collar workers have any private savings, exclusive of housing and pensions; and three, union workers do not reduce savings and investment in housing because they have pension plans. If these propositions are correct, union workers will save more in total than otherwise comparable nonunion workers, increasing the nation's savings rate and ultimately its investment rate as well. The evidence for the first proposition is, as noted earlier, overwhelming. David Wise (1988) has documented the second proposition as part of his analyses of the potential for Individual Retirement Accounts (IRAs) to increase savings. The third proposition is a near correlate of the other two; it would be invalid only if union workers invested less in housing than other workers, which seems highly implausible. Private pension funds—roughly half of which are for union workers—owned some 12 percent of corporate equity and 27 percent of corporate bonds in 1980 (Freeman, 1985b, p. 113). If the key to investment and economic growth is additional savings, unionism contributes positively by raising the savings of workers.

Explaining the Decline in Union Density

Limited and ineffectual penalties for breaking the law have produced the growth of unfair management practices associated with NLRB elections in the 1970s and 1980s.

If the net effects of unionism on society are positive, as I contend in *What Do Unions Do?* and ensuing analyses generally confirm, why is union density declining so sharply in the U.S. private sector?

The decline is due in large part to the inability of unions to gain new members through NLRB elections—a failure resulting from management opposition induced by the negative effect of unions on profits (Freeman, 1985a, 1986c, 1990; Blanchflower and Freeman, 1990). Diverse studies show that management opposition affects the degree to which unions win members through NLRB outcomes (see Summary in Freeman, 1985a). While it is difficult to pin down motivation, it seems natural to view the opposition as being at least partially motivated by the profit calculus, though desire for authoritarian control of workplaces and ideological considerations may also enter into management opposition. However, because the rate of new organization through NLRB elections was extremely low even by the mid-1970s, the inability of unions to organize new workers cannot account for the accelerated drop in density of the 1980s (Bronars and Deere, 1989). The growing gap in employment growth between existing union and nonunion workplaces was the main factor. If union firms are less profitable than nonunion firms, management may invest less thus depressing expansion and job growth. Alternatively, unions may be concentrated in older plants, with little employment growth even without unionism. Deregulation of trucking and airlines—which enhanced the potential return to management from anti-union activity in those sectors—and the aggressive actions of nonunion employers in construction would also appear to have contributed to the slower growth of union employment. Of course, these changes occurred under a legal system that gives management the *de jure* right to conduct massive legal campaigns against unions at workplaces. Limited and ineffectual penalties for breaking the law have produced the near exponential growth of unfair management practices associated with NLRB elections in the 1970s and 1980s.

Comparing the economic effect of unions in the United States with the effects of unions in other countries, one finds that much of the decline in U.S. union density is attributable to the incentives to employers to remain non-union (Blanchflower and Freeman, 1990). Unions raise wages (relative to nonunion wages) more in the U.S. than in other countries. The U.S. differentials are at least three times larger than in other countries (except for Canada). The adverse effects of wages on profits presumably are also larger. On the other hand, beneficial union voice effects do not appear to be larger in the U.S. than overseas. For example, the decrease in turnover due to unionism appears greater in Australia than in the U.S. (Kornfeld, 1990). If the U.S. had a political "labor party" to help enact legislation beneficial to workers as other industrialized countries do, larger collective voice effects might be observed in the U.S.

More detailed analyses of particular countries further highlight the effects of unions on profits and of the legal environment on management actions that can reduce union density. In Japan, the profits crunch following the oil shock seems to be a major cause of the fall in density from the mid-1970s through the 1980s (Freeman and Rebick, 1989). In the United Kingdom, Thatcher's industrial relations legislation greatly weakened the organizing ability of unions, leading to a large fall in density (Freeman and Pelletier, 1990). By contrast, union density rose in the 1970s and stabilized in the 1980s in Scandinavia, Belgium, and Australia, where national bargaining "takes wages out of competition" and thus eliminates most of the profit incentive for employers to fight unionization. The continued strength of unions in Canada appears largely due to labor laws limiting the ability of management to fight unions (Weiler, 1983; Chaison and Rose, 1988), rather than the modesty of the union wage effect. In Canada, private sector union density has begun to fall in manufacturing, where one might expect the profit-driven incentive to remain nonunion to be strongest (Freeman, 1988c).

While the story of union decline told in *What Do Unions Do?* holds up to continuing evaluation, the book missed one broader aspect of the changing situation of American unionism in the latter half of the twentieth century: the linkage between the successes of American unions from the 1950s through the early 1970s in the U.S., and the overall position of the United States in the world economy. When the U.S. had a technological and productivity lead over the rest of the world, American producers had potential "monopoly rents" that unions could extract for workers

The continued strength of unions in Canada appears largely due to labor laws limiting the ability of management to fight unions.

with little adverse effect on investment. Unions bargained with management in the steel and auto industries for sizeable wage gains as part of the workers share of the good fortune of these industries. However, after the oil shock, the loss of the U.S. productivity edge, and the deregulation of the 1970s and 1980s, unions could no longer simply bargain for workers' share of a company's economic rent. The rent was no longer there. From this sweeping perspective, the slow adjustment of unions and unionized firms to the loss of American economic dominance contributed to the decline in union density. What worked for unions in the 1950s and 1960s did not work in the 1970s and 1980s. Labor and management were too slow to reassess their strategies and explore alternative union institutions and activities in other industrial countries, where unions weathered the post–oil shock era better. In my view, a similar lack of historical and international perspective is the major weakness of *What Do Unions Do?*

> *What worked for unions in the 1950s and 1960s did not work in the 1970s and 1980s.*

Assessing the Decline

In light of the research summarized in this volume, should the nation view the declining unionization of the labor market as good, bad, or irrelevant? In *What Do Unions Do?*, we concluded that the falling union density of the 1970s was a bad development for the economy and for society more broadly defined:

> While we are not sure what the optimal degree of unionization is in this country, we are convinced that current trends have brought the union density below the optimal level. In a well-functioning labor market there should be a sufficient number of union and nonunion firms to offer alternative work environments to workers, innovation in workplace rules and conditions, and competition in the market. Such competition will, on the one hand, limit union monopoly power and on the other, limit management's power over workers. (Freeman and Medoff, 1984, pp. 250–51)

At the time that the above passage was written (1980), the latest figures on private sector density stood at 24 percent. The research reviewed in this essay and in the other chapters of this volume has shown that *What Do Unions Do?* neither understated the economic costs of the monop-

166

oly face nor overstated the economic benefits of the voice face of unionism. Therefore, the drop in private sector density to roughly half the 1980 level—and the likely fall to single digits by the mid-1990s—necessarily strengthens the conclusion that declining unionization has gone too far in this country. A return to "ghetto unionism" in the U.S. private sector implies that labor turnover will increase; employee benefits will fall; the protection of workers against arbitrary management decisions will weaken (absent governmental interventions); inequality in earnings will increase; and productivity in many instances will fall lower than it might otherwise be. Moreover, if the allegations that U.S. management is overly concerned with maximizing short-run profits are valid, the decline in density will produce an economic system even less beneficial to workers than are the nonunion systems in which management claims to represent workers as well as shareholders, as in Japan (Aoki, 1984).

Although Scandinavian levels of unionization seem to me to be infeasible and undesirable in a large, diverse country like the United States, the post–*What Do Unions Do?* research supports the view that greater unionization of the U.S. workforce is needed to give workers alternatives to the market or to governmental intervention in workplace arrangements. However, the research and labor market developments of the 1980s clearly indicate that the unionism of the 1990s and into the twenty-first century will have to differ in major ways from the unionism that developed under the Wagner Act. To succeed, unions will have to enhance their voice role in defending workers, providing democracy at the workplace, and improving workplace conditions, as well as play a larger role in the investment and other business decisions of firms than in the past; they will lessen their monopoly wage role. *What Do Unions Do?* recommended policies strengthening the voice/response face of unionism and weakening the monopoly face to enhance the social value of unionism. The evidence from the 1980s suggests that these changes are necessary, not only for society to obtain the greatest benefit from the union institution, but also for unions to rejuvenate themselves.

Greater unionization of the U.S. workforce is needed to give workers alternatives to the market or to governmental intervention in workplace arrangements.

Endnotes

[1] See U.S. Bureau of Labor Statistics, *Employment and Earnings*, January 1990, Table 58. I added figures for service occupations, precision production and operators, fabricators, and laborers to obtain the blue collar statistic.

[2] By social output, I mean not only the production of material goods and services but also the social well-being of workers and others that is not measured in the GNP. Thus, if unions have no effect on productivity, but alter fringe benefits or work rules in ways that increase well-being, social output is increased.

[3] In this discussion I do not consider the effect of unions on the political process, spillovers of union gains to nonunion workers, or the effect of unions on job satisfaction. I treat the effect of unions on the cyclical and secular adjustment of wages and employment in terms of the effects on wages and turnover, rather than as a separate issue.

[4] This 1960s movie, starring Peter Sellers, spoofed British union leaders.

[5] The Lawrence and Lawrence endgame bargaining model of union wage settlements makes logical sense. I know of one case in which union leaders consciously followed such a policy. But I believe that Lawrence and Lawrence are incorrect in applying the model to the steel industry. The United Steelworkers have not only given major concessions to save jobs, but have also sought to buy steel companies for the same purpose.

[6] I write "little reason" rather than "no reason" because workers might increase their labor participation and reject nonunion jobs in the hope of getting a higher paying union job, increasing the rate of unemployment.

[7] The unemployment rate averaged 4.5 percent in the 1950s; 4.8 percent in the 1960s; 6.1 percent in the 1970s; and 7.2 percent in the 1980s. While demographic factors explain some of the upward trend, the economic recession of 1982–83 created the highest rates of joblessness since the Great Depression at a time when union density was dropping rapidly.

[8] Freeman and Medoff, 1984, p. 179.

[9] In the public sector, the evidence for a positive union productivity effect is weaker. My 1986 survey found that most studies of public sector productivity show little if any difference by union status (Freeman, 1986b, Table 11). More recent work has obtained positive productivity effects for teachers' unions on student performance (Kleiner and Petree, 1988; Eberts and Stone, 1984), though without any obvious route for the union effect; and a mixed picture in the hospital sector. One of the two studies cited by Belman found higher productivity among unionized workers, while the other study did not. Still, few, if any, studies find evidence that unionism reduces productivity in the public sector.

[10] See *British Journal of Industrial Relations*, July 1990.

11 Hirsch discounts his analysis of changes because his early period union density figures are particularly weak, and I agree with this assessment. Still, if unionism had a tremendous adverse effect on productivity growth, something might have turned up in the change analysis. In future work, it would be valuable to contrast future and past productivity changes in companies that have changed from union to nonunion status in the 1980s.

12 If unionism does not adversely affect the profitability of R&D by nonunion firms, its aggregate effect on R&D will be less than its effect on union firms. If nonunion firms see a competitive advantage from making an R&D or other investment that union firms will not match, the effect of unionism will be to raise their R&D, offsetting the adverse effect on unionized firms.

PART II

The
POSITIVE ROLE
of UNIONS

Unions and Contemporary Innovations in Work Organization, Compensation, and Employee Participation

Adrienne E. Eaton and Paula B. Voos*

Introduction

The 1980s have been a decade of experimentation in work organization, compensation systems, and labor-management relations in the United States. The goal, explicit or implicit, has generally been to improve the ability of firms to compete in their respective markets. Specifically, these efforts have been aimed at increasing productivity and improving firm financial performance. Evidence suggests that at least some types of programs meet these goals.

Further, many innovations seek to increase worker involvement in decisionmaking. While to some extent increased involvement has been seen as a worthy end in itself, it is more often viewed as crucial to achieving the larger economic goals. In fact, many managers, labor leaders, and government officials have come to believe that tapping worker knowledge and energy is the key to overcoming our problems of competitiveness.

This paper describes the nature of these efforts, focusing on organized labor's response to and role in them—potential as well as actual. We find that U.S. unions in the 1980s have facilitated the implementation and healthy functioning of workplace innovations and have not been

> *Many managers, labor leaders, and government officials have come to believe that tapping worker knowledge and energy is the key to overcoming our problems of competitiveness.*

*Rutgers University and University of Wisconsin, respectively. The authors gratefully acknowledge the assistance of the U.S. General Accounting Office in providing unpublished data for this study; the GAO is not responsible for any of the views expressed herein.

173

hindrances to such programs. We do not claim that changes in work organization or compensation are always appropriate or desirable. Elsewhere we discuss why workers and their labor organizations have sometimes opposed programs that undermined collective bargaining, excessively increased production speeds, or were otherwise detrimental from the perspective of workers (Eaton and Voos, 1989; Eaton, 1989). Despite such occasional opposition, evidence from a variety of sources indicates that there are few differences in the amount or intensity of innovation between the union and nonunion sectors. This should not be particularly surprising. Contemporary experimentation with innovative practices in the union sector is consistent with a long tradition of productivity bargaining in this country in which unions have agreed to productivity-enhancing technologies and methods while also protecting the economic security of members.

> **We argue that unions bring both protections for workers and an organized collective voice to the workplace that are necessary to ensure the genuine participation of workers in decisionmaking.**

Finally, we argue that unions bring both protections for workers and an organized collective voice to the workplace that are necessary to ensure the genuine participation of workers in decisionmaking. In this way, unions have the capacity not only to improve the likelihood that innovation will result in greater industrial democracy, but also that they will deliver on their potential to improve work methods and increase productivity.

Specifically, we find that:

*   unionized companies make more extensive use of workplace innovations. In particular, union companies are more likely to employ team production systems, productivity gainsharing or quality of worklife (QWL) committees and are at least as likely to have employee participation programs. Nonunion companies are more likely to have a profit-sharing program;

*   the workplace programs that predominate in the union sector are more likely to increase productivity than the one program, profit-sharing, which is more likely to be found in the nonunion sector;

*   implicit productivity bargaining provides an explanation for this phenomenon. Unions and management often initiated these programs as part of an effort in an increasingly competitive economic environment to avoid both layoffs and wage concessions by continuously increasing productivity. In contrast, the nonunion sector lacks institutions for exchanging more

174

productive work for higher wages, which is one reason why nonunion workers are less productive;

* participative programs, or team systems, have greater ultimate potential in a unionized environment. One reason is that union workers have more job security and therefore are less subject to management reprisal when voicing their concerns. A second reason is that unions provide a mechanism for workers to influence the design and implementation of programs—an aspect of unionism that has been termed "collective voice." One result is that programs are more likely to be "better balanced," or result in changes of interest to workers, improving the quality of worklife as well as increasing productivity. This increases the likelihood that programs will survive; and

* finally, unions enable workers to play a role in "strategic" corporate decisions regarding investment, plant location, product design, and technology. Cooperative programs in the union sector are less likely to be limited to the shop floor, and hence they have a much greater potential.

The workplace programs that predominate in the union sector are more likely to increase productivity than the one program, profit-sharing, which is more likely to be found in the nonunion sector.

Which "Workplace Innovations" Matter?

Innovations in work organization, compensation, and employee involvement take a variety of shapes, the most prominent of which are various types of *employee participation* (including quality circles, employee involvement groups, most quality of worklife efforts, and what is termed strategic participation); *team concept* plants with new forms of flexible work organization; *gainsharing; profit-sharing; employee stock ownership*; and some other miscellaneous efforts.[1] (Please see the glossary for an explanation of individual terms.) These innovations are not created equal—some are relatively minor interventions and some involve major restructuring of the workplace. Not surprisingly, the more far-reaching ones typically yield the greatest improvements in productivity.

In Table 1, we provide a brief description of each major type of program and a summary of what is now known about its typical effectiveness in enhancing productivity.

TABLE 1
Description of Selected Innovations in Work Organization, Compensation, and Employee Involvement

Note: See also the glossary. The Appendix contains a more extensive description and references to research regarding program effectiveness.

Program & Variants	Description	Effectiveness
I. Employee Participation or Involvement	A general term used for a variety of different programs that attempt to involve employees in decisionmaking. Small group meetings usually are used to motivate employees, to share ideas on how to improve quality, reduce waste, otherwise enhance productivity, or achieve a higher quality of worklife. There is great variety in the range of issues open to discussion and the degree of authority afforded groups.	Most research finds increased job satisfaction, reduced absenteeism and turnover. Small to moderate productivity effects, with more extensive efforts (more involvement, more scope, linkage to other organizational changes) yielding greater results.
IA. Quality Circles (QCs)	Volunteers from a particular work area meet to suggest methods to improve quality and productivity. Issues and authority are limited and there are no direct monetary incentives apart from compensation for time in meetings.	Effects are positive but small and limited in duration. Most QC programs disband after a few years.
IB. Quality of Work Life (QWL)	Various usage. Sometimes refers to workplace level, consultive groups which address a wider range of issues than QCs. In a union setting often refers to a structure with both workplace level groups and joint union-management committees.	More extensive, multi-level programs have larger effects.
IC. Strategic Participation	An attempt to extend participation to involve workers in higher level, strategic decisions like those involving capital investment, technology, or product design. Successful examples of which we are aware (Xerox—see the Appendix and Cutcher-Gershenfeld, 1988) are from the union sector and involve considerable union-management cooperation.	Sizeable increases in productivity or large cost savings are potentially available.

Program & Variants	Description	Effectiveness
II. Teams	Both a type of participative program characterized by a high level of involvement over a wide range of issues and a new, flexible form of work organization. Usually includes a reduction of job classifications, cross-training of individuals for most jobs in a work group, and team responsibility for such previously separated functions as material handling, maintenance, quality control, and certain personnel decisions. Compensation may also be changed to a "pay-for-knowledge" system.	Can increase productivity substantially according to most studies. However, one study found positive effects due to high levels of employee participation rather than concomitant changes in work organization or compensation.
III. Gainsharing	Groups of workers receive bonuses according to a prearranged formula when productivity increases, costs fall, or other performance indicators improve. Typically incorporates some form of employee participation, often through suggestion committees and union-management cooperation if the firm is organized. Examples are Scanlon, Rucker, and Improshare plans, with the latter relying more exclusively on altered compensation.	Moderate to large potential productivity gains. For these to be realized, plans must actually deliver higher earnings for increased productivity.
IV. Profit-sharing (PS)	Bonuses are paid as a function of company profits either immediately (non-deferred PS) or in increased company contributions to pensions (deferred PS). The latter is considerably more common and here these plans resemble ESOPs (Blasi, 1989 and 1990). Often payment is contingent on profits surpassing a threshold level.	Little agreement among researchers; probably small, possibly moderate gains. Deferred plans have smaller effects. Profits are affected by many things besides employee work effort, so there is general agreement that it is a less effective motivator than gainsharing.
V. Employee Stock Ownership Plans (ESOPs)	A mechanism whereby employees accumulate employer's stock until retirement or departure from the company. Usually only a small percentage of company stock is held by employees. But companies may be entirely employee-owned through ESOPs; even here, however, there is great variation in the degree of control exercised by workers over management decisions.	Little evidence that ESOPs typically have much impact on productivity.

Program & Variants	Description	Effectiveness
VI. Other innovations	This is a miscellaneous group of lesser magnitude programs.	Little evidence of any systematic effects; effects are probably small at best for all of the following programs.
VIA. Survey feedback	Worker input is solicited on an individual basis through formal written surveys. Results are discussed with employees and personnel or work practices may be altered.	
VIB. Information Sharing	There is regular communication of business information and strategies.	
VIC. Job enrichment or enlargement	Duties are added to individual jobs, presumably to make them less alienating and more satisfying.	
VID. Job rotation	Jobs are rotated between workers, providing variety and understanding of relationships between tasks.	
VIE. Suggestion systems or suggestion boxes	Rewarding of cost-saving ideas with a one-time bonus for individual employees.	

Team production systems and gainsharing are particularly potent programs according to most evaluations.

This is important because it turns out that some types of innovations are more common in nonunion than union companies and vice versa.

A large empirical literature, of decidedly mixed quality, now exists regarding the outcomes associated with various workplace innovations.[2] Based on our review of this literature, presented in the Appendix, we classify programs according to their potential for enhancing productivity as follows:

I. **High Potential.** Team production systems and gainsharing are particularly potent programs according to most evaluations. Although very different in some respects, teams and gainsharing similarly incorporate major changes in both work organization and compensation, along with an emphasis on moving decisions downward through employee participation, supplemented by joint union-management committees in the organized company. As Blinder (1990), Levine and Tyson (1990),

Weitzman and Kruse (1990), and many others emphasize, the most potent innovations combine substantive employee participation with the sharing of economic rewards from that effort. Teams and gainsharing plans typically do both, albeit in different ways.

II. **Intermediate Potential.** More extensive or more substantive employee participation and quality of work-life committee efforts probably have the potential to yield intermediate increases in productivity, although frankly this is a judgment call insofar as research evidence is mixed.

III. **Lesser Potential.** In the usual instance, employee stock ownership, profit-sharing, and quality circles are much more limited efforts with relatively less potential. Levine and Tyson (1990) note that the half-life of quality circles is under three years and conclude that "quality circles and other purely advisory shopfloor arrangements are not likely to achieve sustainable improvements in productivity." Most profit-sharing plans in the U.S. are deferred and resemble ESOPs in providing benefits upon retirement or other separation from the firm (Blasi, 1990), and indeed may be adopted primarily as a pension substitute (Cheadle, 1988, cited in Mitchell et al., 1990, p. 57).[3] Like ESOPs they tend to be relatively ineffective motivators in the absence of significant employee participation, partly because benefits are deferred and partly because so many things influence profits besides employee work effort (Levine and Tyson, 1990; Conte and Svejnar, 1990; for a dissenting view see Mitchell et al., 1990). Unions often oppose profit-sharing plans which are substitutes for less risky defined-benefit pension plans. Even when it is nondeferred, however, unions may oppose profit-sharing because of the considerable uncertainty of payment and the fear of manipulative management accounting practices.

Obviously, the manner in which a program is implemented also matters—in many instances, high potential efforts fail to produce lower costs, higher productivity, or otherwise improved economic performance. But in general it appears from studies of program effectiveness that more extensive and far-reaching innovations—team production systems, gainsharing plans, or really far-ranging and extensive employee participation—typically yield greater improvements in productivity than do less major efforts

Employee stock ownership, profit-sharing, and quality circles are much more limited efforts with relatively less potential.

179

that involve tinkering with pension benefits, or involve other relatively small compensation premiums. It is important to keep this in mind when considering the record of the union sector, as opposed to the nonunion sector, in implementing these innovations.

Were or Are Nonunion Companies the Chief Innovators?

It is sometimes claimed that nonunion companies are now the progressive leaders in human resource management, that they lead union companies in new productivity-enhancing work organization, compensation systems, employee participation, or other innovations (Lawler and Mohrman, 1987). In this section, we review evidence from a variety of sources on the current extent of such innovations in the union and nonunion sectors. We focus in particular on our own analysis of survey data gathered by the U.S. General Accounting Office in 1987 because we regard it as the best evidence to date on the extent of such programs. We find that the nonunion sector clearly leads the union sector with regard to only one practice: profit-sharing. On the other hand, unionized companies are more likely to employ team production systems or quality of worklife (QWL) committees, and are at least as likely to use quality circles and other mechanisms of employee participation. While the GAO data indicate gainsharing is equally prevalent in both sectors, other evidence persuades us that gainsharing is more common in unionized companies. The programs that predominate in the union sector make on average a greater contribution to increasing productivity than the one program, profit-sharing, which is more likely to be found in the nonunion sector.

Before reviewing this new evidence, however, we examine the history of these efforts, in part because that history produced the still widespread impression that somehow the nonunion sector is providing leadership in this area, and previously published evidence on the types of productivity-enhancing innovations in place in union and nonunion companies.

History

Employee participation programs of various types, and associated changes in work organization and compensation,

180

first appeared on the U.S. scene a bit more than two decades ago and only became widespread in the 1980s.[4] According to the prevailing wisdom, these innovations began initially in the 1960s in nonunion firms like Proctor and Gamble, or in nonunion plants of partially unionized companies. These same firms were committed to keeping new facilities unorganized, a stand consistent with "the deep-seated opposition to unions embedded in the ideology of American management and the culture of many American firms" (Kochan, Katz, and McKersie, 1986, p. 56).[5] This association of innovation, particularly employee participation, with nonunion companies and facilities initially created a climate of hostility and suspicion within the labor movement.[6] While opposition continues in some cases today, in general union leaders have become much more diversified in their views and less oppositional in the 1980s (Eaton and Voos, 1989).[7]

Ichniowski, Delaney, and Lewin have recently questioned whether the nonunion sector ever was actually more innovative, based on contemporary survey data indicating that employee participation programs were "virtually nonexistent" in either sector before 1970, and that "the incidence of participation programs has increased at similar rates in both unionized and nonunion business units, suggesting that employee involvement is not solely a phenomenon of the nonunion sector" (1989). A second recent survey of small manufacturing firms in Michigan by Cooke (1988) provides a fuller picture. Of the firms with participative activities (quality circles, QWL programs, or employee involvement), none of the unionized firms and only 6.5 percent of the nonunion firms reported beginning their programs before 1975. From 1975 to 1980 programs were started in 7.1 percent of the union and 9.7 percent of the nonunion companies. In contrast, 92.9 percent of the union plans and 83.9 percent of the nonunion plans began after 1980. Thus, though a small percentage of nonunion firms were early implementers, almost all the action in both sectors is post-1980.

In sum, it appears that while employee participation occurred early in a few nonunion firms, that sector may have been given too much credit as the leader in industrial relations practices.[8] Further, there are indications that the union sector is now catching up and perhaps pushing beyond the nonunion sector.

The programs that predominate in the union sector make on average a greater contribution to increasing productivity.

Current Levels of Innovation:
Previously Published Evidence

Existing academic studies of the current level of innovative activity in the union versus the nonunion sector are inconclusive, but generally indicate few sharp differences in the overall amount of activity. However, these studies do suggest some differences in the predominant types of productivity-enhancing programs utilized by union and nonunion companies. Table 2 contains data from the Ichniowski, Delaney, and Lewin (1989); Delaney, Lewin, and Ichniowski (1988); Cooke (1988); and Finseth (1988) studies.[9] We will briefly survey existing evidence on program extent, even though it is beset with limitations, before analyzing the better GAO survey data because we regard it as important to take into account all the available information on the incidence of these programs.

Ichniowski, Delaney, and Lewin's data come from a set of very large companies; they compared union versus nonunion operations (1) for all respondents and (2) for the subset of companies with both types of facilities. The latter comparison is important because it holds constant relevant company characteristics—for instance, corporate size or primary industry. A number of differences emerged between the union and the nonunion sectors, although these tended to be insignificant for union versus nonunion facilities in the same company.[10] First, the nonunion sector was significantly more likely than the union sector to have either job enrichment, job enlargement, or job rotation, which the authors term "flexible job design" (see the glossary for a further explanation of all terms). However, we doubt this difference is related causally to union status simply because others have found that these practices occur more commonly in the service sector, which is less unionized (Heckscher, 1981). Second, the union sector had significantly more total job classifications (suggesting inflexibility according to the authors), but fewer job classifications per employee. Both statistics probably reflect the fact that the union companies in this study were simply much larger on average than the nonunion companies, again making it hard to ascribe much meaning to the statistics. Finally, more *unionized* operations reported information sharing and the existence of QWL programs, but differences were neither significant nor large.

Cooke collected information on a different set of programs from 131 union and nonunion manufacturing firms

[With regard to employee participation,] there are indications that the union sector is now catching up and perhaps pushing beyond the nonunion sector.

182

TABLE 2
Extent of Innovation—Union versus Nonunion

	Union	Nonunion	Significance of Difference
I. *Ichniowski, Delaney, and Lewin, 1989—495 large COMPUSTAT firms*:			
1) All business units:			
Flexible job design	25.2%	39.7%	***
Number of job classifications	121.0	38.8	***
Job classifications per employee	0.15	0.36	***
Information sharing	64.2%	56.7%	NS
QWL	49.3%	43.6%	NS
2) Firms with both union and nonunion units:			
Flexible job design	25.6%	34.7%	NS
Number of job classifications	151.4	52.3	***
Job classifications per employee	0.19	0.35	NS
Information sharing	62.8%	63.8%	NS
QWL	50.9%	52.8%	NS
II. *Cooke, 1988—131 small manufacturing firms in Michigan*:			
Participative programs	40.0%	51.7%	NS
Profit-sharing	29.4	52.6	***
ESOPs	7.6	8.8	NS
Gainsharing	9.0	1.8	*
Pay-for-knowledge	10.4	24.6	**
III. *Finseth 1988, unpublished; also Kruse 1988—COMPUSTAT firms*:			
Quality Circles	51.1%	31.0%	
Job rotation	22.5	25.6	
Employee surveys	65.1	43.9	
Productivity-related group bonuses	46.3	25.6	
Profit-sharing	46.2	75.0	

NS = not significantly different
* Significantly different at the 0.10 level on a 2-tailed test.
** Significantly different at the 0.05 level on a 2-tailed test.
*** Significantly different at the 0.01 level on a 2-tailed test.

in the state of Michigan; many of the companies in his study were small. He found few differences with regard to participation. Likewise, there were no significant differences between the sectors in their use of ESOPs. The significant differences came in the area of compensation: many fewer unionized firms had profit-sharing plans. Interestingly, however, the union firms made significantly more use of productivity gainsharing. Gainsharing tends to be preferred by unions over profit-sharing partially because it allows more worker control over the costs included in the bonus formulae and the resulting payout when productivity rises. Profits in contrast are often viewed as subject to too much manipulation by management accounting practices. Finally, more nonunion firms had pay-for-knowledge schemes.

Our reanalysis of Finseth's (1988) data supports Cooke's evidence that the nonunion sector utilizes significantly more profit-sharing. There is a negative and significant correlation in his data (-0.479, N$=$ 89) between the percentage of the workforce involved in profit-sharing and the percentage of the workforce unionized. The union sector led in the use of quality circles, employee surveys, and productivity-related group bonuses, although in each case the correlations with the percent unionized were insignificant.[11]

New Evidence on Program Extent

The best evidence we were able to locate on the types of programs currently in use comes from a survey conducted by the General Accounting Office (U.S. GAO, 1987).[12] While the GAO report simply provides overall descriptive statistics, our reanalysis of the data focuses on union/nonunion differences. We find that while the nonunion (or relatively less unionized) companies do indeed use profit-sharing to a greater extent than do companies in which a substantial number of employees are organized, union companies are significantly more likely to use team production systems, quality of worklife committees, and quality circles. Because this last group of programs, along with gainsharing, is more likely to produce substantial gains in productivity than is profit-sharing, we conclude that if anything, the union sector leads the nonunion sector with regard to workplace innovations which substantially contribute to improved economic performance. Tables 3 to 6 present our reanalysis of the GAO data for the 313 respondents who answered the question on union status and agreed to the release of information.

Union companies are significantly more likely to use team production systems, quality of worklife committees, and quality circles.

184

TABLE 3
Extent of Innovation—Partly Union versus Nonunion, GAO Data

(*Standard errors are in parentheses*)

	Portion of Firms with Any Activity		Mean Extent of Activity*	
	Partly Union [179 Firms]	Nonunion [134 Firms]	Partly Union	Nonunion
Quality Circles	71%	48%	2.20** (0.08)	1.92 (0.12)
Other Participation	79	61	2.44 (0.08)	2.27 (0.13)
Union-Management QWL Committees	46	1	1.65*** (0.07)	1.02 (0.02)
Teams	35	19	1.44*** (0.05)	1.29 (0.06)
Profit-sharing	63	66	2.61 (0.14)	3.96*** (0.23)
Gainsharing	33	15	1.44 (0.06)	1.42 (0.11)
ESOPs	65	58	3.77 (0.19)	3.86 (0.24)
Job Enrichment	66	60	2.02 (0.08)	2.09 (0.11)
Survey Feedback	74	62	2.88 (0.14)	3.22 (0.20)
Knowledge/Skill-based Pay	47	29	1.74 (0.08)	1.68 (0.13)

* Respondents were asked how many employees were covered by the various practices. Categories of responses: 1 = None, 2 = Almost None (1–20%), 3 = Some (21–40%), 4 = About Half (41–60%), 5 = Most (61–80%), 6 = Almost all (81–99%), 7 = All (100%). "Any Activity" is defined as a response > 1.

** Significantly greater at the 0.10 level on a 2-tailed test than the corresponding nonunion or partly union mean.

*** Significantly greater at the 0.05 level on a 2-tailed test than the corresponding nonunion or partly union mean.

Table 3 contains a simple comparison of firms classified as either "partly union" or "nonunion." These two sectors are contrasted with regard to the various workplace innovations included in the survey: quality circles, other participation programs, union-management QWL committees, teams, profit-sharing, gainsharing, ESOPs, job enrichment, survey feedback, and knowledge/skill-based pay.[13] About 40 percent of the firms in the GAO study had less than 1 percent of nonmanagerial employees represented by labor unions—these were considered nonunion and the remainder were classified as "partly union," since no companies were 100 percent organized. Obviously, this is a rough division, so we also break down the union companies by extent of unionization in Table 4.

Partially unionized firms are more likely to report some activity in every category than nonunion firms, with the exception of profit-sharing (see Table 3). Comparing firms with different levels of unionization, profit-sharing is most prevalent among the least organized. However, for every other innovation there is either no significant difference or unionized firms have more activity (see Table 4). Union companies on the whole had significantly more quality circles, union-management quality of worklife committees, and teams (see Table 2). Teams, quality circles, and job enrichment are most likely to be found in moderately unionized companies, whereas QWL committees are most prevalent in highly unionized environments (see Table 4).[14] Thus, union firms are making more use of the types of programs that have greater effects on economic performance.

It is possible, of course, that a given innovation has different consequences for productivity or other outcomes in a union than a nonunion company. To date, there have been few studies relating to this matter. Exceptions are Kelley (1989c) and Kelley and Harrison (this volume), who present evidence that joint labor-management committees positively influence job design outcomes for blue collar machinists only in the presence of a union. The GAO questionnaire asked managers about the extent to which the employee involvement programs were successful in improving organizational performance. (Unfortunately, the compensation-based programs were not included in this part of the questionnaire.) Their ratings are presented in Table 5.

> *We conclude that if anything, the union sector leads the nonunion sector with regard to workplace innovations which substantially contribute to improved economic performance.*

TABLE 4
Extent of Innovation by Level of Unionization, GAO Data Mean Extent of Activity*

(*Standard errors are in parentheses*)

	High (> 40% Union)	Moderate (20–40% Union)	Low (< 20% Union)
Quality Circles	2.00 (0.11)	2.56 a (0.18)	2.12 (0.15)
Other Participation	2.30 (0.13)	2.51 (0.14)	2.58 (0.16)
Union-Management QWL Committees	1.81 a (0.12)	1.61 (0.10)	1.44 (0.11)
Teams	1.37 (0.06)	1.67 a,b (0.12)	1.31 (0.09)
Profit-sharing	2.50 (0.21)	2.08 (0.19)	3.32 b,c (0.29)
Gainsharing	1.39 (0.09)	1.43 (0.09)	1.54 (0.13)
ESOPs	3.55 (0.28)	4.09 (0.35)	3.76 (0.38)
Job Enrichment	1.82 (0.10)	2.22 a (0.16)	2.08 (0.17)
Survey Feedback	2.74 (0.22)	2.93 (0.20)	3.02 (0.29)
Knowledge/Skill-Based Pay	1.64 (0.13)	1.74 (0.14)	1.88 (0.17)
Number of Firms	75	54	50

All significance is at the 0.05 level on a 2-tailed test and is coded as follows:
  a = significantly greater than Low Union category
  b = significantly greater than High Union category
  c = significantly greater than Moderate Union category

* Respondents were asked how many employees were covered by the various practices. Categories of responses: 1 = None, 2 = Almost None (1–20%), 3 = Some (21–40%), 4 = About Half (41–60%), 5 = Most (61–80%), 6 = Almost all (81–99%), 7 = All (100%).

TABLE 5
Managers' Evaluations of the Success of Programs in Improving Organizational Performance, GAO Data

(Standard errors are in parentheses)

	Partly Union	Nonunion	High Union	Moderate Union	Low Union
Quality Circles	3.81 (0.07)	3.79 (0.09)	3.71 (0.11)	4.05b,c (0.11)	3.65 (0.13)
Other Participation	3.85 (0.07)	3.83 (0.08)	3.85 (0.11)	3.95 (0.10)	3.76 (0.13)
Union-Management QWL	3.43 (0.08)	3.67 (0.33)	3.58a (0.13)	3.36 (0.15)	3.20 (0.15)
Teams	3.63 (0.08)	3.82 (0.16)	3.68a (0.15)	3.75a (0.11)	3.27 (0.14)
Job Enrichment	3.50 (0.06)	3.67 (0.16)	3.44 (0.09)	3.51 (0.12)	3.58 (0.12)
Survey Feedback	3.78 (0.06)	3.85 (0.08)	3.76 (0.11)	3.93a (0.09)	3.63 (0.12)

Significance: All the partly union, nonunion comparisons are insignificant at the 0.05 level. The high, moderate, and low union comparisons are indicated as follows:

a = significantly greater than $U < 20$
b = significantly greater than $U > 40$
c = significantly greater than $20 <= U <= 40$.

Scaling: Very great = 5, Great = 4, Moderate = 3, Some = 2, Little or No = 1.

There are no statistically significant differences in program effectiveness between nonunion companies and those that are at least partially unionized, at the 5 percent confidence level. Looking across different levels of unionization, however, two programs are rated as significantly more effective in moderately unionized companies (quality circles and survey feedback), and one is rated as significantly more effective in heavily unionized companies (union-management quality of worklife committees). Teams were regarded as significantly more effective in either moderately or heavily unionized firms than in those with less than 20 percent organization.

188

Table 6 presents the managers' evaluations of employee involvement programs on outcomes besides overall performance. Again, union and nonunion companies are highly similar. The nonunion companies were more likely to report that innovations had spread performance-based rewards to lower levels of their business organizations, but the union companies were more likely to indicate that safety and health had been improved as a result of innovation. Overall, there is little evidence that perceived program effectiveness differs much across union status, and insofar as there are differences, moderately unionized companies appear to have the advantage.

In general, then, the GAO evidence is consistent with that of earlier studies. If anything, the union sector is characterized by a distribution of programs that typically have greater effects on economic performance—teams, QWL committees, and, according to Cooke and Finseth, gain-sharing or productivity-related group bonuses—than the profit-sharing that characterizes the nonunion sector. There is little evidence that profit-sharing—the one program where the nonunion sector continues to lead the union sector according to all available studies—is particularly effective in motivating employees to greater performance. In short, the nonunion sector is no longer more innovative than the union sector, if in fact it ever was more innovative. This is not a surprising result when we take into consideration the historical willingness of U.S. unions to engage in productivity bargaining.

The nonunion sector is no longer more innovative than the union sector, if in fact it ever was more innovative.

Workplace Innovations as a Form of Productivity Bargaining

The workplace level programs that are often a part of the new union management cooperation are in some ways a particular manifestation of a very old phenomenon for U.S. unionism: productivity bargaining. Productivity bargaining traditionally refers to union agreement to revise established work practices or work rules in exchange for a better economic settlement. Mills (1982, p. 451) defines it as "the employer's receiving from the union a quid pro quo for a wage increase, in the form of a relaxation or modification of working practice that will result in greater productivity" and briefly surveys its long use in the U.S. (see also McKersie and Hunter, 1973).[15] Recent union agreement to team

TABLE 6
Managers' Evaluations of the Extent to Which Programs Resulted in a Changed Business Environment, GAO Data

	Percent Great or Very Great		Scaled Mean	
	Union	Nonunion	Union	Nonunion
Improved implementation of technology	40.3%	35.1%	2.49	2.66
Eliminated layers of management or supervision	20.1	19.4	1.84	1.93
Changed management style to one that is more participatory	44.7	36.5	2.64	2.65
Improved union-management relations	22.9	0	2.09**	1.00
Moved decisionmaking to lower organizational levels	36.9	26.9	2.41	2.33
Moved performance-based rewards to lower organizational levels	18.5	22.3	1.87	2.13*
Broadened skill development at lower organizational levels	44.1	36.5	2.65	2.64
Increased information flow throughout the corporation	48.7	44.0	2.75	2.86
Increased employee trust in management	45.2	31.3	2.65	2.61
Improved management decisionmaking	38.0	32.9	2.51	2.60
Improved employee safety/health	31.9	14.2	2.32**	1.85
Improved organizational processes and procedures	38.0	37.3	2.50	2.69

* Significantly different at the .10 level on a 2-tailed test.
** Significantly different at the .05 level on a 2-tailed test.

Scaling: Very great = 5, Great = 4, Moderate = 3, Some = 2, Little or No = 1.

production systems, employee participation, or other open-ended innovations on the shopfloor which continuously seek to reduce costs and increase output, is a form of productivity bargaining, with the quid pro quo for labor being lesser reductions in wages or fewer layoffs than would otherwise have been the case.

We would make two points in this regard. First, the highly competitive economic environment of the 1980s clearly stimulated a general reexamination of existing work practices, along with renewed interest in these programs on the part of management, and union willingness to consider them.[16] Employee involvement programs, teams, and the other innovations discussed here were often launched in the same economic climate that produced concession bargaining, if not direct threats to close plants or outsource work, and were often sold as ways to avoid deeper concessions (Kassalow, 1988; Cappelli and McKersie, 1987; McKersie and Klein, 1985). Our second point is that the economic pressures of the era, however, merely reinforced an underlying U.S. union proclivity toward exchanging more productive work for higher wages. Union workplaces possess—and nonunion workplaces lack—institutions for serious productivity bargaining. Widespread experimentation with these programs in the union sector can be understood in that context.

Union workplaces possess—and nonunion workplaces lack—institutions for serious productivity bargaining.

Union workers can as a group trade harder and/or more productive work for higher wages, or trade increased productivity to prevent reductions in wages when earlier gains are threatened by the forces of competition. Nonunion workers lack the institutions—the collective voice which permits inter-worker discussion and then explicit negotiation with employers—to make these exchanges. More productive work for higher wages is a trade that union workers do not always want to make. But union workers are better off than nonunion workers insofar as the institution of unionism permits them to make, or not make, this exchange.

One can see this by considering the role played by informal work practices in nonunion firms and considering the barriers to productivity bargaining in that environment. Personnel experts assure us that work rules—established ways of doing things—exist in nonunion companies, and are not easily changed (McKersie and Klein, 1985, p. 146; Foulkes, 1980, p. 61). Informal work norms function in nonunion settings to protect workers from stress, poor eval-

191

uations, not being able to sustain the work pace, and adverse social reactions by coworkers (Mathewson, 1931).

The stability of informal work practices is important because the nonunion employer has considerable formal power to reassign both tasks to particular workers and workers to particular jobs—a power frequently termed "flexibility." Employees use work norms in such a context to build some slack into jobs and thus protect themselves against negative outcomes like fatigue or inability to keep up.[17] The power to reassign work and workers, the flexibility so envied by managers in union companies, is not a productivity panacea because it sets in motion protective human behavior. Indeed in some nonunion settings, the company may choose to "buy" individual worker cooperation in ways that are ultimately counterproductive. Supervisors in Foulkes' (1980, pp. 61–66) classic study of nonunion companies complained loudly about overly loose work environments and the difficultly in disciplining workers that resulted from a "people oriented" approach to managing without a union.

The very fact that employee participation programs have been introduced so widely in the nonunion sector is evidence for our view in this regard. In part, nonunion employers are recognizing that the top-down exercise of managerial power may not maximize productivity, both because managers do not know everything and because workers can react to "managerial flexibility" in ways inhibiting productivity. Participation programs focus the ideas and the energy of the work group on production. In organized groups, coworkers can discuss product quality, work flow, and all the details of how work is done and allocated. When coworkers decide together on changes that improve quality or reduce costs, individuals will be more likely to see changes as fair and supported by the work group. But such nonunion workplace participation groups are limited; they do not negotiate wages and hence cannot truly engage in productivity bargaining.

Only with a union can workers exchange more work effort for higher wages. Only with a union—with workplace level groups supplemented by plant or firm level institutions of collective bargaining—do we get real productivity bargaining. Interestingly, in recent years such bargaining has led to considerable experimentation in the union sector with the more serious and far-reaching workplace innovations. While the matter is not without controversy,

The power to reassign work and workers, the flexibility so envied by managers in union companies, is not a productivity panacea because it sets in motion protective human behavior.

the econometric evidence indicates that given a good industrial relations climate, union workers are actually somewhat more productive than nonunion workers (see Belman, this volume, for a review; see Addison and Hirsch, 1989, for a dissenting view). Productivity bargaining is likely one major, if unheralded, reason.[18]

Participation's Ultimate Potential

Not only has innovation been widespread in the union sector, but also a participative program, or team system, has greater ultimate potential when implemented in a unionized workplace. For the rest of this paper, we make a theoretical argument regarding the sources of that greater potential. Three arguments will be developed:

1) First, unions provide workers with important protections against job loss, either for economic reasons or because of managerial reprisal, and this encourages involvement. We review case studies indicating that lack of such protections often limits nonunion participation programs (Witte, 1980; Elden, 1976; Bernstein, 1976). Our argument was developed independently of that made by Levine and Tyson (1990), but is similar in a number of respects; the primary difference involves our systematic examination of the contribution made by union representation. Levine and Tyson agree that job security and guaranteed individual rights are necessary conditions for successful participation and buttress their theoretical arguments with evidence from three foreign cases and one domestic case.[19]

2) Second, unions provide a mechanism whereby workers can utilize their "collective voice" in the design and operation of a program on a long-term basis. One result is that programs in union companies are typically "better balanced" in the sense that they are more likely to be concerned with enhancing the quality of worklife and other direct worker goals, along with increasing productivity. They therefore have greater legitimacy in the eyes of workers and are more likely to survive.

3) And finally, unions can play an important role in extending participation from the shopfloor to the entire enterprise. With unionism, it is possible for participation to become "strategic," so that workers can influence major corporate decisions like plant investment or technology.

Nonunion employers are recognizing that the top-down exercise of managerial power may not maximize productivity.

193

Many argue this is necessary for innovations to be sustained over time (Kochan and Cutcher-Gershenfeld, 1988).

It is instructive to consider the parallel between worker involvement in industry and political democracy. In essence, democracy in either sphere becomes real rather than theoretical with:

1) Adequate guarantees of the rights of individual participants. For instance, free speech is a critical right for political democracy, and similarly the ability to speak up without the fear of retaliation is vital for industrial democracy.

2) Organized interest groups which articulate and push the concerns of individuals within the system. As former Secretary of Labor Ray Marshall explains, "Any viable worker participation system probably requires workers to have some independent power, through organizations they control" (1987, p. 207).[20]

Worker participation plans, team production systems, and other programs that promise extensive worker involvement have greater potential for increasing productivity precisely when they offer genuine industrial democracy.[21] This is more likely to occur in the presence of an independent labor union.

> *A participative program, or team system, has greater ultimate potential when implemented in a unionized workplace.*

Fear of Reprisal

Protection from arbitrary treatment is widely regarded as one of the most significant benefits unions offer workers. Because of contractual requirements and grievance arbitration procedures, managers must have a legitimate reason for firing or otherwise disciplining a worker in unionized workplaces. The importance of such protection for genuine participation should not be underestimated. In the more extensive involvement programs, workers are asked to give their opinions and suggestions about a wide range of issues including potentially their supervisor's role and performance and company policies. In fact, first line supervisors are widely recognized to be one group greatly threatened by employee involvement; middle managers too may be resistant (Klein, 1988). Clearly, workers will be reluctant to participate fully insofar as they have reason to fear retaliation from their superiors (Bernstein, 1980; Levine and Tyson, 1990; Strauss, 1977).

194

There is some evidence to indicate that this dynamic limits the potential of many nonunion programs. Bernstein (1976, pp. 501–2) describes the near-demise of worker participation in the worker-owned American Cast Iron Pipe Company due to the "lack of guarantees against penalties for criticism." Witte (1980) also observed these problems to some degree in the nonunion company he studied, particularly when employee groups were dealing with such core issues as wages.[22]

Thus, there is some anecdotal evidence that fear of reprisal can prevent workers from fully participating in a nonunion setting. At the same time, it is important to recognize that many innovative nonunion companies attempt to provide reassurances against arbitrary treatment. Their "complaint systems" include "open-door" policies, "speak up" programs and ombudsman offices as well as more formal grievance procedures resembling those in unionized settings (Foulkes, 1980; Kochan and Katz, 1988). While the final decision is typically made by a highly placed company official, a tiny minority of these procedures end with a decision by a neutral third-party arbitrator (Ichniowski, Delaney, and Lewin, 1989; Delaney, Lewin, and Ichniowski, 1988).

Research suggests that nonunion grievance procedures, with arbitration or not, produce mixed results. Managers themselves report problems such as delays, inconsistency in outcomes, and lack of worker awareness of the procedure (BNA, 1979). Perhaps the most significant problem mentioned in several studies of nonunion settings is worker fear of reprisal for utilizing the procedure (BNA, 1979; Lewin, 1987b; Witte, 1980, pp. 87–88 and 200, note 1)! Other studies (Lewin, 1987b, cited in Kochan and Katz, 1988; Foulkes, 1980) indicate low usage rates and very low rates of appeal. Thus, while it cannot be said that all nonunion companies lack protection against arbitrary treatment, nor that all unions provide ironclad insurance, there clearly is a significant difference in the protections offered in the two sectors. The situation is similar with regard to another factor limiting participation according to a number of studies: economic insecurity.

Protection from arbitrary treatment is widely regarded as one of the most significant benefits unions offer workers.

Economic Insecurity

Workers' concerns regarding their economic security in the face of an innovation aimed at improving work methods and productivity also can be a barrier to participation (Witte, 1980, pp. 153). Job loss, reduced amounts of employment, and wage reductions are all feared.[23] As Levine and Tyson (1990, p. 210) explain, "Most directly, workers are unlikely to cooperate in increasing efficiency if they fear that by so doing they jeopardize their jobs." Examples abound in both the union and nonunion sectors of involvement programs that were undermined by economic insecurity. The Maxwell House plant in Hoboken, New Jersey, implemented a QWL program in its freeze-dried division in 1976. The experiment ended when, for reasons beyond the plant management's control, the workforce in that department was laid off. Current efforts to build participation and cooperation are frequently met with the call to "remember freeze-dried!"[24]

For this reason labor and management have begun to combine workplace innovations and employment security guarantees in the union sector (Kochan and Cutcher-Gershenfeld, 1988). Recent national agreements, including the current ones between GM and the UAW, and Ford and the UAW, provide for employment guarantees and retraining assistance. Similarly, innovation at unionized facilities of Boeing, Boise Cascade, and Xerox were all accompanied by no-layoff agreements or retraining provisions.[25] Eaton's research (1990) suggests that only a minority of unions are powerful enough to obtain formal guarantees against harmful economic outcomes. On the other hand, in the nonunion sector, companies' commitment to job security is even less enforceable.[26]

Collective Voice

The union is the one institution that has the potential to bring the "collective voice" of the workforce into the participative or cooperative process. That is, the union can provide worker views regarding the initial structuring of the participation process, as well as facilitate its continued operation.

Worker input is perhaps both most needed, and most often absent, in the earliest stages of setting up innovative programs.[27] The undemocratic imposition of a participatory system, political or industrial, may be flawed. Management risks failure where it must "guess" or "assume" that workers want participation as well as the forms that participation should take (Heckscher, 1988, p. 106).[28] Elden (1976) examined a case where a nonunion company attempted to set up a new plant with self-managing work teams. He reports considerable frustration and disappoint-

Workers' concerns regarding their economic security in the face of an innovation aimed at improving work methods and productivity also can be a barrier to participation.

ment within the workforce regarding the actual amount of control and discretion teams were able to exercise. This frustration appeared to stem, in part, from the lack of worker input in the implementation process itself. "Self-management," in fact, became viewed by workers "as something imposed on them from above, something, ironically they were not allowed to participate in managing" (p. 291).

One specific way in which unions may serve a constructive role in structuring a program concerns the spread of an innovation throughout a plant or company. Unions, through their traditional commitment to equity, may help spread the program throughout the plant, eliminating the many problems inherent to experiments limited to single workgroups or parts of a plant (Goodman, 1979; Wells, 1987). Lawler suggests that, in fact, "[m]uch of the credit for [the spread of change throughout an organization] goes to the union because it is the first to raise issues of equality of treatment" (1986, p. 131).

At the same time, unions may help to create environments in which workers may opt into *or out of* innovative work systems. Without entering into the debate on this issue, we think it is sufficient to state that some workers probably want more input into workplace decisions and others do not, and, it appears that unions often push firms to accommodate both types of workers.[29] For instance, participation in QC and QWL programs in unionized settings is typically voluntary. Traditionally oriented workers may even be accommodated in more far-reaching changes in work organization, like team systems. For instance, the GM-Fiero agreement with the UAW, "allowed workers to choose between working under the pay-for-knowledge compensation plan and flexible work systems, or under a traditional pay system" (Kochan and Cutcher-Gershenfeld, 1988, p. 12). From a social vantage point, such flexibility is preferable to simply not hiring workers who prefer the traditional system, a practice frequently recommended by consultants and apparently more commonplace in the non-union sector (Grenier, 1988; Lawler, 1986, pp. 206–7). Workers who dislike participation should not become unemployable! Furthermore, a worker who initially prefers a more traditional system may come to like a new system and, "as a convert," be the best advocate for that system.

A union can provide input from the workforce not only during the implementation of a program, but also in the course of an ongoing program. One consultant has sug-

The union is the one institution that has the potential to bring the "collective voice" of the workforce into the participative or cooperative process.

gested that the union is absolutely essential to the success of plant-level programs (Shay, 1989). First, the union is tied to the plant while managers may come and go. Cutcher-Gershenfeld (1988, p. 24) notes that at Xerox, "The very existence of a union ... proved critical in sustaining and diffusing many of the innovations—particularly when there was managerial turnover." Second, there is general agreement that the payoffs from innovative programs tend to come over the long run (Lawler, 1986, p. 233). However, plant managers tend to be rewarded based on their short-run performance, while the union is an institution that is committed to the long run. As such, it can provide the necessary institutional stability for a program to succeed. In fact, results from a GAO survey indicate that the single greatest barrier to employee involvement efforts is "short-term performance pressure."[30]

> *A union is an ideal and much-needed vehicle for articulating and prioritizing both issues of greatest concern and the degree of desired involvement.*

A union, particularly one that actively organizes for and participates in the program, is an ideal and much-needed vehicle for articulating and prioritizing both issues of greatest concern and the degree of desired involvement (Witte, 1980; Elden, 1976). Unions have always set common collective bargaining goals after allowing workers and work groups with different objectives to each express their own particular demands; scholars term this intra-organizational bargaining. Union experience in aggregating worker views aids the smooth functioning of participative programs.[31]

Program Balance and Legitimacy

The very fact that unions can say "no" to participative and cooperative programs should lead to changes in those programs that increase their long-run viability by making them better balanced—attractive to workers, as well as vehicles of greater productivity. This may be one reason why quality circles (a type of participation) have higher survival rates in the union sector (Drago, 1988). Ironically, it is precisely because unionized workers can say "no" as a group that they can also collectively say "yes" to such efforts. This potentially provides participative and cooperative programs with a greater degree of legitimacy (Cutcher-Gershenfeld, McKersie, and Wever, 1988, p. 11).

It would be disingenuous to pretend that the union's collective voice will never be in opposition to participation in general or to specific directions it may take. At times, collective opposition to a program may be appropriate. Elsewhere (Eaton and Voos, 1989), we have suggested that union opposition to participative and cooperative programs is reasonable and to be expected where management appears to be using a program to interfere with the union's role at the workplace or simply as a method to speed up production. Unions might also appropriately oppose programs that were posed as solutions for problems that do not exist or were the wrong solution for problems that do exist (Heckscher, 1988, p. 105).

However, the possibility of union opposition, along with union participation in the structuring of participative programs, should bring balance to those programs. While management is likely to be most interested in increasing productivity, unions are more likely to see quality of worklife and job satisfaction as inherently important goals in themselves. In fact, many unions explicitly state that the balancing of these disparate goals is a precondition to their participation and support. For instance, the "Statement of Principles" that governs the joint QWL program between ATT and CWA provides that the "[t]he goals of the process include both human satisfaction and economic efficiency." Lawler (1986, pp. 133–34) presents evidence that QWL committees often recommend changes that promote job satisfaction. He notes, "QWL committees often recommend changes in the workplace that are desired by employees. In particular, they make changes in the physical environment: parking lots, cafeterias, restrooms, and time clocks."

Participation programs in the union sector must be carefully crafted to garner the workforce's continuous collective support. This ultimately increases their effectiveness.

Participation programs in the union sector must be carefully crafted to garner the workforce's continuous collective support. This ultimately increases their effectiveness. Effectiveness is also enhanced, we argue in the next section, because union workers can participate more fully in important decisions at higher organizational levels.

Participation at Higher Organizational Levels

In nonunion companies, participation tends to be limited to the workplace level of decisionmaking, and rarely extends to the plant or corporate level. This reduces its ultimate effectiveness because many of the important decisions that affect workers' productivity, lives on the job, and ultimately the viability of participation itself, are made at higher organizational levels. Involvement programs in union companies allow for relatively greater input at the plant and corporation levels.[32]

Without a union, individual workers often lack the information and knowledge necessary to be effective at higher levels of decisionmaking. While Witte (1980, p. 153) reports that the nonunion workers in his case study were generally as competent to deal with lower level issues as managers, they were more likely to be outdone at higher levels by professional managers with access to a large staff.

In nonunion companies there is usually no institution able to coordinate the activities of shopfloor participative groups. Heckscher suggests that nonunion firms "rarely create mechanisms for linking different groups; each problem-solving team remains distinct, obscuring common issues and interests" (1988, pp. 112–13). Elden (1976, p. 290) found that even though joint worker-management task forces were used to study and propose solutions to plant-wide problems, full participation was "limited by the absence of regular and continuous means of involving workers in decisionmaking beyond the immediate work group and team."

In contrast, union involvement at various levels of the organization is probably the dominant model of QWL programs in unionized firms (Lawler, 1986, p. 122). The typical structure involves workgroup or department level committees, which may or may not include union representatives as such, combined with a plant level "steering" committee that oversees the program as a whole and includes plant management and local union leaders. This is also the model of the successful and long-lived Scanlon Plan.

What is more rare, but nevertheless important, is strategic participation at the corporate level. In fact, union involvement at that level may be key to the ultimate success at other levels. Kochan and Cutcher-Gershenfeld (1988, p. 21) argue that "broader and deeper union roles at the strategic level of management decisionmaking are necessary if the innovations in employee participation, work reorganization, and introduction of new technologies and work systems are to be sustained over time." For instance, strategic decisions like closing a plant or laying off a significant portion of a workforce may undermine plant level participation and cooperation efforts as described above.

Union involvement in decisionmaking at this level is both rare and relatively new in the United States.[33] At the low end of the strategic participation spectrum would be a case where management is simply sharing information about long-term corporate plans and goals. An intermediate level of participation might take the form of management consultation with union leaders. At the high end would be

Involvement programs in union companies allow for relatively greater input at the plant and corporation levels.

actual representation on corporate boards of directors such as Chrysler, Western Airlines, or Northwestern Steel and Wire. A different type of high level participation that may be equally or more effective would involve joint strategic planning of products or business units; the involvement of the United Automobile Workers in the Saturn project is probably the best-known example of such extensive joint planning from an early stage.

While this kind of participation is rare in the union sector, it appears to be growing. We know of no examples of this level of worker involvement in nonunion companies, except for a handful that are heavily employee-owned.[34] It is difficult to conceive of such involvement without 1) the institutional structuring of representation, and 2) the institutional resources and expertise a union provides.

Union strategic participation at the corporate level may be key to the ultimate success at other levels.

To summarize, unions clearly have the potential for improving the implementation and functioning of participative programs. This is due in part to the protections unions typically offer members against arbitrary treatment and economic insecurity and in part to their traditional function of organizing and articulating a collective voice in the workplace. Unions may play a constructive role in the structuring of participation to meet the needs of all parties and would appear to be a necessary partner in any attempts to involve labor in decisions at higher levels of management.

Conclusion

In this paper we have attempted to demonstrate that productivity-improving human resource management innovations are in wide usage in the union sector and that, in fact, the use of the most truly productivity-enhancing innovations is, if anything, more common in the union sector than in the nonunion sector. Moreover, workplace innovations have greater potential in the union sector not only for enhancing productivity but for increasing job satisfaction and genuine worker participation in a wider variety of decisions in the workplace.

This greater potential results from two major factors. The first is the role of the union as an agent for explicit productivity bargaining. Unions in the U.S. have long bargained to improve productivity in ways that do not hinder change while protecting their members' interests. Union involvement in innovative programs is consistent with this experience. The second factor consists of the protections and voice for workers that unions bring to any innovative program, but especially to participative programs. Union protections and voice should improve and deepen the potential of innovations to improve production and create a better working environment.

Workplace innovations have potential in the union sector . . . for increasing job satisfaction and genuine worker participation.

Endnotes

[1] We recognize that programs with a given designation (for instance, quality circles) may differ greatly in implementation from plant to plant, and that these categories are not entirely exclusive. For example, teams involve both work reorganization and employee participation (Katz, Kochan, and Keefe, 1987a). Nonetheless, some categorization of innovations is needed to draw major distinctions.

Our categories are adapted from Kochan and Cutcher-Gershenfeld (1988), who use the following list: employee participation, flexible forms of work organization, participation in new technology decisions, employment security, gainsharing, and participation in management decisions. We also made use of Lawler's (1986) categories: quality circles, survey feedback, job enrichment, work teams, union-management quality of worklife programs, gainsharing, and new-design plants.

[2] Mitchell et al., 1990; Levine and Tyson, 1990; Conte and Svejnar, 1990, 1988; Cotton et al., 1988; Weitzman and Kruse, 1990; Russell, 1988; Miller and Monge, 1986; Locke and Schweiger, 1979; see also the Appendix, which references better studies regarding the effectiveness of different programs.

[3] Mitchell et al. point out, "Under the current regulatory system for pensions and profit-sharing, an incentive exists to substitute profit-sharing for pensions. Profit-sharing gives the firm more flexibility in the size of its annual contribution than a defined contribution pension plan does, and the rules regarding fund investment are looser" (p. 58).

[4] Scanlon plans and union-management cooperation, of course, have a much longer history. See Lesieur, 1958; Slichter, 1941; Slichter, Healy, and Livernash, 1960; and Jacoby, 1983.

[5] So while many of these programs came to be associated with nonunion human resource management, to some extent this may be a spurious association. That is, many of these practices, especially the most participative systems, were begun in new facilities that, for a variety of reasons, tended to open and remain nonunion. Managers appeared to be making the reasonable assumption that innovations could be more easily and successfully implemented in new facilities. As a long-time observer of work innovations explains,

> the processes of innovation (diagnosing, planning, inventing, and implementing) are significantly different for new and existing units. In established facilities, the level of aspiration for change and the time frame allotted for achieving it must be much more modest than in new facilities. . . [t]he main job of planners in old facilities is defrosting the old work culture and creating a sense of potential for change. (Walton, 1979, p. 98)

[6] In one example, UAW organizers are reported as complaining that the situation resembled that of the 1920s when companies effectively used employee representation plans to keep independent unions from organizing (Eiger, 1989, p. 4).

[7] Leaders of major unions such as CWA, USW, and the UAW have all strongly supported some types of participative and cooperative activities, but others have not. William Winpisinger of the Machinists, for instance, opposed quality circles as duplicating the local union's functions. The UAW, which is involved in many innovative programs, recently had a major debate at its 1989 convention regarding joint programs, and passed a resolution that reflects what is probably the current majority position on these programs among trade unionists:

> In the workplace, the UAW supports increased worker input and expanded influence on business decisions at all levels. . . At the same time we oppose efforts by companies to use democratic-sounding programs as a smokescreen designed to undermine collective bargaining and workers' rights.

Overall we see more support for innovation among union leaders at top levels than there was ten years ago. Much less is known about attitudes at the local level. Surveys of local leaders involved in participative programs tend to report majority support for such programs, with roughly a quarter to a third opposed. (Kochan, Katz, and Mower, 1984). Such opposition may result from negative experiences with these programs as well as ideology (Eaton, 1989).

[8] To the extent that innovation did begin in the nonunion sector, it is not so much that unions opposed innovation as innovative companies with new facilities and new work practices opposed unionization.

[9] Juravich and Harris (1989) have conducted a study of employee involvement programs in Pennsylvania. Their early results indicate that three quarters of these programs are in unionized firms; it was not possible to include this study in Table 1 because data analysis was incomplete.

[10] The results on the relative importance of merit in promotions and layoffs in the union and nonunion sectors, the use of performance appraisals, and grievance procedures discussed in the paper are not included in our overview because these are long-standing differences related to the very nature of collective bargaining, not differences in innovations.

Using the same data as in their other study, Delaney, Lewin, and Ichniowski (1988) report that more employee involvement programs in totally nonunion firms provide high decisionmaking authority to participative groups than those in totally unionized firms. Looking at firms with both union and nonunion facilities, however, more unionized operations provided high authority, although not significantly more.

Cooke's data also dealt with the intensity of participative programs, but in a different way. He looked at the percentage of the workforce participating in the program, the hours of participation-related training received, and the percentage of the workforce receiving training. There were no significant differences between the two sectors on any of these dimensions.

[11] The correlations were quality circles (-0.114, N $= 75$), group bonuses (0.029, N $= 71$), job rotation (0.026, N $= 70$), and employee surveys (-0.024, N $= 67$).

204

[12] The GAO data are better than those used in earlier studies because the survey authors obtained a relatively good response rate (47.6 percent) for a sample of large, nationwide corporations, the Fortune 1000 companies. This increases our confidence that the data is indeed representative, and contrasts sharply with the 6.5 percent response rate of the Ichniowski, Delaney, and Lewin study, or the exclusively Michigan focus of the Cooke report.

[13] A difference of proportions test is not used to determine whether or not the proportions are statistically different from one another because the mean extent data provide a better summary of overall differences between the two sectors.

[14] It should be noted that there is no information in the GAO survey that indicates specifically whether unionized workers are involved in innovative programs; nonunion workers in partially unionized firms may be partially or even primarily involved.

[15] For further historical discussions of union management cooperation and productivity bargaining see Jacoby (1983) and Slichter (1941). The dominant U.S. union response to productivity-enhancing technological change has been to share in the economic benefits, rather than to block innovation itself. Well-known examples include the Mineworkers' agreements in the 1950s and the Longshoremen and Warehousemen's contracts in the 1960s.

[16] Management made a major push on work rules in the early 1980s. Even in 1986 and 1987, management often went into negotiations attempting to reduce what was viewed as "restrictive work rules"—according to the BNA survey of employer bargaining goals, a greater percentage of firms emphasized this than planned on seeking cutbacks in holidays, vacations, sick leave, personal leave, or other paid time off, special early retirement incentives, switches from defined benefit to defined contribution pension plans, or other reductions in nonwage compensation covered by the survey (BNA, 1985, pp. 16–17; BNA, 1986b, pp. 13–14).

[17] In an environment where work is variable, first-level supervisors too may have an incentive to build some slack into jobs, insofar as it will protect their future ability to meet surges in work.

[18] Earlier discussions of this phenomenon have emphasized the greater accumulation of firm-specific human capital in the union sector (with fewer quits and more training being offered by the average union employer) and more professional management subsequent to executives being "shocked" by the union's appearance on the scene (Freeman and Medoff, 1984). To date, however, there is little conclusive evidence on the actual mechanisms through which unions raise productivity. Our view that productivity bargaining is important is consonant with the research done by industrial relations scholars indicating that the union productivity effect depends in part on the industrial relations climate, with a cooperative union-management relationship being more likely to manifest greater productivity than is a highly adversarial relationship (Ichniowski, 1984a; Freeman and Medoff, 1984).

[19] Levine and Tyson also contend that two other characteristics are necessary for successful participation: some form of profit-sharing or gainsharing, and measures to build group cohesiveness, including reduced pay and status differentials between workers and managers. We would like to point out that unionized workers have advantages in both respects. Union bargaining power guarantees that they will ultimately share in the gains from greater productivity, indirectly if not directly, through some gainsharing or profit-sharing plan. And it is well known that unions compress pay differentials within firms, and in particular elevate the pay of blue collar employees relative to their supervisors (Freeman and Medoff, 1984). Levine and Tyson reference a number of studies that support the view that narrow wage dispersion increases worker cohesiveness and productivity.

[20] Turner (1988a) has recently produced evidence that workplace innovations in the U.S. automobile industry are more likely to result in enhanced productivity in the presence of strong local unionism than in its absence.

[21] It is probably worth noting at this point that these preconditions are necessary for some kinds of participation or cooperation but may not be for others. Turner (1988a, p. 13), for example, points to the differences between "one Japanese management approach to consensus in which top management makes a decision and then groups of lower managers and workers discuss it until they all agree with the decision [and] a more genuinely participative approach." In the first case, workers are made to feel a part of the process, but the information and decisions are still top-down. This type of "participative" process can operate without protections or organized interest groups but it is probably not something most U.S. workers would regard as genuine involvement.

[22] Grenier (1988) observed a nonunion "team" program operating during a union organizing drive. In this case, fear and isolation of union supporters became an explicit goal of the team meetings, a goal that was orchestrated through the comments of team facilitators and the use of peer pressure.

[23] Consequently, union leaders frequently mention employment security as an issue that must be addressed before becoming involved in a participative program.

[24] This was a union situation; the discussion is based on an interview with Maxwell House personnel management, 8/1988. Kochan, Katz and Mower (1984, p. 77) document a similar case in the steel industry but conclude that while other plants in that industry have also suffered job losses, the effect has been "to slow the growth of the [participative] process rather than seriously threaten its existence."

[25] In fact, successful innovations in crisis situations may save jobs without any formal guarantees; the threat of job loss itself may be sufficient to stimulate participation in these cases. On the other hand, Kochan and Cutcher-Gershenfeld argue that employment guarantees are not sufficient to drive participative innovations on their own.

[26] Only 14 percent of the eighty-six local unions in Eaton's study were able to win contractual guarantees against layoffs, for instance. Foulkes (1980) found that

"employment stability" was a key management goal in many of the large non-union companies he studied. Nine of the twenty-six companies studied claimed to have never laid off any regular workers.

27 Local union leaders frequently complain that management springs fully formed programs on them, leaving little room for union input into that program. The Saturn project stands in clear contrast to that approach.

28 Heckscher explains this well: "A major reason that leadership in a managerialist system is so difficult and rare is that it tries to substitute for an adequate form of representation. Somehow, in order for the system to work, the doubts and resistances of employees must be accounted for and dealt with in formulating principles and strategies. If there are no adequate mechanisms for employees to express their concerns, it falls to a leader to guess them" (p. 106).

29 These kinds of differences have been documented among workers in various unionized facilities (Kochan and Cutcher-Gershenfeld, 1988, p. 7).

30 Short-term pressures were viewed as being of great or very great importance by 43 percent of the respondents. No other factor came close to that weight. Only 9 percent of the respondents indicated that short-term pressures were of little or no importance; other factors were much more frequently viewed as unimportant. In fact, managerial turnover was viewed as unimportant by 71 percent of the respondents.

31 Klingel and Martin (1988) describe a process at Harrison Radiator where the union developed and prioritized cost-saving ideas on its own before submitting them to management.

32 It is important to note that collective bargaining itself constitutes limited worker representation at a plant or higher level.

33 Western European countries that have legally required worker representation on Boards of Directors are heavily unionized, and elected representatives, particularly of production workers, are typically either union leaders or persons close to the labor movement.

34 A few such firms have worker representatives on their Boards of Directors, including Polaroid, Fastener Industries, and Reuther Mold (Blasi, 1989).

Glossary

Discussions of contemporary innovations in work organization, compensation, and employee participation use a variety of terms. We constructed a glossary of the most important ones by augmenting the description of terms at the end of the U.S. General Accounting Office's 1987 *Survey of Corporate Employee Involvement Efforts* [in quotes, referenced by GAO below] with our own explanations, based on our knowledge and a variety of other sources. The GAO descriptions are quoted exactly because these definitions were given to persons who answered the survey analyzed in the paper.

Employee Involvement. "A process that provides employees with the opportunity to make decisions affecting their work and work environment [GAO]." See employee participation.

Employee Participation. This is a very general term that is used to encompass many programs, all of which attempt to involve employees in decisionmaking by holding regular meetings, usually of small numbers of persons in the same work groups. Attendance may be voluntary or involuntary, compensated or uncompensated, and training may or may not be provided. Programs vary greatly in the issues to be addressed by groups and the degree of authority afforded. Quality circles, most quality of worklife programs, and employee involvement groups are all considered employee participation programs.

Employee Participation Groups other than Quality Circles. "Any employee participation groups, such as task teams or employee work councils, that do not fall within the definition of either self-managing work teams or quality circles [GAO]."

Employee Stock Ownership Plan (or ESOP). "A credit mechanism that enables employees to buy their employer's stock, thus giving them an ownership stake in the company; the stock is held in trust until employees quit or retire [GAO]."

Employee Surveys. See survey feedback.

Flexible, Cafeteria-style Benefits. "A plan that gives employees choices in the types and amounts of various fringe benefits they receive [GAO]."

Flexible Job Design. Term used by Ichniowski, Delaney, and Lewin (1989), and Delaney, Lewin, and Ichniowski (1988) to designate the use of *job rotation* (moving workers between jobs), *job enlargement* (adding tasks to a job), or *job enrichment* (see below).

Gainsharing. "Gainsharing plans are based on a formula that shares some portion of gains in productivity, quality, cost effectiveness, or other performance indicators. The gains are shared in the form of bonuses with all employees in an organization (such as a plant). It typically includes a system of employee suggestion committees. It differs from profit-sharing and an ESOP in that the basis of the formula is some set of local performance measures, not company profits. Examples include the Scanlon Plan, the Improshare Plan, the Rucker Plan, and various custom-designed plans [GAO]."

Information-Sharing. Sharing of information on the firm's business performance and business plans with employees or employee representatives.

Job Classifications. Jobs formally designated as separate by an organization.

Job Enrichment or Redesign. "Design of work that is intended to increase worker performance and job satisfaction by increasing the skill variety, autonomy, significance and identity of the task, and the performance feedback [GAO]." See also flexible job design.

Knowledge/Skill-based Pay. "An alternative to traditional job-based pay that sets pay levels based on how many skills employees have or how many jobs they potentially can do, not on the job they are currently holding. This includes training and learning opportunities for employees to support knowledge development. Also called knowledge-based pay, pay for knowledge, and competency-based pay. (This does not include merit pay.) [GAO]"

Participative Programs. A general term that refers to any program including employee participation groups. See employee participation and quality circles.

Pay for Knowledge. See Knowledge/Skill-based Pay.

Productivity-related Group Bonuses. See gainsharing. This designation is somewhat broader than gainsharing and may include programs which do not have a system of employee suggestion committees.

Profit-sharing. "A bonus plan that shares some portion of company profits with employees. It does not include dividend sharing [GAO]."

Quality Circles (QC). "Structured type of employee participation groups in which groups of volunteers from a particular work area meet regularly to identify and suggest improvements to work-related problems. The goals of QCs are improved quality and productivity, there are no direct rewards for circle activity, group problem solving training is provided, and the groups' only power is to suggest changes to management [GAO]."

Quality of Worklife (QWL). A general term that in some contexts refers to any program, especially those involving employee participation, that makes improved quality of worklife at least a partial program goal (often in addition to improved product quality, improved productivity, reduced wastage, etc.), and in other contexts refers to a structure that includes both workgroup-level participation groups and joint union-management committees devoted in part to this goal. See union-management quality of worklife (QWL) committees.

Self-managing Work Teams. "Also termed autonomous work groups, semi-autonomous work groups, self-regulating work teams, or simply work teams. The work group (in some cases, acting without a supervisor) is responsible for a whole product or service, and makes decisions about task assignments and work methods. The team may be responsible for its own support services such as maintenance, purchasing, and quality control, and may perform certain personnel functions such as hiring and firing team members and determining pay increases [GAO]."

Suggestion System. "A program that elicits individual employee suggestions on improving work or the work environment [GAO]."

Survey Feedback. "Use of employee attitude survey results, not simply as an employee opinion poll, but rather as part of a larger problem solving process in which survey data are used to encourage, structure, and measure the effectiveness of employee participation [GAO]."

Teams, Team Concept, or Team Production Systems. See self-managing work teams.

Union-Management Quality of Worklife (QWL) Committees. "Joint union-management committees, usually existing at multiple organizational levels, alongside the established union and management relationship and collective bargaining committees. QWL committees usually are prohibited from directly addressing contractual issues such as pay, and are charged with developing changes that improve both organizational performance and employee quality of worklife [GAO]."

Appendix: Research Regarding the Impact of Various Programs on Productivity

Employee Participation Programs

Although many of these programs are generically referred to as QWL, the primary goal is often to increase firm performance. In the General Accounting Office (U.S. GAO, 1987) survey of employee involvement programs used elsewhere in this paper, managers stated that a major reason for implementation was "to improve productivity" (cited by 70 percent of all respondents as being true to a great or very great extent). The other most frequently cited goals were "to improve quality" (72 percent), "to improve employee motivation" (58 percent), and "to improve employee morale" (54 percent). There are a variety of mechanisms through which participation supposedly stimulates efficiency. Primarily, it is believed that participation encourages workers to share their ideas on how to "work smarter," with each other and with management. In addition to changing actual work practices, workers may become more satisfied and/or may identify more with the company and therefore work more productively. A final hypothesized mechanism for increasing productivity is through reduced conflict (Katz, Kochan, and Gobeille, 1983).

Quantitative evidence as to whether or not employee participation actually increases productivity is mixed. The first studies tended to indicate that participation typically has little or no positive impact on productivity, but does improve employee job satisfaction (for a review of the literature see Locke and Schweiger, 1979). However, newer studies usually report at least small positive effects on specific aspects of performance. For instance, in a well-designed longitudinal study, Marks et al. (1986) find a quality circle program to have positive and significant effects on participants' productivity and absenteeism. Griffin (1988) finds that quality circles have positive effects on performance evaluations, job satisfaction, and organizational commitment for a period of about eighteen months after program implementation, but that these gains tended to diminish over time, a phenomenon also frequently mentioned in the nonquantitative literature (Lawler and Mohrman, 1985). Katz, Kochan, and Keefe (1987a) report a positive and significant relationship between participation and reduced labor hours in the U.S. automobile industry (Katz, Kochan, and Gobeille, 1983). Using survey data across companies, Voos (1987) and Cooke (1988) both report that managers perceive employee participation programs to have positive productivity effects. The recent qualitative literature is summarized by Lawler (1986). Of the programs examined, quality circles, semi-autonomous work teams, and "new design plants" are found to enhance quality and increase productivity through improving work methods.[1]

Participation in Strategic Management Decisions

This option represents a pairing of participation with extensive union-management cooperation that permits the union to be involved in strategic decisions, including those involving capital investment, technology, or product design (Kochan, Katz, and McKersie, 1986, pp. 178–205). Perhaps the best-known form is union representation on a board of directors, although this in and of itself does not guarantee a high degree of union influence (Wever, 1988). More commonly, management consults informally on a regular basis with union leaders regarding the current financial health of the business and the prognosis for the future. Sometimes this occurs through a standing joint committee.

A well-documented case in Rochester, New York, illustrates how strategic participation can yield important gains to both workers and firms (Cutcher-Gershenfeld, 1988). In October 1981, the Amalgamated Clothing Workers faced a potential loss of about 180 jobs if the Xerox Corporation went ahead with its plan to reduce costs by subcontracting the assembly of wire harnesses. The union asked Xerox to set up a Joint Study Team of six affected employees, one engineer, and one manager to determine if sufficient cost savings could be achieved to save the jobs. The company agreed. It had built up a good working relationship with the union based on considerable mutual trust; more recently both parties had gained valuable experience in the operation of employee participation groups. The team found sufficient savings (over $3 million) through physical redesign of the work area, upgraded equipment, and massive work reorganization to convince the company to agree to retain the work in-house. Further extensions of cooperation eventually produced a company commitment to build a new xeroxing-machine toner plant in the Rochester area, rather than constructing it in the South as the initial company study suggested.

This example demonstrates that while major gains from strategic participation typically accrue to unions and their members, management may also benefit to the extent that union leaders and workers 1) gain a more realistic understanding of actual problems, bringing extensive indirect benefits to the company insofar as it affects union decisions in current and future collective bargaining, and 2) bring another constructive voice or viewpoint into the decisionmaking process, resulting in cost-saving or revenue-enhancing innovations. (See Klingel and Martin, 1988, for other examples of joint cost-saving efforts). Furthermore, the Xerox case demonstrates the interrelationship among workplace innovation, strategic participation, concession bargaining, and the adverse economic climate of the 1980s.

"Autonomous" or "Self-Managing" Work Teams

As is explained in the text, this is a very extensive innovation involving high levels of employee participation, changed work methods and job classifications, changed compensation systems, and a changed role for the first-level supervisor.

Most evaluations of teams indicate they can potentially increase productivity substantially. For instance, at NUMMI, the joint GM-Toyota venture in southern California, teams have been associated with a 40 percent reduction in the number of labor hours required for each car (Brown and Reich, 1989, cited in Levine and Tyson, 1990). Indeed the main criticism of team systems is that they achieve this by driving workers to work harder as well as smarter (Parker and Slaughter, 1988). This is accomplished by reducing the amount of time individuals are idle. In consequence, work pace is an important source of the intra-union debate surrounding team systems, especially in the auto industry. It is important to understand, however, that productivity gains do not come solely from "speedup" under the team approach; Just-in-time inventory and production techniques, extensive union-management consultation, job rotation, and balancing of work assignments to equalize work load are all important features. One important avenue of enhanced productivity is the elimination of whole classifications of indirect labor, including the reduction of supervisory labor consequent to greater self-management on the part of the workforce.

Lawler (1986) finds that team efforts can yield much better results than limited participation programs like quality circles. Krafcik and MacDuffie (1989) conclude that the type of management used in automotive assembly plants is the most critical factor for productivity; their measure of the degree to which management strategy is "fragile/lean" includes team production as a component. McKersie and Klein (1985), conclude that team production systems, or other socio-technical approaches to large-scale work reorganization, have much larger potential productivity payoffs than less extensive efforts that focus primarily on greater worker involvement—with estimated increases of 30 to 40 percent over a period of several years, as opposed to perhaps 10 to 20 percent. The only important dissenting study is Katz, Kochan, and Keefe (1987a), who find little positive effect of team organization after controlling for the increased participation that usually accompanies it. Thus, the main academic debate about teams is not whether or not they increase productivity, but whether their large effects are primarily due to participation, changed work methods, or other aspects of their operation.

Gainsharing

Gainsharing plans attempt to measure gains in efficiency against a base ratio of inputs to outputs; variants include the Scanlon Plan (traditional and modified), the Rucker Plan, and the Improshare Plan, each characterized by a different formula (Schuster, 1984). Bonuses, over and above regular wages, are paid if future ratios show improvement over the base, giving workers a direct incentive to increase productivity. The Scanlon Plan, which originated in the union sector in the late 1930s and was popularized in the 1950s, adds to this a philosophy of union-management cooperation and a committee structure to organize worker suggestions for productivity improvement; it is perhaps best described as a combination of participation and gainsharing (Lesieur, 1958).

Gainsharing is not feasible in all work situations. Where a viable plan can be established, and actually delivers higher earnings for greater work effort, gainsharing can apparently produce considerable gains in productivity. Probably this is because it combines the considerable power of money as a motivator, the stimulus of group participation and support for individual work effort, and in union firms, the added benefits of union-management cooperation (Schuster, 1984). The U.S. General Accounting Office (1981) found a reduction of labor costs averaging 29 percent for firms with gainsharing plans that had been in place more than five years. And Bullock and Lawler (1984) estimate that productivity is enhanced to some extent in 50 to 80 percent of reported cases. In her study of unionized Wisconsin firms, Voos (1989 and 1987) found gainsharing to be relatively rare (in about 6.6 percent of the unionized Wisconsin companies studied) but consistently evaluated to have larger effects on productivity, flexibility in utilizing labor, and firm performance than many other programs, including employee stock ownership plans, profit-sharing plans, joint in-plant committees addressing specialized issues, or local area labor-management cooperation committees.[2]

Profit-sharing

There are relatively few careful studies measuring the effectiveness of profit-sharing per se, and unfortunately, studies usually fail to distinguish between deferred and nondeferred plans, a distinction that is of major significance. Weitzman and Kruse (1990) provide a wide-ranging listing of relevant studies, many on non-U.S. cases, but they tend to blur the distinction between gainsharing and profit-sharing; considerable profit-sharing research has been done in a context of employee ownership or participation, providing further problems of interpretation. Nonetheless, Weitzman and Kruse conclude, "Taken as a whole, the many different parts add up to a fairly coherent picture of a weak positive link between profit-sharing and productivity."

References to a few of the better studies follow. Cable and FitzRoy (1980a and 1980b) and FitzRoy and Kraft (1986 and 1987) provided econometric evidence that profit-sharing—accompanied by considerable substantive worker participation—increases productivity in a German context. The programs they evaluated differ so markedly from the deferred profit-sharing plans, absent worker participation, which are common in the U.S. that it is difficult to conclude much from their studies. Kruse (1988a) and Mitchell et al. (1990) produced econometric evidence that U.S. profit-sharing programs have positive productivity effects, although both studies are beset with limitations. For instance, Mitchell et al. used sales per worker to measure productivity, an index that confounds quantity and price effects, were unable to control for worker quality or capital inputs, and used a survey with an extremely low response rate, raising the specter of selection bias. They simultaneously reported that, "The limited case research on profit-sharing plans suggests that these programs are much less effective than gainsharing plans in influencing individual or group performance" (p. 72). Voos (1989 and 1987) found that managers agree that the gains from profit-sharing are generally smaller than those from gainsharing, which is also Blinder's (1990) summary view. See also Mitchell and Broderick (forthcoming) for a survey of management opinions regarding the relative efficacy of these plans. Lawler (1986, p. 164) described some successful uses of profit-sharing but concedes that "in most organizations, profits are so far beyond the direct influence of most employees that profit-based bonuses are simply not likely to be effective motivators."

Employee Stock Ownership Plans

Detailed descriptions of these programs and useful reviews regarding their effects include Blasi (1988) and Conte and Svejnar (1990). Conte and Svejnar (1988) provided econometric evidence from the estimation of production functions that ESOPs improve productivity, but in their 1990 review of extant studies, the authors admit that whether or not ESOPs aid company productivity is unclear, but positive effects are more likely where ownership is combined with participation. Rosen, Klein, and Young (1986) made a positive evaluation of ESOPS, but admit that the typical plan is one that provides only a small percentage of ownership, consequently only small financial incentives for increased work effort, little employee exercise over management, or sense of participation. Consequently, they function more as an additional fringe benefit than a true "stake" in the enterprise, and have little measurable impact on productivity. Voos (1989 and 1987) found ESOPs to have the smallest positive effects of any program studied. Blasi (1990) concludes that, "The evidence shows that employee ownership in ESOPs is not bad for companies and has a positive effect on productivity if combined with formal, organized labor-management problem solving in participation groups." Blasi also points out, however, that employee involvement is "only thinly sprinkled" among current ESOPs, that unionized and part-time employees are often excluded from the plan, and that stock is typically distributed according to relative salaries, "with huge premiums for higher-paid employees."

Other Innovations

Few academic studies systematically measure productivity effects for *information-sharing, job enrichment, job enlargement*, or *job rotation*. One exception is Kleiner and Bouillon (1988) who report no statistically significant relationship between information-sharing and productivity, according to a survey of 106 executives. From qualitative evidence, we would judge them to have small effects at best. *Suggestion boxes* or *suggestion systems* are not judged by most experts to bring large or regular productivity increases.

Appendix Endnotes

[1]   "New design plants" are newly opened plants which, in Lawler's view, are designed to maximize workers' involvement in their jobs and in decisionmaking. Thus, they tend to bring together the elements of many of the other programs including work teams and gainsharing.

[2]   In some of Voos' published work gainsharing and profit-sharing plans were reported together because of small sample size for the gainsharing plans alone. However mean effects for the gainsharing programs were always greater than for the profit-sharing plans; means were 1.04 versus 0.67 for productivity, 0.76 versus 0.16 for flexibility, and 0.72 versus 0.33 for profitability.

Industrial Relations and the Reorganization of Work in West Germany: Lessons for the U.S.

Lowell Turner

Introduction: Japanese Success Spurs Work Reorganization

In recent decades, the extraordinary rise of Japanese manufacturing, the general intensification of world market competition, and the rapid advance of microelectronic technology have posed competitive problems for U.S. industry. Central to Japanese success are patterns of work organization and industrial relations quite different from those in the U.S.: on the one hand, the flexible deployment of shop-floor labor, often in teams; on the other hand, harmonious labor-management relations in which managers build consensus with enterprise unionists.[1] The outcome is high productivity and top-quality production. How can traditional U.S. industry—with its clearly spelled out work rules, authoritarian management, and combative labor-management relations—compete with "team Japan"?[2]

Some have suggested that to compete in the new world economy we must not only adopt Japanese production practices but also abandon Western traditions of independent unionism. When U.S. trade unionists naturally resist, they are criticized as "adversarial." My argument is that U.S. managers do not need to break the unions or to transform them into subordinate enterprise unions in order to gain the benefits of new work organization. Rather than looking only to Japan for ways to get us out of our current competitive predicament, we should also look to Europe. A particularly useful example is West Germany, whose world-class export

Rather than looking only to Japan for ways to get us out of our current competitive predicament, we should also look to Europe.

strength is widely recognized. Here we find an approach that is more compatible with our own industrial relations traditions; and hence more likely to be acceptable to U.S. workers and thus viable in the long run. As the West German case suggests, and as this chapter demonstrates, productivity-enhancing work reorganization, including various forms of participation and teamwork, is not only compatible with but may even be enhanced by strong, independent unionism.

It is important to consider the West German experience because of the increasingly obvious limitations to the wholesale adoption of the Japanese approach in the U.S. In the past ten years or so, American managers have been both frightened by and infatuated with the Japanese model. In the scurry to make firms and plants more competitive, managers have introduced new technologies, redesigned products, reorganized production and supplier networks, moved toward "lean production systems" (Krafcik, 1988), and in some cases attempted to introduce new shopfloor teamwork and cooperative employee or labor-management relations (Katz, 1985; Kochan, Katz, and McKersie, 1986; Luria, 1986). With both the success of the Japanese and the pressure of intensified competition in mind, American managers have moved to reorganize work and to adopt new innovations in employee compensation and participation.[3] The new wisdom suggests that we need to motivate workers, to draw out their input and commitment rather than treat them as cogs in a machine. Where firms are able to avoid unions, they do so, arguing that the old adversarial unionism is incompatible with new participation and teamwork.[4] Where unions are entrenched, managers have often tried to trade some union engagement in managerial decisions in return for a loosening of work rules.

There is, however, an inherent instability in the attempts of managers either to challenge unions directly, to move around them, or to transform local unions into Japanese-style enterprise unions. This instability lies in the fact that, in spite of the long-term decline of union membership density in the U.S., a tradition of strong, independent unionism remains firmly entrenched throughout much of U.S. manufacturing. Managerial initiatives that aim to weaken union strength and independence meet with resistance; and the conflicts that are played out, even if management is successful in the short run, often undermine the trust neces-

> *The new wisdom suggests that we need to motivate workers, to draw out their input and commitment rather than treat them as cogs in a machine.*

sary to build genuine worker participation and cooperative industrial relations over the longer term.[5]

It has also become increasingly evident that for workers and society there are serious problems with the Japanese approach. These include speedup, intensely competitive intra-workforce relations, and the absence of independent representation in a system where unions function as an arm of management (Kamata, 1973; Dohse, Jürgens, and Malsch, 1985; Deutschmann, 1987; Fujita, 1988). While we may need elements of the Japanese system in order to get U.S. industry back on sound competitive footing, we do not want or need the whole model.

What we need, rather, is to develop our own approach, starting from the institutions already in place. I would suggest that as we cast about for new ideas—for elements of other models that can be incorporated at home—we look not just to Japan but to Western Europe as well, with its traditions of independent labor organization that are closer to our own.[6]

While we may need elements of the Japanese system in order to get U.S. industry back on sound competitive footing, we do not want or need the whole model.

The Argument: Look to Europe as well as to Japan

Not too long ago, it was fashionable in policy and academic circles to view Europe as a region of the advanced industrial world that was in decline. The tired "old country" European societies had spent their postwar economic miracles and were now beset by the demands of special-interest groups, especially labor. Burdened by high wages, rigid labor markets, and supposedly excessive welfare spending, the countries of Western Europe, in this view, had stagnated and could no longer muster the resources for research and development, new investment, and technologies required in today's markets (Olson, 1982; Scott, 1985). "Eurosclerosis" became a catchword to describe the decline, as policymakers in Washington looked to their own free market approaches or to the competitive challenge from Japan.

Just as suddenly, it seems, Eurosclerosis has vanished from the discourse, replaced by concerns with the "European juggernaut" as 1992 approaches.[7] Among other things, exciting developments in new work organization, technological change, and industrial relations have come into focus in these societies (Kern and Schumann, 1984,

1989). In particular, West Germany stands out as a major industrial power with large export surpluses, coping well so far with the Japanese trade challenge, with an active welfare state, and a strong labor movement to boot.[8]

As an indicator of contrasting patterns of industrial relations, we will consider evidence from the West German and U.S. auto industries, comparing stable and successful industrial relations practices in West Germany with more problematic developments in the U.S., to see what lessons there might be from this non-Japanese source. The West German auto industry in the 1980s offers an example of ongoing work reorganization, excellent industry performance, stable but changing industrial relations, and a strong union role, in which independent, unionized works councillors were increasingly integrated into processes of managerial decisionmaking (Jürgens, Malsch, and Dohse, 1989; Streeck, 1989). In order to generalize the argument, we will also look briefly at two other industries: telephone services and apparel.

For a general picture, we look first at the nature of industrial relations in West Germany (for which the auto industry, as in the U.S., often plays a pattern-setting role). To understand how this system actually works in the contemporary period, we then look in some detail at the politics of work reorganization in West Germany's largest autoworks: the Volkswagen plant in Wolfsburg.[9] We contrast the German approach with that to date in a variety of U.S. auto factories, including the well-known New United Motor Manufacturing, Inc. (NUMMI) plant in Fremont, California. The detailed comparison allows us to ponder what the U.S. can learn from German experience.

Industrial Relations in West Germany

In some ways, the development of postwar industrial relations in West Germany parallels developments in Japan. In both countries, resurgent socialist labor movements were defeated by conservative, probusiness forces in the early 1950s as a new industrial relations order took hold. When the Adenauer government passed the Works Constitution Act in 1952, the West German labor movement lost a major political battle. This Act set up a dual system, in which plant-level works councils were legally separated from union control.[10] As the years went by, the labor movement's stated his-

The West German auto industry in the 1980s offers an example of ongoing work reorganization, excellent industry performance, stable but changing industrial relations, and a strong union role.

220

toric mission of the transformation of society gave way to negotiations with employers, employer associations, and political groupings within the capitalist system for immediate worker gains and modest social reforms (Bergmann and Müller-Jentsch, 1983; Markovits, 1986).

But the "taming" of the West German labor movement was a far cry from the defeat of independent unionism and the incorporation of organized labor into enterprise unions in Japan. West German labor retained its independence through a structure of sixteen national industrial unions, organized into one labor federation (the *Deutscher Gewerkschaftsbund,* or DGB).[11] Although the allied occupation forces would not let West German unions have a *centralized* labor movement (the DGB is formally decentralized, as is the AFL-CIO in the U.S., with power residing in the member unions), unionists settled for a *cohesive* labor movement (see below). In spite of the perceived danger of company unionism (called "yellow unionism" in Germany) inherent in the dual system, the works councils, especially in the auto industry, came to be dominated by members of DGB unions and increasingly became vehicles for the expression of union interests.

The structure and postwar evolution of industrial relations in West Germany have been well described at length elsewhere (for useful recent English-language presentations, see Bergmann and Müller-Jentsch, 1983; Markovits, 1986; Katzenstein, 1987; Thelen, 1987; and Berghahn and Karsten, 1987; for the best English-language study of industrial relations in the West German auto industry, see Streeck, 1984). The structure—required and permissible activities of works councils, unions, and managers—within this system is well regulated by law, but the actual behavior of the parties as well as the negotiated outcomes are very much the product of political and organizational decisions and the relative success of contending strategies within the legal framework. It is both the laws *and* the outcomes of particular strategies, conflicts, and negotiations that have shaped the current institutional arrangements.

The key characteristics of contemporary industrial relations in West Germany, in its actual workings, are:

1. Works councils legally independent of both union and management, democratically elected by the entire workforce, empowered by law, precedence, and plant- and firm-level agreements to consult with manage-

> *The "taming" of the West German labor movement was a far cry from the defeat of independent unionism and the incorporation of organized labor into enterprise unions in Japan.*

221

ment *prior* to the implementation of decisions affecting personnel (including work organization and the use of new technology). In many cases, they participate actively in managerial decisionmaking processes (with veto rights), especially in matters of personnel policy (such as hiring, firing, training and retraining, and reassignment in the event of work reorganization and technological change);

2. Close union–works council relations, with the works councils usually dominated by union members, who are chosen to run either individually or as part of a list from the ranks of the union-organized shop stewards; works councillors are thus often union activists who work closely with the local union office as well as the shopfloor union representatives (in representational work that is significantly overlapping);

3. Regional collective bargaining that is nationally coordinated by centralized unions and employer associations and that establishes guidelines for pay levels and groupings as well as working hours and conditions, setting the framework within which managers and works councillors operate and negotiate for the contractual period; and

4. A cohesive labor movement, organized into one principal labor federation, the DGB, composed of sixteen industrial unions. Although the DGB is formally decentralized (Wilensky, 1976, p. 51), the federation and labor movement as a whole are given relative cohesiveness by the small number of unions, the industrial (and often multi-industry) and centralized nature of these unions, and perhaps most importantly, the centralizing role of one dominant union: the Metalworkers' Union (IG Metall).[12]

> **There are simply many things that management cannot do without first consulting the works council.**

How does this industrial relations system work in practice? From a management point of view, there are simply many things, especially in areas of personnel policy, training, and work organization, that management cannot do without first consulting the works council. In areas such as the introduction of new technology and job design, management is required to give information to the works council and listen to comments and suggestions prior to implementation (Works Constitution Act, Article 90). Once the consultation obligation is fulfilled, however, management often does what it wants in these areas, regardless of the wishes of the works council. But in other areas, such as staffing, pay levels, and training for the new jobs (Articles 87, 95, 98, 99), management must either get agreement from the works council or, in the event of stalemate, face the prospect of labor board proceedings. In spite of West German industry's often-cited shopfloor flexibility, there are myriad personnel issues involved and management is not free to reorganize work without extensive discussion and negotiation with the works council. While management decisionmaking along with the implementation of new work organization may be slowed down in this consensus-building process (and the actual content of decisions may be changed), once agreement is reached, management has an important ally in the works council for winning workforce acceptance of the changes and smoothing implementation.

Works councils are often in a position to force managers to consider the interests of the workforce and occasionally broader social interests.

From the point of view of worker representation, there are two institutional vehicles for the expression of interests in this dual system: the union and the works council. For the works council, consultation and codetermination rights guaranteed in the Works Constitution Act (first established in 1952 and subsequently amended and strengthened in 1972) ensure an integration of sorts into the processes of managerial decisionmaking. This integration can range from marginal to a rather deep penetration, depending on the particular industry, firm, and/or plant. Works councillors are elected by the entire workforce, serving part-time in smaller plants, with a mix of both part-time and full-time councillors in larger plants. They work under a "peace obligation" (Article 74) and a "trustful cooperation" clause (Article 2), which together require that they work with management in the interest of a smoothly running production of goods or services. The integration into managerial decisionmaking processes and the fact that they are elected by a plant workforce combine to mean that works councillors generally consider closely the interests of the firm and/or plant.

On the other hand, as the most strongly organized presence among the workforce, the dominant union in a given industry is usually in a position to select candidates and win most of the positions on the works council.[13] Works council majorities are thus typically made up of active unionists with histories of participation in the internal politics and education of rather centralized national unions. Thus, active unionists operating from bases in national industrial unions in the dual system find themselves in a position to directly influence firm decisionmaking—to promote workforce interests as well as national union and broader working-class interests as well as to facilitate the smooth operation of the firm by supporting negotiated conditions of work and terms of change. In practice, works councils are often in a position to force managers to consider the interests of the workforce and occasionally broader social interests. Managers, on the other hand, are in a position to force works councillors to consider the interests of the firm and/or plant. The result is negotiated solutions to plant- and firm-level problems.[14]

> *The expansion of the use of works councils as arenas for the expression of union positions has arguably contributed to the flexibility and continued strength of West German unions.*

The union, for its part, must consider the interests and point of view of its most influential members at the local and often regional and national levels: the works councillors. This is another way of saying that unions must closely consider firm interests. On the other hand, the union has two important avenues for interest articulation within the industrial relations arena: regional (nationally coordinated) collective bargaining at an industrywide or even multi-industry level; and the works councils at the plant and firm levels. Unions thus have effective instruments for the expression of interests both at a centralized level (in negotiations and sometimes open conflict with the highly centralized employer associations of West German industry) and at a decentralized level (through union influence at the plant and firm levels embodied in the dominant corps of union-oriented works councillors. In an era of shopfloor work reorganization, the role of the works councils has expanded along with the efforts of the unions to disseminate information and exert influence at this level. One can identify a decentralizing trend within West German industrial relations and the building of plant- and firm-level "productivity coalitions" (Streeck, 1987). But as Thelen (1987) has persuasively argued, centralization and decentralization, at least in the case of IG Metall, are no zero-sum game. Far from undermining central union strength, the expansion of the use of works councils as arenas for the expression of union positions has arguably contributed to the flexibility and continued strength of West German unions in a period of worldwide union weakness.

Auto workers make up 40 percent of the membership of IG Metall and play a leading role in policymaking and pattern setting within the union. Among the auto workers, negotiations at Volkswagen have often produced breakthroughs and set patterns for negotiations at other firms. In the postwar period, a distinctive "social partnership" model of industrial relations has evolved at VW, based on and rooted in the West German system of industrial relations.

Social Partnership at Wolfsburg: The VW Model[15]

Like all German auto firms, Volkswagen is a product of special historical and market circumstances.[16] Created by the Nazis in 1938, the Volkswagen plant at Wolfsburg (then and now the largest auto plant in West Germany) entered the postwar period with no union tradition. It was located in a rural company town (near the northern border of what was previously East Germany), with a workforce demoralized by the war and military defeat, fearful that the plant would be shut by British military occupation authorities.[17] The result was a company-dominated works council at Wolfsburg after the war (analogous to company unionism in the U.S.), with IG Metall membership of around 20 percent in the early 1950s and a cooperative labor-management relationship dominated by common survival fears and company paternalism.

But IG Metall turned things around at Wolfsburg in the 1950s and 1960s. Working within the framework of labor-management cooperation, IG Metall made use of the dual system to run candidates in the works council elections, securing its first works council majority in 1955 (Koch, 1987, pp. 89–91). From that date forward, the union has steadily increased membership levels in the plant and extended its domination of the works council, winning its biggest majority in the 1987 elections.[18] IG Metall has managed to do this without disrupting a labor-management "partnership," one that the workforce has supported since the early postwar period.

The key elements of the VW model are:

— cooperative or "social partnership" relations between labor and management;

— the close association of the union and the works council;

— considerable engagement of the works council in the processes of managerial decisionmaking;

Working within the framework of labor-management cooperation, IG Metall made use of the dual system to run candidates in the works council elections, securing its first works council majority in 1955.

— unity within the works council and union, so that differences regarding critical issues such as policy and candidate selection are hammered out internally and a united front is presented in negotiations with management;

— a high rate of union membership and a strong union shopfloor presence (over 1,000 shop stewards out of 62,000 employees);

— virtual lifetime pay and employment security for the workforce;

— a management (from top to bottom) that is trained to listen to the concerns of workforce representatives and to seek consensus prior to the implementation of policy;

— and last but not least, a firm that is highly successful in world markets, whose management and labor representatives at least in the past have regarded "cooperative conflict resolution" at VW as a source of competitive advantage in the marketplace.[19]

> In the VW Model, organizational and technological changes were preceded by extensive negotiations between management and works council.

How has the model fared in the past decade and a half of intensified market pressure? On the whole, the answer is "quite well." VW survived the market crises in 1973–75 (the demise of the Beetle; worldwide economic recession) and from 1979 to 1982 (an even deeper recession and a general crisis for automakers in advanced industrial societies) without either major union concessions, layoffs (workforce reductions occurred principally by means of early retirement and voluntary buy-outs), or plant closures. Both the works council and management have come up with new production and/or organizational concepts that have been successfully implemented, as the following two examples show. The works council promoted a new pay grouping agreement (called LODI) that took effect in 1981 and was designed to trade pay protection for the workers against greater flexibility in labor allocation for management.[20] For its part, management has rapidly introduced new technology, including the famed Halle 54 (the most automated final automobile assembly line in the world), and has introduced new job design concepts such as the *Anlagenführer* ("systems monitor"), who supervises the technology and intervenes when necessary, in a production job that reintegrates tasks and has proven popular with workers (Kern and Schumann, 1984, pp. 40ff.; 1989; Jürgens, Malsch, and

226

Dohse, 1989, pp. 306–10). All of the above organizational and technological changes were preceded by extensive negotiations between management and works council; implementation was based on prior consensus and was facilitated by both sides.[21]

The model, however, is currently facing new sources of stress. In part the new tension is a result of current and predicted intensified market competition, as Japanese and Korean firms expand market share in the European market and older competitors such as Fiat and Peugeot show new strength, and everyone braces for 1992. The new tension is also a result of past success, both for VW as a firm and for the VW industrial relations model. Along with the firm's market success has gone increased employment levels, so that VW now finds itself in a position of potentially serious cost disadvantage. For example, from 1978 to 1986 in Europe, Ford increased production volume by 17 percent while reducing employment by 20 percent; Fiat increased production by 15 percent and reduced employment by 40 percent; but VW increased production by 5 percent while *increasing* employment by 22 percent (*Der Spiegel,* March 1989, p. 130).

VW now finds itself in a position of potentially serious cost disadvantage.

In spite of record sales in 1988, therefore, management is determined to cut costs and employment levels in the coming years. Currently under discussion and negotiation between management and the works council is management's 21-point cost-cutting program, first submitted to the works council in October 1987. In addition to anticipated steady workforce reductions through attrition, management proposes significant workforce concessions in such areas as break time. The responses of worker representatives vary. On the one hand, they recognize the competitive needs of the firm (as they always have; this is a hallmark of the VW model) and will thus go along with what they think necessary for market success, including gradual workforce reductions. On the other hand, they see these proposals as part of a new managerial aggressiveness, the product of a new breed of younger VW managers (many brought in from outside the VW "family") more attentive to market pressures than to VW traditions and the cooperative industrial relations model. Works councillors and shop stewards worry about the increased possibility of future conflict if the "new managers" push too hard.

For their part, worker representatives have also displayed a new willingness to take initiative and mobilize the workforce when it is considered necessary. The VW model, as we have seen, has been based on cooperative relations and engagement between management and the works council; for the most part this has not included the workforce directly. But since the extensive shopfloor discussions and mobilization around the shorter workweek demands in 1984 (although the national IG Metall strike did not include VW), the works council at Wolfsburg has shown an increased propensity to involve the workforce.[22]

The increased willingness of both sides to push in the present period raised talk of a possible strike over contract negotiations in 1990. Both of the groups were clearly testing each other in the new climate and jockeying for position as market developments made clear the need for major adjustment and ongoing work reorganization. In the meantime, both sides have moved forward with new teamwork-oriented organization initiatives. Management has initiated quality circles, which the works council accepted in 1986 after a two-year debate and after the inclusion of strong provisions to include union and works council in the implementation. They have begun to set up production teams in the stamping plant and teams of systems monitors—always after extensive discussion with works councillors. From the union/works council side, the major organizational initiative of the past two years is the campaign for group work.

> As is true for all U.S. and West German auto firms, VW management is pressing toward team forms of organization.

As is true for all U.S. and West German auto firms, VW management is pressing toward team forms of organization in the search for lower costs, higher productivity, production flexibility, and better product quality (inspired by Japanese success). As management enters a period of what it perceives to be trial-and-error adjustment in which new forms of work organization are tried out in various parts of the plant, company concepts regarding the specific shape of teamwork remain rather vague. The works council, on the other hand, has adopted a set of well-developed, IG Metall–promoted group work concepts and is bargaining with management for implementation.

The union framework proposal for group work, developed at national union headquarters for the entire auto industry, includes twelve main principles:[23]

1. a broad assignment of varying tasks for the group (with long cycle times);

2. group competence in decisionmaking in such areas

as job rotation, division of work, quality control, and training needs;

3. decentralization of the plant decisionmaking structure;

4. selection of production organization and technology suitable for group work (based on decentralized technology and production concepts);

5. equal pay for group members;

6. equal opportunity for all to participate in group work, including special training where necessary for the disabled and the socially disadvantaged ("group work as solidaristic work organization");

7. support for the personal and occupational development of individuals and the group;

8. regular group meetings, at least one hour per week;

9. representation of group interests within the established plant system of interest representation;

10. voluntary participation in the groups;

11. pilot projects to test the functioning of group work before broader implementation;

12. a joint steering committee at the firm level, with equal labor and management representation, to oversee and coordinate the implementation of group work and the activities of the groups.

The general works council (for all the VW plants) adopted the IG Metall group work concept in 1988.

The general works council (for all the VW plants) adopted the IG Metall group work concept in 1988. In a remarkable forward to the twelve principles (Riffel and Muster, 1989), the general works council makes the following argument for its promotion of union-developed work reorganization:[24]

We need to move toward group forms of organization both because Japanese and American auto firms are doing this and to get rid of Taylorism. We are conscious of the particular role of VW (as a model), and of the general position of West Germany as an export nation now facing serious competitive challenges from countries with much weaker social rights (including

229

weaker unions). We need to develop a democratic work culture to show the way for modern democracies; our task is to meet world market risks with our own strengths, those that emerge from a democratic firm culture (as at VW) based on social progress. Good performance and top quality do not come in the long run from pressure or incentives but from interesting work, good teamwork, and appropriate opportunities for input.

The prospects for work "humanization" at Wolfsburg and other VW plants look better than ever.

As of 1990, the council at Wolfsburg was engaged in active negotiations with management toward both the adoption of a plant-level agreement on group work and the establishment of pilot projects in the plant.[25] At the same time, the Wolfsburg works council was beginning to spread group work discussions down through the ranks of the shop stewards and the workforce, to include the workers in the campaign and in the formulation of the precise shape of group work proposals for particular areas of the plant.[26] The works council strategy is to engage shop stewards and workers in the design and implementation of new group organization. There appears to be an active process now in motion that management will curtail only with great difficulty. In any case, it dovetails in important ways with managerial goals for improving productivity, product quality, and worker responsibility.

Both sides at Wolfsburg recognize that new forms of teamwork are coming in one form or another.[27] Both sides appear to agree that the works council has taken the primary initiative in this regard (so that management is negotiating changes in the union/works council plan, as opposed to vice versa), and both sides claim to be optimistic that a settlement will be found, based on overlapping interests and a joint learning process as pilot projects are examined. This is a period of uncertainty for both the VW industrial relations model and the future of work organization. Given the past track record and current cooperative negotiating processes, it is also a period when the prospects for work "humanization" at Wolfsburg and other VW plants look better than ever and when the odds for successful adjustment and work reorganization at VW are good (especially in comparative perspective).

One cannot claim, of course, that the industrial relations model at Volkswagen is primarily responsible for firm success in the past decade. In fact, Fiat—another very successful European auto firm of the 1980s—went on the attack against its unions, and successfully marginalized much of the previous influence of worker representation. At VW, the move upmarket toward "high quality, diversified production" (Sorge and Streeck, 1988), the development of appropriate designs, good marketing, and investment decisions (including the purchase of SEAT in Spain for low-end market production) were all probably necessary for continuing firm success. In addition, VW has benefitted from access to the protected markets of some of its trade partners. France and Italy, for example, have largely excluded Japanese auto imports while leaving their markets open for other Common Market members such as West Germany. In Germany itself, an informal "understanding" has slowed down the rate of Japanese automobile import penetration. On the other hand, Japanese market share for autos has risen steadily in West Germany to 15 percent and in Western Europe as a whole to 11 percent; and the rate is much higher in traditional German markets such as Belgium, the Netherlands, and Denmark.

VW has benefitted from access to the protected markets of some of its trade partners. France and Italy, for example, have largely excluded Japanese auto imports.

But the industrial relations model at VW arguably made all of these possible, as works councillors and managers engaged in ongoing consensus-building negotiations that resulted in smooth implementation of production decisions, including model changes, new technology, and work reorganization. VW and Fiat together—the two current sales leaders in the European market—perhaps show that in a period of intense work reorganization, worker interest representation must either be integrated into managerial decisionmaking or it must be marginalized. In this regard, the U.S. auto industry is a middle case. Interest representation in some cases is being integrated in core plants but in other cases is being marginalized, as in many parts supplier plants and some of the Japanese transplants.

How characteristic is VW-Wolfsburg of industrial relations and work reorganization at West German auto plants? There are clearly differences from firm to firm and plant to plant. At Opel-Bochum, for example, management has a more hard-line (GM-style) tradition and the works council is deeply divided into two contending factions. Thus, management takes a freer hand in work organization decisions. What is remarkable in the West German auto industry, however, is the narrow range of plant-level outcomes.[28] Everywhere, IG Metall and works councils are bargaining for the union-developed group work concepts, union-dominated works councils are gaining greater voice in managerial decisionmaking, and work reorganization proceeds apace based on negotiated plans. The narrow range of outcomes and the stability of worker representation are particularly noteworthy in comparison to the wide range of outcomes in the U.S. auto industry.

Work Reorganization in the U.S. Auto Industry: A Great Diversity of Outcomes

U.S. auto firms—General Motors in particular—have a head start of several years over West German firms in the radical shift toward shopfloor teamwork. Nonetheless, none of the American Big Three have achieved a smooth companywide transition. Managerial initiatives and union/workforce responses have resulted in a wide range of outcomes throughout the auto industry, from new nonunion plants (Japanese transplants), to plants with traditional, conflictual industrial relations, to plants with traditional but more cooperative industrial relations, and finally to plants in which team organization is accompanied by an integration of the union into new levels of managerial decisionmaking. The latter cases offer variants on a new model for the U.S. auto industry. The problem is in attempting to spread the model to established plants and greenfield sites alike. We will look first at the widely heralded new "best practice" model at NUMMI, then briefly review representative efforts at innovation at other facilities.

The old GM plant in Fremont opened in 1962 and closed in 1982. During its twenty years of operation, the plant typified work organization and industrial relations in the U.S. auto industry. Standardized goods (with many options) were produced for usually dependable mass markets in a production system notable for the many job classifications (well over 100), a seniority-based system of "job control," high absenteeism, very high grievance rates, and an adversarial industrial relations system that could be termed an "armed truce" (from Harbison and Coleman, 1951). The workforce at Fremont earned a reputation as one of GM's most militant, but this militance was not at all unusual for the U.S. auto industry.

U.S. auto firms—General Motors in particular—have a head start of several years over West German firms in the radical shift toward shopfloor teamwork.

In 1982, with three weeks' notice for the workforce, the plant shut down and stayed closed for two and a half years. When it reopened, it did so as a joint venture of GM and Toyota, called New United Motor Manufacturing, Inc. (NUMMI).[29] GM provided the plant and dealer networks, while Toyota provided the management system. The UAW (United Auto Workers) bargained hard to secure union recognition prior to the plant opening and insisted that former workers be rehired. Although the workforce size was scaled down considerably (because the new plant had only one production line instead of two in the old plant, was run more efficiently, and because of greater outsourcing, such as seat production), and some screening took place, in the end most workers from the old plant who wanted jobs at NUMMI were hired, including former union activists.[30]

The workforce had been traumatized by its long period of dislocation and returned to work with a willingness to try new ways of doing things. What they found was a completely new system of work organization and industrial relations, one that so far has retained the loyalty of the majority, as indicated in subsequent union election outcomes.

Within one production and two skilled-trades classifications at NUMMI, workers are divided into teams, usually of four members and one leader. The production team leader—a union member—is carefully selected using a detailed set of criteria decided by the local union and management, and is trained to play a genuine leadership role—coordinating work, checking parts and equipment, problem solving, doing some repair work, filling in for absent members, keeping records, leading team meetings, looking for ways to encourage quality and productivity, and encouraging members to provide input. Each team member usually rotates through at least two jobs and is expected to maintain high work standards and provide input into ways to do a better, safer, and more productive job. Management has considerable flexibility in job assignment; jobs are given to the most qualified (although these judgements can be rather arbitrary), with seniority used only to break a tie. At least in theory, group leaders (first-line management) oversee several teams as facilitators and problem solvers rather than drill sergeants. Union coordinators (who are also full-time workers) are elected to solve labor-management problems on the shopfloor. With a just-in-time parts delivery system and cooperative labor-management relations (including union leaders who sit in regularly at man-

Within one production and two skilled-trades classifications at NUMMI, workers are divided into teams, usually of four members and one leader.

233

agement meetings and participate at various levels of firm decisionmaking), the system runs smoothly and efficiently with high productivity and high-quality output.[31] Contracts provide the workers with pay comparable to other UAW-organized assembly plants, as well as employment security except in the most adverse market circumstances. The firm has made good on this promise, even when sales have slumped badly (for reasons unrelated to the quality or cost of the product).

What should we make of this system, so different from the traditional U.S. auto assembly plant? My own impression is generally favorable. There is no disputing the outcome in quality and productivity, and in the interviews I have done with NUMMI workers (including several with supporters of the more critical People's Caucus), I have yet to hear anyone say they liked the old GM system better. People like the fact that they are treated with respect, can take pride in a high-quality product, work in a clean, efficient environment, and often find their input and concerns actively solicited. Team leaders in particular are grateful for the opportunity to have more than just a job.

On the other hand, this is clearly no utopia for the workforce. The People's Caucus has built itself into a strong opposition within the union and a visible force in the plant around four issues: the pace of work and the constant pressure to work harder; the very close collaboration between union and management (the critique is that they are indistinguishable and the union no longer provides strong representation for its members); favoritism in the assignment of training, off-line jobs, and special projects; and a union that is not run democratically by its elected leaders (with too many closed-door meetings and deals made between union and management). Since 1986, the opposition has consistently gained around 40 percent of the workforce vote in union elections (about once a year, either for convention delegates or for union offices).

The extent to which these charges are true is a subject of lively debate within the union and workforce, and the way in which these issues will influence the future shape of work organization and industrial relations at NUMMI remains to be seen. What is remarkable, I think, is that many supporters of the People's Caucus are also supporters of NUMMI and see their role as striving to improve the system (by making it more humane and democratic), and that NUMMI is blessed by a lively union/workforce debate at this Toyota-run plant,

In the interviews I have done with NUMMI workers . . . I have yet to hear anyone say they liked the old GM system better.

whose management clearly aimed for and would be more comfortable with a tamer enterprise union.

What is the basis for NUMMI's success in reorganizing work? GM managers like to point to the "significant emotional event" as workers faced two years of plant closure and then returned humbled and grateful to their new jobs. But while this may or may not have been a necessary condition, it clearly was not a sufficient one. Other plants have been closed and then reopened without nearly the same kind of organizational success. What is critical is what the workers faced when they returned to work, and at NUMMI they found jobs and conditions that in many ways exceeded their expectations of life in an auto plant. The key to NUMMI's success lies in the structure and policies of management, and especially the approach to the workers taken by management from top to bottom: the emphasis on garnering input, treating people with respect, gaining consensus within the organization, offering tangible and unusual benefits such as employment security in return for worker and union cooperation, and successfully winning over key union leaders and incorporating them into the process.

NUMMI's success so far has rested very much on the ability of management to provide a system of work and rewards that has held the loyalty of the majority of the workforce and union leadership.

But the system in practice at NUMMI is not exactly the one envisioned by Toyota management. Lively local union politics demonstrate one deviation, with the clear potential to push organizational developments down a new path. Another example is NUMMI management's position in early contract bargaining that no full-time union representatives would be necessary in a consensual labor-management system. The UAW bargained hard on this subject and earned the right to have fifteen full-time representatives, in addition to the many shopfloor union coordinators. Although the Administration Caucus union leadership has not projected an independent vision of where work organization should be heading at NUMMI, this is not by any means a docile enterprise union. NUMMI's success so far has rested very much on the ability of management to provide a system of work and rewards that has held the loyalty of the majority of the workforce and union leadership.

Since 1984, GM has flown large numbers of managers from all over the country to view the Toyota-led organizational success at NUMMI. But the problem has been successfully adapting the lessons. A primary cause of failure has been the inability of plant-level management to change its traditional ways. At GM–Van Nuys, for example, GM made perhaps its most extensive effort to transfer the

NUMMI model (Mann, 1987; Turner, 1988b; Brown and Reich, 1989). But it did so by intervening in union politics in a divisive way: threatening the workforce with plant closure if it did not vote for the new contract; forcing the workforce, under even greater pressure, to vote a second time when the first effort failed; and raising worker expectations through limited "human relations" training (for the team concept) but then dashing these expectations when workers returned to the shopfloor to find many of the same old-school managers and management practices in place. The outcome was predictable: continuing intra-workforce and intra-union conflict over the new system; continuing labor-management conflict; an absence of the high-trust relations necessary for a successful team system with cooperative industrial relations (although all of this exists on paper); no great upsurge in productivity and product quality; and continuing uncertainty over the plant's future.

At its Hamtramck assembly operation in Detroit, GM made an earlier attempt, beginning in 1984, to introduce team organization along with advanced technology at this new showplace plant. But what happened here was typical of developments at several other GM plants. Workers received new training for team organization and were taught that the old ways were wrong: they would now be respected and their input in questions of production, quality, and working conditions would be actively sought on the shopfloor and in team meetings. But as soon as production problems developed, and managers felt the pressure from above to keep up steady production, they reverted to their old ways. Teams were ignored, job rotation dropped by the wayside, and management went back to ordering people around. When I visited the plant in 1988, management and the union were still trying to work out a consistent relationship, redefine the teams, and put a working team system back into place. In the meantime, Hamtramck had become a symbol for the failure of GM's expensive advanced automation solution.

Across the range of GM plants, there are positive outcomes besides NUMMI. At the Lansing plant where the Pontiac Grand Am is made, a successful team system has evolved in a process of give and take between workforce, union, and management (Turner, 1988b). Rather than attempting a wholesale "revolution," as at NUMMI, Van Nuys, and Hamtramck, labor and management have gradually developed a cooperative relationship and brought in new forms of work

236

organization on the basis of existing practices and respect for workforce rights. Participation in the teams, for example, is voluntary, and seniority remains the central criterion for job assignment (including the selection of "team coordinators"). This sort of "homegrown" solution may offer the most realistic prospect for work reorganization and new industrial relations in the U.S.[32]

At many of its other plants, GM has made less ambitious attempts at organizational innovation, often to lay the groundwork for more extensive change. But so far for GM, still the dominant U.S. auto firm, the pattern of outcomes is noteworthy for its great variation: from dramatic reorganizational success to dramatic failure; from new industrial relations to old; from innovative union roles to traditional.

Although Ford and Chrysler have shown greater organizational stability than GM (since 1979–1981, when both almost failed), these firms too are heading toward the uncertainty of team organization. Chrysler has a "Modern Operating Agreement" (for a team system) that it has negotiated for gradual implementation at some of its plants. But at other plants the agreement has been rejected by the union or workforce, causing Chrysler to put in place a "modified" MOA. Ford has been the most successful of U.S. auto firms in recent years, blessed by earlier streamlining and fortunate product decisions. But Ford, too, has seen teams as the future, and has begun to negotiate with the union for the introduction of innovative work organization in sections of its plants, without yet articulating a clear strategy.

Traditions of top-down management persist in the auto and other industries in the U.S., even where a veneer of participation and cooperation has been added on. But for organizational innovations to work, management must not merely pretend to change. Especially in heavily unionized industries such as autos, work reorganization will more likely succeed if management abandons old authoritarian traditions and works with the union to build a genuine and mutually beneficial relationship of trust. The evidence from NUMMI, Lansing, and West Germany makes it clear that independent unionism, when accepted by management, is compatible with contemporary organizational success.

In the U.S., we are still very much in an experimental stage, as demonstrated by the wide range of plant-level variation. Combining what we learn from both NUMMI and Lansing, we see that homegrown solutions including a sub-

For organizational innovations to work, management must not merely pretend to change.

237

stantial role for independent unions in managerial decision-making processes are needed. Firms appear to stand now at a critical historical juncture where the possibility exists to build new relationships and institutions of partnership with labor; but the possibility will be lost if initiatives are insincere and indirectly aimed at undermining union influence.

Lessons from Abroad?

This analysis should not be interpreted either as belittling the very real accomplishments of the UAW in the 1980s or as overlooking the intractable and growing problems faced by IG Metall. The UAW remains a pattern-setter and innovator for the U.S. labor movement, and if a new U.S. model of industrial relations emerges that promotes both market success and new union vitality it may well come out of the sea of labor-management experiments currently underway in the auto industry. At the same time, IG Metall faces high and enduring unemployment in West Germany as well as new managerial aggressiveness on issues such as flexibility of working hours and work reorganization. A shift in the locus of influence to the works councils has arguably contributed to a new "plant syndicalism" (Hohn, 1988), which has made it possible for West German managers to begin to learn the art (well-developed at U.S. auto firms) of playing one plant's workforce off against another. Moreover, the dramatic unification of Germany raises a host of new problems and uncertainties as well as opportunities for West German unions.

But the cross-national outcomes do contrast rather sharply, and these differences make clear the very real constraints faced by the UAW, regardless of leadership decisions or strategy. In fact, the UAW efforts may be a "best-case" scenario in the U.S. industrial relations climate of the 1980s. This is clear from a brief look at the telephone services and apparel industries, which together exemplify the broad (as opposed to industry- or firm-specific) nature of the U.S.–West German contrast.

In telephone services (part of a larger "information industry" that now includes telecommunications and computers), union influence in the U.S. has been challenged and undermined in the competitive turmoil subsequent to the 1984 divestiture of AT&T. National bargaining has broken down, and the unionized AT&T must now compete with nonunion MCI and US Sprint. The seven regional "Baby

Bells" pursue a range of industrial relations approaches, from adversarial to "social partnership." In this uncertain and high-pressure environment, union membership density has declined as the CWA (Communications Workers of America) fights to retain influence. In West Germany, by contrast, because the union (DPG) is integrated into management decisionmaking processes (through the personnel councils) and at the same time belongs to a more cohesive labor movement, it has been able to lead a successful coalition to prevent U.S.-style deregulation. As a result, union membership density remains high and stable while union influence in matters such as work organization grows. While new technologies and services are not introduced as rapidly in West Germany as in the U.S., the Bundespost continues to provide stable national and local telephone services and to accelerate the pace of technological and organizational change.

In the apparel industry, unions in both the U.S. and West Germany have been battered over the past two decades in the face of the massive market penetration of low-cost imports. In both countries, total employment has declined precipitously as some firms have failed and others have rationalized production. In the U.S., firms have moved to Sunbelt states, in part to get away from unions in the North. Thus, union membership density has dropped seriously, as has union influence. In West Germany, by contrast, where the law obliges firms and (union-dominated) works councils to negotiate substantial compensation for laid-off workers, the union used the crisis to build up membership density.[33] Compared to the plant location and union-avoidance strategies in the U.S., firm rationalization strategies in West Germany have contributed to a substantially greater rise in productivity in the West German apparel industry.

Parallel contrasts between the U.S. and West Germany can be seen across a range of industries, regardless of market circumstances and firm or union structure. It appears we could profitably learn from West Germany as well as Japan. These European lessons may be ones that are at once easier for us to assimilate and more appropriate for our political economy.

The lessons can be summarized as follows. Most importantly, entrenched and independent unionism is not incompatible with good production outcomes; a stable industrial relations settlement that allows for ongoing innovation is the important thing. Managers should be encouraged to

Compared to the plant location and union-avoidance strategies in the U.S., firm rationalization strategies in West Germany have contributed to a substantially greater rise in productivity.

pursue genuine strategies of workforce and union incorporation (as in West Germany, and as at NUMMI and Lansing)—they will likely be pleasantly surprised at the results, including genuine cooperation and participation.

Unions also can learn from the West German experience. It would appear that current world markets and imperatives to reorganize work require that unions, in the interest of their own survival, become integrated into processes of managerial decisionmaking. For local unions there may be a danger of loss of independence akin to enterprise unionism; but there is no viable alternative to entering into ongoing discussions and negotiations regarding critical issues such as technological change and work reorganization. The more cohesive the national labor movement as a whole, the less promising will be managerial strategies to avoid or weaken unions, and the better the chances for specific union influence (the West German experiences, in contrast to the U.S., make this apparent).

> **We can only use lessons from abroad if we adapt them for use on the basis of our own institutions.**

We can only use lessons from abroad if we adapt them for use on the basis of our own institutions. But in response to the imperatives of world market change, our institutions and practices are changing, and different futures appear to stand before us. For industrial relations in the U.S., there are at least three distinct possibilities consistent with successful work reorganization:

1. the exclusion of unions, as in the UAW's recent organizing loss at the Smyrna, Tennessee, Nissan plant, although the historical ups and downs of the labor movement in the U.S. make one wonder if such union-free environments really can continue into the indefinite future;

2. the integration of subordinate local unions into managerial processes. The Japanese model, which poses current dangers for unions in the U.S., is probably the model that NUMMI management had in mind until union politics intervened; and

3. a model that incorporates strong, independent unions that bring along their own vision of work reorganization and function as partners, albeit adversarial at times, as opposed to subordinates.

It is possible, of course, for all three models to exist alongside one another in different parts of the economy, and to some extent this is what is happening in the U.S. But it is likely that over time a dominant model will emerge, and we should not be indifferent to the outcome. Because it is closest to our own industrial relations traditions, the third scenario arguably offers the best prospects for a stable labor-management settlement in the U.S. If this is true, then we can probably learn more from the West Germans than from the Japanese as we attempt to incorporate lessons from abroad into our own domestic solutions. What the West German case demonstrates, above all, is that labor-management cooperation, shopfloor teamwork, and union integration into managerial decisionmaking processes are not incompatible with assertive, independent unionism. The argument here is that both of these are necessary for a future that combines economic success with lively industrial and political democracy.

We can probably learn more from the West Germans than from the Japanese as we attempt to incorporate lessons from abroad into our own domestic solutions.

Endnotes

[1] Quite often in Japan, in the auto industry for example, lower-level managers are the union leaders.

[2] It goes without saying that industrial relations is not the only factor contributing to competitive success; public policy and other aspects of firm strategy, which are not the topics of this essay, are also critically important. But the past decade has witnessed a growing awareness of the pivotal role of industrial relations for firm success in contemporary world markets (Altshuler et al., 1984; Dohse et al., 1985; Dyer et al., 1987; Marshall, 1987).

[3] For a useful survey of managerial programs, implemented in both union and non-union environments, see Eaton and Voos, this volume.

[4] This is certainly the Japanese view. Japanese firms that open plants in the U.S. typically adopt plant location strategies that allow them to avoid unionization. In California, for example, of seventy-five Japanese-run plants, only three include union representation.

[5] Unions, for their part, have grappled with new managerial initiatives, sometimes endorsing, sometimes questioning, often having heated internal debates, as they seek to preserve a position of influence in new working arrangements. From the union viewpoint, in spite of the growth of participatory programs, the past decade has witnessed an upsurge in adversarial management, as firms have either avoided unions, challenged them directly, or sought to undermine their influence in the workplace. Management-led cooperative or participatory programs are themselves often perceived on the workforce/union side as elements of a hidden agenda: to weaken union independence and workforce conflict potential.

[6] Katz and Sabel (1985) and Marshall (1987), for example, have done just that. But the problem with both of these perceptive analyses is a tendency to lump together a "German-Japanese model." There is, nonetheless, as these authors recognize, a very substantial difference in the role of unions and the level of industrial democracy in Japan and West Germany.

[7] This occurred well before the dramatic events of 1989 and 1990 that have opened up Eastern Europe.

[8] For the best available study in English of the contemporary West German political economy, see Katzenstein (1989).

[9] Evidence presented on the VW-Wolfsburg plant as well as for several U.S. auto plants (later in the paper) is based on a reading of contracts, agreements, newspaper articles, and other materials supplied by labor and management; a visit to each plant; and most importantly, a series of in-depth interviews with union representatives and managers at each plant.

242

10 Labor had wanted a structure of works councils that would be run by the unions. Business wanted legally independent works councils, in the hopes that these would be firm-identified and less independent. In the political battle of the early 1950s, business got its way: the strategy backfired, however, as unions came to dominate the works councils in the succeeding years (see below).

11 There are three other labor federations in West Germany: the *Deutscher Beamten Bund* (DBB), for civil servants; the *Deutsche Angestellten Gewerkschaft* (DAG), for white collar workers; and the *Christlicher Gerwerkschaftsbund Deutschlands* (CGB), a Catholic workers organization. But these three other federations have had small membership totals and have played only a minor role in West German industrial relations.

12 (a) IG Metall has served as a pattern setter in wage bargaining and in the more recent emphasis on the shorter workweek and on work reorganization; and this union is by far the largest in West Germany and within the DGB. In 1986, IG Metall had 2.6 million members out of 7.8 million total in the DGB (Kittner, 1988, pp. 54, 66, 67).

(b) Not included in this list of the four principal characteristics of postwar industrial relations in West Germany is codetermination at the top level of the firm— the legally mandated inclusion of unionists on company supervisory boards. Whereas the works councils—the other pole of codetermination—engage in daily discussions, negotiations, and representation, the supervisory boards meet only a few times a year. For the worker representatives on these boards, this is an occasion to hear of company financial and strategic planning. Boards are not an insignificant forum, and the access to information and the ability to speak out directly at the top levels has sometimes served union and works council interests, as well as smooth labor-management negotiations. But except in the iron, steel, and coal mining industries, which have parity representation on the supervisory boards, the minority position of labor on the boards has meant that codetermination at this level plays a minor role compared to the daily activities through the works councils. As Markovits (1986, pp. 59–60) puts it: "If real codetermination exists anywhere in West Germany, it does so at the plant level."

13 According to union sources, over 80 percent of all works councillors are union members, and the overwhelming majority of these are members of one of the sixteen industrial unions of the DGB.

14 Even when well integrated into a national union structure, local unions in the U.S. and elsewhere have always had to consider the interests of the plant and/or firm; if the plant closes or the firm goes under, the workforce also goes under. This was recognized long ago in the U.S. industrial relations literature (Barnett, 1926). But because they have been excluded from full information sharing, consultation, and firm decisionmaking processes, local unions have rarely had to consider firm interests as closely as do works councils in West Germany.

¹⁵ There are six large VW auto plants in West Germany, and two of these assemble cars: Wolfsburg and Emden. Wolfsburg is the original and by far the largest plant. Volkswagen has its headquarters here as does the general works council (an increasingly important body made up of representatives from each of the six individual plant works councils). As of March 1989, the Wolfsburg plant had 62,200 employees and produced about 4,000 cars per day: 2,600–2,700 Golfs, 700–800 Jettas, and 500–700 Polos (data provided by Volkswagen AG in Wolfsburg).

¹⁶ One continuing difference is that, unlike other West German auto firms that bargain collectively with the IG Metall at the regional level as members of an employer association, VW bargains separately with the regional-level union. This difference is rooted in a tradition of public ownership at VW; the firm was handed over to the federal government by the British military authorities in 1949 (Streeck, 1984, p. 40). In 1960, against the opposition of the union, the government moved to "privatize" (Koch, 1987, pp. 92ff.), selling 60 percent of the shares to small owners. But even in a minority ownership position, government influence has been important, if only because the government has had a vested interest in industrial peace at this "flagship" West German auto firm. In the 1980s, the conservative CDU/CSU-FDP government under Kohl moved to sell off its remaining shares. Although the state of Lower Saxony retains control of 20 percent of the shares, the sale of the shares of the federal government as a form of privatization has contributed to new managerial pressure on the workforce and works council (see below).

For Ford and Opel, the special circumstances are their respective positions as German subsidiaries of U.S. firms (Ford and GM, respectively); for Daimler-Benz, BMW, and Porsche, the special circumstances are the upmarket, high cost, and quality market niches they occupy as specialty producers.

¹⁷ For a useful history of industrial relations at Volkswagen, see Koch (1987). For much more condensed versions in English see Brumlop and Jürgens (1986); and Streeck (1984, pp. 40ff).

¹⁸ As of 1988, IG Metall membership at Wolfsburg was 95 percent (98 percent hourly; 85 percent white collar). In the 1987 works council elections, 87 percent of blue collar workers voted and 90 percent of these chose the IG Metall list; 81 percent of white collar workers voted and 75 percent chose IG Metall. IG Metall members won sixty-two of sixty-nine seats. (Data supplied by the IG Metall in Wolfsburg and the VW-Wolfsburg works council.)

¹⁹ Volkswagen's market success is well known in Europe, but this point is worth stressing for readers in the U.S., where declining sales make VW look like a market loser. Although VW has largely abandoned the small car market in the U.S. to the Japanese and others, the company has more than made up for this loss by success in other markets, particularly in Europe, where VW has led the field in sales volume in recent years. (VW was number one in sales in Europe for the combined years 1985–1990.)

²⁰ As shopfloor resistance to reassignment has undermined managerial flexibility, managers today complain that LODI has benefitted the workers more than management. But there are no plans to roll back LODI, and works councillors claim that management has failed to develop a unified concept and to organize itself adequately for the proper use of LODI flexibility.

²¹ The works council, however, had little advance input into managerial decision-making regarding new technology and production concepts (Article 90 of the Works Constitution Act requires only that they be informed and consulted). But the works council did agree to the changes and actively negotiated the terms of change regarding effects on the workforce prior to implementation. The current trend is toward increased advance input on the part of the works council, as we will see below in the discussion on group work.

²² This is demonstrated in: (1) the community and shopfloor campaign (which included work stoppages) in 1985–86 against the Kohl government's amendments to the Works Promotion Act (AFG article 116—the changes weaken regional/national strike potential); and (2) the spread of works council–promoted discussions among the workforce concerning proposed new work organization, in particular group work, beginning in 1989. In part, these changes result from a new generation of works council leadership; both the Wolfsburg and general works councils were led from 1984 to 1990 by Walter Hiller (who officially took office in 1986), a "new breed" counterpart to the younger, tougher managers, apparently more willing than his predecessors to engage in internal union and workforce debate and to take a strong stance toward management if necessary.

²³ These *Eckpunkte zur Gruppenarbeit* have been widely circulated to the works councils in the form of (unpublished) educational material. The presentation here is a summary translation based on Muster and Wannöffel (1989, pp. 39–54).

²⁴ This is a summary translation of the content.

²⁵ In negotiations for the first Wolfsburg pilot project in 1989, the works council and management could draw on the experience of several ongoing group work pilot projects at three other VW auto plants in Northern Germany (Muster, 1988).

²⁶ As one example, the works council held an intensive week-long seminar in January 1989—for shop stewards and works councillors from the Wolfsburg paint shop—to discuss management's plans for new technology (essentially, the building of a new paint shop) and works council plans for group work organization. On the first day, key planning managers attended and presented detailed plans for technology and organization in the new paint shop. The rest of the week was devoted to a discussion of IG Metall group work concepts, organizational and health and safety problems in the paint shop, and detailed proposals by the shop stewards (working in small groups) for the implementation of group work in their particular work areas.

For a lengthy report on this seminar, see Riffel and Muster (1989). The conference took place at the Hustedt conference grounds near Celle in Lower Saxony; I attended for three days as a participant/observer.

27 For the works council, group work appears to be an issue whose time has come. In view of the current competitive, cost-cutting needs of the firm, the works councillors cannot reasonably expect to provide the workforce with steadily increasing pay and employment levels as they have done in the past. Rather, incumbent works councillors hope to be able to advertise major gains in working conditions, in part through the coming of group work. The fact that group work proposals also include labor savings (thereby cutting costs and possibly also employment levels for the firm) gives the works council a strong negotiating position toward a management whose own teamwork concepts are not yet so well-defined.

28 During my year in West Germany, 1988–89, I studied the politics of work reorganization at five auto assembly plants, and took a background look at several others. The narrow range of work organization and industrial relations outcomes in comparison to the U.S. is quite apparent.

29 Information presented here is based mainly on in-depth interviews and discussions with workers, union representatives, and managers at NUMMI between 1987 and 1989. The following sources are also useful: for a favorable account, Krafcik (1987); for a critical interpretation, Parker and Slaughter (1988, pp. 100–22); for comparisons of NUMMI with other GM plants, Turner (1988b) and Brown and Reich (1989).

30 3,300 former GM-Fremont workers applied for the new jobs; 2,500 total were hired, about 80 percent of these from the former workforce. Compare this to the screening at other Japanese auto assembly transplants, where typically 100,000 to 200,000 applicants compete for 2,000 to 3,000 jobs.

31 NUMMI's productivity has been estimated at 40 to 50 percent higher than that of the GM-Fremont plant (cf. Krafcik, 1987) and is higher than that of any other GM plant. In quality rating studies, such as those done by *Consumer Reports* and J.D. Power, NUMMI products (first the Chevy Nova, then the Nova and Toyota Corolla, now the Geo Prizm and Corolla) are consistently rated at or near the top.

32 I have made this argument earlier, in Turner (1988; 1989).

33 This paragraph is based on data from Silvia (1987). In the women's and children's apparel segment in the U.S., for example, unionization dropped from 53 percent in 1975 to 34 percent in 1985; in West Germany, total union density in apparel grew from 22 percent in 1971 to 40 percent in 1983.

Unions, Technology, and Labor-Management Cooperation[1]

Maryellen R. Kelley and Bennett Harrison

Introduction

The introduction of new institutional arrangements for promoting collaborative problem solving between managers and workers has been one of the more widely recognized transformations in the management of American corporations since the early 1970s. Sometimes referred to as "employee participation" (EP) or "employee involvement" (EI) programs, these arrangements have taken a variety of forms in name, structure, and focus.[2] A particularly crisp analytical definition of "participation" that succeeds in covering this multitude of forms is offered by Wagner and Gooding, who see EP as a process in which "influence or decision-making is shared between hierarchical superiors and their subordinates" (Wagner and Gooding, 1987, p. 241).

In the early 1970s, EP/EI programs were initiated as experiments in improving the "quality of working life." Management reformers were concerned about worker alienation and the attendant problems of low morale, high absenteeism, and an antagonistic labor relations climate (Cole, 1982; Foulkes, 1980; Walton, 1979). This organizational innovation seems to have become even more widely utilized in the 1980s, especially among manufacturing workplaces. In one survey-based study of ninety-two large unionized manufacturing plants, over 90 percent of the EP/EI programs in place in 1986 were established after 1980 (Cooke, 1990). The wider utilization of employee involvement programs in the 1980s seems to have been

> *A particularly crisp . . . definition of "participation" is as a process in which "influence or decisionmaking is shared between hierarchical superiors and their subordinates."*

triggered by changes in external economic conditions (e.g., the heightened threat from foreign competition) and by a greater willingness on the part of managers to try any new approach that promises to stem the secular squeeze on corporate profits and stagnating productivity (Baily and Blair, 1988; Blinder, 1990; Bowles, Gordon, and Weisskopf, 1986; Glyn, Hughes, Lipietz, and Singh, 1989; Harrison and Bluestone, 1988; Kochan, Katz, and McKersie, 1986).

From management's perspective, the ultimate goal of all EP/EI programs is the improvement of work group, workplace, or company-level performance in productivity or product quality. Some programs have such explicit goals. Others are designed to achieve these goals more indirectly by focusing on improving the quality of the relationship between supervisors and employees—an objective that has been characterized by one industrial relations scholar as "reducing the adversarial nature of labor-management relations" (Cooke, 1990).

On the other hand, other objectives may be more important to the employees. Indeed, union leaders (such as Irving Bluestone of the United Automobile Workers, who has been among the strongest advocates for employee involvement in industrial decisionmaking) have argued that the goal of such programs from the union's perspective was to improve the quality of the worklives of their members. One example of this is as a way of influencing the redesign of work around new technology so as to add new skills and a greater variety of tasks to their jobs. At the very least, employees and their union representatives have expected some *quid pro quo* for their participation in joint problem-solving activities. One commonly cited expectation is that of greater job security, as manifested in policies that commit management to avoid subcontracting out of work that was previously performed inside the plant.

Many empirical studies have been conducted over the course of the last ten years, seeking to measure the level, significance, and direction of employee participation on various performance measures. But reviews of the evidence from this body of research indicate that—while EP/EI programs may positively influence the *perceptions* of both employees and managers that conditions in the workplace have improved—there is mixed evidence that participation has any tangible effects on the *behavior* of managers or workers (Cotton et al., 1988; Wagner and Gooding, 1987). Moreover, the existing research has severe methodological

> *While EP/EI programs may positively influence the perceptions of both employees and managers, there is mixed evidence that participation has any tangible effects on the behavior of managers or workers.*

248

limitations. For example, studies evaluating the effects of employee participation programs have been limited mostly to comparisons among workplaces that vary in the extent of EI/EP, or to case study reports of successful EI/EP and the changes that occur after the inception of a program. Rare is the study that systematically compares workplaces with EI/EP programs to those that have *not* instituted this innovation. An exception is the doctoral dissertation by Cooke (1990, 1989), who makes a comparison of the perceptions of managers regarding productivity changes in plants with and without EI/EP. But his comparison is limited to large unionized manufacturing plants. The majority of workplaces—even in manufacturing—are nonunion, and very small. Thus, quite apart from the fact that Cooke is measuring perceptions of change rather than actual behavioral or physical changes in output and working conditions, his research design restricts the generalizability of his findings.

In this paper, we present new empirical results in which we formally test for the influence of EP activity.

In this paper, we present new empirical results in which we formally test for the influence of EP activity. We use original data from a size-stratified random sample of over a thousand large and small establishments in the U.S. metalworking and machinery sectors. The sample includes both union and nonunion workplaces, and plants with and without an EI/EP problem-solving structure (Kelley, 1990b; Kelley and Brooks, 1988). We operationalize EP as the presence in a plant of formally constituted committees in which managers and blue collar workers meet regularly to deal with problems concerning the implementation of new technology, quality control, and other issues having to do with production. In 1986–87, almost half of the U.S. plants in this key sector had such joint labor-management problem-solving committees.

If EI/EP programs are successful innovations, we should (we will argue) expect to find higher levels of productivity, greater job security, and a tendency toward more egalitarian systems of power-sharing and control over work processes in organizations that have introduced such programs. But our multivariate regression analyses reveal no statistically significant evidence that EI/EP *by itself* has any such effects.

It is notable that few of the existing studies on the impacts of EP explicitly account for the presence or absence of unions. In some studies (Cooke, 1989, 1990), *all* of the workplaces are unionized. In other papers (for example, those reviewed by Levine and Tyson, 1990), unionization was never explicitly taken into account. Since a union is itself constructed to be an employee-initiated instrument for influencing management decisions, it would seem to us that the presence or absence of unions in the workplace should matter in determining the impacts of EP/EI programs. Although the presence of a union is popularly characterized as indicative of an adversarial or conflict-ridden and non-cooperative relationship between management and its work-force, it is also true that the presence of a union involves a number of formal mechanisms for conflict resolution through which collaborative problem solving can occur. For example, negotiation between union officials and managers is itself a form of joint problem solving and occurs routinely in the day-to-day handling of grievances, and periodically in collective bargaining over new contract terms.

Distinguishing the EP-productivity-unionization nexus in large and small companies and workplaces has been a major consideration in our research. If EP is in part a managerial response to crisis, then theories of bureaucratic control in complex organizations, and of the inflexibility of such organizations in the face of heightened global competition and accelerating product cycles, would lead us to expect the incidence and effectiveness of EP to vary by type of organization. Among relatively larger bureaucratic organizations—that is, in the branch plants (BPs) of multi-unit companies—this management innovation is particularly popular. More than 70 percent of BPs have such structures. Unions are also more apt to be available to employees as a formal mechanism for influencing management decisions in such complex organizations. And the combination of a union with a labor-management committee (LMC) is most commonly found in the largest plants of big corporations. When we speak of the importance of the "employee participation–union nexus" in American industry, we are therefore talking mainly about large corporations.

Our conclusions are straightforward, robust, and sufficiently against the grain to warrant further research and discussion. We find no evidence whatsoever that the presence of an LMC, by itself, is cross-sectionally associated with higher levels of efficiency in plants that have introduced computer-controlled automation technologies, as measured by lower machining production time per unit of output. Nor does the presence of an LMC, alone, increase the probable employment security of production workers, as indicated by a lower likelihood that management outsources machining work. Finally, the presence of such an

Distinguishing the EP-productivity-unionization nexus in large and small companies and workplaces has been a major consideration in our research.

EP structure, by itself, has no significant effect on whether plants in which management has introduced the latest generation of computer-controlled machine tool technology also permit blue collar workers to program their own tools.

By contrast, among branch plants of more complex organizations, unionized operations are significantly more efficient than operations (plants) that use the same technology, are organized similarly, make the same product(s), pay the same average wages, and require the same skills—but have no unions. Moreover, when production workers in such plants *are* involved with a union, their managers are significantly less likely to outsource production work, implying a higher degree of employment security for unionized workers. Among both small and large plants that have adopted the new computer-controlled technology for the first time in the past five years, the combination of a union and an LMC is associated with a higher probability of production workers having responsibility for writing programs on their own machines, compared with plants having LMCs but no unions and with nonunion plants with no LMCs.

Among branch plants of more complex organizations, unionized operations are significantly more efficient than . . . [plants that] have no unions.

Why Might Employee Participation Matter?

What the U.S. Postal Service, AT&T, GM, and Cummins Engine have in common is that they are all multi-site, complex organizations with a highly specialized division of labor. They also currently all have EI programs. Why?

All four firms are in some sense classical Weberian bureaucracies. The efficiencies available in principle to such organizations are well known. However, there are also well-known difficulties engendered by the bureaucratic form of organization itself that stand in the way of realizing these advantages. Similar to other recent efforts to redesign such organizations to better fit changes in the external environment, EI/EP may be viewed as a managerial attempt to circumvent the barriers to productivity and quality improvements that are latent within highly bureaucratized structures, resulting from hierarchy and overspecialization.

In particular, we now know of the severe limits to the classical advantages of ever-increasing job specialization. Dividing a set of tasks into a larger number of more narrowly specialized and simplified jobs does not always result in productivity improvements. From experimental studies of job design and group problem-solving exercises, we have learned that workers performing such simplified tasks may, individually, know too little about the overall product or service to identify mistakes, to figure out how to correct them, or to develop new rules of thumb that improve on existing methods. Management cannot rely on individuals to generate solutions to problems of which they are unaware.

Moreover, for workers in narrowly specialized jobs, deviation from procedures may be motivated less by a desire to develop a better method of working than to introduce novelty or relief from the tedious nature of a task. In these circumstances, mistakes proliferate, particularly for products and services in which there are many steps to completion. Tracing the "causes" of quality control problems back to their source is deemed infeasible, especially since no one individual knows enough about all the steps in a particular process to figure out where problems are occurring. The bureaucratic solution to the quality control problem—adding a new layer of specialized inspecting and testing occupations to check output and to identify mistakes—just adds extra costs that do not necessarily pay for themselves.

Much of what workers do to accomplish tasks efficiently in bureaucratic organizations does not conform to the rules and procedures that detail how they are supposed to carry out their jobs. Often, the extent to which such informal violations of established procedure are responsible for the level of efficiency achieved in a bureaucracy is unknown and goes unrecognized. Such incremental modifications and improvements to established procedures (whether formally sanctioned by management or not) accumulate over time and become part of the tacit knowledge or craft "art" that many observers have come to recognize as a key difference between high and low productivity operations (Bohn and Jaikumar, 1986; Pavitt and Patel, 1988; Skinner, 1986).

Yet from a management perspective, there may be considerable uncertainty and difficulty in relying on this informal system of problem solving for generating new ideas that only slowly percolate up the hierarchy. In a complex bureaucratic organization, knowledge of technical operations and ways in which to improve them is fragmentary and distributed unevenly among workers in different positions. Even among those holding the same position, there are individual differences in training, work experience, and motivation that affect the quality and swiftness with which problems may be resolved. Moreover, some managers unfa-

The extent to which . . . informal violations of established procedure are responsible for the level of efficiency achieved in a bureaucracy is unknown and goes unrecognized.

miliar with the details of how tasks are actually performed by those in subordinate positions may fail to recognize good ideas when they see them, or may insist upon adhering to what they know (established procedures), rather than opting for change.

Even if it were possible to generate good ideas that management recognized as such and was willing to implement, sustaining the flow of ideas and incremental changes in practices would still be problematic. As Burawoy has observed (1979), the successful perpetuation of an informal system of problem solving involves the complicity of managers and coworkers to "bend the rules" in ways that are expected to promote efficiency but that also accommodate individual workers' interests and desire for flexibility in how rules are applied to them. Examples include the taking of breaks when workers want to, "slacking off" on certain days, rearranging work schedules to accommodate individual preferences, taking on new responsibilities, and being otherwise rewarded (e.g., with higher compensation) for contributing to the joint problem-solving effort. However, the more *ad hoc* and individualized these accommodations become, the more the informal system threatens to undermine the fairness principle—that rules apply to everyone—by which the management of bureaucratic organizations legitimates its authority and continues to engender loyalty and effort among most employees.

The complicity of managers and coworkers to "bend the rules" . . . threatens to undermine the fairness principle—that rules apply to everyone.

Formalizing a system of employee participation in joint problem-solving programs has the virtue of incorporating into the bureaucratic structure a mechanism for generating ideas about new and better ways of accomplishing tasks. When it works well, management is able to tap the tacit knowledge of workers about the labor process, yielding incremental modifications to procedures that lead to improvements in productivity. If structured as a group participation process, an EI/EP program also has the quality of pooling individual expertise and compensating for the adverse consequences of overspecialization. Moreover, there is sufficient evidence from laboratory experiments to believe that group-generated solutions produce superior results—especially when the problem-solving process permits members to question conventional wisdom and to experiment with new methods, rather than merely to offer suggestions or to affirm solutions proposed by those in authority or leadership positions.[3]

In a bureaucracy, individuals derive their power from

their position in the organizational hierarchy. In an egalitarian system of group problem solving (in which subordinates and supervisors participate), position-based power is likely to be challenged. Yet narrowly restricting the definition of the "problems" open for discussion in order not to threaten these authority relationships excludes from consideration more fundamental solutions to the bureaucratic dilemma. Moreover, the "fairness" issue does not disappear with the formalization of the problem-solving process. The questions concerning the distribution of rewards (i.e., gain-sharing) that result from improvements in performance remain. Indeed, new questions arise, such as how to handle the more open expression of individual dissent and intra- (and inter-) group conflict that is likely to arise under a more egalitarian problem-solving process.

Simply put, what happens when convergence on a single solution or consensus over the choice among competing alternatives does not occur? Falling back on authoritarian decisionmaking—that is, leaving the decision up to those who have greater position power within the bureaucracy—undermines employee trust in a participatory process. If the power to influence decisions is too one-sided and this becomes apparent over time as conflicts between the groups arise, then the subordinate group will have little incentive to continue the participatory problem-solving "game."

In a recent paper, Levine and Tyson (1990) attempted to capture this problem. They suggest that the efficacy of EP/EI programs can be characterized in terms of "a prisoner's dilemma"; i.e., a conflictual situation in which cooperation would benefit both groups, but where there are barriers on both sides to initiating the game. However, once the game gets started—once the participatory problem-solving process is in place—the experience of arriving repeatedly at mutually acceptable solutions leads to the development of trust as the players gradually learn the advantages of cooperation.

Levine and Tyson's formulation points to the analytical relevance of the unequal position of the two parties in the game. In such a situation, there is always a temptation for the more powerful party (management) to impose a solution unilaterally, especially when the solutions proposed by the subordinate party (employees) would result in a diminution of the power of the dominant group. If experience in the game shows that solutions consistently favor one party

Leaving the decision up to those who have greater position power within the bureaucracy—undermines employee trust in a participatory process.

more than the other, then over time subordinates learn that EI/EP does not really pay off for them after all, and the trust necessary for an effective, cooperative problem-solving process becomes undermined.

Why Might Participation—If It Matters At All—Be More Effective in Unionized Settings?

Unionization has long been viewed by industrial relations specialists, political economists, and sociologists (Dunlop, 1958; Hirschman, 1971; Lipset, Trow, and Coleman, 1962; Marshall, this volume) as a system of workplace governance that provides a counterbalance to managerial power, especially in large bureaucratic organizations. As such, the "contentiousness" and the give-and-take which characterize the relationship between managers and workers in a unionized workplace may actually be an advantage (as long as the positions of the two with respect to a particular issue are not so extreme as to preclude a compromise solution). In their willingness to challenge management's proposals, unionized workers may be more apt to come up with "radical" solutions to problems than would be generated in a nonunion workplace where challenge by blue collar workers is perceived as more threatening to managerial activity. Indeed, Cole (1989) argues that the managers of many large companies actually find it *easier* to implement radical organizational changes when there are strong unions with whom they can negotiate (that is, of course, a central tenet of the German, Austrian, and Scandinavian systems of codetermination).

If a union is an effective vehicle for voicing the interests of workers, we would expect it to influence management decisionmaking in ways that enhance the power of the membership. Hence, we might expect to find the outcomes associated with EI/EP *and* a union to strongly reflect the blue collar workforce's concerns, particularly with respect to employment security and control over new technology.

In Levine and Tyson's review of twenty-nine studies of EI/EP, they suggest that formal participation programs instituted in the context of unionization are likely to be more productive than their nonunion counterparts. In studies reporting a positive relationship between EP and productivity, a plant or firm usually has profit- or gainsharing arrangements, relatively narrow wage differentials, long-

In Levine and Tyson's review of . . . EI/EP, they suggest that formal participation programs instituted in the context of unionization are likely to be more productive than their nonunion counterparts.

term employment guarantees, and rules protecting workers from unjust dismissal by management (Levine and Tyson, 1990). The latter two conditions represent an acceptance by management of limitations on its power to terminate an employment relationship. Such restrictions are well-known to be strongly associated with the presence of unions, as are narrow wage differentials (Freeman, this volume; Freeman and Medoff, 1984).[4] In other words, Levine and Tyson's synthesis can easily be reinterpreted as implying that EP sometimes demonstrably enhances productivity, and that when it does, it is usually in the context of a set of institutional arrangements commonly associated with the presence of unions.

Moreover, there are strong theoretical reasons why we should expect the presence of unions to promote efficiency; i.e., equivalent production at lower unit cost, or greater production with the same level of resource use (see Belman, this volume, for a theoretical discussion and review of the empirical evidence). In the "monopoly" model as Freeman and Medoff describe it (1984), unions are able to extract a wage premium from those firms that are relatively sheltered from competition. The higher cost of unionized labor induces such firms to make greater investments in new technology, which in turn leads to productivity improvements.[5] There is also what might be called a "morale effect." True, the union wage pressure may (according to Freeman and Medoff) lead to higher short-run aggregate costs of production than in the absence of a union. But because they have "voice"—the power to ensure that managers will treat them more fairly and to otherwise influence management decisionmaking—unionized workers experience higher morale and therefore tend to be more productive.

Unionized workplaces have a greater ability to attract and retain more highly skilled and experienced workers, due to both higher average wages and to the opportunity for exercising "voice." As a result, a unionized workforce is, on average, likely to be more productive. Additionally, the regulatory process and grievance mechanisms that are part of the normal collective bargaining relationship serve to alert management to sources of organizational inefficiency that might otherwise go unnoticed (Clark, 1980a).

A third way that unionization affects productivity is through the retention of workers with accumulated specific training. By promoting loyalty to the firm, the presence of a union increases job tenure which can, in turn,

There are strong theoretical reasons why . . . the presence of unions [promotes] efficiency.

256

indirectly enhance productivity. This process is now widely thought to be a significant factor in explaining the relatively higher productivity and longer-term planning horizons of large Japanese companies (Aoki, 1987).

In the context of a union, EP/EI is another avenue for promoting dialogue and joint problem solving. For all of these reasons, we would expect to find that plants with EP/EI that also have unions will attain higher levels of productivity than settings where EP/EI is the only formal mechanism through which workers can influence management decisions, and by which management can take advantage of the tacit knowledge of workers about production problems.

Previous Empirical Research on the Effectiveness of EP

In studies from organizational sociology, labor economics, and industrial relations, some researchers report significant positive effects, some find no effect, and a few even report negative impacts of participation on one or another outcome measure (Cotton et al., 1988). In a recent review of no less than seventy different quantitative organizational studies (not all of them addressed specifically to workplace settings), Wagner and Gooding (1987) drew several important generalizations. Participation seems to affect the *attitudes* of the actors more than observable changes in behavior. Discrepancies in findings among published studies are systematically related to the choice of outcome measure and to the method of statistical association used by the researcher. When these sources of discrepancy are accounted for as best as possible, Wagner and Gooding conclude that there is little empirical support for the proposition that EI/EP materially affects outcomes.

The economics and industrial relations literature displays a similarly equivocal set of findings with respect to productivity and labor relations. Investigations of Quality of Worklife (QWL) efforts in the auto industry by Kochan, Katz, and Mower (1984) led the researchers to conclude that these joint activities have, at best, very small effects on performance and labor relations. By contrast, in a sample of unionized companies in a variety of industries, Voos (1989) found that nearly all kinds of collaborative activities have significant positive effects. In a study of large manufacturing plants, 57 percent of which had an EI/EP program and

We . . . expect to find that plants with EP/EI that also have unions will attain higher levels of productivity than settings where EP/EI is the only formal mechanism through which workers can influence management decisions.

257

all of which were unionized, Cooke (1989, 1990) found that the intensity of interaction between management and workers or union officials participating in problem-solving teams or committees significantly increased the perception of managers that both productivity and the "labor climate" are improving. And in their survey of twenty-nine different studies of firms or plants with some kind of EP program, Levine and Tyson (1990) found that in two studies, EP actually harmed productivity; fourteen showed a positive impact; and thirteen were inconclusive.

Our own review of this body of research indicates that even when results are as hypothesized, there are serious methodological and data problems that cause us to question the generalizability of the finding that EP/EI has an effect. In nearly every study, *all* of the observations are on plants or firms having some kind of EP activity (Levine and Tyson, 1990), thus making it impossible to differentiate the effects on productivity (or other outcome measures) of the presence or absence of EP. From the program evaluation (benefit/cost) literature, it is well known that before-and-after studies are generally unreliable (except under the most careful experimental conditions) since so many other properties of the environment are changing simultaneously. And those studies in which *all* the cases are unionized preclude the possibility of observing whether or not the effects of EP differ in union and nonunion environments.

Moreover, generalizability is compromised by the fact that most of the existing research is in the form of case studies of *large* plants or firms. Where representative surveys *have* been conducted, the sample response rates are sometimes quite low by common scientific standards, as with the 6.5 percent effective response rate in the Columbia University Business Unit Data Set employed by Mitchell, Lewin, and Lawler (1990).

Finally, outcomes may be poorly measured and may even systematically incorporate bias. For example, in an effort to model changes over time in the attitudes of plant or personnel managers with respect to the severity of adversarial relations in the workplace, Cooke asked the question: "Is the adversarial relationship between supervisors and workforce in this plant 'much higher,' 'modestly higher,' 'about the same,' 'modestly lower,' or 'much lower' than during the five-year period preceding the introduction of the 'most important' joint labor-management problem-solving activity?" Not a single manager out of the 194 who returned usable ques-

Our own review of . . . research indicates that . . . there are serious methodological and data problems that cause us to question the generalizability of the finding that EP/EI has an effect.

258

tionnaires answered "much higher," and only 4 percent answered "modestly higher." These responses might be valid, but we are skeptical. As worded, the question presumes that the "normal" situation (absent EI/EP) must be riddled with conflict. Moreover, by coupling the perception of change specifically to the timing of the introduction of the EI/EP activity, the question suggests to the respondent that there *should* be a connection between EI/EP activity and the labor-management climate. Such a formulation may induce a biased response (and as a result, a spurious correlation) associating the presence of EI/EP programs—whatever their intended focus—with the expectation of an improvement in the labor-relations climate.

As for the impact of unions, there is consistent empirical evidence showing that these institutions reduce turnover as well as intra-firm and intra-establishment wage inequality (Freeman, this volume). In so doing, they contribute to longer job tenure, and with it, the accumulation of specific human capital within the workplace. By reducing intra-firm and intra-establishment wage inequality, unions apparently do promote cooperation and the sharing of tacit knowledge among workers employed in the same company or plant, which indirectly increases productivity.

That unions directly enhance productivity has been documented in a host of papers (Belman, this volume, provides a comprehensive review). But with the exception of Clark's study of the cement industry (1980a) and Ichniowski's analysis of the paper industry (1986), most existing models are not fitted to process-specific data at all, but rather are conducted at the industry level of analysis. This may be too high a level of aggregation. Unlike some other major industrialized countries, such as the Federal Republic of Germany, industry-level bargaining between an association of employers and a national union is very rare in the United States. A union represents workers employed by particular companies, and when employment is tied to a specific workplace, representation by the union is also determined at the establishment level. Within most industries, there is considerable heterogeneity among plants and firms in management investment strategies, in work rules, and in the skills and training of workers that also can be expected to account for variation in productivity levels. It is at the plant- and process-specific level of analysis where work practices, technology, and labor relations conjoin to shape the level of productivity. Industry-level statistical indicators ignore

By reducing intra-firm and intra-establishment wage inequality, unions . . . promote cooperation and the sharing of tacit knowledge among workers employed in the same company . . . which indirectly increases productivity.

259

these within-industry variations in the sources of productivity differences among plants.

Data Description and Methods

In the following synthesis of results obtained from Kelley's ongoing research, the data come from a nationally representative size-stratified random sample of establishments belonging to twenty-one 3-digit manufacturing industries.[6] In 1986, 25 percent of all U.S. manufacturing workers were employed in these industries. The industries were chosen because they account for nearly 100 percent of all *machining* activity in American industry. All sample establishments use machine tools for some aspect of production operations in their plants. This is a production process which Kelley and her colleagues have been investigating for several years (Harrison and Kelley, 1991; Kelley, 1986, 1989a, 1989b, 1990a, 1990b; Kelley and Brooks, 1988, 1991a, 1991b; Kelley and Harrison, 1990; and Kelley and Xue, 1990).

In order to ensure a sufficient number of cases within each plant size category, establishments were randomly sampled by size in order to yield a data set with an equal number of establishments from each size stratum. Since the distribution of establishments by employment size in U.S. industry is highly skewed—with fewer than 10 percent of all plants employing 100 or more workers in the industries studied—this procedure guarantees a sufficient number of large-size plants to allow for variation among them in the use of technology, type of product, etc. This permits comparisons of the characteristics of particular subgroups among the large plants to the more typical small-size establishment of the population—a comparison which, to our knowledge, is unique in the literature on employee participation. In all of the statistical procedures that follow, each establishment in the sample is weighted by the reciprocal of the probability of selection of that case for inclusion in its appropriate plant size stratum.

Production managers in the plants were surveyed by Kelley and Brooks (1988) between October 1986 and March 1987. All told, 1,015 plant managers were successfully interviewed by mail, yielding a 50 percent response rate. Half of the nonrespondents were then contacted by telephone and asked questions which, apart from their substantive value, confirmed the absence of response bias in the mail survey. The data base includes information on the size of the parent company (as measured by corporatewide employment) and considerable detail on the organizational, technical, and economic characteristics of each plant.

The indicator used to signify that there is an employee participation program comes from a list of questions on the mail survey instrument addressed to the plant manager, asking: "At this plant, have you established committees made up of *both* blue collar workers *and* managers who meet regularly to deal with problems concerning the implementation of new technology? quality control? other production problems? other issues?" (Emphasis as in the original questionnaire.) If the production manager checked "yes" to any of these, then the plant was treated as having employee participation through some type of formal joint labor-management problem-solving committee structure.[7] With respect to unionization, plant managers were asked simply: "Are production workers at this plant unionized?" If the answer was "yes," the plant's workforce was considered to be covered by the terms of a collective bargaining agreement and to be able to avail themselves of the grievance procedures and other mechanisms for influencing management decisionmaking through the union. No attempt was made to discover whether more than one union had jurisdiction within the plant.

Information on union status and on joint labor-management problem-solving committees was available from 92 percent of the completed questionnaires. As shown in Table 1, joint labor-management problem-solving committees (LMCs) are far more common than are unions as a mechanism by which workers get to participate in management decisionmaking. More than 47 percent of the plants in the industries studied have such joint committee arrangements, while only 13 percent of the manufacturing plants are unionized.

The typical manufacturing plant is a small firm. 81 percent of the establishments in the industries studied are single-plant enterprises (SPEs) with an average of 31 employees in the company. Of these SPEs, 54 percent rely wholly on an informal system of communication and problem solving, having neither a union nor a formal committee of workers and managers established for dealing with production issues.

Only 19 percent of the establishments in the manufactur-

Establishments were randomly sampled by size in order to yield a data set with an equal number of establishments from each size stratum.

261

TABLE 1
Proportion of Plants in the U.S. Metalworking and Machinery Sector in 1986–87 with Joint Labor-Management Problem-Solving Committees, with Unions, with Both, and with Neither

for single-plant enterprises and the branch plants of multi-plant firms

	GOVERNANCE STRUCTURE IN THE PLANT			
	pct. of plants with unions alone	pct. of plants with formal joint labor-management problem-solving committees alone	pct. of plants with both	pct. of plants with neither
all metalworking and machinery sector plants in the U.S.	4.9%	39.4%	8.1%	47.6%
single-plant enterprises (mean employment in the company = 31)	3.6%	37.9%	4.3%	54.1%
branch plants of multi-plant firms (mean employment in the parent company = 15,000	10.5%	45.9%	24.8%	18.9%
	PROPERTIES OF THE LABOR-MANAGEMENT ENVIRONMENT IN THE PLANT:			
average plant employment	1,610	520	4,300	19
average firm employment	3,633	2,581	14,706	233
pct. of plants belonging to multi-plant firms	39.8%	21.6%	56.5%	7.4%
average hourly wages rates	$11.91	$9.91	$11.18	$9.49
pct. of plants in which job assignment and promotion are governed by seniority rules	54.7%	41.3%	67.9%	26.6%

Estimated from a stratified random sample of 1,015 manufacturing plants in 21 industries covering 25 percent of all manufacturing employment in 1986–87. For details, see Kelley and Brooks (1988, 1991a).

ing industries studied are branch plants (BPs) of multi-unit corporations. These companies employ an average of over 15,000 workers in their operations throughout the United States. Branch plants of such large companies are 1.7 times more likely than SPEs to have some combination of a union, an LMC, or both. Nearly 71 percent of BPs have established LMCs, with or without a union.

When we compare the characteristics of plants that *do* have LMCs (with or without unions) to plants that have neither unions nor an LMC, it is easy to see that employee participation is powerfully correlated with the presence of bureaucratic forms of business organization (see Table 1). Plants with LMCs are from nearly three to more than twenty-two times larger (on average) than nonunion plants with no such EP program. The parent firms of plants with LMCs are between eleven and sixty-three times larger. Plants with LMCs are from three to nearly eight times more likely to belong to multi-plant organizations, and from one and one-half to two and one-half times more likely to have internal job assignments and promotions for the production workforce be regulated by seniority rules. It would certainly seem that—as we suggested earlier—the introduction of employee participation into U.S. manufacturing workplaces has mainly been part of an effort by managers in large bureaucracies to overcome the rigidities associated with this organizational form.

Our research objective is to compare plants with and without formal employee participation programs for collaborative problem solving, with and without a union, and with and without the joint occurrence of these two institutional arrangements for employee voice. Using various multivariate regression techniques, we specify models that take into account a number of indicators reflecting a plant's technological profile, capacity utilization, and the capabilities and competencies of its management and its blue collar workforce.

We have chosen to model three outcome indicators. Each indicator measures a *tangible manifestation of actions* by managers and employees, rather than (as in so much of the literature) changes in the *perceptions* of managers or their employees. We are able to evaluate whether the presence of EP (with or without a union) is associated with: (1) higher levels of efficiency (i.e., shorter machining production time per unit of output); (2) a greater degree of employment security for machining workers (resulting from a lower

Employee participation is powerfully correlated with the presence of bureaucratic forms of business organization.

likelihood that the plant outsources machining work); and (3) a higher degree of worker control over new technology, as measured by the likelihood that, following the introduction of computer-controlled machine tools into the plant, blue collar machining workers get to write and debug their own programs (in the form of numerical control [NC] and computerized numerically controlled [CNC] machine tools and flexible manufacturing systems, programmable automation [PA] is a relatively recent machine tool technology). All results are summarized in the Appendix A tables, together with complete citations to the respective scientific papers on which the synthesis presented here is based.

Machining production time per unit of output—measures whether plants with LMCs are more efficient.

The first of these indicators—machining production time per unit of output—measures whether plants with LMCs are more efficient, i.e., make a product of given attributes using the same machine tool technology in less time than a plant without joint problem-solving committees.[8] The time it takes to make any one of these machined parts or products will vary with the quality, size, and precision specifications of that output. We account for variation in these key product attributes, in capital intensity and vintage, and in other factors that compare how well or poorly establishments operate with different labor relations. The complete list of explanatory variables is given in Appendix Table A1. This model is estimated on the subsample of plants that had already adopted PA by the time of the survey.

The second outcome indicator measures whether or not management outsources machining work. In plants where management reports that they do *not* usually "farm out" machining work, we infer that workers have greater employment security than in plants where that process is partly performed in-house and partly "on contract." All the firms upon which this analysis is based are already engaged in precision metal-cutting operations at the plants studied. As such, they all have the option of doing additional machining work in-house or sourcing it from the outside.

Outsourcing is pursued for several different reasons. Sometimes managers outsource to obtain specialized capabilities that might otherwise have been generated in-house through new investment in capital equipment, via the hiring of additional workers with the needed skills, or by retraining existing workers. In these cases, outsourcing clearly decreases the employment security of existing employees. Contracting out to reduce short-run costs also blatantly threatens job security of in-house workers. On the other hand, when plant managers deliberately pursue a strategy of buffering their in-house workers from cyclical variations in product demand (thereby preserving their supply of skilled labor from one upswing to another) by "farming out" production in excess of normal capacity, the security of the "permanent" in-house workforce is not threatened.

In the Kelley-Brooks sample, only 21.6 percent of those plant managers who *do* outsource report that their only reason for doing so is a capacity constraint (Harrison and Kelley, 1991; Kelley and Harrison, 1990). We therefore infer that, when subcontracting occurs in these industries, it does so for reasons that usually *do* threaten the employment security of workers employed in the plants where the decision to subcontract originates. A list of explanatory variables in addition to those having to do with the governance of labor relations in the plant is provided in Appendix Table A2. Here, we use the entire sample, including plants with no PA.

The third outcome measure concerns changes in blue collar work roles associated with PA technology. Kelley and Brooks asked managers whether or not blue collar workers have major responsibility for creating the computer programs used to run the new machines. To a large extent, skills in the manual operation of machine tools are automated away when PA is deployed. But blue collar occupations could be redesigned to include major responsibilities for writing programs on such computer-automated machines. Were machine operators permitted to program these machines, conceptual skill demands would be increased and the locus of control over the technology would remain on the shop floor. The research question considered here is whether or not plants with EI/EP are more or less likely to permit such blue collar programming, and whether or not the presence or absence of a union influences this result. For a complete list of other variables in the model, see Appendix Table A3. Again, the relevant subsample is restricted to plants with at least some PA technology in place.

In plants where management reports that they do not usually "farm out" machining work, we infer that workers have greater employment security.

Are Plants with Collaborative Problem-Solving Committees More Efficient?

Unionization in the branch plants of multi-unit companies is positively . . . associated with plant-level efficiency.

A regression equation for production time per unit of output was estimated by ordinary least squares (OLS) for single-plant enterprises (SPEs) and for the branch plants of multi-unit companies (BPs), using sixteen explanatory variables (Kelley, 1990c; Kelley and Xue, 1990). The dependent variable is measured as the sum of programming time (when the machine is computer-controlled), setup time, and run time, all divided by the quantity of physical output. In the regression results presented in Appendix Table A1, a negative coefficient therefore indicates a lower production time per unit of output, i.e., a *positive* effect on efficiency.

The control variables include measures of product attributes, technological capabilities, and capacity utilization. For SPEs, eleven of the sixteen variables are statistically significant at the 0.10 level, according to a two-tailed test. In the BP equation, ten of the sixteen explanatory variables are significant. Many of the variables that previous research has been criticized for omitting—such as skill requirements, wages, and the age of the technology and the capital equipment in the plant—are explicitly included as controls in these efficiency models.[9] The overall explanatory power of the two regressions is quite high, with an R^2 of 0.70 for SPEs and 0.75 for the sample of BPs.

Taking into account these various constraints on productivity differences, and having also controlled for variation in the skill requirements and the wages of machining occupations across plants, the results for both the SPE and BP equations strongly indicate that employee participation has not been associated with greater efficiency in U.S. metalworking operations, as might have been expected from previous scholarly and popular treatments of the subject. Indeed, we find that plants with labor-management problem-solving committees are significantly *less* efficient than those without such organizational innovations. In contrast, unionization in the branch plants of multi-unit companies is positively (and significantly) associated with plant-level efficiency.

To demonstrate these propositions, we use the regression results contained in Appendix Table A1 to calculate the discrete differences in efficiency for each LMC-union "regime," relative to the base category—plants with neither labor-management problem-solving committees nor unions. Tables 2 and 3 display the percentage differences in the estimated average machining production time per unit of output associated with each regime: (1) plants with LMCs alone; (2) plants with unions alone; and (3) plants with both LMCs and unions. Each is measured relative to the base category of plants with neither LMCs nor unions. This is done first for single-plant firms and then for the branch plants of multi-plant enterprises (see Appendix B for details on the methodology).

Among single-plant firms (Table 2), we estimate average production time per unit of output to be the highest when there is a labor-management problem-solving committee structure but no union in the plant. Hence, it is indicative of the *lowest* efficiency among the four alternative labor-management governance regimes. Unions neither interfere with nor promote efficiency, either alone or in combination with LMCs. Since only 11 percent of SPEs that employ computer-controlled machines are unionized, these inferences about the role of unions should perhaps be interpreted with some caution.

Among single-plant firms, we estimate average production time per unit of output to be the highest when there is a labor-management problem-solving committee structure but no union in the plant.

TABLE 2

Increments to Average Production Time per Unit of Output in Different Employee Involvement–Union Regimes, Relative to Plants with Neither EI Nor Unions

single-plant metalworking firms

		Union Present	
		NO	YES
Joint Labor-Managment Problem-Solving Committees Present	NO	base category	+1.8%
	YES	+32.8%	−0.3%

See Appendix B for the derivation of these figures.

Note: Positive numbers indicate relatively longer production time per unit of output, i.e., *lower* level of efficiency, *cet. par.*

Table 3 displays the effects estimated for the sample of PA-using branch plants, 40 percent of which we know to have been unionized. These are the plants belonging to multi-plant, primarily corporate organizations. Here, it is the unionized plants *without* an LMC in which the average production times are estimated to be the lowest (again with all other factors held constant). When the labor-management relationship is mediated solely by a joint problem-solving committee structure without a union—which, among branch plants, is as prevalent as unionization—we find average production times per unit of output to be the *highest*, indicating this regime to be the *least* efficient compared to any of the other alternatives shown in the table. Moreover, unionized plants with LMCs also have an efficiency advantage over nonunionized plants with LMCs. In sum, employee participation through a nonunion labor-management problem-solving structure does not compensate for whatever inefficiencies may arise as a consequence of over-specialization and hierarchical systems in multi-plant (and therefore typically more highly bureaucratic) organizations.

> *Table 3 displays the effects estimated for the sample of PA-using branch plants. . . . Here, it is the unionized plants <u>without</u> an LMC in which the average production times are estimated to be the lowest.*

TABLE 3
Increments to Average Production Time per Unit of Output in Different Employee Involvement–Union Regimes, Relative to Plants with Neither EI Nor Unions

branch plants of multi-plant companies

		Union Present	
		NO	YES
Joint Labor-Managment Problem-Solving Committees Present	NO	base category	− 48.9%
	YES	+34.9%	+8.7%

See Appendix B for the derivation of these figures.

Note: Positive numbers indicate relatively longer pruduction time per unit of output, i.e., *lower* level of efficiency, *cet. par.*

268

Our models also enable us to address directly the long-standing debate among labor scholars about the net impact of unions on efficiency (see Belman, this volume). That is, we may compute the effect of a union in the workplace, independent of whether or not there is a joint labor-management problem-solving committee present as well as the difference in efficiency associated with the presence of LMCs, whether or not there is a union. The results of evaluating the effects of unionization and the presence of LMCs for single-plant enterprises and for branch plants of multi-unit companies are shown in Table 4 (see Appendix B for details). Plants with LMCs are estimated to be substantially *less* efficient than plants without such innovations in labor-management relations, *ceteris paribus*. In particular, branch plants with LMCs are estimated to be 62 percent less efficient than identical branch plants with no LMCs. In dramatic contrast, plants that are unionized are *more* efficient (i.e., have significantly shorter average machining production times per unit of output) than plants without unions, other things equal. Among branch plants, the union-nonunion differential is estimated to be 31 percent.

Plants with LMCs are estimated to be substantially <u>less</u> efficient than plants without such innovations. . . . In dramatic contrast, plants that are unionized are <u>more</u> efficient.

TABLE 4
Union and Labor-Management Cooperation Effects on Average Production Time per Unit of Output, by Organization of the Metalworking Firm

	single-plant firms	branch plants of multi-plant enterprises
UNION EFFECT	−10.1%	−32.6%
COOPERATION EFFECT	28.7%	61.9%

See Appendix B for the derivation of these figures.

Note: Positive numbers indicate relatively longer production time per unit of output, i.e., a *lower* level of efficiency, *cet. par.*

269

Employee Participation, Unionization, and Outsourcing

When a joint labor-management problem-solving committee was present, we expected to find management less likely to subcontract out machining work.

Restrictions or limitations on contracting out have become agenda items in recent years for both labor-management problem-solving committees and for unions. In all of the most well known cases relating EI/EP to restrictions on outsourcing, such as that of the Xerox Corporation (Whyte, 1989), a union is also present. Indeed, in the wake of U.S. Supreme Court decisions in the early 1980s that in effect validated the farming out of production work formerly performed on the premises unless such actions are expressly prohibited by contract, more and more unions have actively sought to insert language on such prohibitions into collective bargaining agreements (Clark, 1989).

In specifying our own binomial logistic regression models, we originally hypothesized that managers would be more likely to contract out work if a union was present, to escape either the higher wages or restrictive work practices that are sometimes codified in collective bargaining agreements.[10] On the other hand, we expected the presence of joint labor-management problem-solving committees to signify that a new collaborative partnership had been forged between managers and their workers, as suggested by Kochan, Katz, and McKersie (1986). Rather than seeking greater flexibility by contracting out, management (we thought) could achieve greater internal flexibility through the cooperative problem-solving mechanism. The *quid pro quo* for collaboration of this sort could well be at least a tacit agreement on the part of managers to refrain from contracting out. Thus, when a joint labor-management problem-solving committee was present, we expected to find management less likely to subcontract out machining work. Our econometric models also include an interaction term to test for the combined effect on managers' decision to outsource when there is both a union *and* a collaborative problem-solving structure at the plant.

The findings are presented in Appendix Table A2. About 60 percent of the managers of both single-plant firms and the branch plants of multi-plant companies told the interviewers that they "usually" contract out machining work. For the sample of single-plant companies, six of ten explanatory variables were statistically significant (at the 0.10 or higher level), while for the sample of branch plants, only four of the ten independent variables were found to matter.[11] The partial effects of having a union, a joint labor-management problem-solving committee, or both on the likelihood of outsourcing do vary somewhat between the two types of firms in the sample. What is clear in every instance is that our "priors" were quite incorrect.

Among single-plant enterprises, the presence of LMCs is associated with a significantly *greater* likelihood of outsourcing (relative to the baseline case of the non-bureaucratic SPE with neither LMCs nor a union), and therefore presumably greater job *in*security. As before, among these generally small, simply structured enterprises, unionization is statistically irrelevant to whether or not managers outsource.

For workplaces attached to a more complex form of business organization (the branch plants of multi-unit companies) the presence of an LMC without a union is again associated with a higher likelihood of outsourcing, and therefore a heightened threat to the job security of blue collar workers employed in such plants. In contrast, a joint F-test on the union and union-LMC interaction terms shows that the presence of a union is significantly associated with a *lower* likelihood of outsourcing, *ceteris paribus*.

Among single-plant enterprises, the presence of LMCs is associated with a significantly greater likelihood of outsourcing.

Collaborative Labor-Management Problem Solving and Blue Collar Control over Programming

Programmable automation is a relatively recent technology whose main application has been in the process of precision metal-cutting. Technologists expect that this innovation will eventually diffuse to other industrial operations because of its ability to greatly reduce unit operating costs, improve product quality, and increase economies of scope (Piore and Sabel, 1984).[12] As of the Kelley-Brooks survey in 1986–87, some type of PA technology—either NC or CNC machine tools, a flexible manufacturing system, or some combination of these three—had been adopted by 43 percent of the sample plants.

There is no question of the effect of programmable automation on tasks involving the exercise of manual skill. To a large extent, these are automated away. Rather, concern centers on the implications for blue collar occupations, i.e., on whether these jobs will be redesigned to include major responsibility for writing the programs that control these machines. Were machine operators permitted to program these machines, conceptual skill demands would be increased for these occupations and the locus of control over the technology would be decentralized to blue collar workers on the shop floor.[13]

In 56 percent of the plants using PA technology, at least some blue collar machining occupations were found to include major programming responsibilities.[14] Expanding blue collar occupations to include new cognitive skills is indicative of an "enrichment" approach to job design. Improvements in the quality of worklife of this type were often cited as the goals of the early reform-minded advocates of EP programs. Moreover, such an increase in responsibilities also suggests that management is willing to permit a greater degree of power sharing, in this case having to do with control over technology. It seems a reasonable test of the efficacy of such programs for enhancing the quality of working life in such subordinate occupations to consider whether or not, in plants with collaborative problem-solving committee structures, we find a greater propensity of management to enrich blue collar jobs with these new responsibilities.

A binomial logistic regression model was estimated, with the dependent variable set equal to unity if any blue collar job involving the setup and operation of programmable machines also included the responsibility to create new parts programs on a regular basis, and to zero otherwise. Eleven variables were hypothesized to be predictors of the approach of management to job design. The results are presented in Appendix Table A3. For the sample that includes all plants that have adopted any PA technology, 6 of the 11 variables were found to be significant. Among those "recent adopters"—all of whose programmable tools are less than five years old and therefore presumably embody the latest generation of PA technology—8 of the same 11 variables were significant predictors of an enrichment job design strategy.

The size and complexity of the firm largely explain why responsibility for writing programs for these machines is decentralized in some workplaces and not others. Small, single-plant enterprises are workplaces where major responsibility for programming is most likely to be assigned to blue collar workers. The more complex the organization, the greater the pull toward centralization of

The size and complexity of the firm largely explain why responsibility for writing programs for these machines is decentralized in some workplaces and not others.

272

control over the technology and the lower the probability that management will design blue collar jobs to incorporate programming responsibilities. In general, among large plants of multi-plant enterprises, the chances of blue collar programming are very small.

Among the sample of all PA users taken as a whole, we find that a job enrichment strategy is not significantly associated with a collaborative problem-solving committee structure. And here, when there is a union present, management is significantly *less* likely to assign new responsibilities to blue collar occupations that come under the protection of the collective bargaining agreement. In other words, in a sample that includes plants using older vintages of the technology, collective bargaining by itself provides no protection against the deskilling of blue collar occupations.[15]

The bureaucratic imperative to centralize control is very strong. If organizational size and complexity were the only determinants of job design, the majority of workers in machining occupations presently employed in large multi-plant enterprises would stand little chance of ever having their jobs upgraded by the addition of major programming responsibilities. However, the development of new institutional arrangements and the evolution of the technology itself may counter that bureaucratic imperative. We can see this most clearly by studying the practices of establishments that use only the most recent generation of PA technology.

Among workplaces with less than a five-year history of PA use, i.e., "recent adopters," there is a significantly higher incidence of blue collar programming than occurs among "experienced users" of the technology. Two-thirds of recent adopters design machining occupations to include parts programming.[16] Among these recent adopters of programmable automation, joint labor-management problem-solving committees are indeed associated with improvement in the quality of blue collar occupations (as measured by the addition of new skills). But this effect of LMCs occurs only when there is also a union present.

In general, among large plants of multi-plant enterprises, the chances of blue collar programming are very small.

How to Explain the "Perverse" Effects of Employee Participation

Only in the case of recent adopters of programmable automation is the presence of EP/EI statistically significant in the expected direction—and then, only if the plant is also unionized.

Only in the case of recent adopters of programmable automation is the presence of EP/EI statistically significant in the expected direction—and then, only if the plant is also unionized. Indeed, in four of the six regression models we estimated, EP/EI—operationalized here as the presence in the plant of a formal joint labor-management problem-solving committee—is actually associated with *worse* outcomes: *lower* levels of productivity and *greater* job insecurity. What are we to make of these "perverse" effects?

That the presence of joint labor-management committees is positively associated with contracting out is of course a perverse outcome only from the perspective of employees. After all, if managers are interested in "cooperation" because it promises to give them greater flexibility in resource allocation, then that same desire for enhanced flexibility would naturally enough lead many managers to outsource as well.

We cannot determine from these data *when* formal committees for collaborative problem solving were first introduced into these plants. It has been suggested to us that LMCs may have been inserted into work settings that had already (previously) been plagued with severe productivity problems. Even if such plants were to achieve dramatic reductions in average production time per unit of output as a consequence of the introduction of EI/EP, they might (it is argued) still be less efficient than would be relatively trouble-free plants, where management did not have such an impetus to introduce employee participation. This explanation may be plausible for SPEs, among whom participation is not the norm. But for the branch plants of (generally large) corporations, fully 70 percent of all establishments have such formal problem-solving committee structures. Were *all* of them in trouble prior to introducing EI/EP programs? Perhaps, but it seems likely that, among the big firms, something else is going on.

Consider the results showing those plants that are more efficient. Some indicators of the kinds of management practices that would reflect the existence of "trouble" have in fact already been included in all of these models. Troubled plants would probably be making fewer investments in new technology, which would in turn be reflected in their hav-

274

ing a smaller percentage of their machine tools being computer-controlled. Disinvestment would be reflected by an aging capital stock. The number of tools per worker in troubled plants would probably be lower. It is possible that some additional unspecified variable (such as the degree of vulnerability of the sample plants to foreign competition) could turn out to be both indicative of low productivity operations and correlated with our indicator of employee participation (the presence of formal LMCs). But it does not seem plausible that such a hidden correlation would be *so* strong as to reverse the findings presented here.

Alternatively, one may view the unexpected results for LMCs as a reflection of the infancy of this organizational innovation. In other words, we are making our observations too early in the learning process. As we said earlier, the implementation of such programs is likely to be fraught with difficulty, especially in defining the objectives and limits to participation and in engendering and sustaining employee trust in the process. Meetings also take time away from productive activity that would otherwise occur in a smoothly running bureaucracy. Hence, we should perhaps not be too surprised that such a popular but poorly understood management innovation does not yield the expected benefits. This critique points to only one remedy: wait and collect additional information as the innovation further diffuses. The aforementioned resurvey of the same plant managers in 1991 should provide some answers to this question.

But there is a third possibility. Earlier, we speculated that LMCs were a management innovation aimed at modifying the contradictory consequences of over-bureaucratization. Our empirical results seem to support this hypothesis. The type of workplace in which management is most likely to have introduced EP/EI programs tends to be large, to belong to a large multi-unit company, and to have a bureaucratically structured internal labor market that is regulated by seniority rules.

In these complex organizations, it could well be that the formal collaborative problem-solving committee structure that was intended to be a reform has itself become subject to rules and procedures that limit its scope and possibility for change. Perhaps, in the pursuit of a better, more congenial atmosphere, a "don't rock the boat" norm develops in EI programs that precludes anyone from proposing controversial solutions or raising too basic or too difficult prob-

We speculated that LMCs were a management innovation aimed at modifying the contradictory consequences of over-bureaucratization. Our empirical results seem to support this hypothesis.

lems which would threaten the positions of various organizational members or lead to conflict between groups. If this type of "group think" is present, any topic likely to spark conflict is simply taboo.

In other words, rather than being a vehicle of liberation from bureaucratic structure, LMCs may simply have become another grafted-on layer of the bureaucratic structure itself, which helps sustain commitment to the status quo. By taking precious time away from productive activity, and by failing to generate radically new, more productive methods, EI just *adds* to costs.

> **LMCs may simply have become another grafted-on layer of the bureaucratic structure . . . and by failing to generate radically new, more productive methods, EI just adds to costs.**

Conclusion

In early 1990, former *Business Week* labor reporter John Hoerr commented on an intriguing coincidence. Under the title "The Strange Bedfellows Backing Workplace Reform" (Hoerr, 1990), he made evident the "extraordinarily strong" endorsement of employee involvement that had just been issued by the National Association of Manufacturers (NAM). In the same month, reports Hoerr, the editors of a union-affiliated journal, *Labor Research Review* (LRR), openly endorsed EI (Banks and Metzgar, 1989)—thereby applauding the initiatives of such unions as the United Auto Workers, for whom employee participation programs have become almost a standard component of workplace governance along with the grievance procedure and other more traditional mechanisms for the expression of employee voice.

But Hoerr's "strange bedfellows" are actually offering quite different prescriptions. There is no mention of unions anywhere in NAM's report. By contrast, the LRR editors propose what they call "a union-empowering model of worker participation in management," and urge that "unions get involved in—and in fact take control of—participation programs." Our evidence strongly suggests that the difference is important. For the sake of comparison, consider as a baseline the nonunion workplace that has EI—the paradigm that NAM is now promoting as the "wave of the future." How do organized workplaces compare to this standard?

Compared to NAM's baseline—EI but no union—certainly among the branch plants of multi-plant firms, unionized plants tend to be more efficient and to provide greater employment security to employees in the form of a lower probability that managers will engage in outsourcing. With respect to job design, we find that among those plants that have adopted the new technology within the last five years and when there is both a union and a collaborative problem-solving committee structure, blue collar workers have a significantly better chance of having their jobs redesigned to include the new skill-enhancing responsibility of programming.

By contrast, nonunion workplaces with joint labor-management problem-solving committees are significantly *less* efficient and *less* likely to provide employment security than is a traditional union-based system of workplace governance. For collaborative problem solving to succeed, it must be possible for employees to achieve outcomes that also empower them. In management-initiated schemes, the narrow focus and limited objectives for which these programs were designed are quite possibly frustrating these aspirations, undermining the trust and commitment so necessary for success.

Nonunion workplaces with joint labor-management problem-solving committees are significantly <u>less</u> efficient and <u>less</u> likely to provide employment security than is a traditional union-based system of workplace governance.

Endnotes

1   This paper was originally prepared for and presented to the August 1990 Washington, D.C., Annual Meeting of the American Sociological Association, as part of Thematic Session # 10: "The Transformation of the Large Corporation." The authors acknowledge the research assistance of Lan Xue and Todd Watkins. For comments and suggestions for revision, we thank Linda Babcock, Barry Bluestone, Harvey Brooks, John Engberg, Chris Farrell, P. Davis Jenkins, Larry Mishel, Walter Powell, and Paula Voos. The survey data for this paper were collected in conjunction with a research project directed by Kelley and Brooks, through the Center for Business and Government, John F. Kennedy School of Government, Harvard University, with support from the National Science Foundation (Grant No. SES 8520174) and the U.S. Office of Technology Assessment (Contract No. 633-2470-0). The Sloan Foundation subsequently provided a grant to Kelley for further analysis of the data on efficiency (Grant No. B1989-17). The questionnaire was administered by the Center for Survey Research of the University of Massachusetts-Boston, under the direction of Dr. Mary Ellen Colten. When this research was conducted, Harrison was on a leave of absence from MIT as a visiting professor of political economy at Carnegie Mellon University.

2   For example, in "quality circles," the meetings of engineers and managers with workers are focused on problems in achieving acceptable product quality standards; the group discussion is akin to a "brainstorming" session designed for the purpose of eliciting suggestions from the group about how to improve quality. "Work teams," by contrast, are groups within the same unit or department of an organization established to encourage the development of a peer group or "self-management" process in which the group assigns particular tasks to individuals and decides on group goals for performance standards and conducts individual and group performance reviews.

3   For a survey of the evidence on this question, see Gordon (1987).

4   On the other hand, profit-sharing or gainsharing are not consistently associated with unionization (Freeman, this volume).

5   While Freeman and Medoff could be described as taking an institutionally informed neoclassical approach, there is also substantial Anglo-American post-Keynesian literature on the long-run virtues of wage-led growth. This material is surveyed in Bowles, Gordon, and Weisskopf (1986) and Harrison and Bluestone (1990).

6   The industries surveyed include: nonferrous foundries (SIC 336); cutlery, hand tools, and hardware (SIC 342); heating equipment and plumbing fixtures (SIC 343); screw machine products (SIC 345); metal forgings and stampings (SIC 346); ordnance and accessories, not elsewhere classified (SIC 348); miscellaneous fabricated metal products (SIC 349); engines and turbines (SIC 351); farm and garden machinery and equipment (SIC 352); construction and related

machinery (SIC 353); metalworking machinery and equipment (SIC 354); special industrial machinery, excluding metalworking (SIC 355); general industrial machinery and equipment (SIC 356); miscellaneous machinery, excluding electrical (SIC 359); electrical industrial apparatus (SIC 362); motor vehicles and equipment (SIC 371); aircraft and parts (SIC 372); guided missiles and space vehicles (SIC 376); engineering and scientific instruments (SIC 381); measuring and controlling instruments (SIC 382); jewelry, silverware, and plateware (SIC 391). Half of the sample establishments were in SICs 354 and 359.

[7]   Managers were not asked how long such committees had been in place, so no learning curve effects can be evaluated with these data. In a follow-up survey of the same plants surveyed by Kelley in the winter of 1990–91 (again under the auspices of the National Science Foundation, under Grant No. SEF8911141), managers were asked about when these programs were first instituted. Questions were added about the presence or absence of employee stock ownership or profit-sharing plans, following Paula Voos' suggestion that these material benefits from cooperation may be more likely to promote productive efficiency than joint committees as such (see also Levine and Tyson, 1990). Results from the follow-up survey will begin to be available late in 1991.

[8]   In the pretest of the survey instrument, Kelley and Brooks learned that metalworking establishments typically make a wide variety of products. Rather than asking managers to select a "typical" product from this array, Kelley and Brooks asked for a small sample (from one to four) of the products usually made in different lot sizes with different technologies. Concerning programmable machines, production managers were asked to describe two different products; i.e., specific jobs that were primarily manufactured using that technology, one of which was usually made in small-sized lots and another usually made in large-sized lots. For products made with conventional, nonprogrammable machine technology, a similar request was made for information on two jobs primarily manufactured on conventional machines—one usually made in a small-sized lot and another in large-sized lots.

Respondents had the option of providing information on only one product if a plant specialized in only large or small batch production and used only one type of machine tool technology. Respondents were asked to name each product or job so identified, to tell the interviewer how many of the same items were manufactured in one production run (or batch) at a time, and to answer all questions specifically in reference to the named product. From the sample of 627 plants using some programmable automation technology, detailed information was compiled on 1,602 different "jobs" or products from the machining process.

The regression analyses were conducted on the complete records within this sample of products for these plants. Of the plants using PA technology, 85 percent provided information on at least two different batch jobs—one made mainly on conventional machine tool technology and another machined mainly with programmable tools. Information on the sample of products was pooled and matched to establishment characteristics. In the statistical procedures reported here, the sample establishment weight described earlier was divided by the number of products named by each plant manager, in order to avoid giving more weight to those plants that report on more products.

9   The explicit inclusion of this set of substantive plant- and product-specific factors influencing efficiency makes it unnecessary to include zero-one ("dummy") variables for each industry, as is common in econometric models where no such microdata are available to the researcher.

10   This literature is reviewed in some detail, and then our own empirical results presented, in Harrison and Kelley (1991) and Kelley and Harrison (1990). Research in the field consists overwhelmingly of case studies. We have been able to identify only a handful of scientifically acceptable surveys—notably a remarkably detailed survey of retrospective information on *trends* in industrial subcontracting in Malaysia, designed and successfully implemented by an official of the International Labour Office in Geneva (Standing, 1989).

11   There is a perfectly plausible explanation for why the equation for single-plant enterprises performs better than the equation for the branch plants. Unlike efficiency and job design outcomes, whether a plant that is part of a larger, more complex company does or does not regularly practice outsourcing will almost always depend on decisions made at the headquarters of the firm, rather than by any particular plant manager. Since most of the explanatory variables available in the Kelley-Brooks data set pertain to the plant (and process) level, we are simply unable to incorporate into this model much information about corporate-level decisions with respect to contracting out. Precisely this aspect of modern decision-making in the large firm—that decisions with implications for the shop floor are increasingly made at different levels within the company—constitutes the central theme of the new theory of industrial relations articulated by Kochan, Katz, and McKersie (1986).

12   Economies of scope are said to exist when, due to the presence of technical synergies or indivisibilities in production, or to economies in such organizational arrangements as supervision, it is less expensive at the margin for the firm to make multiple products (often with the same equipment, in the same plant) than to specialize narrowly in only one product and purchase other products or components through external markets.

13   The alternative approach is to designate programming to be the exclusive responsibility of white collar work roles, through the creation of a specialized white collar occupation called "programmer," or by attaching these tasks to existing managerial and engineering work roles. Such an approach centralizes control over the technology in a few jobs located at the upper levels of the occupational hierarchy at the plant.

14   The survey questions distinguished among different degrees of programming responsibility. For five types of machining occupations, two questions were asked: 1) how often do workers in this occupation edit or alter a program created

280

by someone else?; 2) how often do workers in this occupation create new parts programs? The possible answers to these two question are: "never," "on occasion," or "frequently." Only if a production manager answered "frequently" to this last question for an occupation involving the setup and operation of programmable machine tools at a plant were blue collar jobs considered to be *designed* to include *major* programming responsibilities.

This definition is deliberately restrictive, excluding work roles in which programming functions are ancillary to the main tasks of machine setup and operation, such as those cases in which workers are reported to only edit programs originally created by a programming specialist or are only occasionally called upon to write programs. Only if the new responsibility of programming is substantial; i.e., involves the creation of new programs and is performed regularly by those who set up and operate the technology, are the cognitive skill demands of the work role assumed to have been substantially increased. If there is any bias in the perspective of production managers as to the extent to which blue collar workers actually perform such programming responsibilities, it would be a tendency to underestimate the informal exercise of programming responsibilities. However, there is no reason to assume that production managers who are well-informed about the technology generally are poorly informed about programming responsibilities when they are formally sanctioned by management and explicitly incorporated into these work roles as frequently performed duties.

[15] For a more exhaustive discussion of the industrial relations implications of this finding, see Kelley (1989c).

[16] The lack of user friendly, menu-drive software in early stages in the development of PA may have made managers reluctant to delegate programming responsibility to blue collar workers, but that technical obstacle is no longer present for the latest generation of PA technology. Moreover, in workplaces that have only adopted the technology for the first time within the past five years, there is no pre-existing hierarchical division of labor derived from the earlier generations of technology that management would have to dismantle in order to decentralize control over programming.

APPENDIX TABLE A1

Complete Results of the OLS Regressions on the Log of
Machining Production Time per Unit of Output

Interviews conducted Fall 1986–Spring 1987

explanatory variables	dependent variable: log of machining production time in hours per unit of output	
	single-plant firms	branch planets of multi-plant enterprises
Mean of dependent variable	2.8 hours	4.6 hours
Plant unionized (0–1)	.018	−.672***
	(.228)	(.196)
plant has formal joint labor-mgmt problem-solving committees (0–1)	.284***	.299**
	(.108)	(.138)
Plant has both (0–1)	−.305	(.315)
	.456**	(.227)
log hourly wage of machining workers	.563***	−.161
	(.154)	(.232)
log machining employment	−.231***	−.237***
	(.082)	(.054)
pct. of tools that are programmable	−.285***	−.308***
	(.080)	(.064)
product was manufactured with programmable tools (0–1)	−.331***	−.058
	(.097)	(.101)
50 percent or more of output is produced in batch sizes of fewer than 10 units a plant makes 50 or more different parts or products (0–1)	−.112	.025
	(.118)	(.124)
log of annual physical volume of output for particular product	−.563***	−.574***
	(.025)	(.023)
log of unit cost of materials per item in batch ($)	.180***	.238***
	(.024)	(.024)
log of number of tool changes required to make one item	.599***	.418***
	(.069)	(.058)
machining workers are required to have at least two years of post-secondary technical education (0–1)	.433***	−.048
	(.138)	(.174)
number of machine tools per machining worker	−.213***	−.228***
	(.051)	(.048)
product must meet high precision	−.045	.162
	(.129)	(.119)
all tools in the plant are less than 5 years old (0–1)	.049	−.483
	(.336)	(.431)
machining workers follow written orders (0–1)	.386***	−.281***
	(.116)	(.109)
Intercept	1.202	3.466
R—squared	.695	.753
N	539	584

(standard errors in parentheses)

**Significant at the .05 level (2-tailed test)
***Significant at the .01 level (2-tailed test)

NOTE: Sample restricted to plants with at least one programmable machine tool.
References for details: Kelley (1990b); Kelley and Xue (1990).

APPENDIX TABLE A2

Complete Results of the Logit Regressions on the Probability of Outsourcing

Interviews conducted Fall 1986–Spring 1987

explanatory variables	dependent variable: plant usually outsources machining work (yes = 1, no = 0)	
	single-plant firms	branch plants of multi-plant firms
mean of dependent variable	.59	.62
plant unionized (0–1)	1.022 (.701)	−.183‡ (.455)
plant has formal joint labor-mgmt. problem-solving committees (0–1)	.599*** (.225)	.671** (.335)
plant has both (0–1)	−1.354 (.845)	−.641‡ (.537)
plant makes 50 or more different parts or products (0–1)	.555** (.252)	1.321*** (.298)
pct. of total physical production made in batches of fewer than 10 units	−.005* (.003)	.001 (.004)
pct. of machine tools that are more than 10 yrs. old	.034 (.046)	.096 (.060)
pct. change in sales of the 3-digit SIC industry with which this plant principally identifies, 1983–86	.014 (.015)	−.013 (.015)
log of machining employment in 1986	−.718*** (.180)	−.002 (.111)
log of mean hourly wage of machining workers in the plant	.693** (.335)	.475 (.600)
log of employment in the parent firm in 1986	.290** (.144)	.102* (.061)
Intercept	−1.318	−2.609
−2 log likelihood	554.75	389.26
N	443	321
Chi-square (10 d.f.)	31.10***	42.48***

(asymptotic standard errors in parentheses)

***Significant at the .01 level (2-tailed test)
**Significant at the .05 level (2-tailed test)
*Significant at the .10 level (2-tailed test)
‡Jointly significant at the .05 level (2-tailed test)

NOTE: Sample includes plants with and without PA.
References for details: Harrison and Kelley (1991); Kelley and Harrison (1990).

283

APPENDIX TABLE A3

Complete Results of the Logit Regressions on the Probability that Blue Collar Workers Regularly Program Their Own Machine Tools

Interviews conducted Fall 1986–Spring 1987

explanatory variables	dependent variable: blue collar workers regularly write computer programs (yes = 1, no = 0)	
	all plants	plants that only introduced programmable automation in last 5 years
mean of dependent variable	.56	.67
plant unionized (0–1)	−1.158** (.502)	−3.544* (1.972)
plant has formal joint labor-mgmt problem-solving committees (0–1)	.004 (.233)	.236 (.577)
plant has both (0–1)	.340 (.638)	4.145** (2.148)
50 pct. or more of machining output is in batch sizes of fewer than 10 units (0–1)	.437* (.232)	1.315* (.593)
numerically controlled tools as share of all programmable tools	−1.151** (.301)	−1.739** (.658)
machining workers mainly using PA as share of all machining workers	−.741 (.478)	−.597 (1.152)
seniority rules determine job assignments or promotions (0–1)	−.679** (.221)	−.108 (.548)
plant has formal apprenticeship program of at least 3 years duration (0–1)	−.201 (.257)	−1.838** (.557)
organizational complexity (factor scores ranging from −1.8 to +2.4, fitted to firm size, plant size, whether plant is part of a multi-plant firm, and whether, if so, the plant ships output to other plants within the firm)	−.899** (.163)	−1.104** (.402)
managers who develop quality control standards or set production standards must have at least a bachelor's degree (0–1)	.634* (.280)	2.351** (.761)
machining workers are required to follow written orders (0–1)	−.007 (.240)	1.087* (.615)
Intercept	.378	−.598
−2 log likelihood	566.06	113.49
N	506	129
Chi-square (11 d.f.)	128.86***	126.89***

(asymptotic standard errors in parentheses)

***Significant at the .01 level (two-tailed test)
**Significant at the .05 level (two-tailed test)
*Significant at the .10 level (two-tailed test)

NOTE: Sample restricted to plants with at least one programmable machine tool.
References for details: Kelley (1989a,b,c; 1990a).

284

Appendix B

The estimates of the differences in efficiency for each labor-management regime (relative to the regime of no union–no LMC), displayed in Tables 2 and 3, were derived using the following method. The estimated equation was of the form,

(1)
$$\text{Ln} \left[\frac{\text{production time}}{\text{physical output}} \right]$$

$$= a + b\,(\text{UNION}) + c(\text{LMC}) + d(\text{UNION*LMC}) + \Sigma\,h(\mathbf{X}) + \epsilon$$

where UNION = 1 if the plant is unionized, 0 if not; LMC = 1 if the plant has a joint committee, 0 if not; $\mathbf{X}$ is a vector of other explanatory variables; and ϵ is a random disturbance term distributed with zero mean and constant variance. The OLS regression results are presented in Appendix Table A1. Evaluating the fitted equation for each union-LMC regime, the difference in production time per unit of output for plants with unions but no LMCs, vis-à-vis plants with neither, is given by $\hat{b}$, or 0.018 for SPEs and −0.672 for BPs (see Appendix Table A1). For plants with LMCs but no unions, the difference in efficiency relative to the base case is given by $\hat{c}$, or 0.284 for SPEs and 0.299 for BPs. For plants with both unions *and* LMCs, the difference in efficiency relative to the plants with neither is given by $(\hat{b} + \hat{c} + \hat{d})$, or −0.003 for SPEs and 0.083 for BPs.

Technically, these are estimates of differences in the *log* of efficiency between the various union-LMC regimes and the regime characterized by the absence of both unions and LMCs. The *level* of each difference (z) is given by the transformation

$$[\text{antilog}\,(z)] - 1.$$

It is the results of this transformation that are presented in Tables 2 and 3, for single-plant and multiplant firms, respectively. The estimates are presented as percentage differences from the base regime of no union–no LMC.

The reader is cautioned to remember that these are all estimates from *cross-sectional* data. That means that they measure comparisons among qualitatively different classes of plants. They do *not* measure the effect of (for example) "adding" an LMC to a plant that already has a union. That sort of inference must await the longitudinal analysis to be conducted by Kelley and her colleagues when their 1991 reinterviews of the same metalworking plants are completed.

To obtain estimates of the differential effect of the presence or absence of unions, we use estimates of equation (1) and take the difference

$$
\begin{aligned}
&(\hat{a} + \hat{b} + \hat{c} + \hat{d}(\overline{\text{LMC}}) + \Sigma\,\hat{h}\,\bar{\mathbf{X}}) \\
-&(\hat{a} \qquad\quad + \hat{c} \qquad\qquad\quad + \Sigma\,\hat{h}\,\bar{\mathbf{X}}) \\
=&\ \hat{b} + \hat{d}(\overline{\text{LMC}})
\end{aligned}
$$

where, for convenience, we evaluate the variable LMC at its sample mean. For SPEs and BPs, the sample means of LMC taken from the regressions reported in Appendix Table A1 are 0.466 and 0.653. Thus the union effects are -0.106 and -0.394, respectively. Again, these represent differences between estimates of the *log* of production time per unit of output. To get *levels,* we again subtract 1 from the antilog of these estimates, which gives us the figures shown in the first row of Table 4. For ease of interpretation, we present these as percentages.

The identical procedure is followed to obtain the estimates of the cooperation–no cooperation effect. That is, we compute $\hat{c} + \hat{d}(\overline{UNION})$. The sample means of UNION for SPEs and BPs that are embodied in this calculation, 0.106 and 0.402 respectively, were also taken from the (unpublished) statistics associated with the regressions reported in Appendix Table A1. The untransformed LMC effects are therefore 0.252 and 0.482. The transformed values appear in the second row of Table 4.

Work Organization, Unions, and Economic Performance

Ray Marshall

Introduction

The major assumption of this paper is that the future role of more participative work organizations in the economy is not predetermined, but depends heavily on the choices made by employers, workers, and governments.[1] An important lesson from historical experience in the U.S. and abroad is that work organization choices are closely related to, and have important implications for, other economic and social policies.

A second major assumption is that national economic performance depends significantly on the extent to which labor and work organization policies are integrated with other economic policies. This is so because the need for high performance production systems in a more competitive global economy causes work organization to be increasingly important for a nation's economic, political, and social health.

In order to help clarify the context within which these choices must be made, this paper explores the following guiding hypotheses:

(1) Basic U.S. work organization policies are rooted in the mass production/natural resource economy that made the United States the world's leading industrial nation during the first quarter of this century. These policies were reinforced by "Keynesian" macroeconomic policies that

Historical experience in the U.S. and abroad is that work organization choices are closely related to, and have important implications for, other economic and social policies.

were basically designed to sustain the mass production system and make it more equitable.

(2) Mass production and its supporting Keynesian policies have become anachronistic because of changing technology and the globalization of economic activity. In a more competitive global economy, economic viability requires much greater attention to quality, productivity, and flexibility, all of which have been much less important, if not ignored, by mass production systems.

(3) These changes require that companies, unions, or countries that wish to be high-income, world-class players adopt very different work organization and human resource development policies.

(4) The United States is losing its status as a high performance country because its economic and work organization systems and policies have been slow to adjust to this more competitive world. A failure to adapt implies economic decline, growing inequalities in wealth and income, and lower real wages, even though corporations based in the United States might be able to maintain their profits, at least for a while, by continuing their traditional production systems and shifting employment to lower-paid workers, both overseas and in the United States. A restoration of high performance systems will thus require radical changes in U.S. economic and work organization policies. In a more competitive global economy, countries with consensus-based national goals and strategies have important advantages over countries like the United States that follow passive "laissez faire" policies.

> *A failure to adapt implies economic decline, growing inequalities in wealth and income, and lower real wages, even though corporations based in the United States might be able to maintain their profits.*

The Changing Economy

Traditional labor-management relations are deeply rooted in the economic policies and institutions that made the United States the world's strongest economy during the first half of this century. The most important factors in America's economic success were abundant natural resources and the mass production system, which made it possible to achieve relatively rapid improvements in productivity and total output through economies of scale and reinforcing inter-industry shifts.

The mass production system organized work so that most thinking, planning, and decisionmaking was done by managerial, professional, and technical elites. Line work was simplified so that it could be done by relatively unskilled workers. The assumption was that there was "one best way" to perform a task. It was management's responsibility to discover that one best method and impose it on the system through detailed regulations, enforced by supervisors and inspectors. It was assumed that workers would "soldier," or loaf, unless they were closely supervised. Management therefore sought to gain control of the work by standardizing work processes and transferring ideas, skills, and knowledge to managers and machines.

Some of the system's basic weaknesses were gradually worked out by the 1940s. A major problem for mass production companies, once they stabilized the prices of their products through oligopolistic pricing arrangements, was cyclical instability caused when production outran consumption at administered prices. This problem was fixed through so-called "Keynesian" monetary-fiscal policies which manipulated government spending and interest rates to generate enough total demand to keep the system operating at relatively low levels of unemployment. Industrial relations and "welfare" or "income maintenance" policies reinforced these macroeconomic and administered price policies. Unions, collective bargaining, unemployment compensation, and social security were all justified as ways to sustain purchasing power.

The most important factors in America's economic success were abundant natural resources and the mass production system.

Unions and their supporters had the same aversion for competition in labor markets as the oligopolists did for competitive product markets. Early unions learned that competition forced employers to depress wages and working conditions. Workers in all industrial countries therefore organized not only to extend democracy to the workplace, but also to remove labor from competition through collective bargaining and government regulations. Labor theorists, like the Webbs (1897), argued that removing labor from competition through collective bargaining and government regulations increased efficiency by preventing companies from depressing labor standards, thus forcing them to compete by becoming more efficient. The Webbs reasoned that employers who paid less than the living wage were being subsidized either by workers and their families or by society. Such subsidies therefore generated inefficiencies and made it difficult for countries to develop their human resources.

Both the mass production system and demand management policies were justified by the American economy's remarkable performance in World War II. After the war, the combination of economies of scale, abundant natural resources, strong global demand, and a backlog of technology (much of it, including the computer, developed by the military), ushered in the longest period of equitably-shared prosperity in U.S. history. Progressive government policies and collective bargaining counteracted the market's natural tendency to produce inequality.

The System Erodes

Toward the end of the 1960s, the foundations of America's traditional economic system began to crumble. The main forces for change were technology and increased international competition, which combined to render much of the traditional mass production system and its supporting institutions anachronistic. These changes also dramatically altered the conditions for economic viability. In a more competitive world dominated by knowledge-intensive technology, the key to economic success became human resources and a more effective organization of production systems, not natural resources and traditional economies of scale. Indeed, as the work of Theodore Schultz and other economists demonstrated, the process of substituting knowledge and skills for physical resources had been the main source of improved productivity since at least the 1920s (Carnevale, 1983; Schultz, 1981).

Technology makes new organizations of production *possible*, but competition makes them *necessary*. This is so because a competitive internationalized information economy has very different requirements for national, enterprise, organizational, and personal success than was true of largely national goods producing systems. One of the most important changes for public policy purposes is that national governments have less control of their economies. It therefore is no longer possible for a single country to maintain high wages and full employment through traditional combinations of monetary-fiscal policies, administered wages and prices, and fixed exchange rates. In the 1970s and 1980s, internationalization weakened the linkages between domestic consumption, investment, and output that formed the basic structure of the traditional "Keynesian" demand management system. This became very clear when the early 1980s' U.S. tax cuts increased

In the 1970s and 1980s, internationalization weakened the linkages between domestic consumption, investment, and output that formed the basic structure of the traditional "Keynesian" demand management system.

consumption, but also greatly stimulated imports and there-fore produced much smaller increases in the production of domestic capital goods than had resulted from earlier tax cuts in less globalized markets.

The Basic Choice: Low Wages or Higher Quality, Productivity, and Skills

These altered economic conditions do not just change the *magnitude* of the requirements for economic suc-cess—they fundamentally alter the *necessary structures* and *policies*. This is so because in the more competitive global information economy, success requires greater emphasis on some factors that were much less important in traditional mass production systems. These new factors are quality, productivity, and flexibility.

Quality, best defined as meeting customers' needs, becomes more important for two reasons. First, as the mass production system matured and personal incomes rose, consumers became less satisfied with standardized prod-ucts. Second, the more competitive environment of the 1990s is largely consumer driven; the mass production sys-tem was more producer driven, especially after govern-ments and oligopolies "stabilized" prices. In the more com-petitive environments of the 1970s, oligopolistic pricing became anachronistic; flexible prices became more impor-tant. Furthermore, the mass production system depended heavily on controlling national markets; with internationali-zation, American companies have much less market control.

Productivity and flexibility are closely related to quality. The difference is that productivity improvements are now achieved through using *all factors of production* more effi-ciently, not, as in the mass production system, mainly through economies of scale and compatible and reinforcing inter-industry shifts. Indeed, in the 1970s and 1980s, inter-industry shifts lowered productivity growth because they went, on balance, from more productive manufacturing activities to less productive services.

Flexibility enhances productivity by facilitating the shift of resources from less to more productive outputs and improves quality through the ability to respond quickly to diverse and changing consumer needs. Moreover, flexibility in the use of workers and technology improves productiv-ity by reducing the waste of labor and machine time.

In the more competitive global information economy, success requires greater emphasis on some factors that were much less important in traditional mass production systems.

Firms and economies can compete in more global knowledge-intensive markets either by reducing wages or by becoming more productive. Since the early 1970s, American companies have been competing mainly through reducing domestic wages and by shifting productive facilities to low-wage countries. This is one of the reasons why real wages were lower in the United States in 1990 than they were in 1970, and why in 1989 American wages were about tenth among the major industrialized countries (Bureau of Labor Statistics, 1990; Mishel and Frankel, 1991).

> *Since the early 1970s, American companies have been competing mainly through reducing domestic wages and by shifting productive facilities to low-wage countries.*

Worker Participation and Higher Order Thinking Skills

The fundamental issue, of course, is how to arrange production in order to achieve quality, productivity, and flexibility. The answer appears to be to restructure production systems and to develop and use leading-edge technologies. Productivity is improved in work organizations that reduce waste by maintaining better inventory control, promoting the efficient use of labor, and developing more effective quality controls to prevent defects. High performance systems have a significant degree of employee involvement in what would have been considered "management" functions in mass production systems. Indeed, in more productive and flexible systems, the distinctions between "managers" and "workers" become blurred.

A number of features in high performance production systems encourage worker participation. For one thing, these systems require better educated, skilled workers who are less tolerant of monotonous, routine work and authoritarian managerial controls. Secondly, quality, productivity, and flexibility are all enhanced when production decisions are made as close to the point of production as possible. Mass production managerial bureaucracies were designed to achieve quantity, managerial control, and stability, not flexibility, quality, or productivity in the use of all factors of production. Mass production systems are based on managerial information monopolies and worker controls; high performance systems require that workers be free to make decisions. To accomplish this, information must be shared, not monopolized, because in high performance systems, machines do more routine, direct work and people do more indirect work.[2] One of the most important skills required

292

for indirect work is the ability to analyze the flood of data produced by information technology. Workers who can impose order on chaotic data can use information to add value to products, improve productivity, technology, and quality, and solve problems.

Indirect work also is more likely to be group work, requiring more communication and interpersonal skills. These skills are necessary because productivity, quality, and flexibility require close coordination between what were formerly more discrete components of the production process (e.g., research and development, design, production, inspection, distribution, sales, services). These functions were more linear in the mass production system, but are more interactive in dynamic, consumer-oriented production systems.

Another very important skill for high performance systems is the ability to learn. Learning is not only more important than in mass production systems, it also is very different. The simplification of tasks and the standardization of technology and productivity in the mass production system limits the amount of learning needed or achieved. For line workers, mass production systems stressed learning almost entirely by observation and doing. By contrast, more learning is required in a dynamic, technology-intensive workplace and more of that learning must be through the manipulation of abstract symbols.

Learning in more productive workplaces also is likely to be more communal and cooperative. The adversarial relationships inherent in the mass production system impeded the sharing of information between companies and their suppliers. And a preoccupation with price competition and the neglect of quality created less cooperation, and therefore poor learning processes, between workers and managers. A high performance system, by contrast, encourages the sharing of information and cooperative efforts to achieve common objectives between managers, workers, and suppliers. In addition, communal learning becomes more important as a means of building the kind of consensus needed to improve the performance of more highly integrated production processes. High performance workers are not only required to be self managers, but also to be able to perform a greater array of tasks and adapt more readily to change. This requires a reduction of the mass production system's detailed job classifications and work rules. Well-educated, well-trained, highly motivated workers are

In the mass production system . . . a preoccupation with price competition and the neglect of quality created less cooperation, and therefore poor learning processes, between workers and managers.

likely to be much more flexible and productive, especially in supportive systems that stress equity and internal cohesion. Indeed, humans are likely to be the most flexible components in a high performance system.

Other features of high performance workplaces require greater worker involvement. One is the need for constant improvements in technology—or what the Japanese call "giving wisdom to the machine." Technology is best defined as how things are done. The most important fact about technology is not the physical capital itself, but the ideas, skills, and knowledge embodied in machines and structures. Technology becomes standardized when the rate at which ideas, skills, and knowledge can be transferred to a machine or structure becomes very slow. Standardized technology therefore requires fewer ideas and less skill and knowledge than leading-edge technology. High performance organizations emphasize the development and use of leading-edge technologies because standardized technologies are highly mobile and therefore are likely to be employed mainly by low-wage workers. Some American companies have responded to competitive pressure by attempting to combine high technology and low skills through automation, which has proved to be little, if any, more productive than the combination of standardized technology and low-skilled workers. The most productive systems therefore have highly skilled workers who can develop and use leading-edge technology. And the shorter life cycles of products and technologies in a more dynamic and competitive global economy provide important advantages to continuing innovation and creativity. The more mobile technologies become, the more critical participation by highly skilled workers becomes to competitiveness.

The increased need for quality control is another reason high performance systems work better with more worker involvement. In cases where direct contact with customers is required, flexible, highly skilled employees can provide better customer service than highly specialized mass production workers who can only provide their narrow specialized services. In manufacturing systems, moreover, even the most sophisticated machines are idiosyncratic and therefore require the close attention of skilled workers to adapt them to different and specific situations. With the smaller production runs permitted by information technology and required by more competitive markets, workers must control production and be able to override machines.

> **Some American companies have responded to competitive pressure by attempting to combine high technology and low skills through automation.**

The mass production system usually made this impossible. However, the mass production system's long production runs made it possible to amortize start-up defects during the runs. Systems with short production runs cannot afford many start-up defects, and therefore workers must override the machines if defects start to appear. Quality-driven systems also must provide for more self-inspection by workers which is on the basis of visible observation to *prevent* defects rather than inspections to *detect* them at the end of the production process. Quality control is facilitated by just-in-time inventory and other mechanisms that make defects more visible or detectable early in the production processes. Productivity and quality are enhanced by early detection; otherwise those defective components become invisible when they enter the product, and they are discovered as the products malfunction when used by customers.

Incentive Systems

The explicit or implicit incentives in any system are basic determinants of its outcomes. High performance organizations ordinarily stress positive incentive systems. Mass production incentives tend to be negative: fear of discharge or punishment. They also tend to be more individualistic and implicit. Process- and time-based mass compensation systems, for example, are often unrelated to productivity or quality and may even be counterproductive, or perverse, as when workers fear they will lose their jobs if they improve productivity, or when "incentives," especially for managers, bear no relationship to objective performance or equity and therefore create disunity within the work group. Sometimes, moreover, expressed incentives are to improve productivity, whereas the operative implicit incentives stress stability and control, or some component of the production process (e.g., reducing shipping costs or the cost of supplies), which often has negative effects on the whole system. High performance incentives, by contrast, are more likely to be communal, positive, explicit, based on measurable outcomes, and directly related to the stated objectives of the enterprise.

We should note that positive incentives enhance flexibility as well as productivity and quality. It is easier not to pay a bonus for reasons everybody understands than it is to cut wages. Group incentives and job security encourage flexibility by simultaneously overcoming resistance to the

High performance organizations ordinarily stress positive incentive systems. Mass production incentives tend to be negative: fear of discharge or punishment.

development and use of broader skills and providing employers with greater incentives to invest in those skills. Similarly, bonus compensation systems simultaneously provide greater incentives for workers to improve productivity and quality and create a more flexible compensation system. Participative systems therefore in themselves create positive incentives.

It would be hard to overemphasize the importance of internal unity and positive incentives for high performance, knowledge-intensive workplaces. This is so in part because all parties must be willing to go "all out" to achieve common objectives. In traditional mass production systems, workers are justifiably afraid to go "all out" to improve productivity because, at best, they see little relationship between their efforts and their compensation and at worst, fear increasing productivity will cost them their jobs. This is the reason job security is one of the most important incentives a high performance company can have. Similarly, the fragmentation of work within mass production systems gives workers little incentive to control quality—quality is somebody else's responsibility. A high performance system, by contrast, makes quality control everybody's responsibility. Positive incentives are required, in addition, because the effective use of information technology tends to give workers greater discretion (Zuboff, 1988). It is difficult to *compel* workers to think or even to tell whether or not they are doing it. It also is very hard to compel workers to go all out to improve quality and productivity.

> *It would be hard to overemphasize the importance of internal unity and positive incentives for high performance, knowledge-intensive workplaces.*

How Do All of These Developments Affect Traditional Industrial Relations Systems?

Globalization has strengthened employers relative to unions in several important ways. As noted, unions received considerable public support during the 1930s as not only being necessary to protect workers from arbitrary treatment in Tayloristic management systems, but also because they reinforced Keynesian economic policies. In advanced democratic countries, most people recognize the continued need for unions to protect and promote the interests of the workers in the polity and society as well as in the workplace. But they increasingly question the economic value of collective bargaining. This is so in large

296

measure because the reduced efficacy of Keynesian policies has caused a perception that the unions' role in maintaining purchasing power and stabilizing wages and prices is no longer as critical as it was in the 1930s. For the main problems confronting more competitive global economies—the control of inflation and competitiveness—unions and collective bargaining often are seen as negatives. Similarly, many employers who valued the stabilizing functions of collective bargaining see less need to cooperate with unions since traditional collective bargaining processes are less effective in taking labor out of competition. On the other hand, internationalization gives employers greater market, resource, and production options, thereby strengthening companies relative to unions. The reduced public support for unions, together with the pro-employer biases in American laws and policies, have enabled employers to intensify and expand their anti-union activities.

Reduced public support for unions, together with the pro-employer biases in American laws and policies, have enabled employers to intensify and expand their anti-union activities.

Unions also have suffered because they have appealed mainly to skilled manual and mass production workers and less to workers in the rapidly growing service and technical occupations. Most industrial unions have been more adept at administering contracts under largely adversarial relationships than they are at establishing cooperative relationships and improving productivity, flexibility, and quality. Exceptions include unions in the highly competitive garment and clothing industries, which always had to give greater attention to productivity in order to sustain a wage advantage over the nonunion competitors. Another exception is in areas like construction, where unique customer needs made mass production difficult, thus requiring more highly skilled workers and labor-management cooperation to meet customers' needs.

Some people interpret the relative decline of union strength in the United States to mean that unions are, like their related oligopolistic mass production and regulated industries, anachronistic. I read it otherwise. Indeed, according to the latest evidence from the OECD, unions have gained density in *most* industrialized countries since the 1960s. The fact that the relative strength of American unions has declined much more than their counterparts in other countries (especially Canada, where the union strength has increased since the 1960s—see Figure 1), suggests that their problems are due to unique American factors, not to the obsolescence of trade unions *per se*. In fact, a case can be made that unions continue to have a vital role,

297

Figure 1
Union Membership of Nonagricultural Workers as a Percentage of
Nonagricultural Wage and Salary Employees: 1970 to 1986–87

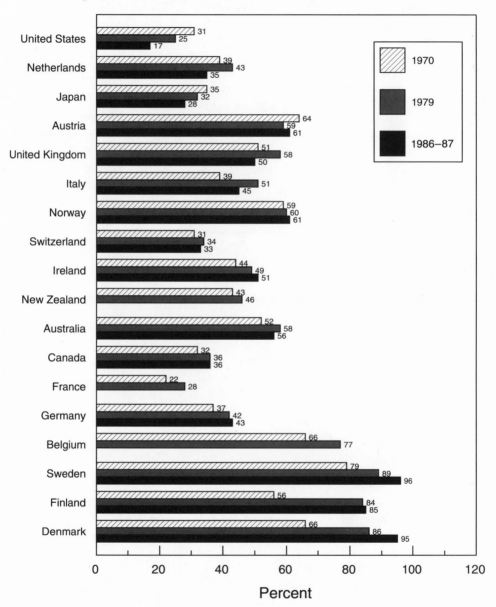

Source: NBER.

though their methods, like those of mass production companies, must be adapted to a more competitive global economy. Genuine worker participation in high performance enterprises, for example, is unlikely unless the workers have independent sources of power to represent their interests. Indeed, unions are an integral part of high performance companies in Sweden, Germany, and even in Japan.

Independent sources of power are essential in more national high performance economies for three major reasons. First, workers are not likely to be willing to go "all out" unless they are able to protect themselves from the adverse consequences of doing so. Second, it is very difficult to have effective participatory, cooperative arrangements between parties with greatly unequal power. This is so because the stronger party ultimately will be inclined to exert unilateral control, thus destroying cooperation and internal unity and causing the weaker party to seek countervailing power. This happened, for instance, during the 1920s and 1930s, when management's unilateral actions encouraged workers to form or seek independent unions. Third, adversarial relations between workers and managers are both inevitable and functional. Unions are needed to represent workers' interests in these relationships. It is not inconsistent, for example, to cooperate to make the pie bigger and to bargain to split it. The trick, of course, is to keep the process from becoming "functionless," to use a German term, i.e., making all parties worse off.

This is not to argue that effective nonunion systems are impossible, but it does imply that they are hard to maintain in the long run. It is especially difficult for these systems to work where management's main motives are to avoid unions or to reduce labor costs. There can be little question that the workers' ability to organize freely and bargain collectively has been an important check on arbitrary and discriminatory actions by companies or unions. I also believe that the right of self-organization has been so diluted in the United States that it no longer provides adequate safeguards to workers.

It might legitimately be asked, however, that if an independent source of power is essential for optimal performance, how does one explain the relatively high performance of nonunion companies like IBM, that generally are regarded as world class. The first explanation, of course, is that the workers' right to organize creates a threat of unionization, which undoubtedly causes IBM to treat its workers

I . . . believe that the right of self-organization has been so diluted in the United States that it no longer provides adequate safeguards to workers.

better than would otherwise be the case. An important policy question, however, is to see to it that the workers' right to organize is real. This right could be diminished if unions became so weak that they could not respond to workers' requests for unionization. There can be little doubt that it is much harder for workers to engage in concerted action in the United States than is the case in Germany, Japan, or most other industrialized democracies. Secondly, there is no doubt that many world class nonunion employers understand that worker involvement is good business. But this is very different where involvement is on terms unilaterally extended by employers than where there is bilateral participation by parties of relatively equal power. My orienting hypothesis is that IBM's unilateral authoritarian decision processes will be better if its employees have an independent source of power to protect themselves in their relationships with management (Mills, 1988). In short, the fact that some nonunion companies have achieved high performance does not prove that they will be more competitive in the long run than their unionized competitors in Europe (especially in Scandinavia and Germany) and Japan—who have gained market share relative to American companies in almost all industries (Dertouzes et al., 1989).

Relatively weak unions in the private sector is one reason why . . . American companies are attempting to compete mainly through lower wages.

We also should note that the existence of relatively weak unions in the private sector is one reason why the Commission on the Skills of the American Workforce found that, relative to their competitors in six other countries studied (Japan, Singapore, Germany, Sweden, Denmark, and Ireland), American companies are attempting to compete mainly through lower wages and Tayloristic work organizations (Commission on Skills, 1990). Less than 10 percent of American companies are attempting to compete through high performance work organizations, whereas most companies in these other countries stressed quality, productivity, and a high degree of worker involvement in work decisions. These differences were not solely because of the presence of strong unions, but unions are important forces for high-wage, high productivity strategies. A major reason for high performance strategies in other countries is a broad consensus that wage competition would cause lower and more unequal wages, thus creating serious political, social, and economic risks.

The distribution of income is important not only because of the threat to national unity and democratic institutions, but also because countries with very unequal income distributions have much greater difficulty solving their economic problems, mainly because the wealthy will resist the equitable fiscal policies needed to promote effective health, education, and other human resource development activities (Sachs, 1989).

Other countries have therefore developed a broad consensus to avoid low-wage strategies. They reason, along with the Webbs, that it is very inefficient for workers or the society to subsidize low-wage industries; a better strategy is to discourage industries that can only compete through lower wages and to provide education and workforce training systems to give workers the kinds of skills needed to participate in high performance work processes.

Evidence

I have argued that greater worker participation will improve productivity, quality, and flexibility. Unfortunately, the evidence for this proposition is difficult to establish because worker participation processes have different meanings, are qualitatively different from place to place, and never occur in isolation from other factors.

There is, however, growing evidence that worker participation and work reorganization are important factors in improving productivity and economic competitiveness (Dertouzes et al., 1989). This should not be surprising, of course, since labor accounts for at least 70 percent of total costs. Small improvements in labor productivity can have a much greater impact on total productivity than larger increases in physical capital. A recent Brookings Institution study, edited by Alan Blinder, acknowledged the positive contribution of worker participation, though Blinder considers such productivity improvements to be "transitory," albeit potentially "impressive" (Blinder, 1990; 1989/90). Blinder, like most economists, believes that "The best way to raise productivity growth, and perhaps the only way to do so permanently, is to speed up the pace of technological innovation" (Blinder, 1989/90, p. 33). The trouble with this view, of course, is the implied assumption that technological innovation is external to the production process and not an integral part of it. This view also fails to recognize that high performance production systems with positive incentives, skilled workers, and a high degree of worker involvement have the capacity for *continuous improvements* in

There is . . . growing evidence that worker participation and work reorganization are important factors in improving productivity and economic competitiveness.

productivity and technology. Nevertheless, the Brookings study shows that incentive compensation systems raise wages about 11 percent an hour more than for other workers, and they do this without reducing fringes or hourly wages (Blinder, 1989/90, p. 37). Blinder concludes that "worker participation apparently does help make alternative compensation plans . . . work better—and also has beneficial effects of its own. This theme was totally unexpected when I organized the conference [that led to these studies]" (Blinder, 1989/90, p. 38).

As might be expected, of course, the mere presence of an employee involvement system is not sufficient to produce high performance—much depends on the degree and quality of worker participation. This was demonstrated by David Lewin and others at Columbia University who studied the relationships between the financial performance of 500 publicly traded companies and the degree of employee involvement. Analysis of the data for 1987 concluded that

> the mere presence of an employee involvement process was not significantly related to positive improvements in any of the financial indicators. However, the further a firm moved up the employee involvement index [measuring degrees of employee involvement] and the more employees were involved in decision-making, the greater the magnitude of financial performance. What appears to be critical is the scope or comprehensiveness of employee involvement and participation programs.
>
> High employee involvement is associated with better financial performance, particularly on the return on investment and return on asset measures. (Economic Policy Council, 1990, p. 16)

In addition, there is abundant case study evidence of the relationship between worker participation and improved quality and productivity. Perhaps the most clear-cut and compelling evidence is from the New United Motor Manufacturing Co., Inc. (NUMMI), a joint venture between Toyota and General Motors in Fremont, California. This was a plant that GM closed in 1982 because its managers could not make it competitive. Toyota reopened the plant as NUMMI in 1984 with a new management system, but with mostly the same UAW members and essentially the same equipment, which was much less automated than in GM's most modern plants. One of the most important changes

Perhaps the most clear-cut and compelling evidence [of the relationship between worker participation and improved quality and productivity] is from NUMMI.

made at NUMMI was to guarantee the workers a high level of job security. Other changes include a reduction in job classifications from about 100 to 4; the elimination of such management perks as private dining rooms, parking lots, private offices, and separate dress codes; and the establishment of work teams of five to ten people who set their own work standards, lay out the work area, determine the work load distribution, and assign workers to specific tasks.

NUMMI's key managerial concept is a commitment to high quality standards by workers and managers. Quality control is built into the production process. NUMMI uses a modified just-in-time inventory system to reduce costs and improve quality by immediately identifying faulty parts. The company also imposes very high quality standards for suppliers, but works closely with those companies to solve quality problems. The inspection function is largely decentralized to line workers.

From a production standpoint, there can be little doubt that NUMMI—which makes Toyota Corollas and the Geo Prism (Chevrolet Novas were discontinued in 1989, and the plant started producing light trucks in 1991)—has been a success. Productivity at the plant is 50 percent higher than at the former GM plant and in 1989 NUMMI ranked first among all GM plants in the U.S. A 1988 MIT study reported that productivity was about 40 percent higher than traditional GM plants and was about equal to that of Toyota's Japanese plants (Krafcik, 1989). *Consumer Reports* judged NUMMI's Chevrolet Nova to be the highest quality of any American-built car. As a result of these successes, there has been strong interest in NUMMI among American managers. GM uses the plant as a managerial training center and other companies have hired NUMMI managers.

Toyota's main objectives at NUMMI were to establish an American production and marketing center and to ascertain whether or not that company's management system could be successfully used with American workers and unions. There is no doubt that Toyota succeeded in demonstrating that this could be done. Toyota has improved on the NUMMI experience with its Camry, produced in its newer plant in Georgetown, Kentucky. In 1990, the Corolla was still ranked as one of the highest quality American-built cars by J.D. Powers & Associates (it ranked ninth and the Camry third), and Toyota's Cressida was ranked first. What makes Toyota's performance so impressive is the fact

NUMMI's key managerial concept is a commitment to high quality standards by workers and managers.

that almost all other cars ranked were luxury vehicles whereas the Corolla and Camry are lower-priced subcompacts (White, 1990).

General Motors' main objective at NUMMI was to learn more about the Japanese management system. GM managers had relied more heavily than Toyota or Ford on automating to improve productivity and competitiveness. NUMMI taught GM that the workers were not the problem; and it learned from many other experiences that machine technology alone was not the answer. The NUMMI experience has helped GM to produce even better results in Shreveport, Louisiana, than at NUMMI and has caused that company to rethink its Saturn strategy.

Saturn was originally designed to leapfrog the competitive advantage enjoyed by Japanese auto companies. The NUMMI experience not only caused GM to change the kind of car it planned to make in its Saturn plant, but also to give much greater attention to worker participation and work organization. In many ways the Saturn agreement improves on the one at NUMMI. Saturn uses the team concept, but the union participates at every level of the management system, not just on the shop floor as at NUMMI. Like NUMMI, job classifications have been greatly reduced to one for production workers and three to five for skilled workers. Saturn also dispenses with management perks, but goes farther: all workers are on salary equal to 80 percent of average UAW wages in other U.S. auto plants. The other 20 percent varies according to such factors as productivity, profits, and quality. Saturn, unlike NUMMI, assigns relief workers to each work team and the work is more self-paced. Moreover, the team leaders at Saturn are elected by members of their work units or through an election designed by the UAW. At NUMMI they are determined by management.

Saturn also follows NUMMI's lead in giving workers job security by providing for no layoffs for 80 percent of workers except for severe economic conditions or unforeseen catastrophic events.

Critics argue that NUMMI has subjected workers to "management by stress" by speeding up the production line and by eliminating easy jobs and slack time. Some workers also have been very critical of NUMMI's very strict absentee policies. Other critics argue that some NUMMI managers have regressed to their former authoritarian ways, and criticize the "team" concept for weakening union solidarity (Parker and Slaughter, 1988).

Saturn uses the team concept, but the union participates at every level of the management system, not just on the shop floor.

Despite these criticisms, the UAW and the overwhelming majority of the plant's workers strongly support NUMMI's participatory processes. As the Saturn agreement demonstrates, however, NUMMI's system can be improved upon.[3] In my view, the participatory systems in Europe—especially in Sweden and Germany—are much more viable than the Japanese system used at NUMMI (see Turner in this volume). As I have demonstrated elsewhere (Marshall, 1987), this is so because European workers have stronger unions and political parties (independent sources of power), and participate at every level in the company structures and in the society. Japanese companies encourage participation because it is good business, not because they are forced to do so by strong labor movements.

The evidence strongly supports the conclusion that restructured production systems emphasizing worker participation can greatly improve productivity and quality as well as the quality of worklife. As noted, in a more competitive global economy, firms can compete either by reducing wages or improving productivity and quality through worker reorganization and increased workforce skills. There also is strong evidence, however, that *genuine* worker participation is much less pervasive in the United States than in Japan or Western Europe. How do we account for this? Several hypotheses might be advanced:

(1) The mass production system was both more successful and more entrenched in the United States, so unions and management are more reluctant to abandon the adversarial and authoritarian systems that it produced than are their Japanese or European counterparts.

(2) Most American employers are not convinced that participatory systems are more effective than traditional mass production systems and authoritarian management procedures. There appears to be enough uncertainty about these new approaches that most American managers apparently believe the risks outweigh the potential benefits.

(3) Government policies in the United States encourage companies to follow low-wage strategies. The United States, for example, has been extremely reluctant to restrain managerial decisionmaking, either by requiring the kind of worker participation processes that exist in almost all other major industrial countries or by strengthening the workers'

Despite . . . criticisms, the UAW and the overwhelming majority of the plant's workers strongly support NUMMI's participatory processes.

305

right to organize and bargain collectively, which has been greatly diluted since the 1940s and 1950s. The U.S. also has been reluctant to interfere with the "employment at will" doctrine which allows American companies to easily shift the costs of change to workers and communities through lay-offs and plant closings. Indeed, U.S. tax and tariff policies actually encourage American companies to shift employment to low-wage countries. As noted earlier, unlike other advanced industrial countries, the United States has not adopted a high-wage, full employment strategy. We have, for example, encouraged the perpetuation of industries that are viable only through low wages; most other indus-trialized countries actively discourage such indus-tries through high minimum or negotiated wages and other restrictions.

> *Perhaps the most serious limitation of American policy has been the lack of a human resource development strategy to produce the skilled workers needed for high performance work systems.*

Perhaps the most serious limitation of American policy has been the lack of a human resource development strat-egy to produce the skilled workers needed for high per-formance work systems. Our mass production school sys-tem and the absence of policies to educate and train the 75 percent of our front-line workers who are not college edu-cated create serious competitive disadvantages for Ameri-can companies. All of our major economic competitors have policies to provide strong basic education and work training for those skills that do not require four years of col-lege. American secondary school graduates, by contrast, consistently score near the bottom on international math and science assessments—even below many developing countries. And we have almost no post-secondary skill training programs for most noncollege-bound youths. A recent report, for example, found that in mathematics, 95 percent of Japanese high school students outperform the top 5 percent of America's students (Council on Competi-tiveness, 1990). Without higher order thinking skills, drop-outs, and even most high school graduates, increasingly are condemned to lives of low wages and joblessness. Our prin-cipal competitors see to it that all young people acquire basic thinking skills by the time they are fifteen or sixteen years old. These basic academic skills provide the founda-tion for further education, professional and technical job training, or work. These countries also have a variety of technical training and education programs for those who do not enter technical college immediately. However, higher education remains an option even for those who elect technical training or work options after completing their basic education.

Role of Labor Movements

Public policies can help create the context within which labor movements operate, but labor movements themselves must develop the strategies, policies, and structures to strengthen their ability to protect and promote workers' interests. Labor movements can do this by being active forces for just, democratic, full employment, high-wage economies. Of course, labor movements in different countries have varying degrees of power to influence national policies. While it is always possible to argue that particular national labor movements have not made the right strategic choices, it is, as a practical matter, impossible to determine the extent to which the outcomes for a particular labor movement are due to context and how much to strategic choice. Critics of U.S. unions, for example, argue that they should have become more "political" and been less wedded to collective bargaining. The failure of the AFL-CIO to obtain enough political support from a Democratic-controlled Congress and the White House to make the National Labor Relations Act more effective and enforceable is often cited as an illustration of the political weakness of the American labor movement. It is highly unlikely, however, given the political structures of the United States, that American unions could ever establish the kind of independent political labor movements that their counterparts have developed in parliamentary systems. The structure of American government makes it very difficult for third parties to get started, gives inordinate power to non-metropolitan areas with low union densities, and makes it possible for willful minorities to block legislation. The failure of labor law reform in the 1970s, for example, had very little to do with how hard the AFL-CIO was willing to push for it or how much it was favored by labor's supporters in the Congress. The bill passed the House of Representatives by almost a 100-vote majority, and had 58 of 100 votes for passing in the Senate, but the bill's supporters were unable to muster the 60 votes needed to break a filibuster by a few anti-union senators at a time when a filibuster delayed

Labor movements themselves must develop the strategies, policies, and structures to strengthen their ability to protect and promote workers' interests.

other important legislation. It is, moreover, difficult to change the filibuster (or "cloture") rule because it gives great power to each senator.

My reading of the international comparison leads to the following list of factors for high performance labor movements, most notably those in Scandinavia and Western Europe, which have maintained and improved their strength in the same international economic environment that has produced large losses for some unions, especially those in the U.S. (Figure 1). The factors strengthening labor movements are closely interrelated, but generally can be classified according to the development of policies that gain strong public support and those designed to strengthen internal unity.

Public Policies

(1) Successful labor organizations have adopted clear goals and objectives, as well as strategies to simultaneously achieve those objectives and to gain greater support from nonlabor groups. Strong labor movements continue to advocate full employment policies, but they also want full employment at high and rising wages. And they advocate policies to prevent wages and incomes from polarizing as much as they have in the United States. These labor movements realize the extent to which international competition has changed the ability to take labor out of competition and maintain full employment by traditional strategies. This means developing policies that permit companies to compete in international markets while maintaining full employment and equity. Successful labor movements have developed different strategies, but generally they recognize the need to limit wage increases to changes in productivity plus or minus the difference between changes in domestic and international prices.

In addition, all of these labor movements are concerned with the creation of wealth, not just its distribution. The policies that flow from this objective include measures to *stimulate national investment* in job- and wealth-creating activities. Sources of investment funds include: private and collective pension funds, lower real interest rates, and measures to promote the development and use of leading-edge technology.

> **Strong labor movements continue to advocate full employment policies, but they also want full employment at high and rising wages.**

308

Successful labor movements give particularly high priority to policies to strengthen education and training, especially for workers. This is done through the support of public education as well as the strengthening of worker education and training through collective bargaining. They also have supported adjustment policies to shift labor and other resources from low-wage to high-wage sectors. Labor movements have always supported universal education, health care, and family support policies. Indeed, it would not be surprising to find a strong correlation between union density and the degree of support for human resource development activities. There can be little doubt that in an age of multinational corporations, investing in people is the best way to strengthen a country's economy.

(2) High performance labor movements also have *global strategies* which are designed to support high wages, full employment, and equity. Unlike groups with ideological commitments to "free markets," labor movements owe their existence to a healthy appreciation of the *limitations* as well as the *strengths* of markets. They understand that markets must operate within the framework of *rules*, especially those that protect basic labor standards. Such standards promote human resource development and force companies to compete by becoming more *efficient*, not by *reducing basic labor standards*. In a global economy, however, labor standards must now be part of *international trade rules*.

Trade-linked labor standards could, in addition, provide global purchasing power by giving Third World workers a way to participate in the economic growth of their countries. It should be emphasized, however, that international labor standards do not imply an international minimum wage—wage differentials are too great for that to be practical. There is, however, a difference between having low wages because of a low level of economic development and suppressing wages to attract capital; the latter would violate international labor standards, the former would not. Labor standards also would allow workers to organize and bargain collectively and protect them from hazardous workplaces, forced labor, child labor, and discrimination because of such factors as race, ethnic origin, or union membership.

> *Successful labor movements give particularly high priority to policies to strengthen education annd training, especially for workers.*

Internal Strengths

Labor movements will have very little ability to represent workers' interests unless they are well organized internally. Some of what is required to strengthen labor movements is fairly obvious, such as organizing, developing internal democracy, and being responsive to workers' concerns. In fact, strong labor movements are sufficiently popular that much organizing of new members is by rank and file members themselves. There is, in addition, a close relationship between a labor movement's public policies and its internal strength. Strong public support greatly facilitates organizing. There are, moreover, a number of factors that all strong labor movements seem to have in common; these include:

Labor movements have articulated a rationale that goes beyond narrow "special interest" concerns like higher wages and better working conditions.

(1) Broad public support because labor movements have articulated a rationale that goes beyond narrow "special interest" concerns like higher wages and better working conditions. Democratic countries generally accept the idea that free and democratic labor movements are essential to democracy but unions have not always been considered in the national economic interest. Unions gained support after the 1930s because they were considered to be essential to help stabilize economies and increase purchasing power, in keeping with prevailing Keynesian policies. The successful labor movements of the 1980s have articulated strategies to be just, full-employment, high-income countries— emphasizing the essential role of worker involvement in high performance enterprises and the importance of human resource development for national welfare. These labor movements have stressed economic growth as well as the equitable distribution of income.

(2) Successful labor movements have therefore been able to develop and implement coordinated goals that attract broad support. Because these labor movements have been led by skilled, well-informed leaders who were able to convince other groups of the importance of their role, they have been able to

participate very effectively in sophisticated tripartite (labor, management, government) decision, forecasting, or information sharing processes.

(3) High performance labor movements have strong local workplace entities, as well as strong national economic and political organizations. Labor movements that are only organized around one of these dimensions (workplace, national, political, or economic) have not been as strong as those that emphasize all of them. In particular, strong labor movements tend to welcome measures to improve economic competitiveness through greater worker involvement in reorganizing work to achieve high performance. This is so because strong unions are not afraid that arrangements like works councils or quality circles will become alternatives to unions. As in Germany and Sweden, strong unions will control the worker participation mechanisms, thereby strengthening their position.

Strong labor movements tend to welcome measures to improve economic competitiveness through greater worker involvement in reorganizing work to achieve high performance.

(4) The strongest labor movements develop mechanisms for interactive communications with their members. These labor movements therefore have extensive education and research services, both to help members gain addition job skills as well as for general education and strengthening labor leaders' ability to participate effectively in national organizations and political processes.

(5) The strongest labor movements also usually have streamlined structures that make it possible to both coordinate national policies, service workers at the shop level and minimize internal jurisdictional conflicts. Sometimes these structures have been possible because countries are relatively small, as in Sweden, but Germany was able to develop more rational structures by starting from scratch after World War II.

Conclusions

The goals, policies, and objectives of labor movements in the democratic industrial countries are rooted in mainly national, mass production economies. This was particularly true for unions in the U.S., where the mass production system was larger and more deeply entrenched than elsewhere. Political and economic conditions in the U.S. have made it more difficult for unions to survive, grow, and adapt. It has particularly been more difficult for unions to establish independent political movements, which is a major difference between unions in the U.S. and elsewhere. However, unions also have faced much greater opposition from employers.

A major factor in the strength of the U.S. unions has been public opinion, which was more favorable during the 1930s and 1940s than during the 1970s and 1980s.

A major factor in the strength of the U.S. unions has been public opinion, which was more favorable during the 1930s and 1940s than during the 1970s and 1980s. At least part of this popularity was due to the belief that unions were good for the economy because they helped maintain purchasing power, in keeping with the prevailing Keynesian policies. However, these policies became anachronistic in a more competitive internationalized information world, which also makes the oligopolistic mass production system less effective. This leads some people to believe that unions have become obsolete. I have argued that this is a false conclusion: high performance organizations require much greater worker involvement, which, in turn, is most effective if workers have an independent source of power to represent their interests.

A major problem in the U.S. is the fact that unions have been so weakened since the 1960s that workers do not, in fact, have effective options to organize in the face of much stronger employer opposition. Part of the reason for intensified employer opposition is the weakening of the mass production Keynesian safety net system that provided mutual accommodations for unions and large scale employers before the 1970s, when the eroding effects of technology and more competitive global markets become more apparent. These changes greatly strengthened international companies relative to unions and made it possible for almost all American companies to respond to change with cost cutting rather than quality and productivity improving strategies. In addition to weaker unions, American companies are not constrained by public policies that restrict their wage-cutting strategies and offer incentives for companies to become high performance organizations. One of the most serious defects in the U.S. policy mix is poor public schools and the absence of the kind of high quality comprehensive school-to-work and worker training systems that exist in every other major democratic industrial country.

The recommendations by the Commission on the Skills of the American Workforce would therefore greatly improve the competitiveness of American companies. These recommendations include:

High performance organizations require much greater worker involvement, which, in turn, is most effective if workers have an independent source of power to represent their interests.

- the adoption of high standards for school leavers;

- the development of an alternative system to allow young people who do not function very well in regular schools to achieve these standards;

- a system where workers who are not pursuing a baccalaureate degree can be trained and certified for technical skills;

- a requirement that all companies devote at least 1 percent of payroll to workplace training; and

- the development of a system of local, state, and national employment and training councils to provide oversight to worker education and training.

Stronger labor movements are clearly in the national interest. The U.S. should therefore modernize its labor relations laws to make it easier for workers to organize and bargain collectively and more difficult for employers to thwart those rights by legal and illegal means. I believe it would be in the national interest to establish works councils along the lines of the German system discussed by Turner in this volume. At a minimum, there should be labor-management safety and health committees.

However, unions must strengthen their internal processes and gain greater public support if more favorable public policies are to be adopted. In achieving these objectives, unions can learn from the experience of those labor movements that have continued to prosper despite a hostile international economic and political environment. These successful labor movements have adopted broad, popular

313

goals for public policies to establish high wages, full employment, and economic justice. These strategies constitute the modern intellectual equivalent of Keynesian economics, which complemented and strengthened the equity, industrial relations, and labor market rationales for unions and collective bargaining. They have, in addition, developed strategies to promote international, national, and enterprise policies and institutions to achieve these objectives. These strategies require strengthening unity among workers within and between countries and promoting national policies to improve productivity, quality, flexibility, and equity. Those who believe in free, democratic, prosperous, just societies have a strong stake in how well unions and their supporters achieve these objectives.

Stronger labor movements are clearly in the national interest.

Endnotes

1   As I use the term, industrial relations refers to the relationships between workers and managers in a production system. The production system includes technology and organizational arrangements as well as workers and managers.

2   Or, more accurately, front-line workers take on some of the indirect functions previously performed by "white collar" or "salaried" staff.

3   Indeed, I believe the management systems in Sweden and Germany are much better than those in Japan. This is so because the systems are more pervasive and give workers control at every level. The Japanese system actually only applies to 15–20 percent of workers; the Swedish and German systems are more universal.

Bibliography

Abowd, John M. "The Effect of Wage Bargains on the Stock Market Value of the Firm." *American Economic Review*, Vol. 79, September 1989, pp. 774–800.

Abowd, John and Richard Freeman. "Introduction and Summary." In John Abowd and Richard Freeman, *Immigration, Trade, and the Labor Market*. Chicago: University of Chicago Press, 1991.

Adams, Walter and Hans Mueller. "The Steel Industry." In Walter Adams, ed., *The Structure of American Industry*. New York: Macmillan Publishing Company, 1986.

Addison, John T. and Barry T. Hirsch. "Union Effects on Productivity, Profits, and Growth: Has the Long Run Arrived?" *Journal of Labor Economics*, Vol. 7, No. 1, 1989, pp. 72–105.

Addison, John and Barry Hirsch. *The Economic Analysis of Unions*. Boston: Allen & Unwin, 1986.

AFL-CIO. *The Economy: Domestic Issues—Employment and Training Trade*. Washington, DC: AFL-CIO, 1988.

Ahlberg, Dennis et al. "Technological Change, Market Decline, and Industrial Relations in the U.S. Steel Industry." In Daniel Cornfield, ed., 1987.

Allen, Steven G. "Productivity Levels & Productivity Change Under Unionism." *Industrial Relations*, Vol. 27, No. 1, Winter 1988a.

Allen, Steven G. "Human Resource Policies and Union–Non Union Productivity Differences." Working Paper No. 2744. National Bureau of Economic Research, 1988b.

Allen, Steven G. "Declining Unionization in Construction: The Facts and the Reasons." *Industrial and Labor Relations Review*, April 1988c.

Allen, Steven G. "Further Evidence on Union Efficiency in Construction." *Industrial Relations*, Spring 1988d.

Allen, Steven G. "Can Union Labor Ever Cost Less?" *Quarterly Journal of Economics*, May 1987.

Allen, Steven G. "Unionization and Productivity in Office Building and School Construction." *Industrial and Labor Relations Review*, January 1986a.

Allen, Steven G. "The Effect of Unionism on Productivity and Privately and Publicly Owned Hospitals and Nursing Homes." *Journal of Labor Research*, Winter 1986b.

Allen, Steven G. "Unionized Construction Workers Are More Productive." *Quarterly Journal of Economics*, May 1984.

Allen, S. and Clark, R. "Unions, Pension Wealth, and Age-Compensation Profiles." *Industrial and Labor Relations Review*, Vol. 42, April 1988, pp. 342–59.

Altshuler, Alan, Martin Anderson, Daniel Jones, Daniel Roos, and James Womack. *The*

Future of the Automobile. The Report of MIT's International Automobile Program. Cambridge, MA: MIT Press, 1984.

Anderson, Richard and Mordechai Kreinin. "Labour Costs in the American Steel and Auto Industries." *World Economy*, Vol. 4, June 1981, pp. 199–208.

Aoki, Masahiro. "The Japanese Firm in Transition." In K. Yamamura and Y. Yasuba, eds., *The Political Economy of Japan*. Stanford: Stanford University Press, 1987.

Aoki, Masahiro. *The Cooperative Game Theory of the Firm*. Oxford: Clarendon Press, 1984.

Ashenfelter, Orley. "A Review Symposium." *Industrial and Labor Relations Review*, Vol. 38, No. 2, January 1985, pp. 244–63.

Babbie, Earl R. *Survey Research Methods*. Belmont, CA: Wadsworth Publishing Company, 1973.

Baily, Martin and M. Blair. "Productivity and American Management." In Robert E. Litan, Robert Z. Lawrence, and Charles L. Schultze, eds., *American Living Standards: Threats and Challenges*. Washington, DC: The Brookings Institution, 1988.

Baldwin, Carliss Y. "Productivity and Labor Unions: An Application of the Theory of Self-Enforcing Contracts." *Journal of Business*, Vol. 56, 1983, pp. 155–85.

Baldwin, Robert. "Determinants of Trade and Foreign Investment: Further Evidence." *The Review of Economics and Statistics*, Vol. 61, February 1979, pp. 40–48.

Baldwin, Robert. *Nontariff Distortions of International Trade*. Washington, DC: The Brookings Institution, 1970.

Banks, Andy and John Metzgar, eds. "Participating in Management: Union Organizing on a New Terrain." *Labor Research Review*, Fall 1989.

Barkin, Solomon, ed. *Worker Militancy and its Consequences: The Changing Climate of Western Industrial Relations*. 2d ed. New York: Praeger Publishers, 1983.

Barnet, Richard and Ronald Muller. *Global Reach: The Power of the Multinational Corporations*. New York: Simon and Schuster, 1974.

Barnett, George E. *Chapters on Machinery and Labor*. Carbondale, IL: Southern Illinois University (first edition, 1926), 1969.

Becker, Brian E. "Concession Bargaining: The Impact on Shareholders Equity." *Industrial and Labor Relations Review*, January 1987.

Becker, Brian E. and Craig Olson. "Unions and Firm Profits." Mimeo. Industrial Relations Institute, University of Wisconsin-Madison, January 1990.

Becker, Brian E. and Craig Olson. "The Impact of Strikes on Shareholder Equity." *Industrial and Labor Relations Review*, Vol. 39, No. 3, April 1986.

Belman, Dale. "Concentration, Unions, and Labor Earnings: A Sample Selection Approach." *Review of Economics and Statistics*, August 1988.

Belman, Dale and K. Wilson. "Time Series Research on Union Productivity Effects: Are Past Results Idiosyncratic?" Working Paper No. 121. University of Wisconsin-Milwaukee, 1989.

Bemmel, Brian. "How Unions Affect Productivity in Manufacturing Plants." *Industrial and Labor Relations Review*, Vol. 40, No. 2, January 1987.

Benvignati, Anita M. "Interfirm Adoption of Captial-Goods Innovations." *Review of Economics and Statistics*, Vol. 64, 1982, pp. 330–35.

Berghahn, Volker R. and Detlev Karsten. *Industrial Relations in West Germany*. Oxford: Berg Publishers, 1987.

Bergmann, Joachim and Walter Müller-Jentsch. "The Federal Republic of Germany: Cooperative Unionism and Dual Bargaining System Challenged." In Barkin, ed., 1983, pp. 229–77.

Bernstein, Paul. *Workplace Democratization: Its Internal Dynamics*. New Brunswick, NJ: Transaction Books, 1980.

Bernstein, Paul. "Necessary Elements for Effective Worker Participation in Decision Making." *Journal of Economic Issues*, Vol. 10, No. 2, June 1976, pp. 490–522.

Betcherman, Gordon. "Technological Change and Its Impacts: Do Unions Make a Difference?" *Proceedings of 1987 Annual Meeting of the Canadian Industrial Relations Association*, 1988.

Blackburn, M.L., D.E. Bloom, and R.B. Freeman. "The Declining Economic Positions of Less Skilled American Men." In G. Burtless, ed., *A Future of Lousy Jobs? The Changing Structure of U.S. Wages*. Washington, DC: The Brookings Institution, 1990.

Blanchflower, David G. "Union Relative Wage Effects: A Cross-Section Analysis Using Establishment Data." *British Journal of Industrial Relations*, Vol. 22, 1984, pp. 311–32.

Blanchflower, David G. and R. Freeman. "Going Different Ways: Unionism in the U.S. and Other OECD Countries." Paper presented at Minnesota Industrial Relations Conference, March 1990.

Blanchflower, David G., N. Millward, and A.J. Oswald. "Unionisation and Employment Behavior." Working Paper No. 3180. National Bureau of Economic Research, 1989.

Blanchflower, David G. and A.J. Oswald. "Internal and External Influences Upon Pay Settlements." *British Journal of Industrial Relations*, Vol. 26, No. 3, November 1988a, pp. 363–70.

Blanchflower, David G. and A.J. Oswald. "The Economic Effects of Britain's Trade Unions." Paper No. 324, Centre for Labour Economics, LSE, 1988b.

Blasi, Joseph Raphael. "Comment." In Blinder, 1990.

Blasi, Joseph R. Personal communication, December 1989.

318

Blasi, Joseph R. *Employee Ownership: Revolution or Ripoff?* Cambridge, MA: Ballinger Books, 1988.

Blinder, Alan S., ed. *Paying for Productivity: A Look at the Evidence*. Washington, DC: The Brookings Institution, 1990.

Blinder, Alan. "Pay, Participation, and Productivity." *Brookings Review*, Winter 1989/90, pp. 33–38.

Block, R., M. Kleiner, M. Roomkin, and S. Salsburg, eds. *Human Resources and the Performance of the Firm*. Wisconsin: Industrial Relations Research Association, 1987.

Bluestone, Barry and Bennett Harrison. *The Deindustrialization of America*. New York: Basic Books, 1982.

Boal, William M. "Unionism and Productivity in West Virginia Coal Mining." *Industrial and Labor Relations Review*, Vol. 43, No. 4, April 1990.

Bohn, Roger E. and Ramchandran Jaikumar. "The Development of Intelligent Systems for Industrial Use: A Conceptual Framework." *Research on Technological Innovation, Management, and Policy*, Vol. 3, 1986, pp. 169–211.

Bok, Derek and John Dunlop. *Labor and the American Community*. New York: Simon and Schuster, 1970.

Bowles, Samuel, David M. Gordon, and Thomas Weisskopf. "Power and Profits: The Social Structure of Accumulation and the Profitability of the Postwar Economy." *Review of Radical Political Economics*, No. 18, Spring/Summer 1986.

Brereton, Barbara. "U.S. Multinational Companies: Operations in 1984." *Survey of Current Business*, Vol. 66, No. 9, September 1986, p. 27.

Brett, Jeanne M. and Stephen P. Goldberg. "Wildcat Strikes in Bituminous Coal Mining." *Industrial and Labor Relations Review*, July 1979.

Bronars, Stephen and Donald R. Deere. "Union Organizing Activity and Union Coverage, 1973–1988." National Bureau of Economic Research Conference on Labor Economics, November 1989.

Bronars, Stephen G. and Donald R. Deere. "Union Membership Rights, Rent-Sharing, and Firm Behavior." Unpublished Manuscript. University of California, 1988.

Brown, Charles. "Firms' Choice of Method of Pay." *Industrial and Labor Relations Review*, Vol. 43, No. 3, Special Issue, February 1990, pp. 165–82.

Brown, Charles and James Medoff. "Trade Unions in the Production Process." *Journal of Political Economy*, Vol. 86, No. 3, June 1978, pp. 355–78.

Brown, Clair and Michael Reich. "When Does Union-Management Cooperation Work? A Look at NUMMI and GM–Van Nuys." *California Management Review*, Vol. 31, No. 4, Summer 1989, pp. 26–44.

Brumlop, Eva and Ulrich Jürgens. "Rationalisation and Industrial Relations: A Case Study of Volkswagen." In Jacobi et al., 1986, pp. 73–94.

Bullock, R. J. and Edward E. Lawler III. "Gainsharing: A Few Questions, and Fewer Answers." *Human Resource Management*, Vol. 23, No. 1, Spring 1984, pp. 23–40.

Burawoy, Michael. *Manufacturing Consent: Changes in the Labor Process Under Monopoly Capitalism*. Chicago: University of Chicago Press, 1979.

Bureau of Labor Statistics. Unpublished data, May 1990.

Bureau of National Affairs. *Basic Patterns in Union Contracts*. Washington, DC: BNA, 1986a.

Bureau of National Affairs. *Collective Bargaining Negotiations and Contracts*. Washington, DC: BNA, 1986b.

Bureau of National Affairs. *Collective Bargaining Negotiations and Contracts*. Washington, DC: BNA, 1985.

Bureau of National Affairs. *Grievance Guide*. 6th ed. Washington, DC: Bureau of National Affairs , 1982.

Bureau of National Affairs. "Policies for Unorganized Employees." In *Personnel Policies Forum*, No. 125. Washington, DC: BNA, 1979.

Bussey, John. "Did U.S. Car Makers Err by Raising Prices when the Yen Rose?" *Wall Street Journal*, April 18, 1988.

Byrnes, Patricia, Rolf Fare, Shawna Grosskopf, and C.A. Knox Lovell. "The Effect of Unions on Productivity: U.S. Surface Mining of Coal." Working Paper 87-8. Department of Economics, University of North Carolina, April 1987.

Cable, John R. and Felix R. FitzRoy. "Cooperation and Productivity: Some Evidence from West German Experience." *Economic Analysis and Workers' Management*, Vol. 14, No. 2, 1980a, pp. 163–80.

Cable, John R. and Felix R. FitzRoy. "Productive Efficiency, Incentives, and Employee Participation: Some Preliminary Results for West Germany." *Kyklos*, Vol. 33, No. 1, 1980b, pp. 100–21.

Callaghan, W. "Trade Unions, Pay, Productivity and Jobs." In J. Philpott and W. Callaghan, eds., *Unions in the 1990's*. London: Employment Institute/Trade Unions Congress, 1990.

Cappelli, Peter and Robert B. McKersie. "Management Strategy and the Redesign of Workrules." *Journal of Management Studies*, Vol. 24, No. 5, September 1987, pp. 441–62.

Carnevale, Anthony. *Human Capital: A High-Yield Corporate Investment*. Washington, DC: American Society for Training and Development, 1983.

Chaison, G. and J. Rose. "Continental Divide: The Direction and Fate of North American Unions." Working Paper No. 309. McMaster University, September 1988.

Cheadle, Allen. "Incentive, Flexibility, or ?: Explaining Patterns of Profit Sharing Activity." Working Paper. University of Washington, Department of Health Services, July 1988.

Clark, Gordon L. *Unions And Communities Under Siege*. Cambridge: Cambridge University Press, 1989.

Clark, Kim. "Unionization and Firm Performance: The Impact of Profits, Growth, and Productivity." *American Economic Review*, Vol. 74, No. 5, December 1984, pp. 893–919.

Clark, Kim B. "The Impact of Unionization on Productivity: A Case Study." *Industrial and Labor Relations Review*, Vol. 33, No. 4, July 1980a, pp. 451–69.

Clark, Kim B. "Unionization and Productivity: Micro-Economic Evidence." *Quarterly Journal of Economics*, Vol. 95 , No. 4, December 1980b.

Clark, Kim B. and Z. Griliches. "Productivity Growth and R&D at the Business Level: Results from the PIMS Data Base." In Zvi Griliches, ed., *R&D, Patents, and Productivity*. Chicago: University of Chicago, 1984, pp. 393–416.

Cohen, Stephen S. and John Zysman. *Manufacturing Matters: The Myth of the Post-Industrial Economy*. New York: Basic Books, 1987.

Cole, Robert E. *Strategies for Learning*. Berkeley: University of California Press, 1989.

Cole, Robert E. "Diffusion of Participatory Work Structures in Japan, Sweden, and the United States." In Paul S. Goodman, ed., *Change in Organizations: New Perspectives on Theory, Research, and Practice*. San Francisco: Jossey-Bass, 1982.

Commission on Skills of the American Workforce. *America's Choice: High Skills or Low Wages!* Rochester, NY: Center on Education and the Economy, 1990.

Connerton, M., R.B. Freeman, and J.L. Medoff. "Industrial Relations and Productivity: A Study of the U.S. Bituminous Coal Industry." Mimeo. Cambridge, MA: Harvard University, 1983.

Connolly, R.A., B.T. Hirsch, and M. Hirschy. "Union Rent Seeking, Intangible Capital, and Market Value of the Firm." *Review of Economics and Statistics*, Vol. 68, No. 4, 1986, pp. 567–77.

Conte, Michael A. and Jan Svejnar. "The Performance Effects of Employee Ownership Plans." In Blinder, 1990.

Conte, Michael A. and Jan Svejnar. "Productivity Effects of Worker Participation in Management, Profit-Sharing, Worker Ownership of Assets, and Unionization in U.S. Firms." *International Journal of Industrial Organization*, Vol. 6, No. 1, March 1988.

Cooke, William N. "Factors Influencing the Effect of Joint Union-Management Programs on Employee-Supervisor Relations." *Industrial and Labor Relations Review*, Vol. 43, July 1990, pp. 587–603.

Cooke, William N. "Improving Productivity and Quality through Collaboration." *Industrial Relations*, Vol. 28, No. 2, Spring 1989, pp. 299–319.

Cooke, William N. "Summary Report of Task 1: Survey of Michigan Business." Report prepared for Michigan Labor-Management Partnership Project, Michigan Department of Commerce. Institute of Labor and Industrial Relations, University of Michigan, 1988.

Cornfield, Daniel, ed. *Workers, Managers, and Technological Change*. New York: Plenum Publishing, 1987.

Cotton, John L., David A. Vollrath, Kirk L. Froggatt, Mark L. Lengnick-Hall, and Kenneth R. Jennings. "Employee Participation: Diverse Forms and Different Outcomes." *Academy of Management Review*, Vol. 13, No. 1, 1988, pp. 8–22.

Council of Economic Advisors. *The Economic Report of the President*. Washington, DC: U.S. Government Printing Office, 1983.

Council on Competitiveness. *Competitive Index*, June 1990.

Cutcher-Gershenfeld, Joel. "Tracing a Transformation in Industrial Relations." U.S. Department of Labor, Bureau of Labor-Management Relations and Cooperative Programs, Report No. 123. Washington, DC: U.S. Government Printing Office, 1988.

Cutcher-Gershenfeld, Joel, Robert B. McKersie, and Kirsten R. Wever. "The Changing Role of Union Leaders." U.S. Department of Labor, Bureau of Labor-Management Relations and Cooperative Programs, Report No. 127. Washington, DC: U.S. Government Printing Office, 1988.

Daniel, W.W. *Workplace Industrial Relations and Technical Change*. London: Francis Pinter, 1987.

DeFina, R. "Unions, Relative Wages, and Economic Efficiency." *Journal of Labor Economics*, Vol. 1, October 1983.

Delaney, John Thomas, Casey Ichniowksi, and David Lewin. "Employee Involvement Programs and Firm Performance." *Proceedings of the Forty-First Annual Meeting of the Industrial Relations Research Association*, New York, December 1988. Madison, WI: IRRA, 1989.

Delaney, John Thomas, David Lewin, and Casey Ichniowski. "Human Resource Management Policies and Practices in American Firms." Paper. Industrial Relations Research Center, Graduate School of Business, Columbia University. New York, 1988.

Dertouzes, Michael L., Richard K. Lester, and Robert M. Solow. *Made in America*. Cambridge, MA: MIT Press, 1989.

Deutschmann, Christoph. "Economic Restructuring and Company Unionism: The Japanese Model." *Economic and Industrial Democracy*, Vol. 8, 1987, pp. 463–88.

Dohse, Knuth, Ulrich Jürgens, and Thomas Malsch. "From 'Fordism' to 'Toyotism'? The Social Organization of the Labor Process in the Japanese Automobile Industry." *Politics and Society*, Vol. 14, No. 2, 1985, pp. 115–46.

Dornbusch, Rudiger, Paul Krugman, and Yung C. Park. *Meeting World Challenges: U.S. Manufacturing in the 1990s*. Rochester: Eastman Kodak, 1989.

Drago, Robert. "Quality Circle Survival: An Exploratory Analysis." *Industrial Relations*, Vol. 27, No. 3, Fall 1988, pp. 336–51.

Dunlop, John T. "Policy Decisions and Research in Labor Economics and Industrial Relations." *Industrial and Labor Relations Review*, April 1977.

Dunlop, John T. *Industrial Relations Systems*. New York: Holt, Rinehart, and Winston, 1958.

Dunlop, John T. *Wage Determination Under Trade Unionism*. New York and London: MacMillan, 1944.

Dyer, Davis, Malcolm S. Salter, and Alan M. Webber. *Changing Alliances*. The Harvard Business School Project on the Auto Industry and the American Economy. Boston: Harvard Business School Press, 1987.

Eaton, Adrienne E. "The Role of the Local Union in a Participative Program." *Labor Studies Journal*, Vol. 15, No. 1 Spring 1990, pp. 33–53.

Eaton, Adrienne E. "'Just Saying No': Local Union Opposition to Participative Programs." Labor Studies Department, Rutgers University, unpublished paper presented at IRRA Poster Session, Atlanta, Georgia, December 1989.

Eaton, Adrienne E. and Paula B. Voos. "The Ability of Unions to Adapt to Innovative Workplace Arrangements." *American Economic Review*, Vol. 79, No. 2, May 1989, pp. 172–76.

Eberts, Randall W. "Teacher Unions and the Cost of Public Education." *Economic Inquiry*, October 1986 pp. 631–43.

Eberts, Randall W. and Joe A. Stone. *Unions and Public Schools: The Effect of Collective Bargaining on American Education*. Lexington, MA: Lexington Books, 1984.

Economic Policy Council of the United Nations Association. *The Common Interests of Employees and Employers in the 1990s*. New York: Economic Policy Council, 1990.

Eiger, Norman. "Organizing for Quality of Working Life." *Labor Studies Journal*, Vol. 14, No. 3, Fall 1989, pp. 3–22.

Elden, Max. "Democracy at Work for a More Participatory Politics: Worker Self-Management Increases Political Efficacy and Participation." Unpublished dissertation. University of California at Los Angeles, California, 1976.

Elias, P. and D. Blanchflower. *Occupations, Earnings, and Work Histories of Young Adults: Who Gets the Good Jobs?* Research Paper No. 68. Department of Employment, London, 1989.

Elkouri, Frank and Edna Asper Elkouri. *How Arbitration Works*. 4th ed. Washington, DC: Bureau of National Affairs, 1985.

Ellerman, David P. "The Legitimate Opposition at Work: The Union's Role in Large Democratic Firms." *Economic and Industrial Democracy*, Vol. 9, 1988, pp. 437–53.

Farber, Henry. "The Analysis of Union Behavior." In O. Ashenfelter and R. Layard, eds., *Handbook of Labor Economics*. Amsterdam, Netherlands: North-Holland Publishing, 1986.

Fedrau, Ruth and Kevin Balfe. *Cooperative Labor-Management Worker Adjustment Programs*. Washington, DC: U.S. Department of Labor, Bureau of Labor Management Relations and Cooperative Programs, BLMR 133, 1989.

Finseth, Eric. "The Employment Behavior of Profit-Sharing Firms: An Empirical Test of the Weitzman Theory." Unpublished senior thesis. Department of Economics, Harvard University, 1988.

Fitzroy, Felix R. and Kornelius Kraft. "Cooperation, Productivity, and Profit Sharing." *Quarterly Journal of Economics*, Vol. 102, No. 1, February 1987, pp. 23–35.

Fitzroy, Felix R. and Kornelius Kraft. "Profitability and Profit-Sharing." *Journal of Industrial Economics*, Vol. 35, No. 2, December 1986, pp. 113–30.

Flaherty, Sean. "Strike Activity, Worker Militancy, and Productivity Change in Manufacturing, 1961–1981." *Industrial and Labor Relations Review*, Vol. 40, No. 4, July 1987.

Flanders, Allan. *The Fawley Productivity Agreements*. London: Faber and Faber, 1964.

Foulkes, Fred. *Personnel Policies in Large Nonunion Companies*. Englewood Cliffs, NJ: Prentice-Hall, 1980.

Frantz, J. "The Impact of Unions on Productivity in the Wooden Household Furniture Industry." Undergraduate thesis. Harvard University, 1976.

Freeman, Audrey. *The New Look in Wage Policy and Employee Relations*. New York: Conference Board, 1985.

Freeman Richard B. "On the Divergence of Unionism Among Developed Countries." In Renato Brunetta and Carlo Dell'Aringa, eds., *Labour Relations and Economic Performance*. Hampshire, England: Macmillan, 1990a.

Freeman, Richard B. "How Much Has De-unionisation Contributed to the Rise in Male Earnings Inequality?" Paper presented at the Russell Sage Conference on Inequality, 1990b.

Freeman, Richard B. "What Does the Future Hold for U.S. Unionism?" *Relations Industrielles*, Vol. 44, No. 1, 1989, pp. 25–46.

324

Freeman, Richard B. "Contraction and Expansion: The Divergence of Private Sector and Public Sector Unionism in the United States." *Journal of Economic Perspectives*, Vol. 2, No. 2, Spring 1988a, pp. 63–88.

Freeman, Richard B. "Union Density and Economic Performance." *European Economic Review*, Vol. 32, 1988b, pp. 707–16.

Freeman, Richard B. *Canada in the World Labor Market*. Report to Economic Council of Canada, October 1988c.

Freeman, Richard B. "In Search of Union Wage Concessions in Standard Data Sets." *Industrial Relations*, Vol. 25, No. 2, Spring 1986a, pp. 131–45.

Freeman, Richard B. "Unionism Comes to the Public Sector." *Journal of Economic Literature*, March 1986b.

Freeman, Richard B. "The Effect of the Union Wage Differential on Management Opposition and Organising Success." *American Economic Review*, Vol. 76, 1986c, pp. 92–96.

Freeman, Richard B. "Why Are Unions Faring Poorly in NLRB Representation Elections?" In T. Kochan, ed., *Challenges and Choices Facing American Unions*. Cambridge, MA: MIT Press, 1985a.

Freeman, Richard B. "Unions, Pensions, and Union Pension Funds." In D. Wise, ed., *Pensions, Labor, and Individual Choice*. Chicago: University of Chicago, 1985b.

Freeman, Richard B. "Unionism, Price-Cost Margins, and the Return to Capital." Working Paper No. 1164. National Bureau of Economic Research, 1983.

Freeman, Richard B. "Union Wage Practices and Wage Dispersion within Establishments." *Industrial and Labor Relations Review*, Vol. 36, No. 1, 1982, pp. 3–39.

Freeman, Richard B. "Unionism and the Dispersion of Wages." *Industrial and Labor Relations Review*, Vol. 34, No. 1, 1980a, pp. 3–23.

Freeman, Richard B. "The Exit-Voice Tradeoff in the Labor Market: Unionism, Job Tenure, Quits, and Separations." *Quarterly Journal of Economics*, Vol. 4, No. 4, 1980b, pp. 643–74.

Freeman, Richard B. "Individual Mobility and Union Voice in the Labor Market." *American Economic Review*, May 1976.

Freeman, Richard B. and Lawrence Katz. "Industrial Wage and Employment Determination in an Open Economy." In Richard Freeman and J. Abowd, eds., *Immigration, Trade, and the Labor Market*. Chicago: University of Chicago Press, 1991.

Freeman, Richard B. and M. Kleiner. "The Impact of New Unionisation on Wages and Working Conditions." *Journal of Labor Economics*, January 1990a.

Freeman, Richard B. and M. Kleiner. "Employer Behavior in the Face of Union Organizing Drives." *Industrial and Labor Relations Review*, April 1990b.

Freeman, Richard B. and James L. Medoff. *What Do Unions Do?* New York: Basic Books, 1984.

Freeman, Richard and James Medoff. "The Impact of Collective Bargaining: Illusion or Reality?" In J. Steiber, R. McKersie, and D. Mills, eds., *U.S. Industrial Relations 1950–1980: A Critical Assessment.* Madison, WI: Industrial Relations Research Association, 1981.

Freeman, Richard and James Medoff. "New Estimates of Private Sector Unionism in the United States." *Industrial and Labor Relations Review,* Vol. 32, No. 2, January 1979, pp. 143–74.

Freeman, Richard B. and J. Pelletier. "The Impact of Industrial Relations Legislation on Union Density in the UK and Ireland." *British Journal of Industrial Relations,* April 1990.

Freeman, Richard and Marc Rebick. "Crumbling Pillar? Declining Union Density in Japan." *Journal of the Japanese and International Economies,* 1989.

Friedman, Milton. *Capitalism and Freedom.* Chicago: University of Chicago Press, 1962.

Fujita, Eishi. "Labor Process and Labor Management: The Case of Toyota." Paper presented at an international symposium on "The Micro Electronics Revolution and Regional Development, Labour Organization and the Future of Post-Industrializing Societies," University of Milan, April 11–13, 1988.

Glyn, Andrew, Alan Hughes, Alain Lipietz, and Ajit Singh. "The Rise and Fall of the Golden Age." In Stephen Marglin and Juliet Schor, eds., *The End of the Golden Age.* Oxford and New York: Oxford University Press, 1989.

Goodman, Paul S. *Assessing Organizational Change: The Rushton Quality of Work Experiment.* New York: Wiley, 1979.

Gordon, Judith R. *A Diagnostic Approach to Organizational Behavior.* 2d ed. Boston: Allyn and Bacon, 1987.

Graddy, Duane B. and Gary Hall. "Unionization and Productivity in Commercial Banking." *Journal of Labor Research,* Summer 1985.

Green, F. and M. Potepan. "Vacation Time in the United States and Europe." Paper given at EMRU Labour Economics Conference, Hull University, April 1987.

Green, F., G. Hadjimatheou, and R. Small. "Fringe Benefit Distribution in Britain." *British Journal of Industrial Relations,* 1985, pp. 261–80.

Greer, Charles W., Stanley A. Martin, and Ted A. Reusser. "The Effect of Strikes on Shareholder Returns." *Journal of Labor Research,* No. 1, Fall 1980, pp. 217–31.

Grenier, Guiellermo. *Inhuman Relations: Quality Circles and Anti-Unionism in American Industry.* Philadelphia: Temple University Press, 1988.

Griffin, Ricky W. "Consequences of Quality Circles in an Industrial Setting: A Longitudinal Assessment." *Academy of Management Journal*, Vol. 31, No. 2, June 1988, pp. 338–58.

Grossman, Gene. "Imports as a Cause of Injury: The Case of the U.S. Steel Industry." *Journal of International Economics*, Vol. 20, 1986, pp. 201–23.

Gruben W. and K. Phillips. "Unionization and Unemployment Rates: A Re-Examination of Olson's Labor Cartelization Hypothesis." Federal Reserve Bank of Dallas, January 1990.

Gunderson, M. "Union Impact on Wages, Fringe Benefits, and Productivity." In M. Gunderson and J. Anderson, eds., *Union-Management Relations in Canada*. Toronto, Canada: Addison-Wesley, 1982.

Gutchess, Jocelyn F. *Employment Security in Action*. New York: Pergamon Press, 1985.

Harbison, Frederick H. and John R. Coleman. *Goals and Strategy in Collective Bargaining*. New York: Harper and Brothers, 1951.

Harrison, Bennett and Maryellen R. Kelley. "Outsourcing and the Search for Flexibility: The Morphology of Production Subcontracting in U.S. Manufacturing." In Michael Storper and Allen J. Scott. eds., *Pathways to Industrialization and Regional Development in the 1990s*. Boston and London: Unwin and Hyman, 1991.

Harrison, Bennett and Barry Bluestone. "Wage Polarisation in the U.S. and the 'Flexibility' Debate." *Cambridge Journal of Economics*, Vol. 14, September 1990, pp. 351–73.

Harrison, Bennett and Barry Bluestone. *The Great U-Turn: Corporate Restructuring and the Polarizing of America*. New York: Basic Books, 1988.

Heckscher, Charles. *The New Unionism: Employee Involvement in the Changing Corporation*. New York: Basic Books, 1988.

Heckscher, Charles. "Democracy at Work: In Whose Interests? The Politics of Worker Participation." Unpublished dissertation. Harvard University, 1981.

Helfgott, Roy. *Computerized Manufacturing and Human Resources*. Lexington, MA: Lexington Books, 1988.

Helkie, William L. and Peter Hooper. "An Empirical Analysis of the External Deficit." In Ralph C. Bryant et al., eds., *External Deficits and the Dollar: The Pit and the Pendulum*. Washington, DC: The Brookings Institution, 1988.

Herzenberg, Stephen. "Whither Social Unionism? Labor and Restructuring in the U.S. Auto Industry." Revised version of a paper prepared for the *Conference on North American Labor Movements: Similarities and Differences*, Center for International Affairs, Harvard University, February 3–5, 1989.

Hicks, Donald. *Automation Technology and Industrial Renewal*. Washington DC: American Enterprise Institute, 1986.

Hilke, John and Philip Nelson. "International Competitiveness and the Trade Deficit." U.S. Federal Trade Commission, May 1987.

Hill, Marvin and Anthony Sinicropi. *Management Rights*. Washington, DC: BNA, 1986.

Hirsch, Barry. "Market Structure, Union Rent-Seeking, and Firm Profitability." *Economics Letters*, Vol. 32, 1990, pp. 75–79.

Hirsch, Barry. "Labor Unions and the Economic Performance of U.S. Firms." Unpublished Manuscript. W.E. Upjohn Institute, 1988.

Hirsch, Barry T. and John T. Addison. *The Economic Analysis of Unions: New Approaches and Evidence*. Boston: Allen and Unwin, 1986.

Hirsch, Barry and R.A. Connolly. "Do Unions Capture Monopoly Profits?" *Industrial and Labor Relations Review*, Vol. 41, No. 1, October 1987.

Hirsch, Barry T. and Albert N. Link. "Labor Union Effects on Innovative Activity." *Journal of Labor Research*, Vol. 8, Fall 1987, pp. 323–32.

Hirsch, Barry T. and Albert N. Link. "Unions, Productivity, and Productivity Growth." *Journal of Labor Research*, Vol. 5, Winter 1984, pp. 29–37.

Hirschman, Albert O. *Exit, Voice, and Loyalty*. Cambridge: Harvard University Press, 1971.

Hoerr, John. "The Strange Bedfellows Backing Work Place Reform." *Business Week*, April 30, 1990.

Hohn, Hans-Willy. *Von der Einheitsgewerkschaft zum Betriebssyndikalismus: Soziale Schliessung im dualen System der Interessenvertretung*. Edition Sigma. Berlin, Wissenschaftszentrum, 1988.

Hyman, Richard and Wolfgang Streeck, eds. *New Technology and Industrial Relations*. Oxford: Basil Blackwell, 1988.

Ichniowski, B. "Human Resource Management Systems and the Productivity of U.S. Manufacturing Businesses." Mimeo. Columbia University, January 1990.

Ichniowski, Casey. "The Effects of Grievance Activity on Productivity." *Industrial and Labor Relations Review*, Vol. 40, No. 1, October 1986, pp. 75–89.

Ichniowski, Casey. "Industrial Relations and Economic Performance: Grievances and Productivity." Working Paper No. 1367. National Bureau of Economic Research, June, 1984a.

Ichniowski, Casey. "Ruling Out Productivity? Labor Contract Pages and Plant Economic Performance." Working Paper No. 1368. National Bureau of Economic Research, June 1984b.

Ichniowski, Casey, John Thomas Delaney, and David Lewin. "The New Human Resource Management in U.S. Workplaces: Is It Really New and Is It Only Nonunion?" *Relations Industrielles*, Vol. 44, No. 1, 1989.

328

Ichniowski, Casey and David Lewin. "Grievance Procedures and Firm Performance." In C. Olson and B. Becker, eds., *Human Resources and the Performance of the Firm*. Madison, WI: Industrial Relations Research Association, 1987.

Jacobi, Otto, Bob Jessop, Hans Kastendiek, and Marino Regini, eds. *Technological Change, Rationalisation, and Industrial Relations*. New York: St. Martin's Press, 1986.

Jacoby, Sanford M. "Union-Management Cooperation in the United States: Lessons from the 1920s." *Industrial and Labor Relations Review*, Vol. 37, No. 1, October 1983, pp. 18–33.

Johnson, G. "Changes Over Time in the Union/Non-Union Differential in the United States." Mimeo. University of Michigan, 1981.

Johnson, G. "Economic Analysis of Trade Unions." *American Economic Review*, Vol. 65, May 1975, pp. 23–38.

Juravich, Tom and Howard Harris. "The Pennsylvania Employee Involvement Database: A Guide to Labor Management Programs in Pennsylvania." Unpublished report. Pennsylvania State University, April 1989.

Jürgens, Ulrich, Thomas Malsch, and Knuth Dohse. *Moderne Zeiten in der Automobilfabrik: Strategien der Produktionsmodernisierung im Länder- und Konzernvergleich*. Berlin: Springer-Verlag, 1989.

Kamata, Satoshi. *Japan in the Passing Lane: An Insider's Account of Life in a Japanese Auto Factory*. New York: Pantheon Books, 1973.

Karier, Thomas. "Unions and the U.S. Comparative Advantage." *Industrial Relations*, Vol. 30, No. 1, Winter 1991.

Karier, Thomas. *Trade Deficits and Labor Unions: Myths and Realities*. Washington, DC: Economic Policy Institute, 1990a. Also in this volume.

Karier, Thomas. "The Determinants of U.S. Foreign Production: Unions, Monopoly Power, and Comparative Advantage." Working Paper No. 34. Jerome Levy Economics Institute, January 1990b.

Karier, Thomas. "New Evidence on the Effect of Unions and Imports on Monopoly Power." *Journal of Post Keynesian Economics*, Vol. 10, No. 3, Spring 1988, pp. 414–27.

Karier, Thomas. "Unions and Monopoly Profits." *Review of Economics and Statistics*, Vol. 62, No. 1, February 1985, pp. 34–42.

Karlson, Stephen. "Adoption of Competing Inventions by United States Steel Producers." *Review of Economics and Statistics*, Vol. 68, No. 3, August 1986, pp. 415–22.

Kassalow, Everett M. "Concession Bargaining: Towards New Roles for American Unions and Managers." *International Labour Review*, Vol. 127, No. 5, 1988, pp. 573–92.

Katz, Harry. *Shifting Gears: Changing Labor Relations in the U.S. Automobile Indus- try.* Cambridge, MA: MIT Press, 1985.

Katz, Harry C., Thomas A. Kochan, and Kenneth R. Gobeille. "Industrial Relations Per- formance, Economic Performance, and QWL Programs: An Interplant Analysis." *Industrial and Labor Relations Review,* Vol. 37, No. 1, October 1983, pp. 3–17.

Katz, Harry C., Thomas A. Kochan, and Jeffrey H. Keefe. "Industrial Relations and Pro- ductivity in the U.S. Automobile Industry." *Brookings Papers on Economic Activ- ity,* Vol. 3, 1987a, pp. 685–715.

Katz, Harry C., Thomas A. Kochan, and Jeffrey H. Keefe. "The Impact of Industrial Relations on Productivity: Evidence from the Automobile Industry." Paper pre- sented at the Brookings Microeconomic Conference, Washington, DC, December 3–4, 1987b.

Katz, Harry, Thomas A. Kochan, and Jeffrey Keefe. "Effects of Industrial Relations on Productivity." *Brookings Papers on Economic Activity,* Vol. 3, Special Issue, 1987c.

Katz, Harry C., Thomas A. Kochan, and Mark Weber. "Assessing the Effects of Indus- trial Relations Systems and Efforts to Improve the Quality of Working Life on Orga- nizational Effectiveness." *Academy of Management Journal,* September 1985.

Katz, Harry and Charles F. Sabel. "Industrial Relations and Industrial Adjustment in the Car Industry." *Industrial Relations,* Vol. 24, No. 3, 1985, pp. 295–315.

Katzenstein, Peter J., ed. *Industry and Politics in West Germany: Toward the Third Republic.* Ithaca: Cornell University Press, 1989.

Katzenstein, Peter. *Policy and Politics in West Germany: The Growth of a Semisovereign State.* Philadelphia, PA: Temple University Press, 1987.

Kaufman, Robert S. and Roger T. Kaufman. "Union Effects on Productivity, Personnel Practices, and Survival in the Auto Industry." *Journal of Labor Research,* Fall 1987.

Keefe, Jeffrey. "Do Unions Hinder Technological Diffusion?" *Industrial and Labor Relations Review,* Vol. 44, No. 7, pp. 261–74, 1991.

Keefe, Jeffrey and Harry C. Katz. "Job Classifications and Plant Performance." *Indus- trial Relations,* Vol. 29, No. 1, 1990, pp. 111–18.

Kelley, Maryellen R. "Plant-Specific and Process-Specific Determinates of Productiv- ity: The Case of Programmable Automation." Paper presented at the International Conference on Investment and Technology, Royal Swedish Academy of Engineer- ing, January 1990a.

Kelley, Maryellen R. "New Process Technology, Job Design, and Work Organization: A Contingency Model." *American Sociological Review,* Vol. 55, April 1990b, pp. 191–208.

Kelley, Maryellen R. "Plant, Process, and Product-Specific Determinants of Efficiency in the Use of New Technology: The Case of Programmable Automation." Paper presented at the International Conference on Investment and Technology in Stockholm, Sweden. Sponsored by the Royal Swedish Academy of Engineering and the Organisation for Economic Co-operation and Development, January 21–24, 1990; available in a substantially revised version as Working Paper No. 90–26, School of Urban and Public Affairs, Carnegie Mellon University, August 1990c.

Kelley, Maryellen R. "Alternative Forms of Work Organization Under Programmable Automation." In Stephen Wood, ed., *The Transformation of Work?* London: Unwin-Hyman, 1989a.

Kelley, Maryellen R. "An Assessment of the Skill-Upgrading and Training Opportunities for Blue Collar Workers Under Programmable Automation." *Industrial Relations Research Association: Proceedings of the Forty-First Annual Meeting*, July 1989b, pp. 301–8.

Kelley, Maryellen R. "Unionization and Job Design Under Programmable Automation." *Industrial Relations*, Vol. 28, No. 2, Spring 1989c, pp. 174–87.

Kelley, Maryellen R. "Programmable Automation and the Skill Question: A Reinterpretation of the Cross-national Evidence." *Human Systems Management*, Vol. 6, No. 3, 1986, pp. 223–41.

Kelley, Maryellen R. and Harvey Brooks. "External Learning Opportunities and the Diffusion of Process Innovations to Small Firms: The Case of Programmable Automation." *Technological Forecasting and Social Change*, Vol. 39, April 1991a, pp. 103–25.

Kelley, Maryellen R. and Harvey Brooks. "Diffusion of NC and CNC Machine-Tool Technologies in Large and Small Firms." In R. U. Ayres and B. Haywood, eds., *The Diffusion of CIM Technologies: Models, Case Studies, and Forecasts*, Vol. III of *Computer-Integrated-Manufacturing: Revolution in Progress*. Vienna, Austria: International Institute for Applied Systems Analysis, 1991b.

Kelley, Maryellen R. and Harvey Brooks. *The State of Computerized Automation in U.S. Manufacturing*. Center for Business and Government, John F. Kennedy School of Government, Harvard University, 1988. Forthcoming from the MIT Press.

Kelley, Maryellen R. and Bennett Harrison. "The Subcontracting Behavior of Single vs. Multiplant Enterprises in U.S. Manufacturing: Implications for Economic Development." *World Development*, Vol. 18, September 1990, pp. 1273–94.

Kelley, Maryellen R. and Lan Xue. "Does Decentralization of Programming Responsibilities Increase Efficiency? An Empirical Test." In W. Karwoski and M. Rahini, eds., *Ergonomics of Advanced Manufacturing and Hybrid Automated Systems, II*. New York: Elsevier, 1990.

Kendrick, John W. "Nonunion Dispute Resolution: A Theoretic and Empirical Analysis." *Journal of Conflict Resolution*, September 1987.

Kendrick, John W. and Elliot S. Grossman. *Productivity in the United States: Cycles and Trends*. Baltimore, MD: Johns Hopkins University Press, 1980.

Kendrick, John W. and Richard B. Peterson. *The Modern Grievance Procedure in the United States*. Westport, CT: Greenwood Press, 1988.

Kern, Horst and Michael Schumann. "New Concepts of Production in West German Plants." In Katzenstein, 1989, pp. 87–110.

Kern, Horst and Michael Schumann. *Das Ende der Arbeitsteilung?* Munich: C.H. Beck, 1984.

Kittner, Michael, ed. *Gewerkshaftsjahrbuch 1988: Daten-Fakten-Analysen*. Cologne: Bund-verlag, 1988.

Klein, Janice A. "The Changing Role of First-Line Supervisors and Middle Managers." U.S. Department of Labor, Bureau of Labor-Management Relations and Cooperative Programs. Report No. 126. Washington, DC: U.S. Government Printing Office, 1988.

Kleiner, Morris M. and Marvin L. Bouillon. "Providing Business Information to Production Workers: Correlates of Compensation and Profitability." *Industrial and Labor Relations Review*, Vol. 41, No. 4, July 1988, pp. 605–17.

Kleiner, Morris M. and Daniel L. Petree. "Unionism and Licensing of Public School Teachers: Impact on Wages and Educational Output." In R. Freeman and C. Ichniowski, eds., *When Public Sector Workers Unionize*. Chicago: University of Chicago Press for NBER, 1988.

Klingel, Sally and Ann Martin. *A Fighting Chance: New Strategies to Save Jobs and Reduce Costs*. Ithaca, NY: Cornell University Press, 1988.

Koch, Günther. *Arbeitnehmer steuern mit: Belegschaftsverstretung bei VW ab 1945*. Cologne: Bund-Verlag, 1987.

Kochan, Thomas A. and Joel Cutcher-Gershenfeld. "Institutionalizing and Diffusing Innovations in Industrial Relations." Report No. 128, U.S. Department of Labor, Bureau of Labor-Management Relations and Cooperative Programs. Washington, DC: U.S. Government Printing Office, 1988.

Kochan, Thomas A. and Harry C. Katz. *Collective Bargaining and Industrial Relations*. Homewood, IL: Irwin, 1988.

Kochan, Thomas A., Harry Katz, and Robert McKersie. *The Transformation of American Industrial Relations*. New York: Basic Books, 1986.

Kochan, Thomas A., Harry C. Katz, and Nancy R. Mower. "Worker Participation and American Unions." In Thomas A. Kochan, ed., *Challenges and Choices Facing American Unions*. Cambridge, MA: MIT Press, 1985.

Kochan, Thomas A., Harry C. Katz, and Nancy R. Mower. *Worker Participation and American Unions: Threat or Opportunity*. Kalamazoo, MI: W.E. Upjohn Institute for Employment Research, 1984.

Kochan, Thomas A., Robert McKersie, and John Chalykoff. "The Effects of Corporate Strategy and Workplace Innovations on Union Representation." *Industrial and Labor Relations Review*, Vol. 39, No. 4, 1986, pp. 487–501.

Kornfeld, Robert. "Effects of Unions on Young Workers in Australia." Mimeo. Harvard University, 1990.

Krafcik, John F. "Triumph of the Lean Production System." *Sloan Management Review*, Vol. 30, No. 1, Fall 1988, pp. 41–52.

Krafcik, John F. "Learning from NUMMI." Cambridge, MA: MIT, International Motor Vehicle Program, September 1987.

Krafcik, John F. and John Paul MacDuffie. "Explaining High Performance Manufacturing: The International Automotive Assembly Plant Study." Unpublished paper. Massachusetts Institute of Technology, May 1989.

Kruse, Doug. "Profit-Sharing and Productivity: Microeconomic Evidence." Working Paper. Institute of Management and Labor Relations, Rutgers University, 1988a.

Kruse, Doug. "Profit-Sharing and Productivity." Chapter 3 of *Essays on Profit-Sharing and Unemployment*. Ph.D. thesis. Harvard University, 1988b.

Kuhn P. "A New Integrated Theory of Unions and Life Cycle Employment Contracts: Voice Malfeasance and Welfare." Ph.D. thesis. Harvard University, 1983.

Kupferschmidt, M. and R. Swidensky. "Longitudinal Estimates of the Union Effect on Wages, Wage Dispersion, and Pension Fringe Benefits." Mimeo. University of Guelph, 1989.

Kwoka, John. "International Joint Venture: General Motors and Toyota." In John Kwoka and Lawrence White, eds., *The Anti-trust Revolution*. Glenview, IL: Scott, Foresman, 1989.

Lawler, Edward E., III. *High-Involvement Management*. San Francisco: Jossey-Bass, 1986.

Lawler, Edward E., III, and Susan A. Mohrman. "Unions and the New Management." *Academy of Management Executive*, Vol. 1, November 1987, pp. 293–300.

Lawler, Edward E., III, and Susan A. Mohrman. "Quality Circles after the Fad." *Harvard Business Review*, Vol. 85, No. 1, January/February 1985, pp. 65–71.

Lawrence, Collin and Robert Z. Lawrence. "Manufacturing Wage Dispersion: An End Game Interpretation." *Brooking Papers on Economic Activity*, No. 1, 1985, pp. 47–106.

Leonard, J. "Employment Variability and Wage Rigidity: A Comparison of Union and Non-union Plants." Mimeo. University of California at Berkeley, 1986.

Lesieur, F. G. ed. *The Scanlon Plan: A Frontier in Labor-Management Cooperation*. Cambridge, MA: MIT Press, 1958.

Levine, David I. and Laura D'Andrea Tyson. "Participation, Productivity, and the Firm's Environment." In Blinder, 1990.

Lewin, David. "Non-union Dispute Resolution: A Theoretic and Empirical Analysis." *Journal of Conflict Resolution*, No. 31, September 1987a, pp. 465–502.

Lewin, David. "Conflict Resolution in High Technology Firms." In Archie Kleingartner and Cara Anderson, eds., *Human Resources in High Technology*. Lexington, MA: Lexington, Books, 1987b.

Lewin, David and Richard B. Peterson. "Behavioral Outcomes of Grievance Activity." Working Paper. Columbia University Graduate School of Business, October 1987.

Lewis, H.G. *Union Relative Wage Effects: A Survey*. Chicago: University of Chicago Press, 1986.

Link, Albert N. "Productivity Growth, Environmental Regulations, and the Composition of R&D." *Bell Journal of Economics*, Autumn 1982.

Link, Albert N. "Basic Research and Productivity Increase in Manufacturing: Additional Evidence." *American Economic Review*, December 1981.

Linneman, Peter and Michael Wachter. "Rising Union Premiums and the Declining Boundaries Among Noncompeting Groups." *American Economic Review Proceedings*, Vol. 76, No. 2, May 1986, pp. 103–8.

Linneman, Peter, M. Wachter, and W. Carter. "Evaluating the Evidence on Union Employment and Wages." *Industrial Labor Relations Review*, Vol. 44, No. 1, 1990.

Linnick, Stuart et al. *The Developing Labor Law*. 2d ed., 3rd supplement, 1982–86. Washington, DC: Bureau of National Affairs, 1988.

Lipset, Seymour Martin, M.A. Trow, and James Coleman. *Union Democracy*. New York: Anchor, 1962.

Locke, Edwin A. and David M. Schweiger. "Participation in Decision-Making: One More Look." In Barry M. Staw, ed., *Research in Organizational Behavior*, Vol. 1. Greenwich, CT: JAI Press, 1979.

Lovell, C.A. Knox, Robin Sickles, and Ronald S. Warren, Jr. "The Effect of Unionization on Labor Productivity: Some Additional Evidence." *Journal of Labor Research*, Vol. 9, No. 1, Winter 1988, pp. 55–63.

Luria, Daniel D. "Technology, Work Organization, and Competitiveness: Automotive Subsystem Cost Reduction, 1986–1992." Ann Arbor, MI: Center for Social and Economic Issues, Industrial Technology Institute, University of Michigan, 1987.

Luria, Daniel D. "New Labor-Management Models from Detroit?" *Harvard Business Review*, Vol. 64, No. 5, September/October 1986, pp. 22–27.

Machin, S.J. "The Productivity Effects of Unionization and Firm Size in British Engineering Firms." *Warwick Economic Research Paper*, March 1988a.

Machin, S.J. "Unions and the Capture of Economic Rents: An Investigation Using British Firm Level Data." Mimeo. Department of Economics, University College, London, 1988b.

Machin, S. and Mark Stewart. "Unions and the Financial Performance of British Private Sector Establishments." Discussion Paper 88–23. University College London, 1988.

Machin, S. and S. Wadhwani. "The Effects of Unions on Organization Change, Investment, and Employment: Evidence from WIRS." Discussion Paper 355. Centre for Labour Economics, LSE, 1989.

McKersie, Robert B. and L. Hunter. *Pay, Productivity, and Collective Bargaining*. London: Macmillan, 1973.

McKersie, Robert B. and Janice A. Klein. "Productivity: The Industrial Relations Connection." In William J. Baumol and K. McLennan, eds., *Productivity, Growth, and U.S. Competitiveness*. New York: Oxford University Press, 1985.

McLaughlin, Doris. *The Impact of Labor Unions on the Rate and Direction of Technological Innovation*. Detroit: Wayne State University, 1979.

Macpherson, David "Trade Unions and Labor's Share in U.S. Manufacturing Industries." Mimeo. Miami University, March 1989.

Macpherson, David and James Stewart. "The Effect of International Competition on Union and Nonunion Wages." *Industrial and Labor Relations Review*, Vol. 43, No. 4, April 1990.

Macpherson, David and James Stewart. "Unionism and the Dispersion of Wages among Blue Collar Women." *Journal of Labor Research*, Vol. 8, No. 4, Fall 1987, pp. 395–495.

Maki, D.R. "The Effects of Unions and Strikes on the Rate of Growth of Total Factor Productivity in Canada." *Applied Economics*, Vol. 15, 1983.

Mann, Eric. *Taking on General Motors: A Case Study of the UAW Campaign to Keep GM Van Nuys Open*. Los Angeles: Institute of Industrial Relations Publications, UCLA, 1987.

Mansfield, E. "Basic Research and Productivity Increase in Manufacturing." *American Economic Review*, December 1980.

Mansfield, Edwin. *Industrial Research and Technological Change*. New York: Norton, 1968.

Mansfield, Edwin. *Research and Innovation in the Modern Corporation*. New York: Norton, 1971.

Mansfield, Edwin. *The Production and Application of New Industrial Technology*. New York: Norton, 1977.

Markovits, Andrei S. *The Politics of the West German Trade Unions: Strategies of Class and Interest Representation in Growth and Crisis*. Cambridge: Cambridge University Press, 1986.

Marks, Mitchell Lee, Philip H. Mirvis, Edward J. Hackett, and James F. Grady, Jr. "Employee Participation in a Quality Circle Program: Impact on Quality of Work Life, Productivity, and Absenteeism." *Journal of Applied Psychology*, Vol. 71, No. 1 February 1986, pp. 61–69.

Marshall, Alfred. *Elements of Economics*. 3d ed. London: Macmillan, 1899.

Marshall, Ray. *Unheard Voices: Labor and Economic Policy in a Competitive World*. New York: Basic Books, 1987.

Mathewson, Stanley B. *Restriction of Output Among Unorganized Workers*. rev. ed. Carbondale and Edwardsville, IL: Southern Illinois University Press (original edition, 1931), 1969.

Mefford, Robert N. "The Effect of Unions on Productivity in a Multinational Manufacturing Firm." *Industrial and Labor Relations Review*, October 1986.

Metcalf, David. "Union Presence, Productivity Growth, and Investment Behavior in British Manufacturing Industry." Working Paper No. 1203. Centre for Labour Economics, LSE, 1990.

Metcalf, David. "Can Unions Survive in the Private Sector?" Working Paper No. 1130. Centre for Labour Economics, LSE, 1989.

Metcalf, David. "Unions and Productivity." Mimeo. Centre for Labour Economics, LSE, 1988.

Metcalf, David. "Unions and the Distribution of Earnings." *British Journal of Industrial Relations*, Vol. 20, 1982, pp. 163–69.

Miller, Katherine I. and Peter R. Monge. "Participation, Satisfaction, and Productivity: A Meta-Analytic Review." *Academy of Management Journal*, Vol. 29, No. 4, 1986, pp. 727–53.

Miller, Richard U., Brian E. Becker, and Edward B. Krinsky. "Union Effects on Hospital Administration: Preliminary Results from a Three State Study." *Labor Law Journal*, August 1977.

Mills, Daniel Quinn. *The IBM Lesson: The Profitable Art of Full Employment*. New York: Times Books, 1988.

Mills, Daniel. *Labor-Management Relations*. 2d ed. New York: McGraw-Hill, 1982.

Millward, N. and M. Stevens. *British Workplace Industrial Relations 1980–1984*. London: Gower, 1986.

Miscimmara, Philip. *The NLRB and Managerial Direction: Plant Closings, Relocations, Subcontracting, and Automation*. Philadelphia: Wharton Shool, Industrial Research Unit, 1983.

Mishel, Lawrence. "The Late Great Debate on Deindustrialization." *Challenge*, January/February 1989, pp. 35–43.

Mishel, Lawrence and David Frankel. *The State of Working America, 1990–91 Edition.* Armonk, NY: M.E. Sharpe Publishers, 1991.

Mitchell, Daniel J. B. and Renae F. Broderick. "Flexible Systems in the American Context: History, Policy, Research, and Implications." In *Advances in Industrial and Labor Relations.* Forthcoming.

Mitchell, Daniel J.B., David Lewin, and Edward F. Lawler III. "Alternative Pay Systems, Firm Performance, and Productivity." In Blinder, ed., 1990.

MIT Commission on Industrial Productivity. *Made in America: Regaining the Productive Edge.* Cambridge, MA: MIT Press, 1989.

Morris, Charles. *The Developing Labor Law.* 2d ed. Washington, DC: Bureau of National Affairs, 1982.

Mulvey, C. "Wage Levels: Do Unions Make a Difference?" In J. Niland, ed., *Wage Fixation in Australia.* Sydney: Allen and Unwin, 1986.

Muramatsu, K. Chapter in M. Aoki, ed. *Economic Analysis of the Japanese Firm.* Amsterdam, Netherlands: North-Holland Publishing, 1984.

Murphy, Kevin. *Technological Change Clauses in Collective Bargaining Agreements.* Washington, DC: AFL-CIO Professional Employees Department, 1981.

Muster, Manfred. "Zum Stand der Gruppenarbeit in der Automobilindustrie in der Bundesrepublik." In Roth and Kohl, eds., 1988, pp. 259–81.

Muster, Manfred and Manfred Wannöffel. *Gruppenarbeit in der Automobilindustrie.* Bochum: Joint publication of the IG Metall Verwaltungsstelle Bochum and the Gemeinsame Arbeitsstelle Ruhr-Universität Bochum, 1989.

Nader, Ralph and William Taylor. *The Big Boys: Power & Position in American Business.* New York: Pantheon Books, 1986.

Nakamura, K., H. Sato, and T. Kamiya. *Do Labor Unions Really Have a Useful Role?* (in Japanese). Tokyo: Sogo Rodo Kenkyujo, 1988.

National Advisory Committee on Semiconductors. *A Strategic Industry at Risk.* Advance Edition. Washington, DC: National Advisory Committee on Semiconductors, 1989.

Neumark, David. "Declining Union Strength and Wage Inflation in the 1980s." Federal Reserve Board, January 1989.

Nickell, S., S. Wadhwani and M. Wall. "Unions and Productivity Growth in Britain 1974–86: Evidence From UK Company Accounts Data." Discussion Paper No. 353. Centre for Labour Economics, LSE, 1989.

Nolan, P. and P. Marginson. "Skating on Thin Ice?: David Metcalf on Trade Unions and Productivity." *British Journal of Industrial Relations*, Vol. 28, No. 2, July 1990.

Norsworthy, J.R. and Craig A. Zabala. "Worker Attitudes, Worker Behavior, and Productivity in the U.S. Automobile Industry, 1959–1976." *Industrial and Labor Relations Review*, July 1985.

Note. "Automation and Collective Bargaining." *Harvard Law Review*, No. 84, 1971, pp. 1822–55.

Olson, Mancur. *The Rise and Decline of Nations: Economic Growth, Stagflation, and Social Rigidities*. New Haven: Yale University Press, 1982.

Osawa, M. "The Service Economy and Industrial Relations in Small and Medium Size Firms in Japan." *Japan Labor Bulletin*, July 1, 1989.

Parker, Mike and Jane Slaughter. *Choosing Sides: Unions and the Team Concept*. Boston: South End Press, 1988.

Pavitt, Keith and Pari Patel. "The International Distribution and Determinants of Technological Activities." *Oxford Review of Economic Policy*, Vol. 4, 1988, pp. 35–55.

Pencavel, J. "Employment and Trade Unions." Draft manuscript. Mimeo. Stanford University, 1989, pp. 25–47.

Petchinnis, Stephen. "The Attitude of Trade Unionists Towards Technological Change." *Relations Industrielles*, Vol. 38, No. 1, 1983, pp. 104–19.

Piore, Michael J. and Charles F. Sabel, *The Second Industrial Divide: Possibilities for Prosperity*. New York: Basic Books, 1984.

President's Commission on Industrial Competitiveness. *Global Competitiveness: The New Reality*, Vols. 1 and 2. Washington, DC: U.S. Government Printing Office, 1985.

Quinn, Dennis P. "Dynamic Markets and Mutating Firms: The Changing Organization of Production in Automotive Firms." BRIE Research Paper #1. Berkeley Roundtable on the International Economy, University of California-Berkeley, 1989.

Rees, A. "The Effects of Unions on Resource Allocation." *Journal of Law and Economics*, Vol. 6, October 1963, pp. 69–78.

Rees, John, Ronald Briggs, and Raymond Oakey. "The Adoption of New Technology in the American Machinery Industry." *Regional Studies*, Vol. 18, No. 6, 1984, pp. 489–504.

Register, Charles A. "Wages, Productivity, and Costs in Union and Nonunion Hospitals." *Journal of Labor Research*, Vol. 9, No. 4, Fall 1988.

Reynolds, L. *Labor Economics and Labor Relations*. 8th ed. Englewood Cliffs, NJ: Prentice Hall, 1982.

Riffel, Michael and Manfred Muster. *Bericht über das Planungsseminar "Neue Lackiererei Wolfsburg" vom 16.01–20.01.1989 in Hustedt/Celle*. Wolfsburg: Betriebsrat der Volkswagen AG, 1989.

Rosen, Corey, Katherine J. Klein, and Karen M. Young. *Employee Ownership in America: The Equity Solution*. Lexington, MA: Lexington Books, 1986.

Roth, Seigfried and Heribert Kohl, eds. *Perspecktive: Gruppenarbeit*. Cologne: Bund-Verlag, 1988.

Roth, Siegfried and Peter Königs. "Gruppenarbeit als Gestaltungsalternative bei CIM-Einsatz." In Roth and Kohl, eds., 1988, pp. 81–94.

Ruback, Richard and M.B. Zimmerman. "Unionization and Profitability: Evidence from the Stock Market." *Journal of Political Economy*, Vol. 92, No. 6, December 1984.

Russell, Raymond. "Forms and Extent of Employee Participation in the Contemporary United States." *Work and Occupations: An International Sociological Journal*, Vol. 15, No. 4, 1988, pp. 374–95.

Sachs, Jeffrey. "Social Conflict and Populist Policies in Latin America." Working Paper No. 2897. National Bureau of Economic Research, March 1989.

Salinger, M.A. "Tobin's **q**, Unionization, and the Concentration-Profits Relationship." *Rand Journal of Economics*, vol. 15, no. 2, 1984.

Salkever, David S. "Unionization and the Cost of Producing Hospital Services." *Journal of Labor Research*, Summer 1982.

Salvatore, Dominick. *The Japanese Trade Challenge and the U.S. Response*. Washington, DC: Economic Policy Institute, 1990.

Scherer, F.M. *Industrial Market Structure and Economic Performance*. New York: Rand McNally, 1980.

Schultz, George and Arnold Weber. *Strategies for the Displaced Worker*. New York: Harper and Row, 1966.

Schultz, Theodore. *Investing in People: The Economics of Population Quality*. Berkeley: The University of California Press, 1981.

Schuster, Michael. *Union-Management Cooperation: Structure, Process, and Impact*. Kalamazoo, MI: W.E. Upjohn Institute for Employment Research, 1984.

Schuster, Michael. "The Impact of Union-Management Cooperation on Productivity and Employment." *Industrial and Labor Relations Review*, Vol. 36, No. 3, April 1983, pp. 415–30.

Scott, Bruce R. "National Strategies: Key to International Competition." In Scott and Lodge, eds., 1985, pp. 71–143.

Scott, Bruce R. and George C. Lodge, eds. *U.S. Competitiveness in the World Economy*. Boston: Harvard Business School Press, 1985.

Scott, Robert. "Trade and Employment in Automobiles; The Short-Run Success and Long-Run Failure of Protectionist Measures." In Laura Tyson, William Dickens, and John Zysman, eds., *The Dynamics of Trade and Employment*. Cambridge: Ballinger Books, 1988.

Shaiken, Harley. *Work Transformed*. New York: Holt, Rinehart, and Winston, 1984.

Shay, Mike. Consultant with Participative Systems Inc., Princeton, NJ. Interview. January 1989.

Sicherman, N. "Overeducation in the Labor Market." Mimeo. Rutgers University, June 1989.

Silvia, Stephen J. "Unions, Industrial Relations Systems, and Crisis: The Impact of Sectoral Decline on West German and American Apparel Unions." Paper prepared for delivery at the 1987 Annual Meeting of the American Political Science Association, 1987.

Simmons, John and William Mares. *Working Together*. New York: New York University Press, 1985.

Simpson, W. "The Impact of Unions on the Structure of Canadian Wages: An Empirical Analysis With Microdata." *Canadian Journal of Economics*, Vol. 18, 1985, pp. 164–81.

Skinner, Wickham. "The Productivity Paradox." *Harvard Business Review*, July–August, 1986, pp. 55–59.

Slichter, Sumner H. *Union Policies and Industrial Management*. Washington, DC: The Brookings Institution, 1941.

Slichter, Sumner H., James Healy, and Robert Livernash. *The Impact of Collective Bargaining on Management*. Washington, DC: The Brookings Institution, 1960.

Sloan, Frank A. and Killard W. Adamache. "The Role of Unions in Hospital Cost Inflation." *Industrial and Labor Relations Review*, January 1984.

Sloan, Frank A. and Bruce Steinwald. *Hospital Labor Markets*. Lexington, MA: Lexington Books, 1980.

Sorge, Arndt and Wolfgang Streeck. "Industrial Relations and Technical Change: The Case for an Extended Perspective." In Hyman and Streeck, eds., 1988.

Spencer, Daniel. "Employee Voice and Employee Retention." *Management Journal*, September 1986.

Standing, Guy. "The Growth of External Labour Flexibility in a Nascent NIC: Malaysian Labour Flexibility Survey." Working Paper No. 35. World Employment Programme Research, International Labour Office, Geneva, November 1989.

Strauss, George. "Industrial Relations: Time of Changes." *Industrial Relations*, Vol. 23, No. 1, Winter 1984, pp. 1–15.

Strauss, George. "Workers Participation in Management: An International Perspective." In Barry M. Staw and L.L. Cummings, eds., *Research in Organizational Behavior*, Vol. 4. Greenwich, CT: JAI Press, 1982.

Strauss, George. "Managerial Practices." In J. Richard Hackman and J. Lloyd Suttle, eds., *Improving Life at Work: Behavioral Science Approaches to Organizational Change*. Santa Monica, CA: Goodyear Publishing, 1977.

Streeck, Wolfgang. "Successful Adjustment to Turbulent Markets: The Automobile Industry." In Katzenstein, ed., 1989, pp. 113–56.

Streeck, Wolfgang. "Industrial Relations in West Germany: Agenda for Change." Discussion paper IIM/LMP 87–5. Wissenschaftszentrum Berlin, April 1987.

Streeck, Wolfgang. *Industrial Relations in West Germany: A Case Study of the Car Industry*. New York: St. Martin's Press, 1984.

Summers, Lawrence. "Why is the Unemployment Rate So Very High at Full Employment?" Brookings Papers on Economic Activity 22, 1986, pp. 339–83.

Sveikauskus, C.D. and L. Sveikauskus. "Industry Characteristics and Productivity Growth." *Southern Journal of Economics*, January 1982.

Sweeney, J. Lecture on the Role of Unions in Health Care. Harvard University Trade Union Program, March 1990.

Taylor, George. "Collective Bargaining." In John Dunlop, ed., *Automation and Technological Change*. Englewood Cliffs, NJ: Prentice-Hall, 1962.

Terleckyi, Nestor. "Comment." In Zvi Griliches, ed. *R&D, Patents, and Productivity*. Chicago, IL: University of Chicago Press, 1984.

Terleckyi, Nestor. "What Do R&D Numbers Tell Us about Technological Change?" *American Economic Review*, May 1980.

Thelen, Kathleen. *Continuity in Crisis: Labor Politics and Industrial Adjustment in West Germany, 1950–1987*. Dissertation in Political Science. University of California-Berkeley, 1987.

Turner, Lowell. "Three Plants, Three Futures." *Technology Review*, Vol. 92, No. 1, January 1989, pp. 38–45.

Turner, Lowell. "Battles for Work Reorganization in the U.S. Auto Industry." Presented at conference "Industrial Relations in Times of Deregulation," Werner-Reimers-Stiftung, Bad Homburg, Federal Republic of Germany, September–October 1988. Mimeo. Max-Planck Institut fur Gesellschaftsforschung, Koln, Federal Republic of Germany, 1988a.

Turner, Lowell. "Are Labor-Management Partnerships for Competitiveness Possible in America? The U.S. Auto Industry Examined." BRIE Working Paper #36. Berkeley Roundtable on the International Economy, University of California-Berkeley, September 1988b.

U.S. Congress, Office of Technological Assessment. *Technology and Structural Unemployment: Reemploying Displaced Adults*. Washington, DC: U.S. Government Printing Office, 1986.

U.S. Department of Commerce, Bureau of Economic Analysis. *Survey of Current Business*. Washington, DC: U.S. Government Printing Office, June 1990.

U.S. Department of Labor, Bureau of Labor Statistics. "International Comparisons of Hourly Compensation Costs for Production Workers in Manufacturing, 1989." Report 787. U.S. Department of Labor, Washington, DC, April 1990.

U.S. Department of Labor, Bureau of Labor Statistics. *Industry Wage Survey: Machinery Manufacturing*. Bulletin 2229, November 1983.

U.S. Department of Labor, Bureau of Labor-Management Relations and Cooperative Programs. *Labor-Management Cooperation: Perspectives from the Labor Movement*. Washington, DC, 1984.

U.S. General Accounting Office. *Survey of Corporate Employee Involvement Efforts*. Mimeo. Washington, DC, 1987.

U.S. General Accounting Office. *Productivity Sharing Programs: Can They Contribute to Productivity Improvement?* Washington, DC, 1981.

Ulph, Alastair and David Ulph. "Labor Markets and Innovation." *Journal of the Japanese and International Economies*, Vol. 3, No. 4, December 1989.

Verma, Anil. "Relative Flow of Capital to Union and Nonunion Plants within a Firm." *Industrial Relations*, Vol. 24, No. 3, 1985, pp. 395–405.

Voos, Paula B. "The Influence of Cooperative Programs on Union-Management Relations, Flexibility, and Other Labor Relations Outcomes." *Journal of Labor Research*, Vol. 10, No. 1, Winter 1989, pp. 104–17.

Voos, Paula B. "Managerial Perceptions of the Economic Impact of Labor Relations Programs." *Industrial and Labor Relations Review*, Vol. 40, No. 2, January 1987, pp. 195–208.

Voos, Paula B. "The Union Impact on Profits: Evidence from Industry Price-Cost Margin Data." *Journal of Labor Economics*, Vol. 4, No. 1, 1986.

Voos, Paula and Lawrence Mishel. "The Union Impact on Profits: Evidence from Industry Price-Cost Margin Data." *Journal of Labor Economics*, Vol. 4, No. 1, January 1986a, pp. 105–33.

Voos, Paula and Lawrence Mishel. "The Union Impact on Profits in the Supermarket Industry." *Review of Economics and Statistics*, Vol. 68, No. 3, August 1986b, pp. 513–17.

Wadhwani, S. "The Effect of Unions on Productivity Growth, Investment, and Employment: A Report on Some Recent Work." Working Paper No. 356. Centre for Labour Economics, LSE, April 1989.

Wagner, John A. III and Richard Z. Gooding. "Effects of Societal Trends on Participation Research." *Administrative Science Quarterly*, Vol. 32, June 1987, pp. 241–62.

Walton, Richard E. "Work Innovations in the United States." *Harvard Business Review*, Vol. 79, No. 4, July/August 1979, pp. 88–98.

Warren, R.S. "The Effect of Unionization on Labor Productivity: Some Time Series Evidence." *Journal of Labor Research*, Vol. 6, No. 2, Spring 1985, pp. 199–207.

Webb, Sidney and Beatrice Webb. *Industrial Democracy*. London: Longman, Green & Company, 1897.

Weikle, Roger. "The Attitude and Preferences of Local Union Leaders for Adjustment to Technological Change." Unpublished Dissertation. University of South Carolina, 1985.

Weiler, P. "Promises to Keep: Securing Workers' Rights to Self Organisation Under the NLRA." *Harvard Law Review*, Vol. 96, June 1983, pp. 1769–1827.

Weitzman, Martin L. and Douglas L. Kruse. "Profit Sharing and Productivity." In Alan S. Blinder, ed., 1990.

Wells, Donald M. *Empty Promises: Quality of Working Life Programs and the Labor Movement*. New York: Monthly Review Press, 1987.

Wever, Kirsten R. "Toward a Structural Account of Union Participation in Management: The Case of Western Airlines." Mimeo. Washington, DC, 1988; also in *Industrial and Labor Relations Review*, Vol. 42, No. 4, July 1989.

Wever, Kirsten R. "Western Airlines and Its Four Major Unions: The Airline Pilots' Association, the Air Transport Employees, the Association of Flight Attendants, and the International Brotherhood of Teamsters." Report No. 129, U.S. Department of Labor, Bureau of Labor-Management Programs and Cooperative Relations, Washington, DC: U.S. Government Printing Office, 1988.

White, Joseph B. "Car Makers Gear Up to Turn Good Marks in Quality Poll to Competitive Advantage." *Wall Street Journal*, July 3, 1990, p. B-1.

Whyte, William F. "Advancing Knowledge Through Participatory Action Research." *Sociological Forum*, Vol. 4, No. 3, 1989, pp. 367–85.

Wilensky, Harold L. *The "New Corporatism," Centralization, and the Welfare State*. London: Sage Publications, 1976.

Willman, Paul. *Technological Change, Collective Bargaining, and Industrial Efficiency*. New York: Oxford University Press, 1986.

Wise, David. "Saving for Retirement: The U.S. Case." *Journal of the Japanese and International Economies*, Vol. 2, 1988, pp. 385–416.

Witte, John F. *Democracy, Authority, and Alienation in Work: Workers' Participation in an American Corporation*. Chicago: University of Chicago Press, 1980.

Zanetich Dan. Personnel Manager, Maxwell House, Hoboken, New Jersey. Interview, August 25, 1988.

Zuboff, Shoshona. *In the Age of the Smart Machines*. New York: Basic Books, 1988.

Index

CETA. *See* Comprehensive Employment and
Training Act
Chrysler Corporation, 237
Clothing Manufacturers Association, 130
Coal industry. *See also* United Mine
Workers
productivity, 51–52, 55, 155, 156
strikes, 66, 69, 74n.12
technology, 58
Cohesive labor movement, 221
Collective bargaining
competitiveness, 1, 2, 4, 10
contracts, 124–29, 270
productivity, 53, 69
technology, 122, 124–29, 134
works councils, 222, 224
Collective voice, 44, 148–51, 175, 193,
196–98
Columbia Tribune decision, 139
Columbia University survey, 258, 302
Commission on the Skills of the American
Workforce, 300, 313
Communications industry, 127, 135, 239
Communications programs, 123, 311
Communications Workers of America
(CWA), 135, 239
Compensation programs, 146, 149,
179–80, 184, 197, 208. *See also*
specific programs, e.g., Pension plans
Competitiveness, 1–12
cost vs. total, 2–4
definition, 2
technology, 294
wages, 1, 4–8, 191, 309
works councils, 227
Comprehensive adjustment programs,
134–35
Comprehensive Employment and Training
Act (CETA), 140n.19
Compustat companies, 137n.2, 156, 159,
183
Computer industry, 6
Computerized automation. *See* Automation
Construction industry, 50–51, 55, 57–58,
156, 159
Contracts, 124–29, 131–32, 235, 270
Cooperative programs. *See* Participation
programs
Corruption, 146
Costs. *See* Labor costs; Price-cost margin;
Prices
Council for a Union-Free Environment,
143–44
CPS. *See* Current Population Survey

Craft unions, 58
Crime, 146
Current Population Survey (CPS), 137n.2,
152, 154
CWA. *See* Communications Workers of
America

Decision bargaining, 124–25
Democracy, 194
Denmark, 231, 300
Department of Commerce data, 32
Department of Labor, 72
Deregulation, 239
DFI. *See* Direct Foreign Investment
DGB unions, 221, 222
Direct foreign investment (DFI), 27–32
Dollar, value of the, 3, 4, 18

Econometric analysis, 21, 36–39, 193
Economic Report of the President (1983),
41
Economy, U.S.
competitiveness, 2, 191
decline/growth, 153–55, 160, 288–91
job security, 195–96
wages, 151–53
work organization, 287–315
Education, 292–95, 306–7, 309
Efficiency, 266–69
Employee participation. *See* Participation
programs
Employees. *See* Job; Workers
Employee stock ownership plans (ESOP),
150, 175, 177, 179, 183–87, 208,
214–15
Employers. *See* Management
Employment Cost Index survey, 152
Employment Service (ES), 140
Encouragement policy, 131
England. *See* United Kingdom
ES. *See* Employment Service
ESOP. *See* Employee stock ownership plans
Europe. *See also* specific countries
exports/imports, 231
participation programs, 9
productivity, 217–20, 239, 300
U.S. trade deficit, 5
wages, 4
Eurosclerosis, 219
Exchange rate, 4
Exit theory, 44, 45, 73n.4
Exports. *See also* Imports
foreign investment, 32
importance, 20, 24

347

Dale Belman is an Associate Professor of Economics at the University of Wisconsin-Milwaukee. He is currently continuing his research on labor relations systems and firm performance.

Adrienne E. Eaton is an Assistant Professor of Labor Studies at Rutgers University. Her publications include articles on unions and employee involvement (EI) programs that have appeared in *Industrial and Labor Relations Review* and *Labor Studies Journal*. She is currently working on a study of factors contributing to the survival of EI programs in unionized workplaces.

Richard Freeman holds positions at Harvard University, the National Bureau of Economic Research, and the London School of Economics. He is co-author of *What Do Unions Do?* (with James Medoff) and co-editor of *When Public Sector Workers Unionize* (with Bernard Ichniowski). He is currently researching the development of unions in industrialized countries.

Bennett Harrison is a Professor of Political Economy at the School of Urban and Public Affairs at Carnegie Mellon University. He is co-author of *The Deindustrialization of America* and *The Great U-Turn*. He is currently conducting research on the relative contributions of large and small firms to economic development, on the extent to which manufacturing companies are again choosing to locate in close proximity to one another, and on the strategic planning capacities of community development corporations serving low-income areas.

Thomas Karier is an Associate Professor of Economics at Eastern Washington University and has recently served as a Research Fellow at the Jerome Levy Economics Institute (1989–1991). He has written numerous articles concerning unions and business behavior which have been published in the *Review of Economics and Statistics, Industrial Relations*, and the *Journal of Post Keynesian Economics*.

Jeffrey H. Keefe is an Assistant Professor of Industrial Relations and Human Resources at the Institute of Management and Labor Relations at Rutgers University. He received his B.A. from Villanova University and his Ph.D in Industrial and Labor Relations from Cornell University. He has published articles in the *Industrial and Labor Relations Review, Industrial Relations*, and the *Brookings Papers on Economic Activity*.

Maryellen R. Kelley is an Associate Professor of Management and Public Policy in the School of Urban and Public Affairs, Carnegie Mellon University, and a Fellow at the Center for Science and International Affairs of Harvard University's John F. Kennedy School of Government. She has published extensively on the economics and sociology of technological change, on the structure of internal labor markets, and on industrial policy. Her forthcoming book on the state of U.S. manufacturing (co-authored with Harvey Brooks) will be published by MIT Press.

Ray Marshall holds the Bernard Rapoport Centennial Chair in Economics and Public Affairs at the LBJ School of Public Policy at the University of Texas-Austin. He served as Secretary of Labor in the Carter Administration (1977–1981) and is the author of numerous articles and books, including *Unheard Voices: Labor and Economic Policy in a Competitive World*.

Lawrence Mishel is the Research Director of the Economic Policy Institute. He is the author of *The State of Working America, 1990–91 Edition* (with David M. Frankel), *Manufacturing Numbers: How Inaccurate Statistics Conceal U.S. Industrial Decline*, and *Shortchanging Education* (with M. Edith Rasell). He holds a Ph.D. in economics from the University of Wisconsin and has published in a variety of academic and nonacademic journals.

Lowell Turner is an Assistant Professor of International and Comparative Labor at Cornell University in the School of Industrial and Labor Relations. A former union representative for the National Association of Letter Carriers, he has a Ph.D. in Political Science from U.C. Berkeley and is a specialist on German and American Labor. His book, *Democracy at Work: Changing World Markets and the Future of Labor Unions*, is scheduled for publication by Cornell University Press in the Fall of 1991.

Paula B. Voos is an Associate Professor of Economics and Industrial Relations at the University of Wisconsin-Madison. She earned her Ph.D. from Harvard University in 1982. She is the author of numerous articles in professional journals and a former member of the Executive Board of the Industrial Relations Research Association.

The Economic Policy Institute was founded in 1986 to widen the debate about policies to acheive healthy economic growth, prosperity, and opportunity in the difficult new era America has entered.

Today, America's economy is threatened by stagnant growth and increasing inequality. Expanding global competition, changes in the nature of work, and rapid technological advances are altering economic reality. Yet many of our policies, attitudes, and institutions are based on assumptions that no longer reflect real world conditions.

Central to the Economic Policy Institute's search for solutions is the exploration of the economics of teamwork—economic policies that encourage every segment of the American economy (business, labor, government, universities, voluntary organizations, etc.) to work cooperatively to raise productivity and living standards for all Americans. Such an undertaking involves a challenge to conventional views of market behavior and a revival of a cooperative relationship between the public and private sectors.

With the support of leaders from labor, business, and the foundation world, the Institute has sponsored research and public discussion of a wide variety of topics: trade and fiscal policies; trends in wages, incomes, and prices; the causes of the productivity slowdown; labor market problems; U.S. and Third World debt; rural and urban policies; inflation; state-level economic development strategies; comparative international economic performance; and studies of the overall health of the U.S. manufacturing sector and of specific key industries.

The Institute works with a growing network of innovative economists and other social science researchers in universities and research centers all over the country who are willing to go beyond the conventional wisdom in considering strategies for public policy.

The research committee of the Institute includes:

Jeff Faux—EPI President
Lester Thurow—Dean of MIT's Sloan School of Management
Ray Marshall—former U.S. Secretary of Labor, currently a Professor at the LBJ School of Public Affairs, University of Texas
Barry Bluestone—University of Massachusetts-Boston
Robert Reich—JFK School of Government, Harvard University
Robert Kuttner—Author; columnist, *New Republic,* and *Business Week;* co-editor, *New Republic*

EPI Reports, Working Papers, Briefing Papers, and Seminars are distributed by *Public Interest Publications.* For a publications list or to order, call 1-800-537-9359.

Shorter **EPI Briefing Papers** are available directly from the Institute / 1730 Rhode Island Ave., NW, Suite 200 / Washington, DC 20036.